中国人民大学2019年度
"中央高校建设世界一流大学（学科）和特色发展引导专项资金"支持

智库丛书
Think Tank Series

国家发展与战略丛书
人大国发院智库丛书

结构调整攻坚期的中国宏观经济

China's Macroeconomy in the Key Period of Structural Adjustment

刘元春　闫衍　刘晓光　著

中国社会科学出版社

图书在版编目（CIP）数据

结构调整攻坚期的中国宏观经济／刘元春，闫衍，刘晓光著.—北京：中国社会科学出版社，2020.6
（国家发展与战略丛书）
ISBN 978-7-5203-6559-8

Ⅰ.①结⋯　Ⅱ.①刘⋯②闫⋯③刘⋯　Ⅲ.①中国经济—宏观经济—研究　Ⅳ.①F123.16

中国版本图书馆 CIP 数据核字（2020）第 087928 号

出 版 人	赵剑英
责任编辑	马　明
责任校对	朱妍洁
责任印制	王　超

出　　版	中国社会科学出版社
社　　址	北京鼓楼西大街甲 158 号
邮　　编	100720
网　　址	http://www.csspw.cn
发 行 部	010-84083685
门 市 部	010-84029450
经　　销	新华书店及其他书店
印　　刷	北京明恒达印务有限公司
装　　订	廊坊市广阳区广增装订厂
版　　次	2020 年 6 月第 1 版
印　　次	2020 年 6 月第 1 次印刷
开　　本	710×1000　1/16
印　　张	24.25
插　　页	2
字　　数	251 千字
定　　价	138.00 元

凡购买中国社会科学出版社图书，如有质量问题请与本社营销中心联系调换
电话：010-84083683
版权所有　侵权必究

摘　　要

　　2019年在中美贸易摩擦全面加剧、世界经济同步回落、国内结构性因素持续发酵、周期性下行力量有所加大等多重因素的作用下，中国宏观经济告别了2016—2018年"稳中趋缓"的平台期，经济增速回落幅度加大，经济结构分化明显。在五大短期周期因素同步回落、三大传统红利加速递减以及两大临时突发事件三重冲击下，中国宏观经济的弹性和韧性得到了全面显现，在以"六稳"为核心的逆周期调节政策和持续的供给侧结构性改革的对冲下，中国宏观经济成功守住底线、完成了预期的目标。但值得注意的是，在经济增速回落的过程中，经济的结构性分化较为严重，升级型的结构调整速度放慢，而萧条型的结构调整却持续加速，从而导致2019年中国经济结构调整步入艰难期。

　　2020年是中国全面建成小康年，中国宏观经济将在延续2019年基本运行模式的基础上出现重大的变化，不必过于悲观。一方面，2019年下行的趋势性力量和结构性力量将持续发力，导致2020年潜在GDP增速进一步回落；另一方面，2019年下行的很多周期性力量在2020年开始出现拐点性变化,随着十大积极因素的巩固和培育,宏观经济下行将有所缓和,下行幅度将较2019年明显收窄。其中,部分周期性力量的反转以及中国制度红利的持续改善将是2020年最为值得关注和期待的新变化。一是随着吏治整顿的基本到位和十九届四中全会精神的全面落实,中国制度红利将全面上扬,TFP增速将明显改善;二是随着各类杠杆率的稳定、应付债务增速的下降、高风险机构的有序处置、金融机构资本金的补足、监管短板的完善使金融风险趋于收敛,化解金融风险的攻坚战取得了阶段性胜利,金融环境将得到明显改善;三是企业库存周期触底反弹,前期过度去库存为2020年企业补库存提供了较大的空间;四是对中美贸易摩擦的恐慌期已经过去,适应性调整基本到位,企业信心将得到明显回归;五是为应对外部冲击而启动的各类战略将有效提升相应部门的有效需求,特别是在关键技术、科技研发体系、国产替代、重要设备等方面启动的战略将产生很好的拉动效应;六是随着全球汽车周期的反转,中国汽车市场可能企稳;七是猪周期反转,猪肉供求常态化,猪肉价格的大幅度下降将为宏观政策提供空间,改善民众的消费预期;八是在基础设施投资持续改善、国有企业投资持续上升以及民营企业家预期的改善的作用下,民营投资将在2020年摆脱底部徘徊的困局;九是新一轮更加积极的财政政策和边际宽松的稳健货币政策将进一步发力,这与2020年全面小康带来的社会政策红利以及全球同步宽松带来的全球政策红利,一起决定了2020年的政策红利将大于前几个年份；十是中国庞大的市场、多元化出口路径、齐全的产业、雄厚的人力资源、开始普及的创新意识和创新竞争、强大的政府及其控制能力决定了，中国经济的韧性和弹性将在2020年进一步强化。

根据上述定性判断，设定系列参数，利用中国人民大学中国宏观经济分析与预测模型（CMAFM模型），预测结果如下。

第一，在全球经贸增速放缓、中美贸易摩擦加剧与内部需求回落等周期性力量与趋势性力量叠加的综合作用下，2019年中国宏观经济延续了2018年以来的疲软态势，呈现"持续趋缓"的态势。预计2019年实际GDP增速为6.1%，较2018年回落0.5个百分点，实现政府预定的6.0%—6.5%的经济增长目标。同时，由于GDP平减指数涨幅降至1.5%，名义GDP增速为7.6%，较2018年显著回落2.1个百分点，短期下行压力加大。

第二，在趋势性因素与周期性因素叠加、国际与国内不利因素强化的作用下，预计2020年经济增速将进一步回缓，但在"六稳"举措进一步发力、改革红利进一步显化、系列短期周期性力量转变的作用下，中国经济的弹性和韧性将持续显现，预计2020年实际GDP增速为5.9%，较2019年增速回落0.2个百分点。同时，由于GDP平减指数涨幅降至1.1%，2020年名义GDP增速为7%，较2019年回落0.6个百分点，下滑幅度明显收窄。在内外需求周期性下行的作用下，2020年投资和消费增速触底企稳，但仍难以有效回升，预计投资增长5.5%，消费增长8.0%；出口增速为-2.0%，进口增速为1.0%。2020年猪肉等食品价格大幅上涨引发的结构性通胀因素将在下半年明显回落，预计全年CPI涨幅将回落至2.3%；同时，在总需求不足和输入型的通缩因素的作用下，2020年工业领域的通缩风险上扬，预计PPI下跌1.0%；综合来看，GDP平减指数涨幅将回落至1.1%。

在上述判断和预测的基础上，报告提出了八个方面的政策建议。

第一，综合考虑现阶段国际、国内的趋势性因素和周期性因素，2020年中国经济增长的区间管理目标宜设为5.5%—6.0%，保守目标为5.8%左右，不仅能够完成"两个一百年"目标的阶段性任务和保证社会就业的基本稳定，也更有利于保持战略定力，按照既定方针推动经济高质量发展。

第二，将中期视角的"预期管理"作为各项宏观政策的统领和重要抓手。在内需增长出现明显下滑和结构分化达到新的临界值的背景下，简单的预调、微调已经不足以应对宏观经济日益面临的加速性下滑风险，而必须借助于中期视角的"预期管理"。2020年宏观政策要有前瞻性、市场主体要有前瞻性。

第三，落实十九届四中全会精神，全面开启新一轮全方位改革开放和新一轮供给侧结构性改革来解决我们面临的深层次结构性与体制性问题。在经济结构转换的关键期和深层次问题的累积释放期，简单的宏观政策调节和行政管控，难以应对基础性利益冲突和制度扭曲所产生的问题，基础性、全局性改革依然是解决目前结构转型时期各类深层次问题的关键。必须以构建高标准市场经济体系为目标，推出新一轮改革开放和供给侧结构性改革。

第四，构建货币政策新稳健的新框架，从哲学理念、目标体系、工具选择、审慎管理、汇率安排、预期管理和政策协调等方面，对新形势下的稳健货币政策的框架进行全面重构。建议2020年M2增速应当高于名义GDP增速的水平，达到8.5%—9.0%；全社会融资总额增速不能过快回调，保持在11%左右符合金融整顿与强化监管的要求。

第五，积极的财政政策需要更加积极有为，在更加积极的同时提高针对性，调动三个积极性。考虑到结构调整攻坚期的外部困局和内部大改革的特殊性，建议2020年财政赤字率可以提高到3.0%以上。减税降费从生产端向消费端和收入分配改革过渡。

第六，"稳投资"的政策方向和政策工具必须做出大幅度的调整，落实党的十九大提出的"发挥投资对优化供给结构的关键性作用"。

第七，民生政策要托底，应对经济下行和民生冲击叠加带来的"双重风险"。

第八，积极应对中美贸易摩擦，全新思考世界结构裂变期中国的战略选择。

关键词：2019—2020年中国宏观经济，增速回落中的结构分化，悲观预期中的利好

Abstract

China's macroeconomy in 2019 left the plateau of "stable but trending down" of 2016—2018. Economic growth declined in a larger scale and its economic structure was significantly differentiated. Intensifying Sino-US trade friction, a slowing global economy, aggravating domestic structural problems, and strengthening downward cyclical forces were among the main reasons for the decline. Confronted with the triple shocks of five weakening short-term cyclical factors, an accelerated decrease of three major traditional dividends and two temporary emergencies, China's macroeconomy nonetheless fully demonstrated its flexibility and resilience. Countercyclical policies with "six stability measures" as the core, along with continued supply-side structural reform as a hedge, helped China achieve its macroeconomic goals. However, in the context of declining economic growth, structural differentiation of the economy was relatively serious. Growth-enhancing types of structural adjustment slowed down, while recessionary and growth inhibiting types continued to accelerate, leading to a difficult period for China's economic structural adjustment in 2019.

In 2020, when the mission of building a moderately prosperous society in all respects will be accomplished, China's macroeconomy will undergo significant changes while continuing the basic operation mode of 2019. There is no need to be too pessimistic. On the one hand, the trends and structural forces leading to the economic downturn in 2019 will continue, which will further reduce potential GDP growth rate in 2020. On the other hand, many cyclical forces that led to the economic downturn in 2019 will begin to reverse in 2020. The reversal of these forces and the continued improvement of China's institutional dividends will be the most noteworthy changes. With the cultivation and consolidation of the following ten positive factors, the macroeconomic downturn will be eased, and the decline will be significantly narrower than that in 2019.

First, with the reorganization of its bureaucracy and the full implementation of the guidelines of the fourth plenary session of the 19th Central Committee of the Communist Party of China (CPC), China's institutional dividend will increase and the growth rate of Total Factor Productivity (TFP) will significantly improve. Second, with the stability of leverage ratios, the decline in the growth rate of debts payable, the orderly closing of high-risk institutions, the replenishment of financial institutions' capital, and enhanced regulations, financial risks will be restrained and financial environment will be significantly improved. Third, the inventory cycle of enterprises will bottom out and rebound. Excessive destocking early in 2019 will provide space for enterprises to replenish inventory in 2020. Fourth, the period of panic over Sino-US trade friction has passed, and adaptive adjustments are basically in place. As a result, business confidence will be restored. Fifth, various strategies launched to cope with external shocks will raise effective demand in several sectors, especially key technologies, scientific and technological research and development, domestic substitution, and important equipment. Sixth, with the reversal of the downturn in the global auto market, China's auto market may stabilize. Seventh, pig market cycle reverses and pork supply and demand return to normal. A sharp drop in pork prices will provide space for macro policies and improve consumer expectations. Eighth, with upgraded infrastructure investment, an increase of state-owned enterprise investment, and improved expectations of private entrepreneurs, private enterprise investment will no longer lag the rest of the economy in 2020. Ninth, a new round of more proactive fiscal policy and a prudent monetary policy with marginal easing will provide further support for aggregate demand. These policies, together with the social policy dividend in 2020 brought about by a moderately prosperous society in all respects, and the global policy dividend from global monetary easing, suggest that the policy dividend in 2020 will be higher than those in previous years. Finally, China's huge market, diversified exports, established industries, abundant human resources, growing acceptance of innovation and competition, and effective government oversight will strengthen China's economic flexibility and resilience in 2020.

Based on the above qualitative judgments, we set a series of parameters and use the China's Macroeconomic Analysis and Forecasting Model of Renmin University of China (CMAFM) to forecast. The results are as follows.

Firstly, under the combined effects of cyclical and trend forces, such as the slowdown of global economic and trade growth, the intensification of Sino-US trade friction, and the fall of domestic demand, China's macroeconomy in 2019 has continued its weak trend since 2018, showing signs of a "continuous slowdown". Real GDP growth rate is forecasted at 6.1% for 2019, 0.5 percentage points lower than that in 2018, achieving the government's economic growth target of 6.0%—6.5%. At the same time, as the growth rate of GDP deflator index is expected to drop to 1.5%, the growth rate of nominal GDP will be 7.6%, 2.1 percentage points lower than that in 2018, adding to the short-term downward pressure on the economy.

Secondly, under the influence of both trend and cyclical factors, and the strengthening of international and domestic adverse factors, economic growthin 2020 is expected to further decline. However, with the effects of the "six stability" initiative, the benefits of the reform dividend, and the transformation of a series of short-term cyclical forces, the elasticity and resilience of China's economy will continue. It is expected that the real GDP growth rate in 2020 will be 5.9%, 0.2 percentage points lower than that in 2019. At the same time, as the growth rate of GDP deflator index is expected to drop to 1.1%, the growth rate of nominal GDP in 2020 will be 7.0%, 0.6 percentage points lower than that in 2019, a significantly smaller decline. Driven by the cyclical downward trend of internal and external demand, growth rates of investment and consumption will bottom out and stabilize in 2020. Investment is expected to grow by 5.5% and consumption by 8.0%; the growth rate of exports will be -2.0% and the growth rate of imports 1.0%. In 2020, the structural inflation caused by a sharp rise in the prices of pork and other food will fall significantly in the second half of the year, and it is expected that annual CPI growth will fall to 2.3%. At the same time, under the influence of insufficient aggregate demand and imported deflation, the deflation risk in industrial sector will rise in 2020, and estimated PPI will fall by 1.0%. Taken together, the growth of GDP deflator index will fall back to 1.1%.

Based on the above judgments and forecasts, this report makes eight policy recommendations.

First, considering domestic and international trends and cyclical factors at the current stage, the target range of China's economic growth for 2020 should be set from 5.5% to 6%, with a conservative target around 5.8%. This rate of growth will not only enable achievement of "two centenary goals" and guarantee the basic stability of social employment, but it will also be conducive to maintaining a strategic focus and promoting high-quality economic development in accordance with established policies.

Second, make medium-term "expectation management" the guiding approach of macro policies. In the context of a significant decline in internal demand growth, with structural differentiation reaching a new threshold, simple pro-cyclical fine-tuning is no longer sufficient to cope with the accelerating risks of macroeconomic decline. Therefore, we must resort to "expectation management" of a medium-term perspective. In 2020, both macro policies and market entities should be forward-looking.

Third, implement theguidelines of the fourth plenary session of the 19th Central Committee of the CPC, that is, to initiate a new round of comprehensive reform and opening up as well as supply-side structural reform to address deep-seated structural and institutional problems. During the critical period of transforming economic structure and addressing cumulative deep-seated problems, simple macro-policy adjustment and administrative control will not be enough to deal with problems caused by conflicts of fundamental interests and distorted institutions. Fundamental and overall reform remains the key to solving various deep-seated problems in the current period of structural transformation. We must initiate a new round of reform, including opening up and supply-side structural reform, with the goal of building a high-standard market economy.

Fourth, construct a new framework of prudent monetary policy. Comprehensively reconstruct the framework from the perspectives of philosophy, target system, tool selection, prudential management, exchange rate arrangement, expectation management, and policy coordination. It is suggested that M2 growth should bequicker than nominal GDP growth in 2020, reaching 8.5—9.0%. The growth rate of total social financing should not be reduced too fast. Stabilizing it at around 11% is in line with the requirements of financial rectification and strengthened regulation.

Fifth, fiscal policy requires new initiatives that are more proactive and targeted. In view of the external difficulties in the critical period of structural adjustment and the particularity of major internal reforms, it is suggested that the fiscal deficit to GDP ratiobe raised to over 3.0% in 2020. The focus of cutting taxes and fees should shift from production to consumption and consider the effects on income distribution.

Sixth, the policy orientation and policy instruments of "stable domestic investment" must be substantially adjusted to implement theprinciple put forward at the 19th national congress of the CPC to "enable investment to play a crucial role in improving supply structure".

Seventh, livelihood policy should play a fundamental supporting role and address "dual risks" posed by the economic downturn and livelihood issues.

Eighth, actively manage trade friction with the United States, and think anew about China's strategic choices during the period of dramatic changes in the structure of global political economy.

Key words: China's Macroeconomy in 2019—2020; Structural Differentiation in the Slowdown of Economic Growth; Positive Factors in Pessimistic Expectations

目 录

一 总论与预测 …………………………………………… (1)

二 增速放缓与结构分化下的中国宏观经济 ……………… (11)

 (一) 全球经济开启新一轮低迷期，中国经济
   增速明显趋缓 ………………………………… (13)

 (二) 在"六稳"举措的提振作用下，中国
   经济综合表现好于市场悲观预期 …………… (27)

 (三) 衰退性的结构分化加剧，升级型的结构
   分化趋于停滞 ………………………………… (41)

三 中期视角下中国经济增长的性质和 2020 年
 运行模式 ……………………………………………… (60)

 (一) 中国宏观经济运行的 4 大趋势性
   因素 …………………………………………… (61)

 (二) 中国宏观经济运行的 5 大周期性
   因素 …………………………………………… (68)

（三）2020年中国宏观经济运行的10大
　　　积极因素 …………………………………………（76）

**四　2020年经济增长目标的确立和需要关注
　　的风险点** …………………………………………（97）
（一）2020年中国经济增长目标的确立……………（98）
（二）2020年宏观经济运行需要关注的
　　　风险点 ………………………………………（105）

五　结论与政策建议 ………………………………（139）

Contents

Chapter One　Overview and Forecast ·························· (163)

Chapter Two　China's Macroeconomy under the Situation of Slowing Growth and Structural Differentiation ························ (178)

Chapter Three　The Nature of China's Economic Growth in 2020 from a Midium-term Perspective ······ (239)

Chapter Four　The Establishment of an Economic Growth Target for 2020 Considering Possible Risks ······ (284)

Chapter Five　Conclusions and Policy Suggestions ············ (338)

一　总论与预测[*]

2019年在中美贸易摩擦全面加剧、世界经济同步回落、国内结构性因素持续发酵、周期性下行力量有所加大等多重因素的作用下，中国宏观经济告别了2016—2018年"稳中趋缓"的平台期，经济增速回落幅度加大，经济结构分化明显。但中国宏观经济的弹性和韧性在"六稳"政策的作用下显示出强大的力量，中国宏观经济依然在预期、可控的区间运行。

第一，GDP平减指数的明显回落、需求端参数的同步下滑表明周期性下行力量依然是2019年中国宏观经济下滑的核心原因。一是企业库存周期自2018年第三季度结束高位运转之后快速步入新的下行期，市场化去库存和政策性去库存叠加带来了明显的加速收缩效应；二是民间投资在投资收益预期下滑、信心疲软、投资空间约束等因素的制约下，难以及时跟进国有企业投资摆脱周期底部运行的困境；三是在金融风险高位缓释、国有企业

---

[*] 本书书稿完成时间为2019年年底。其中对2020年的预测分析未考虑新冠肺炎疫情的影响，作为对未发生疫情下的情景分析和疫情恢复期的比较基准，供读者参考。

持续去杠杆、中小金融机构风险持续暴露等因素的作用下，中国经济主体的偿债能力还没有全面反转，金融周期底部运行的特点十分明显；四是在逆全球化运动和国际冲突全面蔓延的作用下，全球不确定性大幅度上升，国际贸易增速同步回落，全球耐用品和投资品需求明显收缩，导致世界经济低迷期全面重启。

第二，供给端的疲软、各类基础性参数的持续变化以及潜在GDP增速的惯性变化，说明趋势性力量和结构性力量的下滑依然是GDP增速回落的主要因素。一是中美贸易摩擦的全面爆发以及全球经济低迷期的重启决定了中国经济传统动能之一的全球化红利不仅没有呈现企稳回升的态势，反而出现了快速下滑；二是PPI由正转负、工业利润的持续负增长以及制造业份额的持续下滑说明了中国经济传统动能之一的工业化红利递减不仅没有止跌，反而在近期出现加速的态势；三是人口老龄化率的加快、流动性人口的负增长以及储蓄率的持续下滑说明另一中国经济传统动能的人口红利依然处于加速递减期。

第三，中美贸易摩擦的全面爆发以及猪肉价格的暴涨是2019年宏观经济运行中最独特并值得重点关注的两大事件。对美出口关税的不断提升以及中美贸易谈判的高度不确定性对于中国外需变化以及经济主体的预期带来了较为明显的边际冲击，这些冲击是民间投资回落以及其他周期性下滑力量有所加剧的核心原因之一。猪肉价格的飙升不仅对居民消费和消费预期带来了明显的冲击，也对宏观经济政策调控带来了明显的干扰，是中国消费增速的加速回落的核心原因之一。

第四，在短期周期因素同步回落、三大传统红利加速递减以及临时突发事件的三重冲击下，中国宏观经济的弹性和韧性得到了全面显现，在以"六稳"为核心的逆周期调节政策和持续的供给侧结构性改革的对冲下，中国宏观经济成功守住底线、完成了预期的目标。一是就业稳，守住了不发生失业潮的底线；二是金融稳，守住了不发生系统性和区域性金融风险的底线；三是制度红利开始加速上扬，资源配置效率和TFP增速开始有明显改善。

第五，需要注意的是，在经济增速回落的过程中，经济的结构性分化较为严重，升级型的结构调整速度放慢，而萧条型的结构调整却持续加速，从而导致2019年中国经济结构调整步入艰难期。一是虽然第三产业增速依然高于第二产业，但第三产业增速回落幅度明显高于第二产业；二是虽然很多新兴产业和高技术产业增速依然高于传统行业，但新兴产业和高技术产业增速的回落明显加速，开始与传统行业增速有拉平的趋势；三是行业分化、区域分化、不同规模的企业绩效分化较为严重，导致很多行业、区域和中小企业的绩效恶化，开始触及底线，短板效应开始在不断累积。

2020年是中国全面建成小康年，也是中国GDP增速持续回落的一年。中国宏观经济将在延续2019年基本运行模式的基础上出现重大的变化。一方面，2019年下行的趋势性力量和结构性力量将持续发力，导致2020年潜在GDP增速进一步回落；另一方面，2019年下行的很多周期性力量在2020年开始出现拐点性变化，宏观经济下行有所缓和，下行幅度将较2019年明显收窄。

第一，新常态的增速换挡期、动力转换期以及前期风险的释放期尚未结束，决定全球化红利、工业化红利以及人口红利的趋势性力量并没有出现趋稳的迹象，将延续2019年的发展态势。这决定了2020年中国潜在GDP增速将进一步回落，并成为2020年GDP增速跌破6%的重要原因。

第二，2020年是美国大选年也是英国脱欧年，全球地缘政治冲突和世界经济面临的不确定性将进一步上扬，信心低迷、投资下滑、贸易收缩将进一步恶化，2020年中国宏观经济的外部环境并不会出现改善。

第三，部分周期性力量将出现反转以及中国制度红利的持续改善将是2020年最为值得关注和期待的新变化。一是随着吏治整顿的基本到位和十九届四中全会精神的全面落实，中国制度红利将全面上扬，TFP增速将明显改善；二是随着各类杠杆率的稳定、应付债务增速的下降、高风险机构的有序处置、金融机构资本金的补足、监管短板的完善使金融风险趋于收敛，化解金融风险的攻坚战取得了阶段性胜利，金融环境将得到明显改善；三是企业库存周期触底反弹，前期过度去库存为2020年企业补库存提供了较大的空间；四是对中美贸易摩擦的恐慌期已经过去，适应性调整基本到位，企业信心将得到明显回归；五是为应对外部冲击而启动的各类战略将有效提升相应部门的有效需求，特别是在关键技术、科技研发体系、国产替代、重要设备等方面启动的战略将产生很好的拉动效应；六是随着全球汽车周期的反转，中国汽车市场可能企稳；七是猪周期反转，猪肉供求常态化，猪肉价格的大幅度下降将为宏观政策提供空间，改善民众的消费预期；八是在基础设施投资持续改善、国有企业投资持续上升以及民营企业家预期的改善的作用下，民营投资将在2020年摆脱底部徘徊的困局；九是新一轮更加积极的财政政策和边际宽松的稳健货币政策将进一步发力，这与2020年全面小康带来的社会政策红利以及全球同步宽松带来的全球政策红利，一起决定了2020年的政策红利将大于前几个年份；十是中国庞大的市场、多元化出口路径、齐全的产业、雄厚的人力资源、开始普及的创新意识和创新竞争、强大的政府及其控制能力决定了，中国经济的韧性和弹性将在2020年进一步强化。

第四，2020年也是充满不确定性和风险的一年。一是美国大选是否会进一步激化中美贸易摩擦，特别是由于特朗普的个性特征和两党斗争的白热化出现超预期事件的发生；二是猪肉价格下降是否会按照预定的路径进行，是否会在回落中出现通货紧缩，还是在持续价格蔓延中出现物价持续上扬；三是在GDP增速进一步回落中结构持续分化是否会带来局部产业、局部区域以及中小企业的拐点性变化，从而诱发新的局部风险。

综合考虑现阶段国际、国内的趋势性因素和周期性因素，2020年中国经济增长的区间管理目标宜设为5.5%—6.0%，保守目标为5.8%左右，能够完成"两个一百年"目标的阶段性任务和保证社会就业的基本稳定，也更有利于保持战略定力，按照既定方针推动经济高质量发展。

根据上述的一些定性判断，利用中国人民大学中国宏观经济分析与预测模型（CMAFM模型），不考虑2019年国民经济核算方法的调整和第四次全国经济普查对历史数据的修订，设定主要宏观经济政策假设：（1）2019年与2020年名义一般公共预算赤字率分别为2.8%与3.0%；（2）2019年与2020年人民币与美元平均兑换率分别为6.9∶1与7.0∶1。分年度预测2019年与2020年中国宏观经济核心指标，其预测结果如表1所示。

表1　2019—2020年中国宏观经济核心指标预测

预测指标	2016年	2017年	2018年	2019年*	2020年*
1. GDP增长率（%）	6.7	6.8	6.6	6.1	5.9
第一产业	3.3	4.0	3.5	3.2	3.3
第二产业	6.3	5.9	5.8	5.5	5.3
第三产业	7.7	7.9	7.6	6.9	6.6
2. 固定资产投资完成额（亿元）	596501	631684	635636	670596	707479
（增长率,%）	8.1	7.2	5.9	5.5	5.5
社会消费品零售总额（亿元）	332316	366262	380987	411847	444794
（增长率,%）	10.4	10.2	9.0	8.1	8.0
3. 出口（亿美元）	20976	22633	24867	24618	24126
（增长率,%）	-7.7	7.9	9.9	-1.0	-2.0
进口（亿美元）	15879	18438	21357	20289	20492
（增长率,%）	-5.5	16.1	15.8	-5.0	1.0

续表

预测指标	2016年	2017年	2018年	2019年*	2020年*
净出口（亿美元）	5097	4196	3509	4329	3634
（增长率,%）	-14.2	-17.7	-16.4	23.4	-16.0
4. CPI上涨率（%）	2.0	1.6	2.1	2.7	2.3
PPI上涨率（%）	-1.4	6.3	3.5	-0.5	-1.0
GDP平减指数上涨率（%）	1.1	3.8	2.9	1.5	1.1
5. M2增长率（%）	11.3	8.1	8.1	8.5	8.5
M1增长率（%）	21.4	11.8	1.5	3.5	4.0
社会融资规模存量增长率（%）	12.8	13.4	9.9	10.9	10.5
社会融资规模流量（亿元）	178022	223969	192584	235446	240000
6. 政府收入（亿元）	206171	234029	258757	272348	286325
（增长率,%）	6.0	13.5	10.6	5.3	5.1
公共财政收入（亿元）	159552	172567	183352	189403	195085
（增长率,%）	4.5	7.4	6.2	3.3	3.0
政府性基金收入（亿元）	46619	61462	75405	82945	91240
（增长率,%）	11.9	34.8	22.6	10.0	10.0

注：*表示预测值。

数据来源：Wind数据库、中国人民大学中国宏观经济论坛测算。

第一，在全球经贸增速放缓、中美贸易摩擦加剧与内部需求回落等周期性力量与趋势性力量叠加的综合作用下，2019年中国宏观经济延续了2018年以来的疲软态势，呈现"持续趋缓"的态势。预计2019年实际GDP增速为6.1%，较2018年回落0.5个百分点，实现了政府预定的6.0%—6.5%的经济增长目标。同时，由于GDP平减指数涨幅降至1.5%，名义GDP增速为7.6%，较2018年显著回落2.1个百分点，短期下行压力加大。在趋势性因素与周期性因素叠加、国际与国内不利因素强化的作用下，预计2020年经济增速将进一步回缓，但在"六稳"

举措进一步发力、改革红利进一步显化、系列短期周期性力量转变的作用下,中国经济的弹性和韧性将持续显现,预计2020年实际GDP增速为5.9%,较2019年增速回落0.2个百分点。同时,由于GDP平减指数涨幅降至1.1%,2020年名义GDP增速为7.0%,较2019年回落0.6个百分点,下滑幅度明显收窄。

第二,从供给面的角度来看,在总需求不足和全球制造业低迷等因素的作用下,工业增速稳中趋缓,得益于建筑业增速回升的部分对冲,第二产业增速小幅下降,预计2019年第二产业实际增速为5.5%,较2018年回落0.3个百分点。但工业增速的持续下滑抑制了生产性服务业的增长,导致第三产业增长势头放缓,预计2019年第三产业增速为6.9%,较2018年回落0.7个百分点。在猪瘟疫情等因素的影响下,预计第一产业增速放缓至3.2%,较2018年回落0.3个百分点。在趋势性力量的作用下,2020年经济结构深化调整的格局将进一步延续,预计第二产业增长5.3%,第三产业增长6.6%,分别较2019年回落0.2个和0.3个百分点。

第三,从总需求的角度来看,消费、投资、出口三大需求均出现不同程度下滑。在居民收入增长放缓和预期恶化等因素的作用下,2019年汽车等耐用品消费增速明显回落。预计全年社会零售销售总额增长8.1%,比2018年下滑0.9个百分点,扣除价格因素,实际增长6.3%,较2018年回落0.6个百分点。基础设施建设投资增速逐渐企稳回升,但难抵制造业投资的显著回落，全社会固定资产投资增速持续放缓，预计2019年增速为5.5%，较2018年进一步下滑0.4个百分点。在全球经贸增速下滑和中美贸易摩擦升级的影响下，2019年中国出口增速显著回落，但进口增速回落的幅度更大，导致净出口规模显著扩大。预计2019年以美元计价的出口增速为-1.0%，进口增速为-5.0%，净出口规模为4329亿美元，较2018年大幅增长23.4%，为近3年来首次规模扩大。在内外需求周期性下行的作用下，2020年投资和消费增速触底企稳，仍难以有效回升，预计投资增长5.5%，消费增长8.0%；出口增速为-2.0%，进口增速为1.0%。

第四，受猪瘟疫情影响，猪肉价格大幅上涨导致食品价格攀升，带动CPI持续走高，预计2019年CPI上涨2.7%。但中国总需求不足的局面不仅没有得到缓解，反而进一步加剧，非食品CPI、核心CPI持续走低，叠加原油等国际大宗商品价格下行，工业品价格出现显著回落。预计2019年PPI下跌0.5%，比2018年显著回落4.0个百分点。综合来看，GDP平减指数涨幅为1.5%，较2018年回落1.4个百分点，物价水平总体平稳，但价格形势的分化达到新高度。2020年猪肉等食品价格大幅上涨引发的结构性通胀因素将在下半年明显回落，预计CPI涨幅将回落至2.3%；同时，在总需求不足和输入型的通缩因素的作用下，2020年工业领域的通缩风险全面上扬，预计PPI下跌1.0%；综合来看，2020年GDP平减指数将进一步回落，预计涨幅下降为1.1%。

第五，在稳增长与防风险的综合平衡下，2019年货币政策在保持稳健中性的基础上，加快了改革的步伐，从而富有新的内涵。预计2019年M2增速为8.5%，较2018年提高0.4个百分点。得益于货币政策边际宽松和LPR改革，全社会融资总额增速出现较快增长。预计2019年全社会融资总额存量增速为10.9%，较2018年提升1.0个百分点。2020年货币政策仍将保持边际宽松定位，预计M2增速为8.5%，与2019年持平；但经济内生性的紧缩压力加大，预计2020年社会融资总额存量增速为10.5%，较2019年小幅回落。

第六，在经济下行和减税降费的作用下，政府公共财政收入增速持续回落，叠加土地市场的景气消退导致政府性基金收入增速大幅回落，政府总收入增速全面放缓。预计2019年公共财政收入增速为3.3%，达到18.9万亿元，政府性基金收入增速为10.0%，达到8.3万亿元，两项收入合计达到27.2万亿元，增长5.3%，较2018年增速回落5.3个百分点，政府维持收支平衡的压力加大。由于宏观经济基本面和积极的财政政策定位没有发生明显改变，预计2020年财政收入和政府性基金收入增速与2019年基本持平，分别增长3.0%和10.0%，两项收入合计增长5.1%。

二 增速放缓与结构分化下的中国宏观经济

2019年全球经济增速和贸易增速双双大幅下滑,降至近10年来的最低水平。在此背景下,中国宏观经济核心指标也出现一定放缓,但是下滑幅度低于全球和主要经济体降幅,综合表现也好于2018年年底的市场悲观预期。值得关注的是,中国宏观经济总需求不足的问题尚未得到有效缓解,反而有所加剧,新一轮经济下行的内生性紧缩机制已经形成,引发宏观经济加速性下滑风险。

表2　　2019年中国宏观经济指标基础数据

预测指标	2015年	2016年	2017年	2018年	2019年 1—6月	2019年 1—9月
1. 国内生产总值增长率(%)	6.9	6.7	6.9	6.6	6.3	6.2
其中:第一产业增加值	3.9	3.3	3.9	3.5	3.0	2.9
第二产业增加值	6.2	6.1	6.1	5.8	5.8	5.6
第三产业增加值	8.2	7.8	8.0	7.6	7.0	7.0
2. 固定资产投资完成额(亿元)	551590	596501	631684	645675	299100	461204
(增长率,%)	10.0	8.1	7.2	5.9	5.8	5.4

续表

预测指标	2015年	2016年	2017年	2018年	2019年 1—6月	2019年 1—9月
社会消费品零售总额（亿元）	300931	332316	366261	380987	195210	296674
（增长率,%）	10.7	10.4	10.2	9.0	8.5	8.2
3. 出口（亿美元）	22735	20976	22633	24867	11711	18251
（增长率,%）	-2.9	-7.7	7.9	9.9 (7.1)	0.1 (6.1)	-0.1 (5.2)
进口（亿美元）	16796	15879	18419	21357	9900	15266
（增长率,%）	-14.3	-5.5	16.0	15.8 (12.9)	-4.3 (1.4)	-5 (-0.1)
4. 广义货币（M2）增长率（%）	13.3	11.3	8.2	8.1	8.5	8.4
狭义货币（M1）增长率（%）	15.2	21.4	11.8	1.5	4.4	3.4
社会融资规模（亿元）	154086	178022	194430	193000	125100	187378
社会融资规模存量增长率（%）	12.4	12.8	12.0	9.8	10.9	10.8
5. 居民消费价格指数上涨率（%）	1.4	2.0	1.6	2.1	2.2	2.5
工业生产者出厂价格指数上涨率（%）	-5.2	-1.4	6.3	3.5	0.3	0
GDP平减指数上涨率（%）	0.1	1.2	4.1	3.4	2.1	1.7
6. 全国政府性收入（亿元）	194547	206171	234029	258757	139627	203841
增长率（%）	0.1	6.0	13.5	10.6	3.1	4.4
全国公共财政收入（亿元）	152217	159552	172567	183352 (6.2)	107846 (3.4)	150678 (3.3)
全国政府性基金收入（亿元）	42330	46619	61462	75405 (22.6)	31781 (1.7)	53163 (7.7)

注：小括号中为以人民币计价的增长率。

数据来源：Wind数据库、中国人民大学中国宏观经济论坛测算。

二 增速放缓与结构分化下的中国宏观经济 | 13

◇（一）全球经济开启新一轮低迷期，中国经济增速明显趋缓

2019年全球经济出现了剧烈共振。在中美贸易摩擦全面加剧的作用下，全球经济贸易政策的不确定性以及地缘政治风险大幅上扬到历史新高，不仅直接造成中美两大经济增长火车头受挫，也使得全球风险上扬和市场信心低迷，加剧了世界范围内的可贸易品、投资品和耐用消费品的全面收缩，导致全球制造业陷入集体性低迷期，世界经济开启新一轮下行周期。鉴于全球主要经济体增速的普遍放缓和贸易摩擦的不确定性，目前各大国际组织纷纷下调了2019年经济和贸易增长预期。根据国际货币基金组织（IMF）2019年10月的最新报告，2019年全球经济增速预计下滑至3.0%，比2018年大幅回落0.6个百分点，这也是自2010年走出国际金融危机以来的最低水平；2019年全球贸易增速预计下滑至1.1%，比2018年显著回落2.5个百分点，比经济增速回落幅度更大，也是自2010年走出国际金融危机以来的最低水平。

在全球贸易品、投资品和耐用消费品的全面收缩下，全球制造业陷入集体性低迷期。2019年全球制造业陷入集体性低迷期，与服务业的分化达到历史新水平。自2018年开始，全球制造业

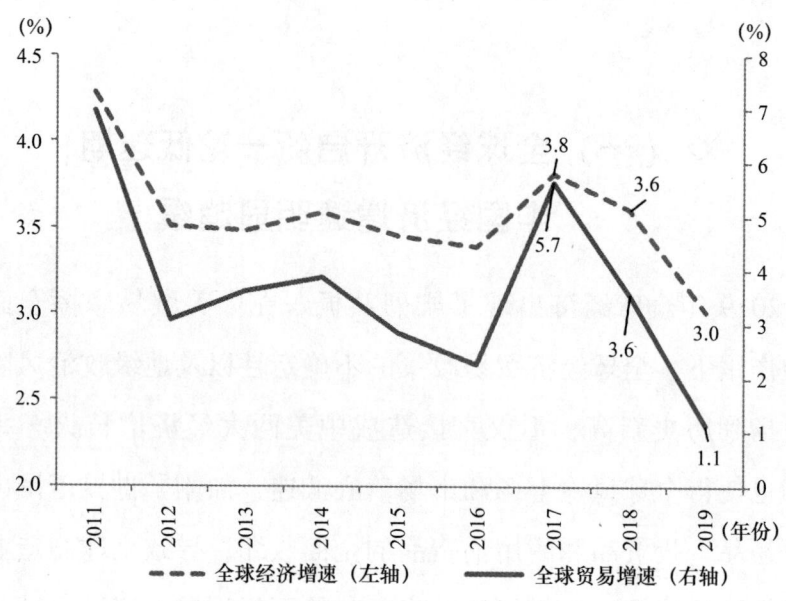

图 1　全球经济增速和贸易增速急剧下滑

PMI 就一路下行，自 2019 年 5 月起，已经连续 5 个月处于 50%以下的紧缩区间，9 月为 49.7%；与此同时，服务业 PMI 也有所下行，但目前依然处于扩张区间，9 月为 51.6%，与制造业 PMI 的缺口在持续扩大。上述情况在欧元区的表现尤其明显，在日本、美国和英国也是如此。自 2019 年 2 月起，欧元区制造业 PMI 就已经跌入紧缩区间，并呈现不断恶化的趋势，截至 10 月，制造业 PMI 已降至 45.7%，但服务业 PMI 依然保持在扩张区间，10 月为 51.8%；其中，德国制造业 PMI 自 1 月起降至紧缩区间，10 月已大幅降至 41.9%，而服务业 PMI 依然保持在扩张区间，10 月为 51.2%。日本制造业 PMI 也是自 1 月起降至紧缩区间，

10月降至48.5%,而服务业PMI依然保持在扩张区间,9月为52.8%。类似的,美国制造业PMI自8月起降至紧缩区间,但下滑速度更快,9月已降至47.8%,而服务业PMI依然保持在扩张

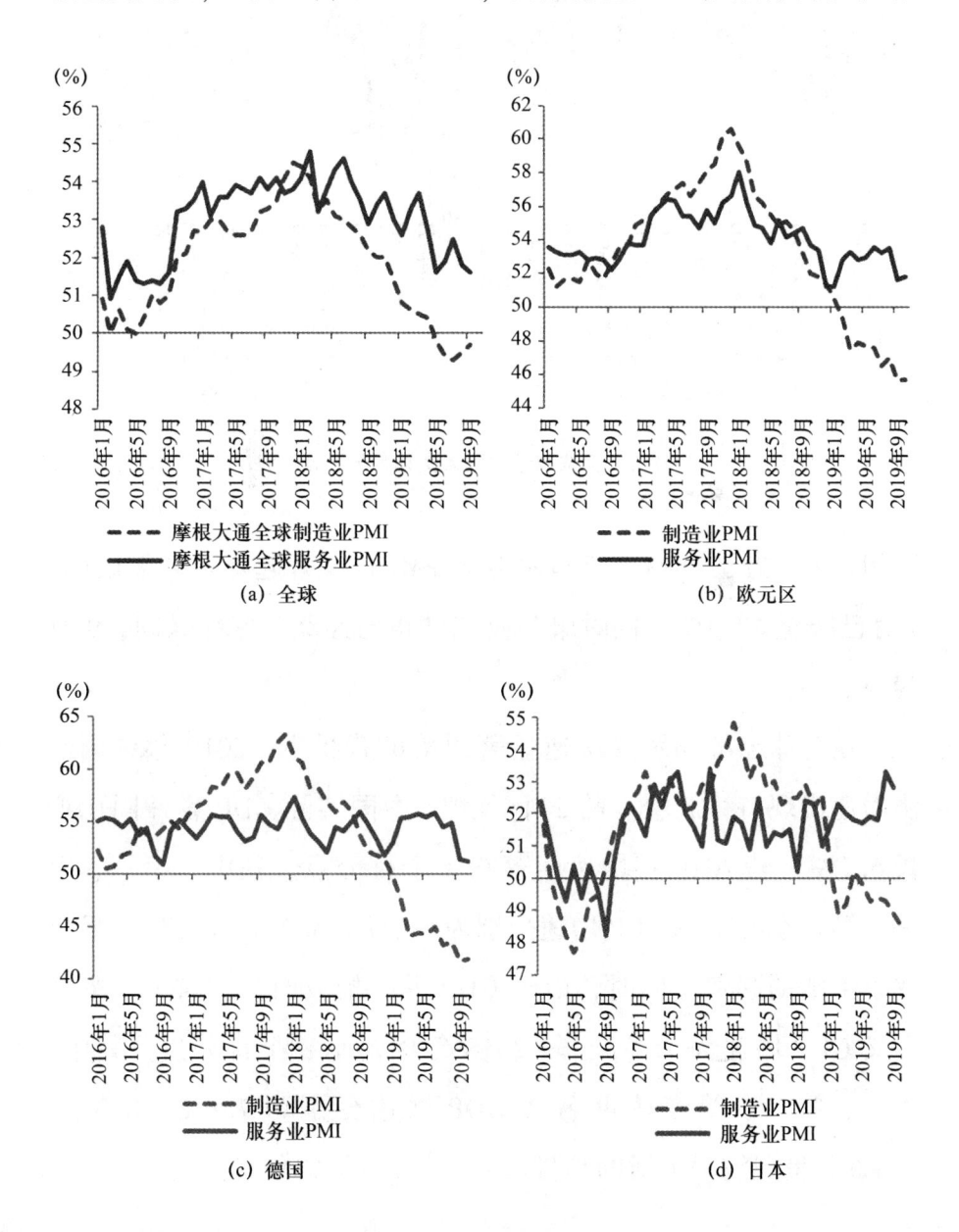

(a) 全球

(b) 欧元区

(c) 德国

(d) 日本

(e) 美国　　　　　　　　　　　　(f) 英国

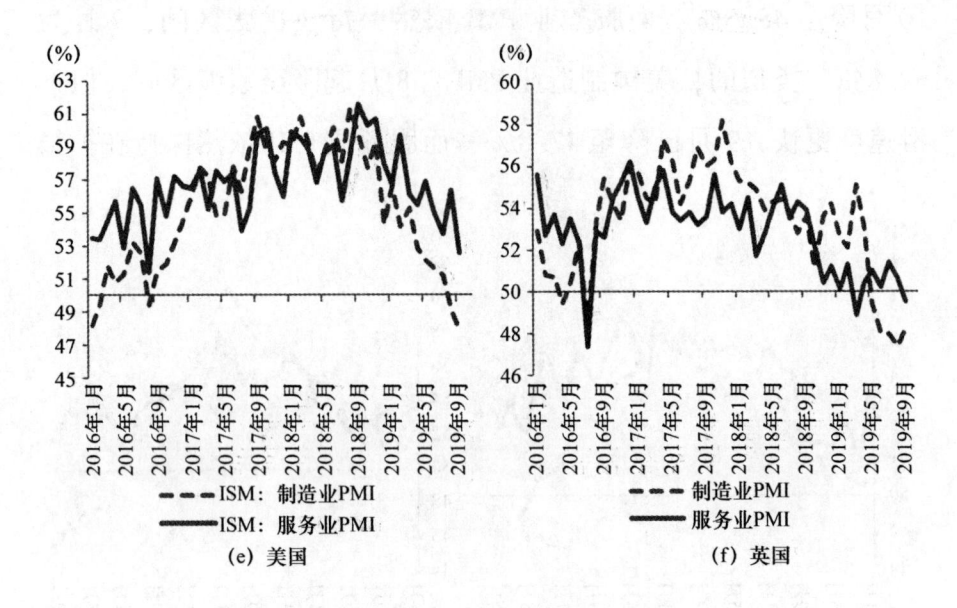

图2　全球制造业陷入集体性低迷期

区间，9月为52.6%。英国制造业PMI自5月起降至紧缩区间，9月已降至48.3%，同时服务业PMI也已经跌入紧缩区间，9月为49.5%。

在全球经济和贸易增速显著回落的背景下，2019年中国经济增速出现持续放缓。前3个季度，中国实际GDP累计同比增长6.2%，较2018年增速回落0.4个百分点。其中，第一、第二、第三季度实际GDP增速分别为6.4%、6.2%、6.0%，呈现逐季下滑的趋势。同时，由于GDP平减指数回落，前3个季度名义GDP增速为7.9%，较2018年回落1.8个百分点。其中，第一、第二、第三季度名义GDP增速分别为7.8%、8.3%、7.6%，呈现波动下滑的趋势。

二 增速放缓与结构分化下的中国宏观经济 | 17

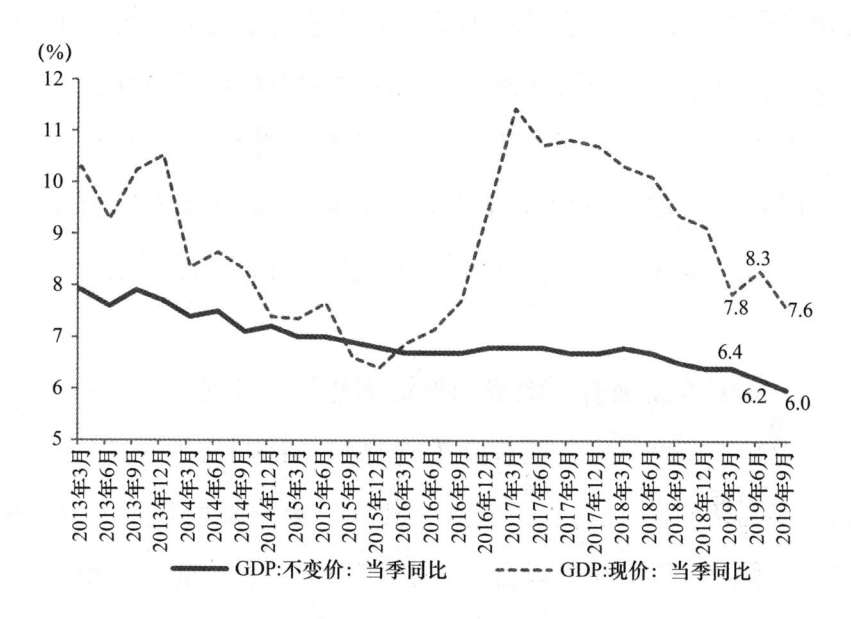

图3 中国经济增速呈现放缓趋势

虽然中国经济下行压力加大，经济增速也在放缓，但相比全球主要经济体的表现，中国经济增长依然最为稳定，领先优势明显。2019年全球GDP增速下滑了0.6百分点，美国、欧元区分别下滑0.6个、0.7个百分点，印度下滑超过1.0个百分点，不少国家陷入技术性衰退，而中国仅下滑了0.5个百分点，经济增速位居全球主要经济体首位。

但是，随着世界经济新一轮低迷期的开启，2019年中国宏观经济不仅延续了2018年下半年以来总需求不足的局面，而且新一轮经济下行的紧缩机制正加速形成，产生了较为强烈的收缩效应，主要表现在：一是消费和投资需求全面回落，与产出的缺口主要是以大幅减少进口来填平，即依靠净出口的短期大幅增长实现脆弱平衡；二是总需求不足开始加速向供给面传导，制造业和服务业增速出现全面下滑，企业绩效和市场预期恶化；三是制造业生产和投资增速的回落趋于同步化，并向生产性服务业传导；四是核心 CPI、PPI 同步下行，并反过来通过价格紧缩效应导致市场主体感受趋冷，导致投资和消费信心越加不足。

1. 从需求面来看，消费和投资增速持续放缓

前 3 个季度，社会消费品零售总额累计同比增长 8.2%，较 2018 年同期回落 1.1 个百分点。其中，第三季度仅增长 7.6%，较第二季度回落 1.0 个百分点。扣除价格因素，前 3 个季度社会消费品零售总额实际同比增长 6.4%，较 2018 年同期回落 0.9

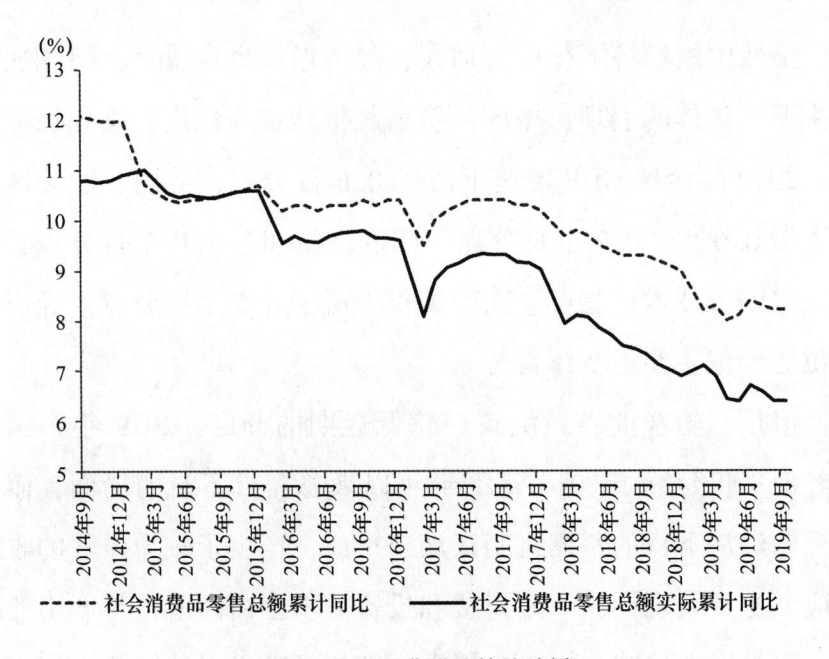

图 4 中国消费增速持续放缓

个百分点。

此外,前3个季度,固定资产投资累计同比增长5.4%,重新回落至2018年同期水平。其中,民间投资同比增长4.7%,较2018年同期大幅回落4.0个百分点,重回加速下滑趋势;房地产投资增长10.5%,较2018年同期回升0.6个百分点,对总投资起到了一定的支撑作用。

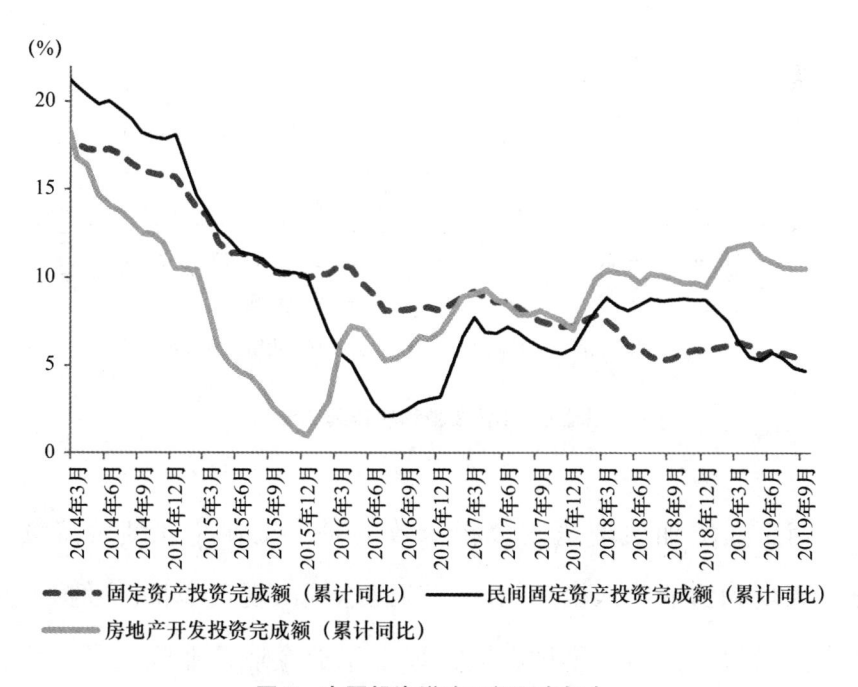

图5 中国投资增速下行压力加大

2. 从供给面来看,总需求持续不足导致工业和服务业增速也屡创新低

前3个季度,规模以上工业增加值同比增长5.6%,较2018年同期增速大幅回落0.8个百分点,且自第一季度以来呈现持续

下滑的态势。其中，制造业增加值同比增长5.9%，也较2018年同期增速下滑0.8个百分点，同样自第一季度以来呈不断下滑的趋势。

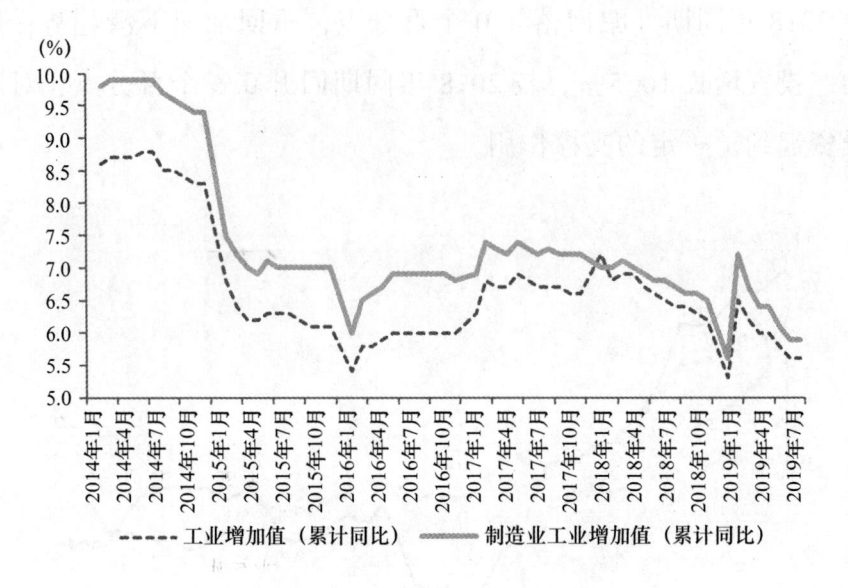

图6 中国工业增速持续下滑

与工业增加值增速放缓相一致的是，工业企业绩效持续恶化，表现为营业收入增速放缓，利润总额出现负增长，亏损面呈现扩大趋势。前3个季度，规模以上工业企业营业收入同比增长4.5%，较2018年增速回落了5.1个百分点；利润总额同比下降2.1%，其中第一季度下降3.3%，第二季度下降1.9%，第三季度下降1.8%，呈逐季收窄态势。前3个季度，营业收入利润率为5.9%，同比降低0.4个百分点。从亏损面看，前8个月，亏损企业家数同比增长5.7%，较2018年增速小幅回落0.5个百分点，但是亏损企业亏损额同比增长 11.6%，较 2018 年增速扩大 6.2 个百分点，说明存在亏损集中化趋势，局部产业和企业可能面临经营风险临界点。

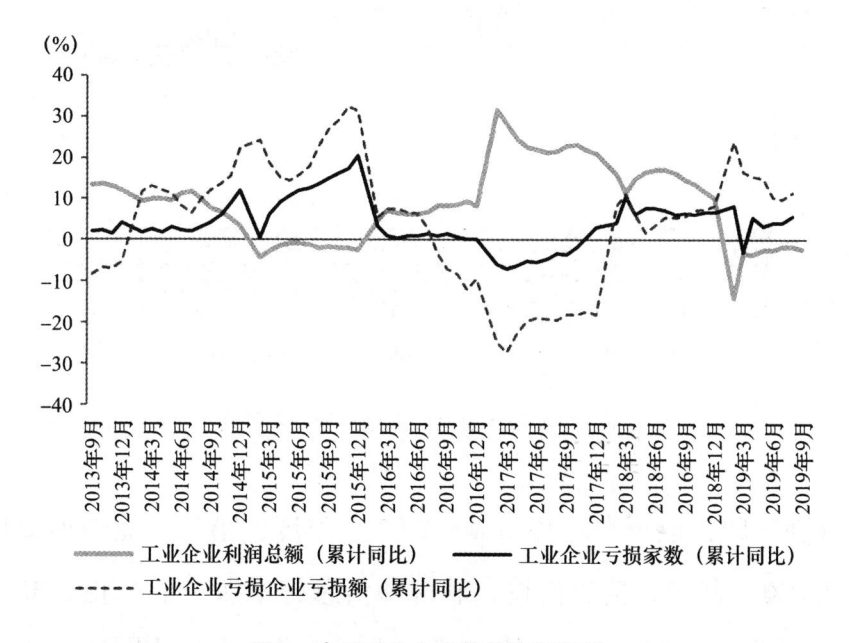

图 7 中国工业企业效益有所恶化

从制造业景气度来看，与全球制造业变化趋势一致，中国制造业 PMI 自 2018 年年中以来呈现下滑趋势，自 2019 年 5 月以来已连续 6 个月处于紧缩区间，10 月为 49.3%。从 PMI 分项指数来看，新订单特别是新出口订单的下行带来了较大拖累作用。10 月，PMI 新订单指数下滑至 49.6%，特别是新出口订单指数下降至 47.0%，自 2018 年 6 月以来已连续 17 个月处于紧缩区间。

从服务业来看，2019 年前 3 个季度，服务业生产仍然保持

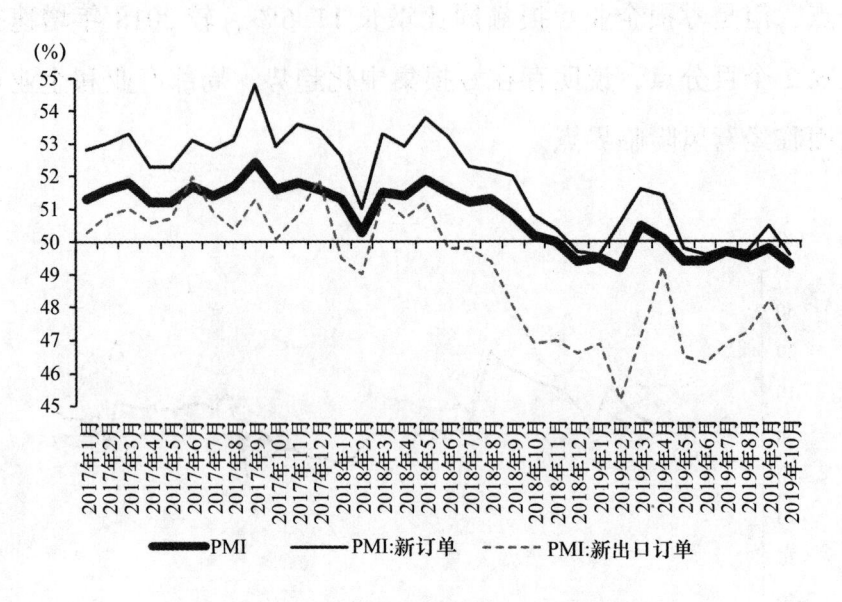

图8 中国制造业 PMI 持续处于紧缩区间

在合理区间，但下滑趋势明显。前3个季度，第三产业增加值增长7.0%，其中，信息传输、软件和信息技术服务业，租赁和商务服务业，交通运输、仓储和邮政业，金融业增加值同比分别增长19.8%、8.0%、7.4%和7.1%，增速分别快于第三产业增加值12.8个、1.0个、0.4个和0.1个百分点。前8个月，规模以上服务业企业营业收入同比增长9.5%，其中，战略性新兴服务业、高技术服务业和科技服务业营业收入分别增长12.1%、11.9%和11.6%，增速分别快于全部规模以上服务业2.6个、2.4个和2.1个百分点。

从服务业景气指数看，服务业 PMI 指数持续运行在扩张区间，与制造业 PMI 指数运行呈现明显分化的态势。但值得关注

二 增速放缓与结构分化下的中国宏观经济

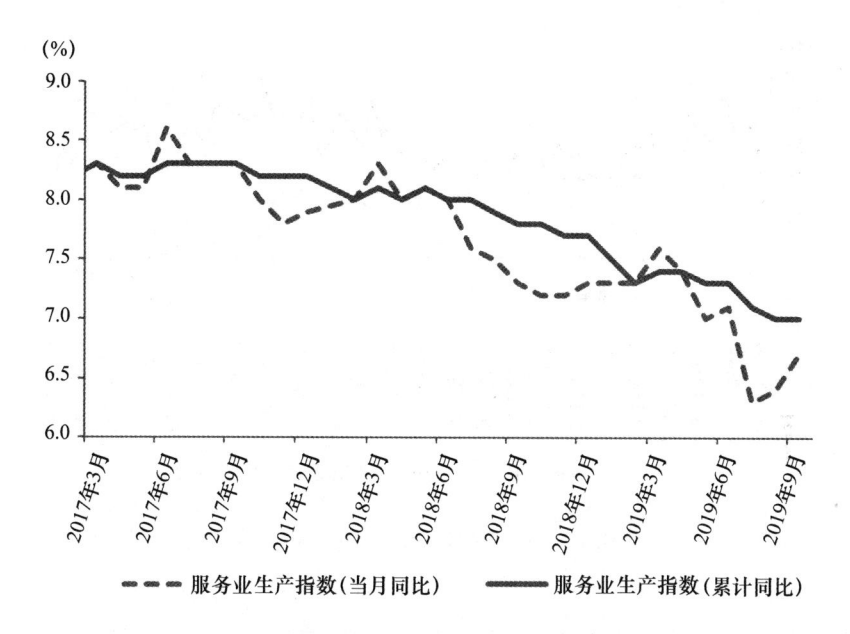

图9 中国服务业生产指数下行压力加大

的是,随着制造业持续疲软,服务业特别是生产性服务业也面临较大的下行压力。前3个季度,服务业生产指数同比增长7.0%,较2018年同期回落0.9个百分点,特别是第三季度服务业生产指数增速首次跌破了7%,其中7—9月分别为6.3%、6.4%和6.7%。10月,服务业PMI指数较9月大幅下滑1.6个百分点至51.4%,显示服务业下行压力进一步加大。

3. 在食品价格结构性上涨的同时,非食品CPI、核心CPI和PPI持续走低,反映了总需求不足带来的加速性下滑压力

2019年年初以来,食品价格出现了轮番上涨,特别是第三

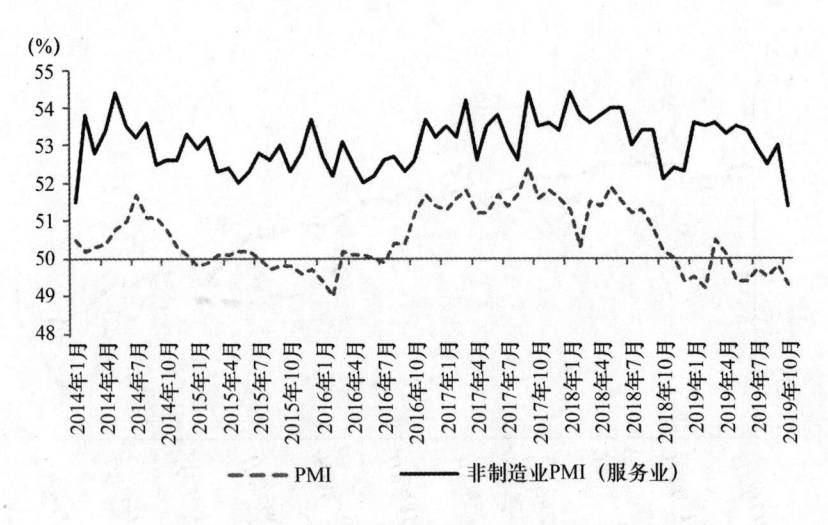

图10 中国制造业与服务业PMI走势

季度在猪肉价格的带动下，食品CPI出现较大涨幅，导致CPI持续走高。9月，食品CPI同比增长11.2%，CPI同比增长3.0%。但是，在食品价格快速上涨的同时，与宏观经济相对应的各类价格指数却在持续下行，反映了总需求不足带来的宏观经济加速性下滑压力，内生紧缩机制已经形成。2019年年初以来，非食品CPI、核心CPI和PPI等物价指数涨幅持续回落，特别是PPI已步入通缩区间。9月，非食品CPI和核心CPI涨幅分别降至1.0%和1.5%，较年初回落了0.7个和0.4个百分点。更重要的是，工业领域出现一定的通缩迹象。进入2019年以来，PPI涨幅由2018年的3.5%急剧回落至近零增长，第三季度以来由正转负，而且跌幅呈扩大趋势。9月，PPI同比下跌1.2%，较8月份跌幅进一步扩大0.4个百分点。

二 增速放缓与结构分化下的中国宏观经济

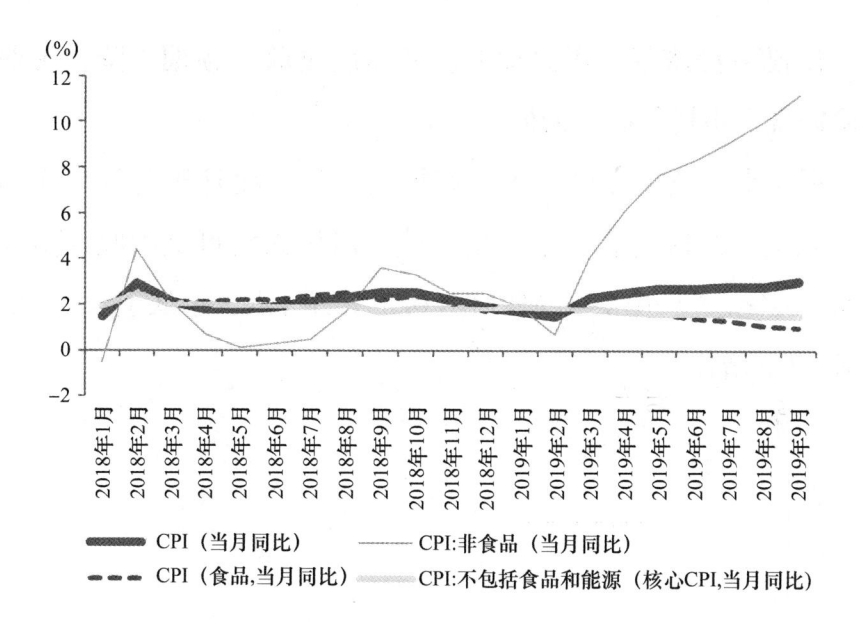

图11 中国食品CPI与非食品CPI走势分化

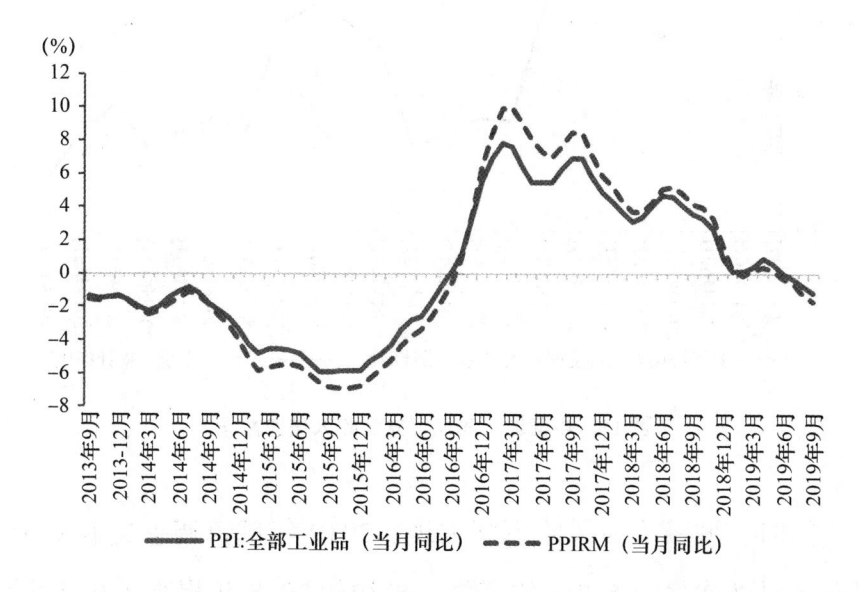

图12 中国PPI指数进入下跌区间

4. 随着经济下行压力加大，城镇居民收入预期下降，失业风险闪现，市场信心较为低迷

近年来，城镇居民收入增速持续放缓，而且显著低于实际GDP增速。2019年前3个季度，城镇居民人均可支配收入实际增长5.4%，较2018年同期回落0.3个百分点，也低于6.2%的实际GDP增速。

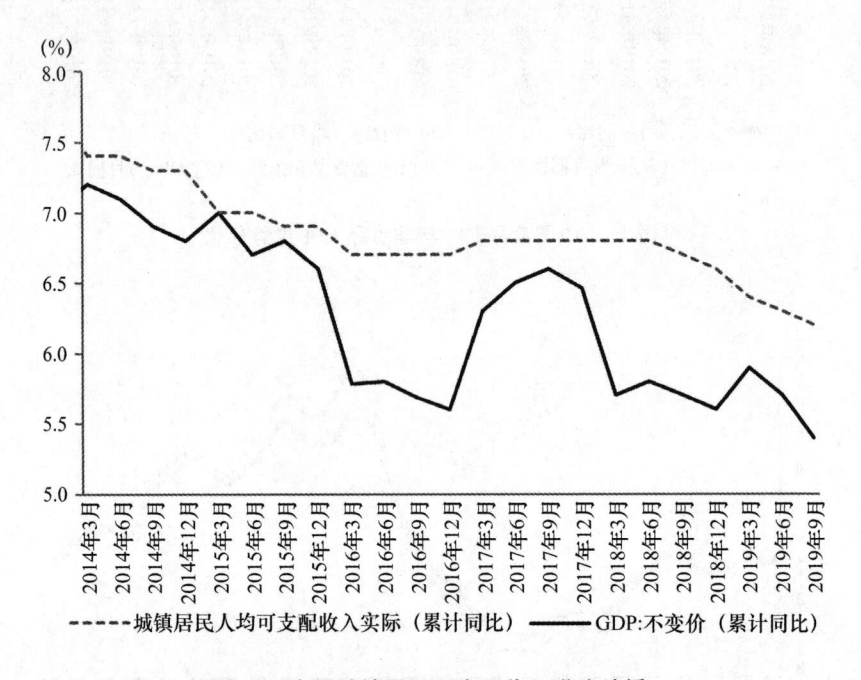

图13 中国城镇居民可支配收入增速放缓

同时，城镇失业风险不断闪现，2019年城镇调查失业率于2月和7月两次攀上5.3%的高位，平均较2018年提高了0.2个百分点。10月，制造业和非制造业PMI从业人员指数分别为

47.3%和48.2%,显示用工景气度处于紧缩区间。在此背景下,第二季度城镇居民未来收入信心指数降至52.6%,为2016年年底以来的低位。

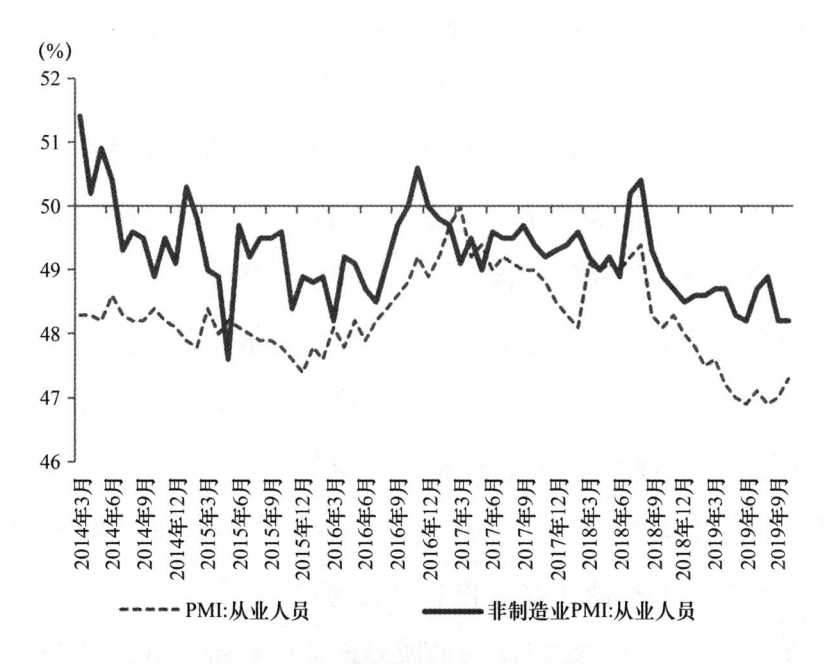

图14 中国就业景气度下行压力较大

（二）在"六稳"举措的提振作用下,中国经济综合表现好于市场悲观预期

面对内外部经济下行压力,中国一方面通过"六稳"政策积极应对,加强宏观政策逆周期调节力度;另一方面,不断出台各类改革举措提高增长潜力,确保宏观经济运行总体平稳。虽然

中国经济各方面下行压力加大，经济增速也在放缓，但是"六稳"举措取得了超预期的成效。中国宏观经济在内外夹击之下保持了超预期稳定，经受住了过去一年多世界经济低迷和中美贸易摩擦的"挤压"，没有出现破底线的状况，充分显示了中国经济的弹性和韧性。

首先，"六稳"政策发力。早在2018年7月，中共中央政治局会议就已经提出和部署"六稳"工作，要求做好稳就业、稳金融、稳外贸、稳外资、稳投资、稳预期工作，反映了当时中央已经对全球经济的发展态势、中美贸易摩擦的走势以及中国经济自身在攻坚期的发展规律，做出了精准的、前瞻性的判断，进而要求对宏观经济政策进行再调整、再定位，强化底线意识、忧患意识。根据中央"六稳"工作精神，各部门各地区相继制定实施了一系列政策举措，多管齐下"稳增长"。

在稳外贸方面，当时中国的贸易增速依然维持在两位数，在世界范围内都属于较高的增长速度，但中央依然提出了要稳外贸。一是贸易多元化。从2013年开始提出"一带一路"倡议，很重要的一点就是要使我们的出口、进口、贸易格局、投资格局真正的多元化。二是以进口博览会为主体，不仅要大规模地出口，还需要大规模地进口，而且要进口一些高品质商品，让高品质的商品在中国进行销售、生产甚至进行国产化替代。三是为了应对美国对中国出口商品的征税，采取了一系列措施。一方面，出口退税率进一步提高，从原来的11%提升到13%；另一方面，在国内进行减税降费，对于一些行业进行专门的扶持。特别是营商环境方面的改善和外贸进出口流程的改善，使交易成本大幅度降低，以此全面应对美国的贸易保护。

在财政政策方面，2019年通过加大减税降费力度和稳定基础设施建设投资，加强财政逆周期调节功能。首先，2019年推出了超2万亿元的减税降费计划，涉及增值税、个税等12个税种，养老保险等19个费种，以进一步减轻企业等市场主体负担，激发市场活力。其中，1月1日起，实施小微企业普惠性减税和个人所得税减税；4月1日起，实施包括制造业增值税税率下降3个百分点的深化增值税改革；5月1日起，实施以企业养老保险费率下调为主的社保降费；7月1日起，清理和规范行政事业性收费和政府性基金。前3个季度，全国累计新增减税降费17834亿元，其中新增减税15109亿元，新增社保费降费2725亿元。在新增减税中，增值税改革新增减税7035亿元，小微企业普惠性政策新增减税1827亿元，个人所得税两步改革叠加新增减税4426亿元。

其次，为了进一步发挥财政政策的逆周期调节作用，2019年前3个季度，相比3.3%的公共财政收入增速，公共财政支出增速达到9.4%；相比7.7%的政府性基金收入增速，政府性基金支出同比增速达到24.2%。因此，2019年前3个季度，财政赤字率达4.0%，政府性基金赤字率达1.2%，两者合计赤字率达5.2%，为近年来的最高水平。

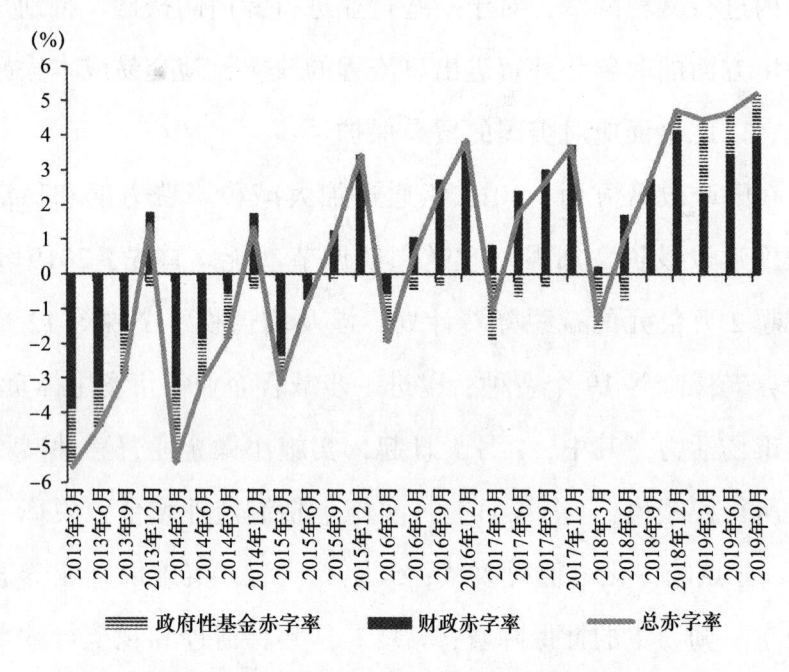

图 15　财政赤字率和政府性基金赤字率大幅提升

最后，积极的财政政策还体现在通过加大和加快地方政府专项债券发行促进基础设施建设投资企稳回升。2019 年安排新增地方政府债务限额 30800 亿元，比 2018 年额度增加 9000 亿元，其中新增一般债务限额 9300 亿元，新增专项债务限额 21500 亿元，分别比 2018 年额度增加 1000 亿元和 8000 亿元。同时，经十三届全国人大常委会第七次会议通过，授权国务院在 2019 年以后的年度，在当年新增地方政府债务限额的 60% 以内，提前下达下一年度新增限额，授权期限为 2019 年 1 月 1 日至 2022 年 12 月 31 日。这意味着 2019 年根据地方项目建设的实际需要，提前下达了专项债的部分新增额度，确保年初即可使用见效，带动有效投资和内需。截至 2019 年 9 月底，新增地方政府债务限额已经基本使用完毕，达到 30367 亿元，比 2018 年同期增加 10254 亿元；其中，一般债务 9070 亿元，专项债 21297 亿元。

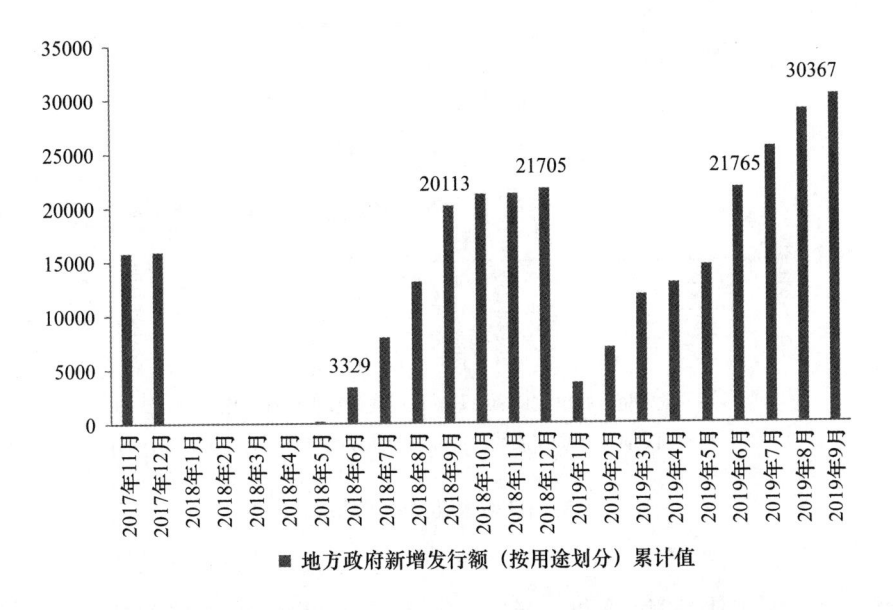

图 16　2019 年地方政府债券发行额提高和发行速度加快

2019 年前 3 个季度，基础设施建设投资同比增长 3.4%，较 2018 年同期增速提高 3.2 个百分点；剔除电力，基础设施建设投资同比增长 4.5%，较 2018 年同期增速提高 1.2 个百分点。尽管基础设施建设投资增速企稳回升，但是由于近年来加强地方政府债务风险管控，特别是推动地方政府融资平台转型，基础设施建设投资回升速度非常缓慢，目前投资增速仍然低于总体投资增速，从而持续拖累投资复苏。

不过，随着新一轮减税降费举措和对房地产市场的持续调

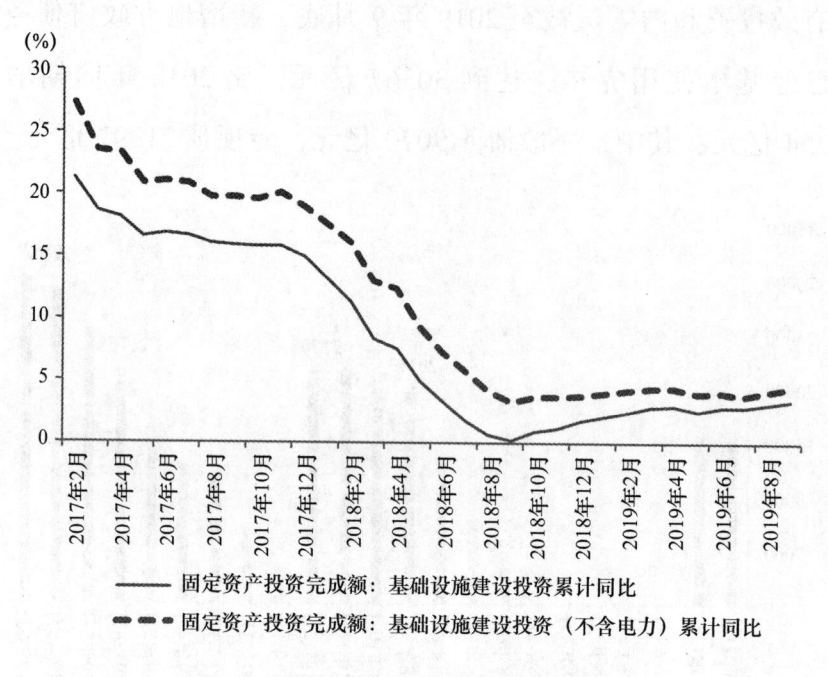

图17 基础设施建设投资增速缓慢回升

控,2019年中国财政收入和政府性基金收入增速双双出现显著回落。前3个季度,公共财政收入同比增长3.3%,较2018年同期增速回落5.4个百分点;其中,税收收入负增长0.4%,较2018年同期增速回落13.1个百分点;全国政府性基金收入同比增长7.7%,较2018年同期增速回落20.3个百分点;财政收入和政府性基金收入合计同比增长4.4%,较2018年同期增速回落9.6个百分点。

2019年货币政策保持稳健中性定位,边际宽松。9月,M2同比增长8.4%,较2018年同期小幅提升0.1个百分点;社会融资规模存量同比增长10.8%,较2018年同期小幅回升0.2个

二 增速放缓与结构分化下的中国宏观经济

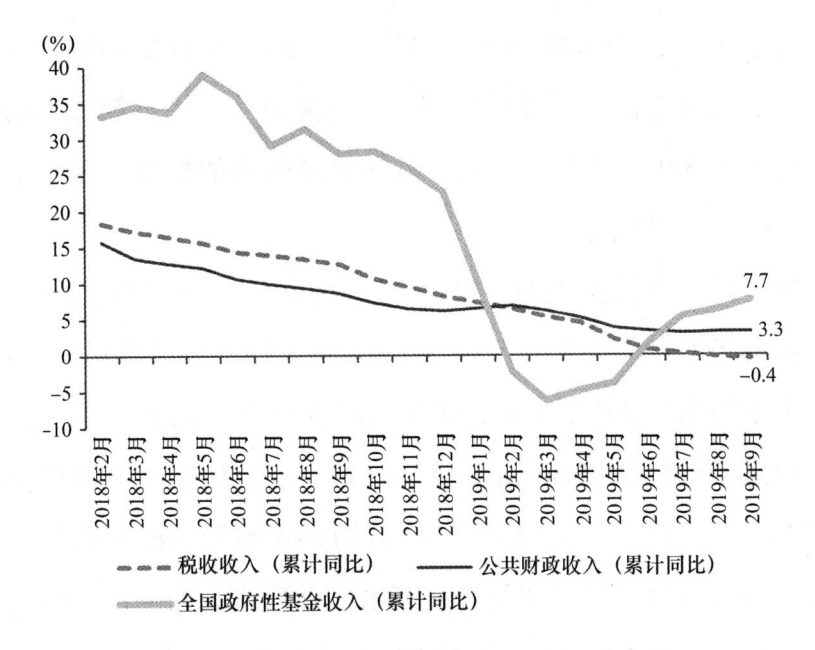

图18 中国财政收入增速明显放缓

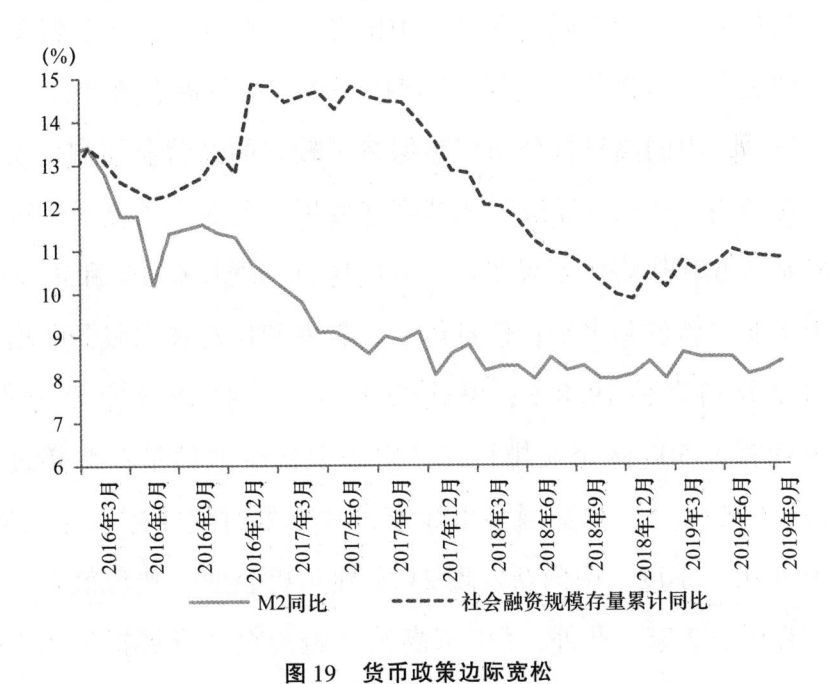

图19 货币政策边际宽松

百分点。不过，M1同比增长3.4%，较2018年同期回落0.6个百分点；从社会融资规模流量同比增速来看，第一、第二、第三季度分别为38%、22%、1%，呈现明显回收的趋势，显示货币政策并未全面转向宽松。

货币政策的边际宽松，体现在市场利率的下行中。2019年信用债的各券种平均发行利率均较2018年同期有所下降。

由于中国自2018年年中就开始部署推进"六稳"工作，特别是通过减税降费和改善营商环境等措施，2019年中国经济的发展态势总体好于2018年年底的市场悲观预期。面对世界经济低迷期的挑战以及中美贸易摩擦带来的前所未有的不确定性，很多悲观论者在2018—2019年对中国经济产生过度悲观预期。

从过去一年的实际情况看，中国经济经受住了世界经济低迷以及中美贸易摩擦的"挤压"，保持了较好的发展态势增长。

第一，中国高科技公司依然保持了较好的经营业绩和发展态势。2019年，"三新经济"依然高速发展。前3个季度，中国高技术制造业和战略性新兴产业利润同比分别增长6.3%和4.6%，好于工业总体盈利水平；信息传输、软件和信息技术服务业增加值同比分别增长19.8%，增速快于第三产业12.8个百分点。2019年世界500强企业排行榜，中国上榜企业数量首次超过美国，达到129家，比美国多出8家，具有划时代的标志性意义。2019年第一季度，中国新发现21家独角兽企业，独角兽企业总数上升至202家。此外，《国家高新区瞪羚企业发展报告2018》

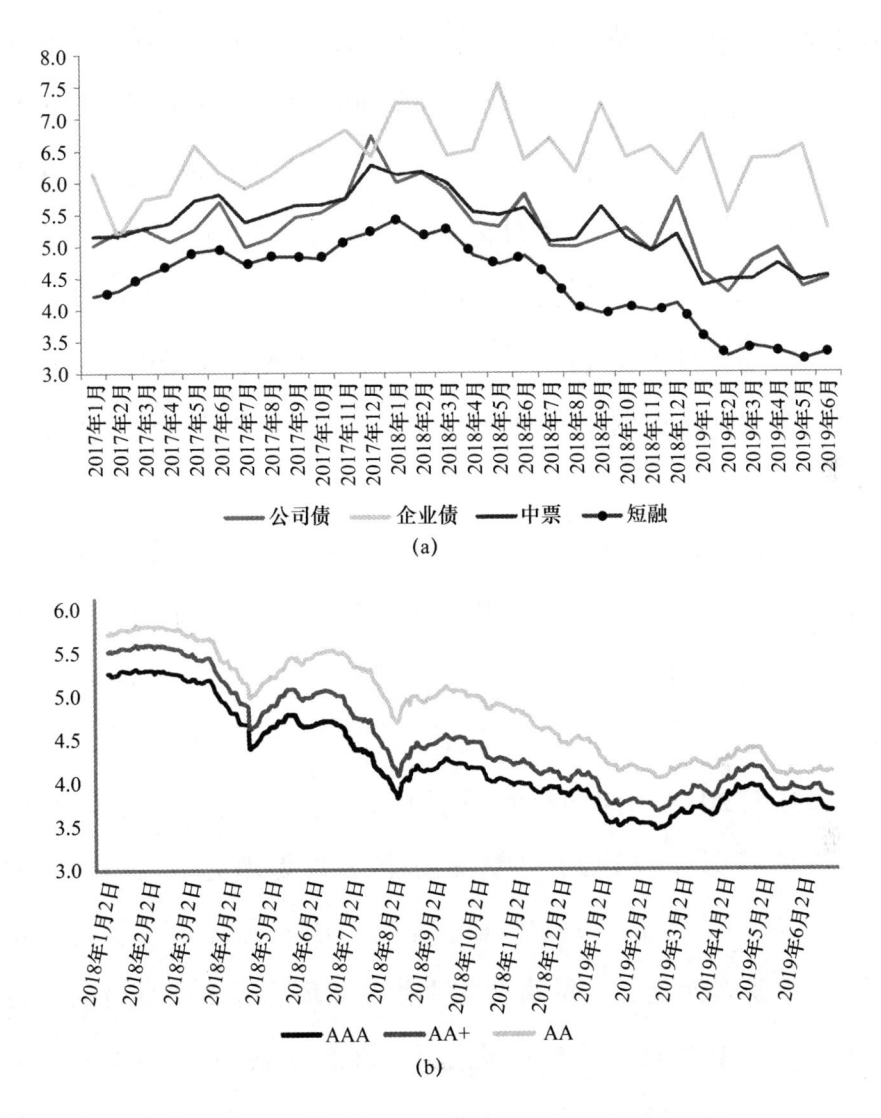

图20 信用债发行利率和3年期中票收益率趋于下行

显示，国家高新区瞪羚企业数量达到2857家。同时，截至2019年10月31日，据lplytics统计，中国厂商的5G标准必要专利（SEP）占36%，领先美国、韩国、芬兰等。其中，华为领跑5G

标准必要专利及标准技术贡献量,其5G标准必要专利申请量为2160件,占比18%,在所有厂商中排名第一。2019年7月30日,华为公司发布了上半年业绩,华为上半年实现营收4013亿元,同比增长23.2%;净利润率为8.7%。华为上半年的智能手机发货量达到1.18亿台,同比增长24%。同时,2019年上半年,华为还签订了30多个5G国际大单。可见,关于中国一些科技型大企业会迅速倒闭的预言落空了,中国企业的韧性比悲观论者想象得要好。

第二,贸易增速保持了正增长,贸易顺差扩大,稳外贸基本实现。2019年前3个季度,中国进出口总额同比增长2.8%;其中,出口同比增长5.2%,进口负增长0.1%;贸易顺差达到20461亿元(2984亿美元),同比增长44.2%(36.1%)。尽管出口增速较2018年同期小幅回落1.3个百分点,但是在全球经济低迷的背景下,特别是考虑到全球贸易增速从2018年的3.6%大幅回落至1.1%,中国稳外贸的成效无疑是显著的。特别是在贸易多元化、减税降费和改善营商环境等多项举措的合力推进下,中国外贸"稳中有进",发展态势良好。2019年上半年,中国与"一带一路"沿线国家货物进出口额合计达4.2万亿元,同比增长9.7%,高出总体贸易增速5.8个百分点,占中国外贸总值的28.9%。

第三,外商直接投资和国际储备出现明显反转,稳外资基本实现。2019年前3个季度,中国实际使用外商直接投资额同比

二 增速放缓与结构分化下的中国宏观经济 | **37**

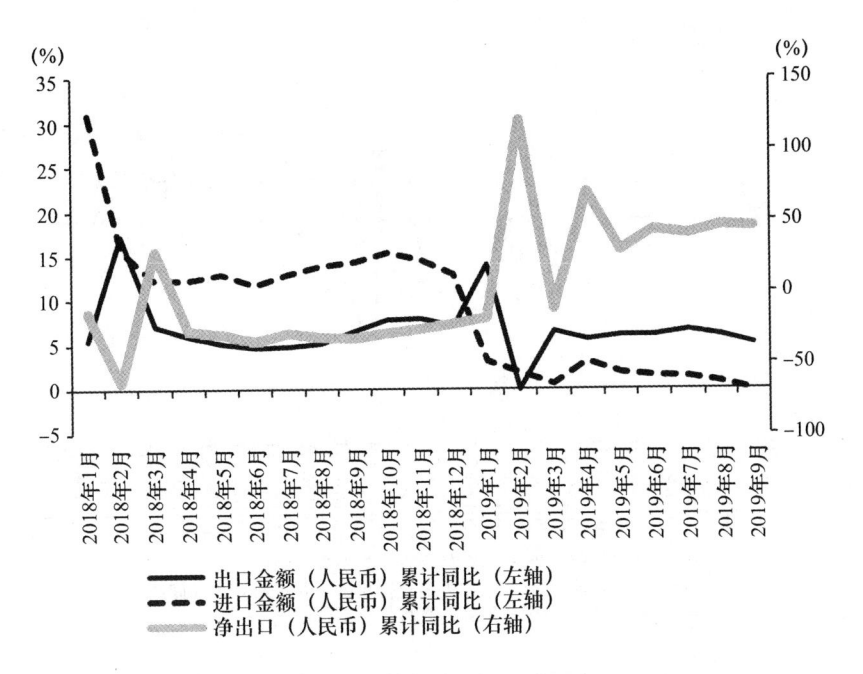

图21 中国贸易增速变化趋势

增长6.5%，较2018年同期增速提高3.6个百分点；以美元计价，外商投资同比增长2.9%，依然保持了正增长。因此，需要客观看待所谓的外资撤离中国论。根据我们的调研，尽管中国一些低端产业的确搬迁到东南亚，但是欧美特别是欧洲、日本、韩国，开始对中国的高新技术和服务业进行大规模投资。2019年前3个季度，中国服务业实际使用外商直接投资额达到718.8亿美元，同比增长9.2%，较2018年同期增速大幅提高6.2个百分点。因为中国市场太庞大了，美国等高新技术企业无法舍弃中国市场。中国巨大的市场、中国产业和技术链的完整性和相对稳定性，是一些东南亚国家所难以替代的。

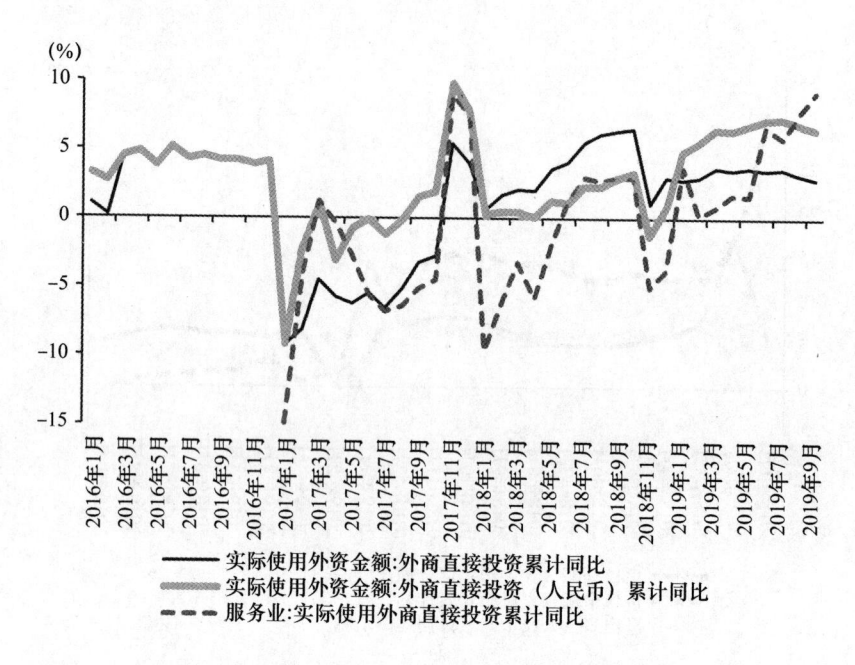

图 22 中国实际利用外资额增长形势稳中向好

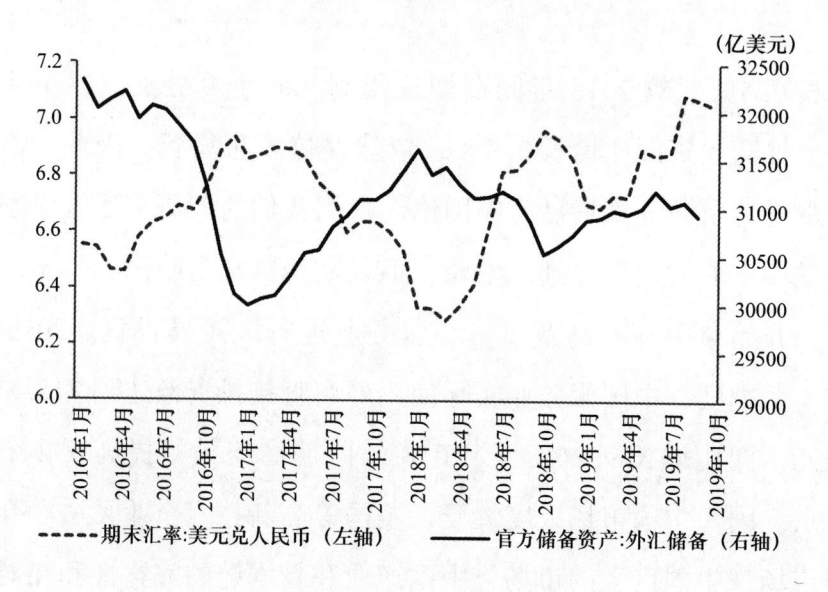

图 23 人民币汇率和官方外汇储备走势

二 增速放缓与结构分化下的中国宏观经济 | **39**

在外贸、外资总体平稳的背景下,人民币汇率总体稳定,外汇储备略有回升。2019年人民币兑美元汇率从1月的6.70波动上升至10月的7.05,但相比2016—2018年的大起大落,总体表现平稳。同时,官方外汇储备从30879亿美元小幅提升至10月的30924亿美元,也比过去3年的走势稳定。

同时,中国重大金融风险攻坚战取得阶段性胜利。各类金融市场保持稳定,债务风险得到较好缓释,各类信用债的违约率较2018年同期大幅减少。

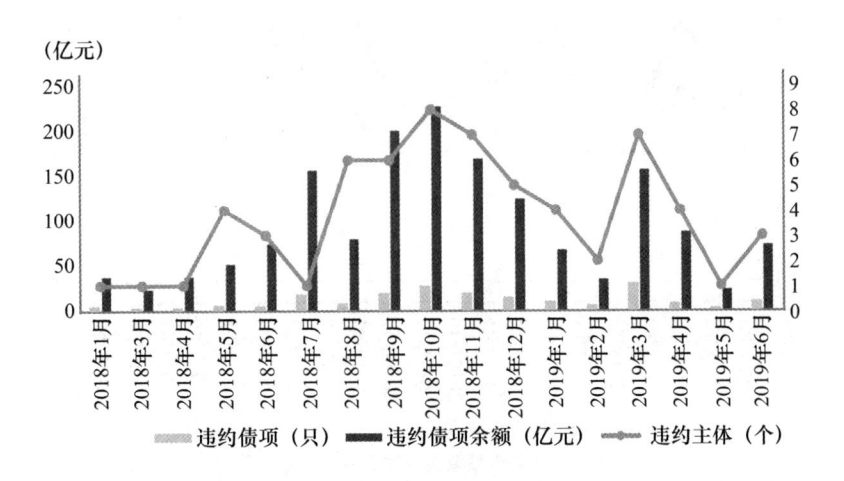

图24 信用债违约情况

注:2018年2月当月没有违约数据,故缺失。

第四,营商环境改善持续,创业创新热情高涨,城镇就业总体稳定,居民收入保持较快增长。2019年前3个季度,全国新登记市场主体数量达到1766万户,日均新设市场主体是6.5万户,同比增长13.1%。2019年前3个季度,城镇新增就业人数达到1097万人，基本提前完成全年1100万人的新增就业目标。9月，全国城镇调查失业率为5.2%，25—59岁群体调查失业率为4.6%，继续保持在5.5%以内的目标区间。前3个季度，中国居民人均可支配收入同比增长8.8%，扣除价格因素，实际增长6.1%。

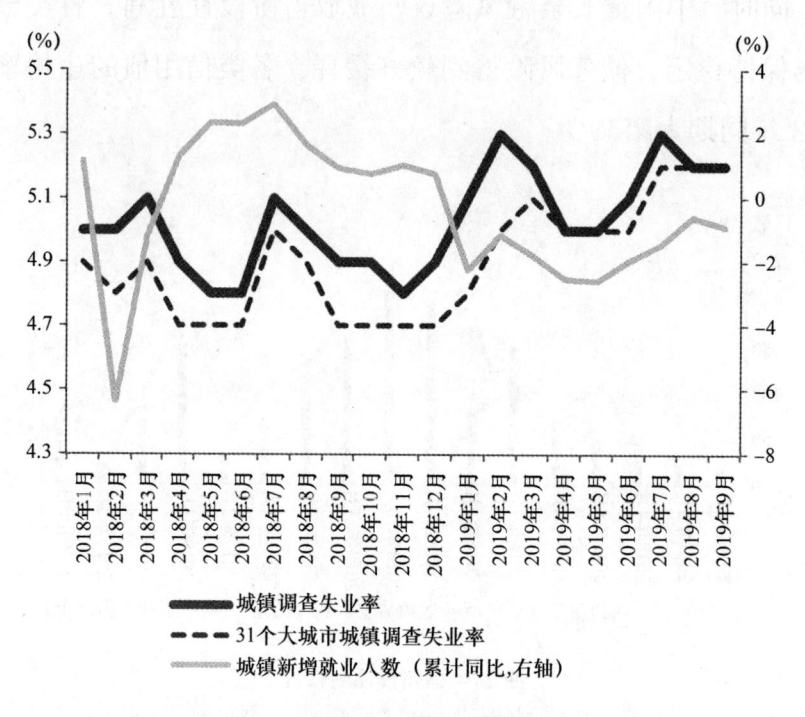

图25 中国城镇调查失业率略有上升

综上可见，在内外夹击之下，中国经济不仅没有出现很多境外人士和悲观人士所预期的极端现象，展示了中国经济的风险抵御能力，而且对比全球主要经济体的表现，中国经济增长仍然保持领先优势：2019年全球GDP增速预计下降0.6个百分点，美国、欧元区分别下降0.6个、0.7个百分点，印度下降超过1.0个百分点，而中国仅下降了0.5个百分点。

◇◇（三）衰退性的结构分化加剧，升级型的结构分化趋于停滞

相比经济增速的回落，更值得关注的是，在中国经济结构调整的攻坚期，出现了"衰退性的结构分化加剧，升级型的结构分化趋于停滞"的现象。近年来，中国经济在不同行业、不同区域、不同规模、不同所有制层面的结构分化现象不仅没有缓解，反而有所加剧，如果继续忽视可能会达到临界点，带来底部效应。因此，要求相应的政策必须更细、更加精准、更有前瞻性。

1. 国民储蓄流向的结构分化

2019年在消费对GDP增长拉动作用大幅减弱的同时，中国储蓄流向也发生了结构变化，集中表现为投资的拉动力进一步下滑，而净出口的拉动力大幅上升，换言之，国民储蓄更多地以净出口的方式流向了海外，而非以投资方式留在国内。前3个季度，资本形成总额对GDP累计同比的拉动从2018年同期的2.1个百分点回落至1.2个百分点，对经济增长的贡献率从2018年

同期的31.8%回落至19.8%；相比之下，净出口对GDP累计同比的拉动从2018年同期的-0.7个百分点提升至1.2个百分点，对经济增长的贡献率从2018年同期的-9.8%提升至19.6%。

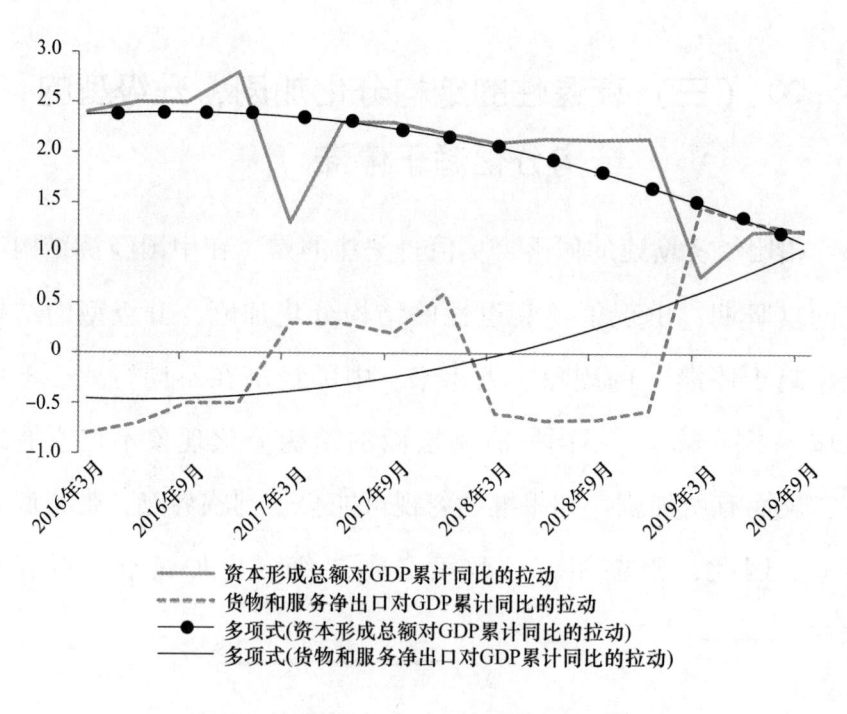

图26 投资和净出口对经济增长的拉动分化

这也反映在2019年中国进出口总额增速与净出口增速的分化上。前3个季度，以美元计价，中国进出口总额同比负增长2.4%，较2018年同期增速回落18.2个百分点，但是中国净出口增长36.1%，较2018年同期增速提升60.5个百分点。由此，净出口对实际GDP增长的拉动达到1.2个百分点，贡献率达到19.6%，分别较2018年同期提升了1.9个和29.4个百分点，在国内最终消费支出和资本形成总额增长放缓的背景下,对总需求增长起到了很好的支撑作用。但是,进出口总额与净出口额增速的分化,不仅加剧了中国经济增长对于外需的依赖,且由于经济循环的萎缩,也加剧了中国经济的脆弱性。

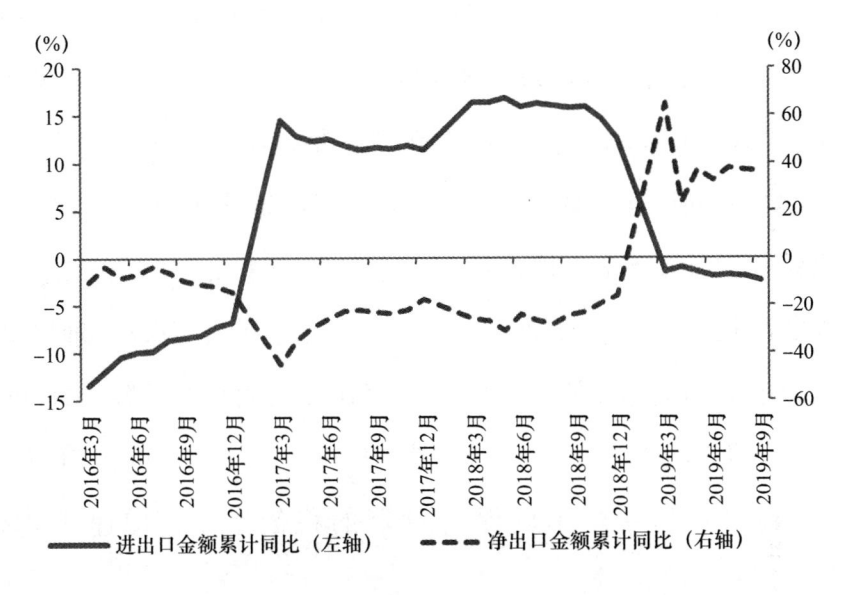

图27 进出口总额与贸易盈余(以美元计价)走势分化

从中长期的视角来看,近年来,中国投资增速持续较快下滑。2003—2012年,中国投资增速长期保持在20%以上,十年平均增速为25.3%。随着投资效率下降和债务率攀升,投资驱动的增长模式变得不可持续。2013年开始,中国经济经历了再平衡调整,投资增速明显放缓,从2012年的20.3%下滑至2015年的9.8%。

理论上,出现一定的投资增速回落是符合中国经济结构转型和高质量发展要求的。据我们测算，现阶段保持8.0%—12.0%的投资增速比较适宜。测算依据在于，假设技术进步率达到2.0%，考虑到劳动就业人数开始出现负增长，如果要保持6.0%左右的长期经济增速，就需要保持8.0%左右的资本存量增长率，而鉴于目前资本存量约是投资额的6倍，考虑到10%左右的资本折旧，现阶段需要保持8.0%—12.0%的投资增速。但是，2016年以来，中国投资增速并没有稳定在这一水平，而是继续快速回落至2018年的5.9%。剔除价格因素，2018年实际投资仅增长0.5%，特别是在"六稳"政策发力之前，前3个季度实际投资负增长0.2%。这一水平已经明显跌破合理区间，甚至低于同期美国投资增速，不仅存在较大的超调风险，还可能带来经济失速风险。作为对比，美国2017年第一季度至2019年第二季度连续10个季度保持投资的稳健增长，增速平均值为6.3%。

随着"六稳"政策发力和大规模减税降费政策落地，2019年中国投资仍未出现明显复苏迹象，前3个季度投资名义增长5.4%，实际增长2.2%。当前投资增速仍远低于合意水平，主要源于企业投资意愿持续减弱。一方面，制造业投资逆转了逐步回暖向好的趋势而重回疲态，成为当前投资下滑的主要拖累；另一方面，"设备工器具购置"投资在连续3年仅3.0%左右的低速增长后，2019年首次出现负增长，前3个季度负增长1.2%；扩建投资自2017年首次出现负增长以来，跌幅不断扩大至2019

二 增速放缓与结构分化下的中国宏观经济 | **45**

年前3个季度的7.2%,显示企业生产性投资意愿不强,投资下行压力仍然较大。

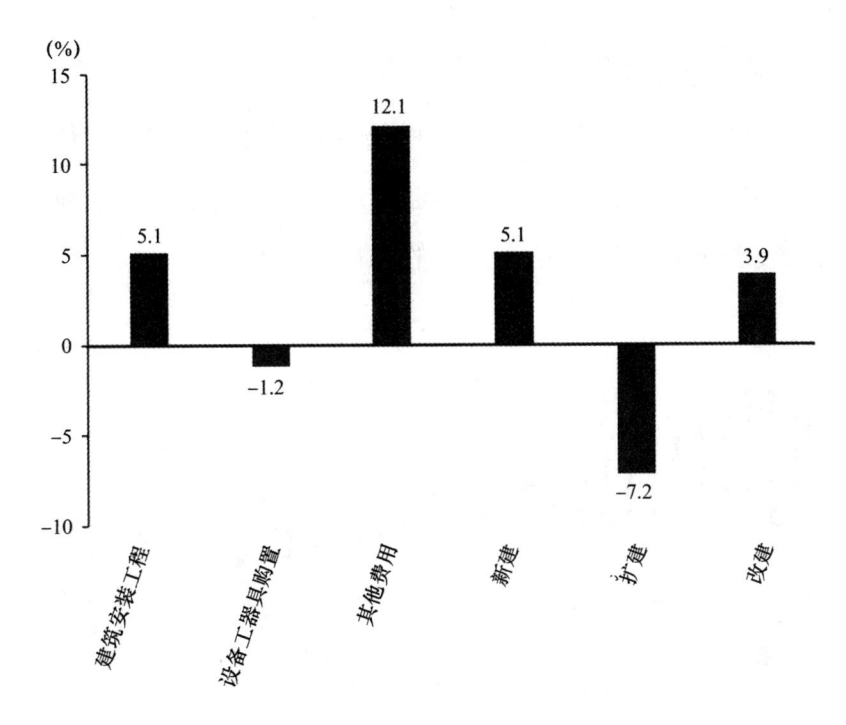

图28 固定资产投资结构分化(2019年前3个季度同比增速)

建筑安装工程 5.1
设备工器具购置 -1.2
其他费用 12.1
新建 5.1
扩建 -7.2
改建 3.9

从中国经济的现实矛盾和未来发展方向来看,以上变化趋势都与中国经济的调整和发展方向不完全相符。在供给方面,供给结构不符合人民群众日益增长的对美好生活的需求。为了解决这一矛盾,发展生产和调整供给结构是当前以及未来一段时间中的重要任务。在此背景下,投资增长和资本形成应该发挥更大的作用。在内外需的对比方面,为了满足人民群众日益增长的对美好生活的需求,以及提高中国经济增长的内生动力和内在稳定性,中国都需要通过经济再平衡调整来降低整体经济对净外需的过度依赖。

2. 区域经济分化

分地区来看，过去几年经济增长较快的地区 2019 年依然保持较好的增长势头，而经历显著经济调整的下滑地区依然延续了过去的疲弱态势，区域经济分化的格局进一步加大。

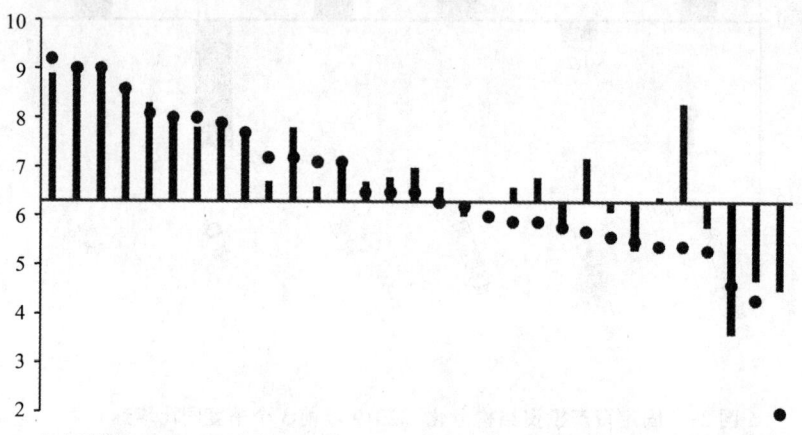

图 29　不同地区增长形势分化

从全国各地区的增长形势图来看，区域分化格局更为明显。2019 年上半年，中部地区和西南地区各省基本继续保持 7.0% 以上的较快增长；东南沿海地区在中美贸易摩擦的冲击下依然保持较为稳健的增长；但是，东北地区、京津冀地区、西北地区、内蒙古、山东、山东、海南及广西，2019年上半年经济增速基本都在6.0%以下，尤其是吉林、黑龙江、天津经济增速分别为2.0%、4.3%、4.6%，均低于5.0%，位居全国后三位。

3. 行业分化

2019年在制造业总体下行的影响下，工业与服务业的分化达到新高度。首先，从增加值增长方面看，第三季度服务业增加值增长7.2%，而工业增加值增长下滑至5.0%，低于服务业增速2.2个百分点。

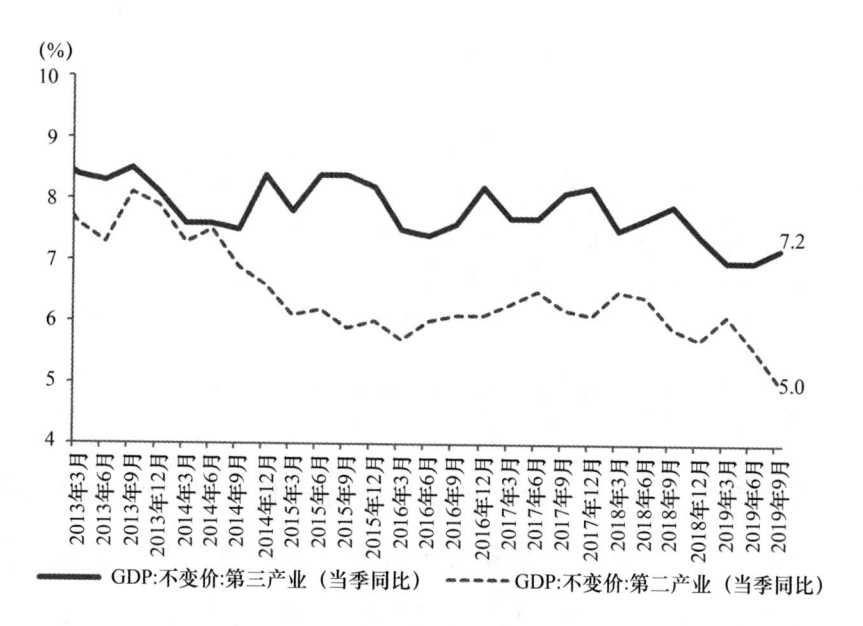

图30 工业与服务业增加值增速走势分化

其次，从投资方面看，以上分化趋势更为明显。前3个季度，第三产业投资增长 7.2%，较 2018 年同期增速回升 1.9 个百分点；第二产业投资增速下降至 2.0%，较 2018 年同期增速回落 3.2 个百分点。第二产业投资增速与第三产业投资增速的缺口达到 5.2 个百分点，重回 2016 年年中以来的扩大趋势。

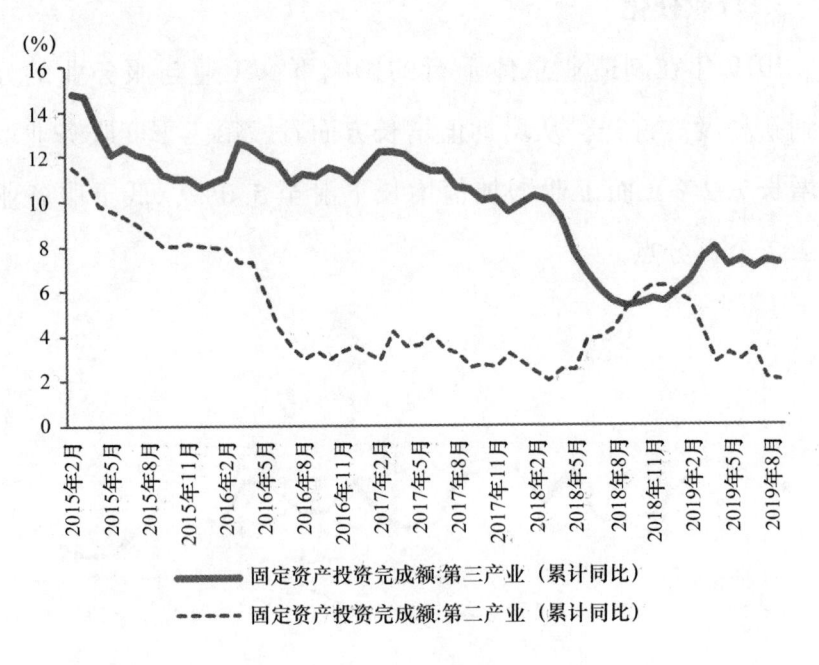

图 31 第二产业与第三产业投资增速走势分化

从盈利水平看，工业特别是制造业与服务业的对比更加显著。2019 年前 7 个月，规模以上服务业企业营业利润累计同比增长 9.2%，但工业企业利润总额同比下降 1.7%，其中制造业企业利润总额同比下降 3.4%。

在制造业内部，企业经营绩效分化也很明显。前 3 个季度，在制造业细分行业中：（1）有 9 个行业利润总额出现负增长，

二 增速放缓与结构分化下的中国宏观经济 | 49

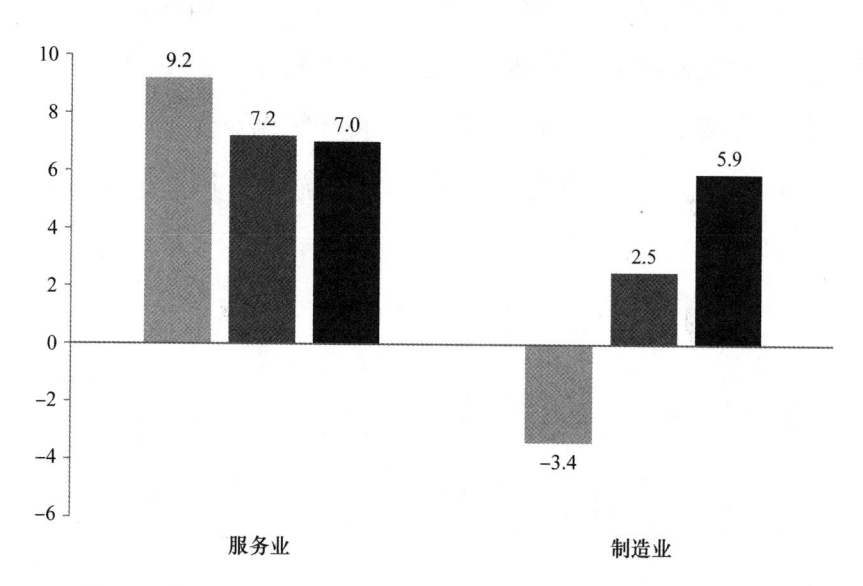

图32 2019年服务业与制造业同比增长对比

包括石油加工、炼焦及核燃料加工业，黑色金属冶炼及压延加工业，化学纤维制造业，造纸及纸制品业，汽车制造业，化学原料及化学制品制造业，木材加工及木、竹、藤、棕、草制品业，纺织业，纺织服装、服饰业，跌幅分别为53.5%、41.8%、29.1%、20.2%、16.6%、13.0%、4.4%、4.3%、1.6%；（2）有8个行业利润总额实现个位数增长，包括通用设备制造业，农副食品加工业，计算机、通信和其他电子设备制造业，仪器仪表制造业，有色金属冶炼及压延加工业，印刷业和记录媒介的复制，皮革、毛皮、羽毛及其制品和制鞋业，废弃资源综合利用业；（3）有12个行业利润总额实现两位数增长，包括医药制造业，金属制品业，食品制造业，非金属矿物制品业，文教、工美、体育和娱乐用品制造业，橡胶和塑料制品业，专用设备制造业，电气机械及器材制造业，酒、饮料和精制茶制造业，家具制造业，烟草制品业，铁路、船舶、航空航天和其他运输设备制造业。

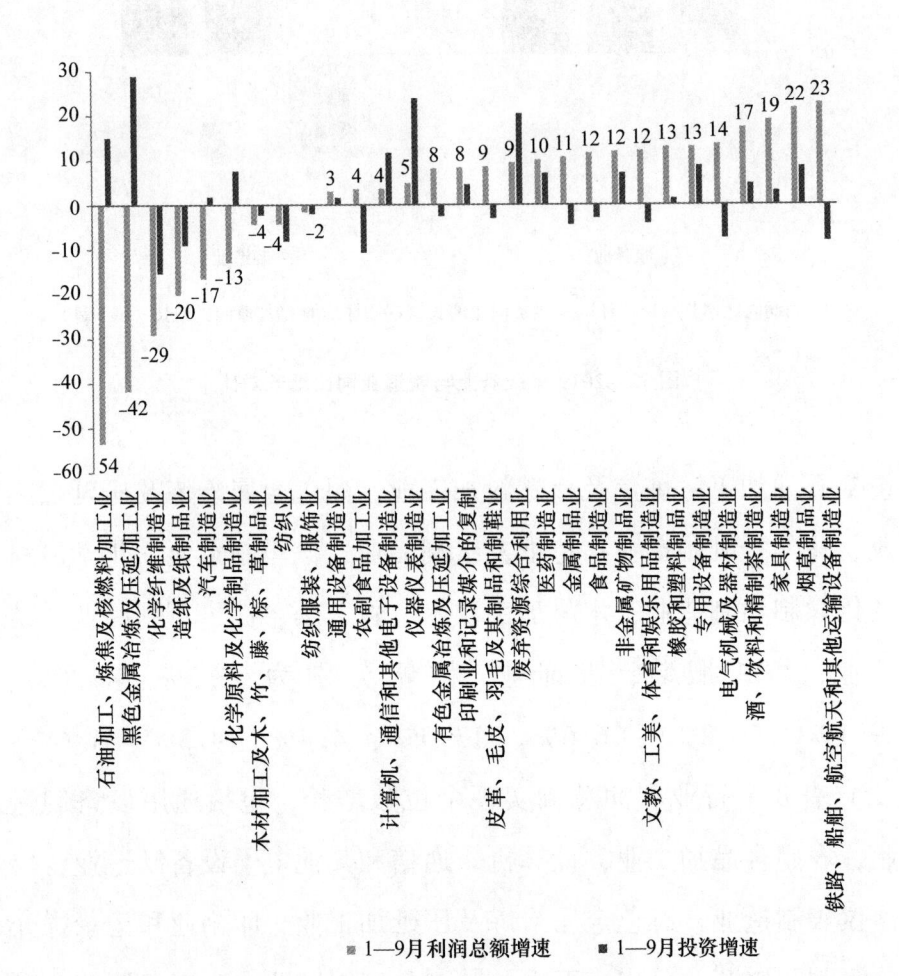

图33 不同行业利润总额和投资增速分化

4. 结构升级动态出现放缓的迹象

在扶持政策的陆续退出、产业周期的调整、区域与行业分化、中美贸易摩擦以及内外需求下滑等多重因素的冲击下，中国新动能增速在2019年下半年加速放缓，从而加剧经济增速下行的压力，新旧动能转换步入艰难期，新动能的培育需要新的思路和新的政策。

从近3年的发展趋势来看，新动能增长速度已经出现明显下滑，并且下滑幅度比传统经济增速下滑的幅度要快得多，已经与传统经济的增速基本接近。(1) 工业战略性新兴产业增加值增速从2017年的11.0%下降到2019年第一季度的6.7%，下滑了4.3个百分点，而同期传统工业增加值增速回落了0.4个百分点，战略性新兴产业增加值增速比全部工业增速仅高0.2个百分点。(2) 高新制造业增加值增速从2017年的13.4%下降到2019年第一季度的7.8%，下降了5.6个百分点，战略性服务业增加值增速从17.3%下降到13%，下降了4.3个百分点。(3) 高技术投资增速从2017年的15.9%下降到2019年第一季度的11.4%，下降4.5个百分点，而所有行业同期投资增速仅下滑了1.1个百分点。(4) 全年网上零售增速从2017年的32.2%下降到2019年1—5月的17.8%，下降了14.4个百分点，而同期全社会消费品零售总额增速下滑了2个百分点。

从总体产业结构调整看，2019年中国工业和服务业的内部结构延续了过去的调整趋势，但是调整动态出现放缓甚至是逆转的迹象。在经济增速总体下滑的同时，制造业和高端服务业出现更大幅度的下滑，而建筑业和金融业增速却出现明显回升。特别是在服务业整体增速下滑中，信息传输、软件和信息技术服务业，租赁和商业服务业等细分行业的增速下降幅度明显大于服务业整体增速，而金融业的增速却大幅提高。这与中国发展高端服务业和解决"脱实就虚"的方向不完全相符。

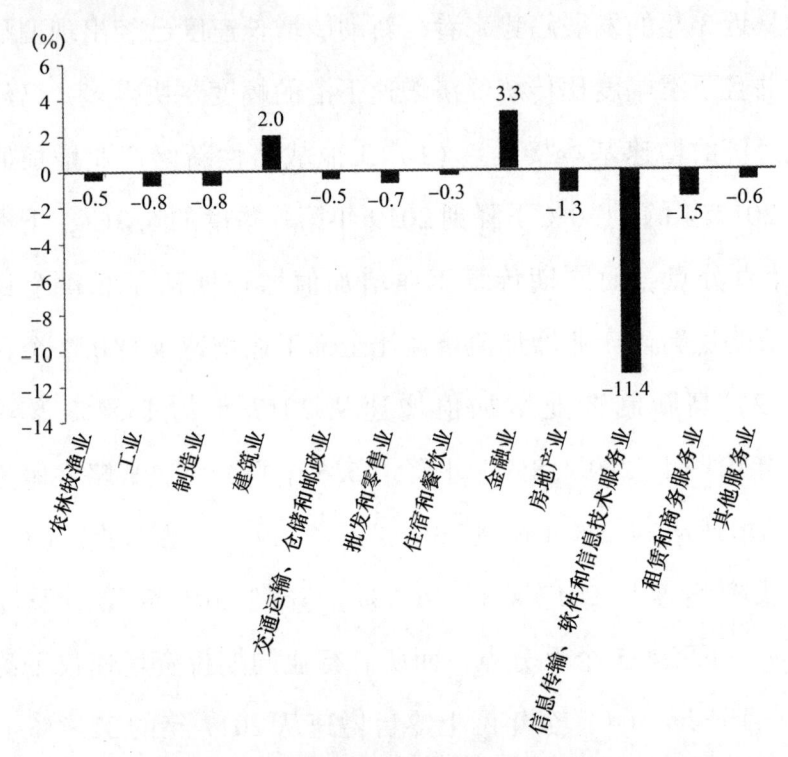

图34 服务业内部结构的优化调整动态出现逆转迹象

从工业部门内部结构调整看,结构优化调整的动态也出现了逆转迹象。与2018年同期相比,2019年前3个季度,规模以上工业增加值增速下降0.4个百分点,制造业增速下降0.8个百分点,高新技术产业的增速下降3.1个百分点,医药制造业增速下降3.4个百分点,通用设备制造业增速下降3.5个百分点,专业设备制造业增速下降3.7个百分点,计算机、通信和其他电子设备制造业增速下降4.3个百分点,汽车制造业增速下降8.5个百分点。这种变化意味着过去几年的工业结构调整趋势有所放缓。

从投资的角度看,在全社会固定投资实现平稳增长的同时,2019年,制造业固定投资增速大幅下滑,较2018年同期下降了6.2个百分点;民间投资增速较2018年下降了4个百分点;高技术制造业固定投资增速较2018年下降了2.3个百分点。民间投资增速未能实现稳定,全社会固定投资增长的内生动力依然薄弱。制造业整体以及高技术制造业投资增速的大幅下滑,与服务业投资增速提升形成鲜明对比,这并不是好的现象。中国在当前及未来较长一段时间内,产业升级不完全是甚至主要不是服务业对制造业的替代,一个非常重要的任务是提升和强化制造业。服务业的过快扩张和制造业的过快萎缩,不符合中国产业发展和调整的方向。高技术制造业投资增速的下滑,不符合提升中国制造业整体实力和竞争力的要求。

从消费的角度看,消费新增长点和新动能的增速出现更大幅度下滑。在消费层面还有一个不好的迹象,2019年网上零售增速较2018年的下滑幅度大于整体增速的降幅。2019年前3个季度，全社会零售品销售名义增速较2018年同期下降了1.1个百分点，而实物商品网上零售额、网上商品和服务零售额增速较2018年同期分别下降了7.2个和10.2个百分点。这意味着过去几年的消费升级趋势有所放缓。例如，虽然实物商品网上零售额占社会消费品零售总额的比重较2018年同期继续提高2.0个百分点，但提升的幅度较2018年同期回落1.5个百分点。

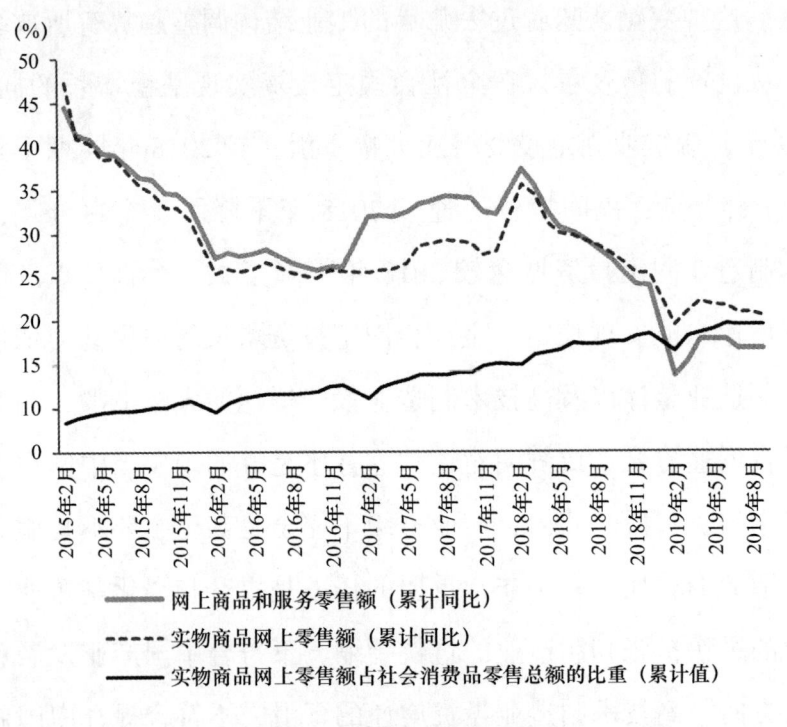

图35　消费升级速度放缓

从贸易的角度看，高新技术产品和机电产品的对外贸易增速出现更大幅度的下滑，让人担忧。2019年1—8月，高新技术产品累计出口增速较2018年同期下降5.7个百分点,远高于整体出口增速的降幅。其中,航空航天技术、生物技术、材料技术和计算机与通信技术累计出口增速的降幅分别是36个、19.6个、15.3个和10.9个百分点。机电产品累计出口增速较2018年同期下降1.4个百分点,也明显高于整体出口增速的降幅。其中,运输工具和机械设备累计出口增速的降幅分别是13.9个和5.2个百分点。高新技术产品和机电产品进口增速的下降幅度也明显高于整体进口增速的降幅。2019年1—8月,高新技术产品累计进口增速较2018年同期下降15.6个百分点,明显高于整体进口增速的降幅。其中,计算机集成制造技术和电子技术累计进口增速分别下降了42.9个和19.1个百分点。机电产品累计进口增速较2018年同期下降了15.7个百分点,也明显高于整体进口增速的降幅。其中,机械设备和电器及电子产品累计进口增速分别下降了20.8个和18.2个百分点。在产品类别上,高新技术产品和机电产品对外贸易出现更大幅度的下滑。在国家分类上,对美贸易出现了更大幅度的下滑。两者结合在一起,在一定程度上反映出中美贸易紧张状况对中国外贸的深层面冲击。这既不利于中国对外贸易产品结构的进一步优化,也会对国内制造业结构的升级过程产生不利影响。

造成中国经济结构升级放缓的原因主要有以下三个方面。

第一,各类战略规划的到期、产业扶植政策的退出以及财政补贴缺口的扩大决定了近期新动能高速发展的政策红利将步入递减期，许多缺乏造血功能的产业和企业将面临严峻的挑战。

过去10年来，中国高技术、战略性新兴产业以及"三新经济"之所以高速发展的核心原因就在于各类战略的陆续出台，各类产业享受了充分的政策红利。但是，这些政策红利在以下几个因素的作用下已快速步入递减期。（1）很多企业已经用完了政策优惠的孵化和扶持期。例如高新技术园区的企业一般享受3—5年的税收优惠和各类补贴支持。（2）大量战略性新兴产业的规划期将在2020年结束，各种政策补贴开始步入退坡期。例如按照《能源发展战略行动计划（2014—2020年）》的规定，到2020年实现风电与煤电平价上网；按照《节能与新能源汽车发展规划（2012—2020）》的规定，2020年将彻底退出新能源补贴。（3）遍地开花的各类产业园区和产业基地已经给很多地方带来较大的财政负担，在今后两年的财政约束下，很多对于战略性产业和高新技术企业的补贴也难以持续。例如2009—2017年中国政府对新能源汽车的补贴累积达到2000亿元，未来3年的补贴也将超过2000亿元，在财政收入增速下滑和政府融资能力下降的当前，财政补贴缺口将大幅度扩大，名惠而实不至使得很多依靠补贴生存的企业和行业难以为继。2017年年底，累积可再生能源发电补贴缺口总计达到1127亿元，而2019年单年度补贴缺口将扩大到1200亿元。

第二，很多不合理的产业布局、行政化的重复建设以及市场虚火驱动下的泡沫将步入问题的暴露期和行业大调整期，从而决定了未来一段时间中国新动能很可能出现一个低谷。

在全国各地新经济和新动能"竞标赛"作用下,各地大上快上了很多项目,兴建了很多园区和产业基地,出现了很多泡沫神话。但是,经过10年的发展,这些市场和行政扭曲必须接受市场需求的裁决。(1)很多没有技术基础、产业基础、人力基础以及市场基础的产业园区和创新基地在行政扶持几年后难以形成自我发展的造血能力,将逐步退出市场。到2018年年底中国有各类园区2.5万个,各类孵化器6000多个,其中70%的园区和孵化器在一些没有任何基础的三四线城市,大量园区和众创空间难以收支平衡,其退出的爆发期将在2019—2020年。(2)很多重复建设的产业在政策"输血"很多年之后依然没有造血功能,在停止"输血"之后必将在激烈的市场竞争中被整合和淘汰。例如中国新能源汽车生产企业已经达到169家,平均每家的市场份额不足10000辆,大量的企业难以在近3年内达到规模化生产的临界点。再例如28个省都把光伏作为主导产业,至少建立了280个地级市或工业园区,提出了打造千亿级新能源或光伏产业基地,导致很多战略性新兴产业出现严重的产能过剩,大量企业没有自我生存的能力。(3)很多市场化资金在新经济泡沫破灭后大规模离场,导致近几年市场资金严重吃紧。这集中体现在摩拜倒塌、P2P爆雷、互联网+草根创业步入迷茫期。例如,2017年中国人工智能企业达到1011家,投融资总额达到277亿美元,占全球募集资金的70%,但是随着一些科技故事的破灭,很多 VC/PC 出现退场，2018 年募集基金同比下滑了 74.85%。

第三，中美贸易摩擦通过关税贸易、产业链、技术卡脖子效应以及市场预期扰乱等方式将在下半年对高新技术产业和新动能产生实质性的冲击。

美国对于 2000 亿美元中国商品征收 25% 的关税，以及签署《确保信息通信技术与服务供应链安全》行政令将华为等公司列入出口管制实体清单，这些举措对中国高新技术产业的发展带来了严重影响。这些影响将在近期全面显化。这集中体现在以下几个方面：（1）高新技术产品出口增速从 2018 年的 19.5% 下滑到 2019 年第二季度的零增长，高新技术产品进口增速从 2018 年的 25.1% 下降到 2019 年 5 月的 9.6%，外部需求和内部产业链受到明显冲击。（2）对于关键技术的出口限制，导致部分高新技术企业业绩下滑。其中最典型的案例就是美国对中兴公司的制裁导致 2018 年该企业利润下滑 252.88%。（3）由于担忧贸易战和技术战导致全球价值链和产业链的重构，许多企业开始计划进行产能和投资转移，从而对高新技术企业的投资带来严重冲击。例如，UBS 对北亚地区跨国公司的 CFO 进行调研发现，2019 年受到中美贸易摩擦的影响，其中有 82% 计划或正在进行企业搬移，很多企业计划在 2020—2021 年将产能的 20%—60% 搬离中国大陆，其中有 20% 计划迁移到美国，25% 计划迁移到越南，22% 迁移到印度。

综合以上因素，第四季度中国经济增速依然能够稳得住，全年主要预期目标能够实现,但更为关键的是2020年。第四季度GDP增速预计能够稳定在6.1%左右,全年经济增速为6.1—6.2%,保持在6%—6.5%的目标区间。一是减税降费效应还在持续,并且在年底会显现得更为明显,因为大量的税收征收和抵扣在年底体现得最为充分;二是前3个季度专项债的发行所带来的投资和增长效应存在一定的滞后期,政策效果将在第四季度进一步体现;三是近期中美贸易摩擦的缓和,对短期市场信心提供了有力支撑。但是,2020年经济增速会不会"破6";如果不"破6",支撑经济增长的基础在哪里;如果"破6",底线在何处;会不会不影响"两个一百年"目标的实现,会不会影响社会和就业的稳定,这需要从中期视角出发,对现阶段中国经济增长的性质和2020年运行模式进行深入分析。

三　中期视角下中国经济增长的性质和 2020 年运行模式

2019—2020 年中国经济下滑是趋势性因素与周期性因素叠加、国际与国内不利因素强化所导致的经济增速持续回落。在 4 大趋势性因素中，目前只有制度性因素开始筑底回升，其所释放的改革红利推动了全要素生产率（TFP）的改善，但还没有承担起拉动经济常态化增长的重任。在 5 大周期性因素中，金融风险的缓释和中美贸易摩擦的阶段性缓和将为 2020 年带来一个相对稳定的金融环境和外贸环境，为重建市场信心提供了一个有利时点。2020 年经济增速的下台阶效应可能还将进一步显化，但也不必过于悲观，部分周期性力量可能出现反转以及中国制度红利的持续改善将是 2020 年最为值得关注和期待的新变化。随着 10 大积极因素的巩固和培育，宏观经济下行态势将有所缓和，下行幅度将较 2019 年明显收窄。

三 中期视角下中国经济增长的性质和2020年运行模式 | **61**

◇◇（一）中国宏观经济运行的4大趋势性因素

从4大趋势性因素来看，影响中国经济潜在增速的趋势性力量并没有步入新的平台期，依然处于回落阶段，经济增速换挡的显化是2019—2020年改革调整攻坚期的主要特征。

第一，改革攻坚期决定了新一轮的改革红利还没有完全出现，近期全要素生产率有所改善，但还没有承担起拉动中国经济常态化增长的重任。随着上一轮改革红利的消失，很多既有的制度体系不仅未能成为推动经济增长的动力，反而成为制约新时代经济高质量发展的障碍。

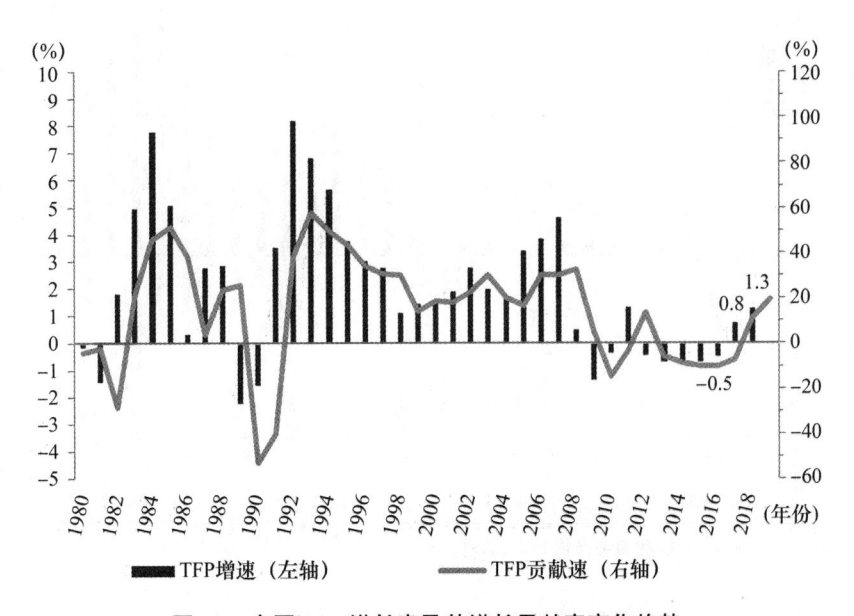

图36 中国TFP增长率及其增长贡献率变化趋势

TFP 增长率从 1992—2007 年的 3.4% 逐步回落到 2008—2016 年的 -0.3%，对经济增长的贡献率从 29.9% 回落至 -4.7%。目前，新一轮的制度红利正在加速构建并开始筑底回升，推动 TFP 有所改善。2017—2018 年 TFP 增长率企稳回升，从 2016 年的 -0.5% 回升至 0.8% 和 1.3%，对经济增长的贡献率从 -7.3% 回升至 11.0% 和 19.5%。但是，目前 TFP 的改善幅度仍难以主导经济高质量发展和承担起拉动经济常态化增长的重任，深化改革调整的任务依然艰巨。

第二，中美贸易摩擦和全球经济大幅放缓决定了全球化红利处于快速下滑期。早在中美贸易摩擦爆发之前，全球化红利已经

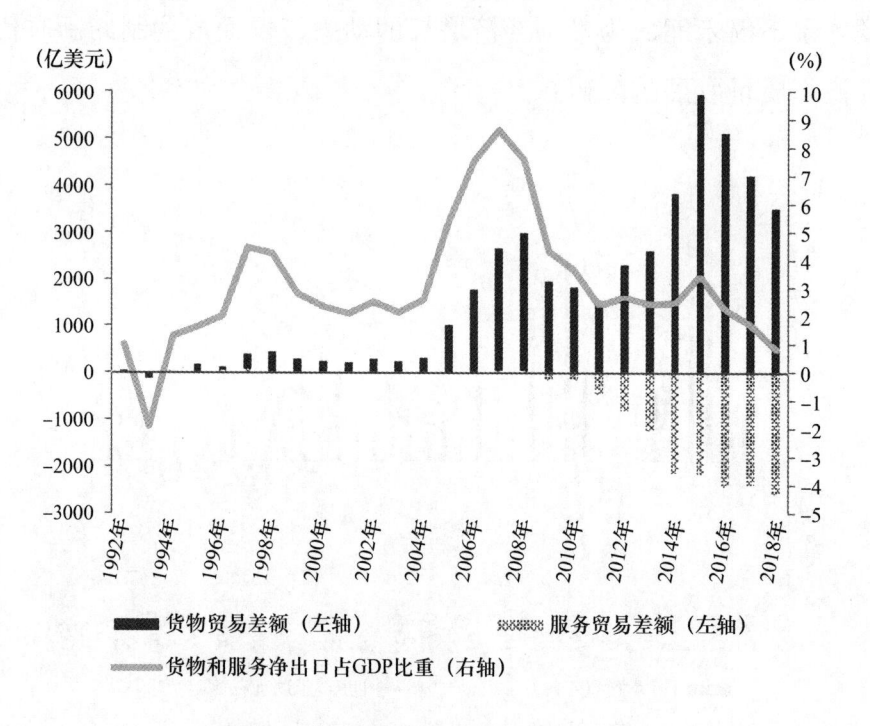

图37 中国货物和服务净出口变化趋势

出现了大幅下滑甚至趋于耗竭的现象。货物和服务贸易顺差占中国GDP的比重从2007年8.6%的峰值逐步回落到2018年的0.8%，其中货物贸易顺差呈现缩小的趋势，而服务贸易逆差则呈现扩大的趋势。近期中美贸易摩擦的加剧进一步加速了全球化红利的衰竭，在中期内恐难以有效提升。

全球贸易增速2018年出现新探底现象，中国外贸环境进入了趋势性新低迷期。从货物贸易看，进出口金额、出口金额、进口金额增速分别从2010年的33.9%、30.5%、38.0%波动下滑至2018年的9.7%、7.1%和12.9%，2019年1—10月又进一步大幅下滑至2.4%、4.9%和-0.4%。尽管2019年实现了较大规模的货物贸易顺差，但仍具有明显的"衰退型"顺差特征，

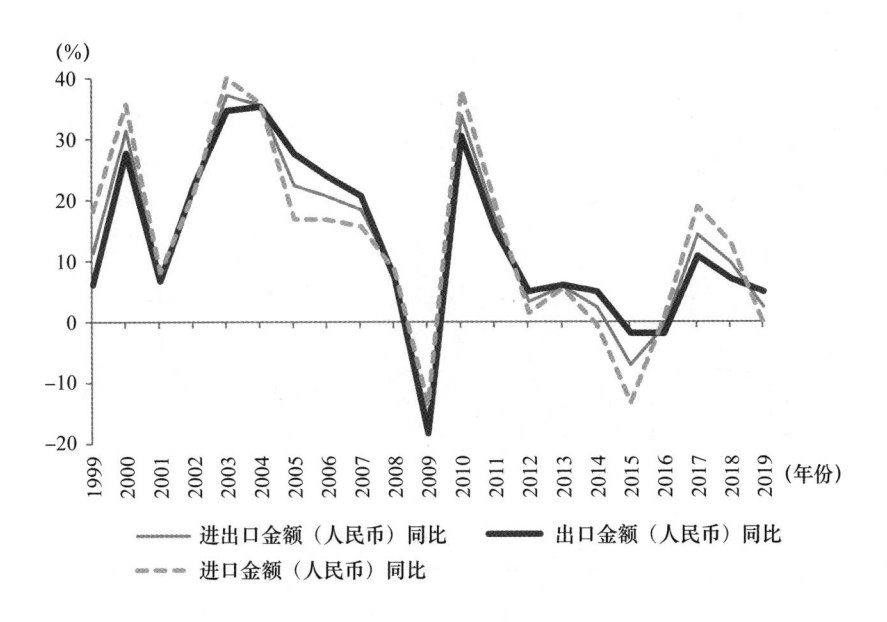

图38 中国进出口变化趋势

而且服务贸易逆差还在持续扩大。

第三，工业化红利开始递减。制造业比重的进一步下滑和第三产业的快速上升决定了工业化红利持续递减。1978—2007年中国工业占GDP比重稳定在40%左右，但自2008年以来，工业占GDP比重从41.3%持续下滑至2018年的33.9%，年均下降超过0.7个百分点，2019年前3个季度又进一步下滑0.4个百分点至33.5%。由此，第三产业占GDP的比重于2008年首次超过工业占比，2019年前3个季度达到54%。同时，第一产业占比已降至6.2%，传统产业转型的增长效应基本耗竭。

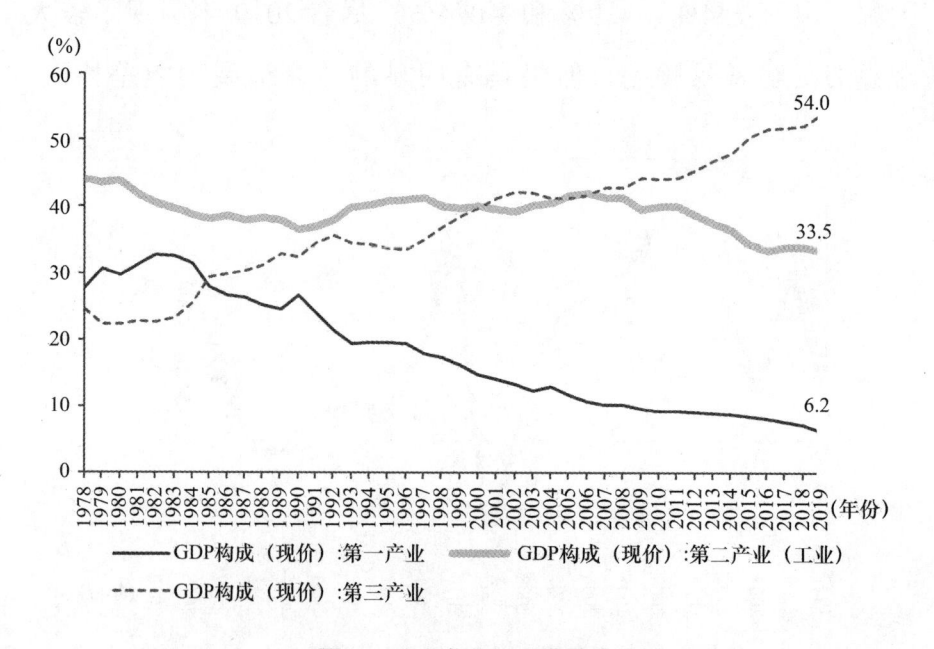

图39 工业化红利开始递减

第四，人口红利大幅度逆转。人口老年化的加速决定了传统

三 中期视角下中国经济增长的性质和2020年运行模式 | **65**

人口红利趋于衰竭。2013年，全国15—64岁人口达到10.1亿的顶点，其中16—60岁劳动年龄人口于2012年达到顶点9.2亿，此后开始持续下降。总人口抚养比于2010年达到34.2%的最低点后开始持续上升，2018年达到40.4%。人口结构的变化导致国民储蓄率于2010年达到51.8%的最高点，此后开始持续回落，2018年为45.3%。

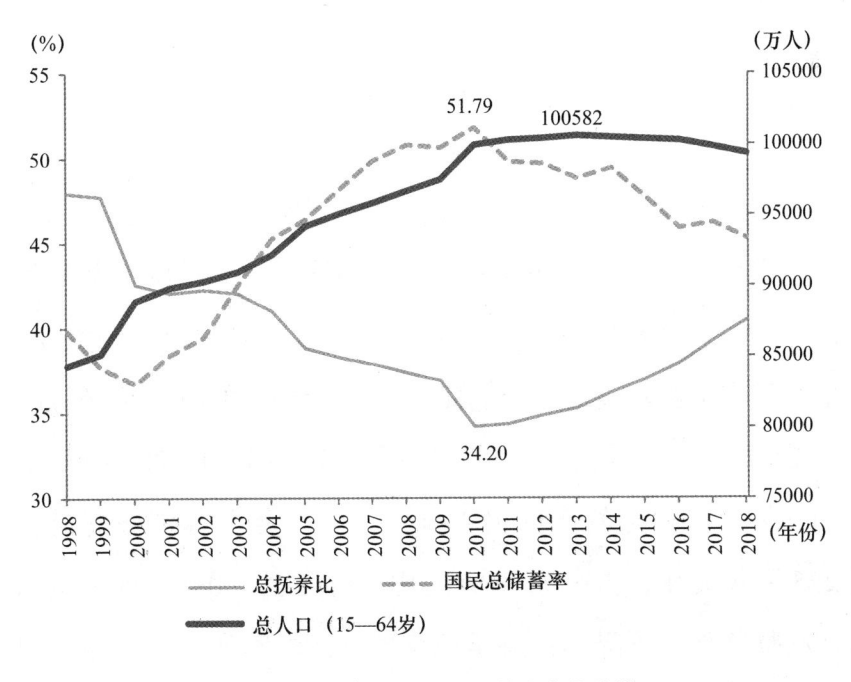

图40 中国人口结构和储蓄率变化趋势

同时，从产业结构和城乡结构转型的角度看，农业劳动力转移速度明显放缓，流动人口总数开始由增长转为回落。特别是2014年以来，全国流动人口规模持续下降，城镇落户意愿低落。

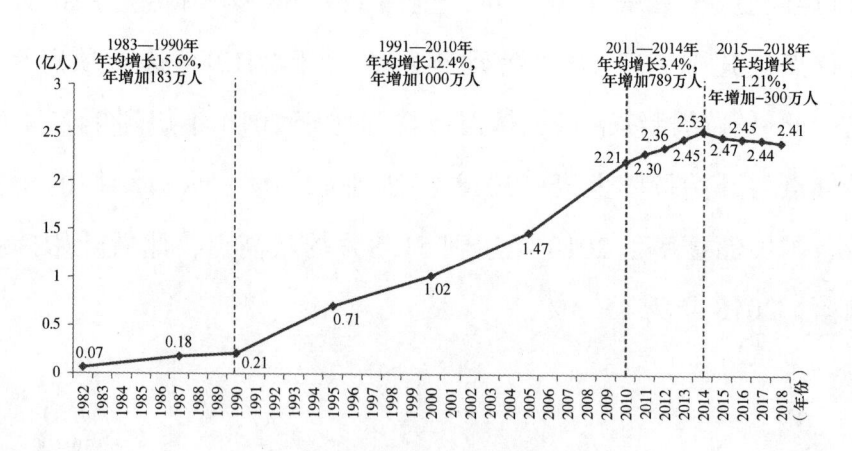

图 41　中国流动人口变化形势

除上述 4 种传统经济增长动力之外，值得重点提及的是，中国经济增长的外部环境恶化具有中长期性，世界经济中长期的趋势性下滑因素仍未见底，中美贸易摩擦引发了新的结构性变化。一是全球技术进步仍处于下行期；二是全球性的收入不平等问题没有得到改善；三是全球债务问题没有得到缓和，2019 年 11 月 15 日国际金融协会发布的报告显示，2019 年全球债务规模将超过 255 万亿美元，占全球 GDP 的比例将升至 330%；四是全球人口红利整体步入下降期；五是逆全球化的时间和深度可能比预期的更长更深。中美贸易摩擦不仅是大国在世界经济低迷期的必然产物，也是霸权周期变迁的产物。遏制中国是美国长期以来一统世界的必然选择，层层加码的谈判技巧说明美国只是利用谈判来推行其单边主义和贸易霸凌主义。中美贸易摩擦直接改变了中国的外部环境，成为中国经济下行压力加大的核心因素之一。

三 中期视角下中国经济增长的性质和2020年运行模式 | **67**

因此,中国经济趋势性下滑的力量并没有得到有效逆转,潜在GDP增速的下滑是导致当前中国经济增速下滑的核心原因之一。在影响中国经济潜在增速的4大趋势性力量中,目前除了制度性因素见底回升并带来TFP改善,其他几大因素都在下行甚至有所加速。过去10年,中国经济增速平均每年下降0.5个百分点,2019—2020年叠加国际国内多重不利因素影响,经济增速的"下台阶效应"将持续显化。

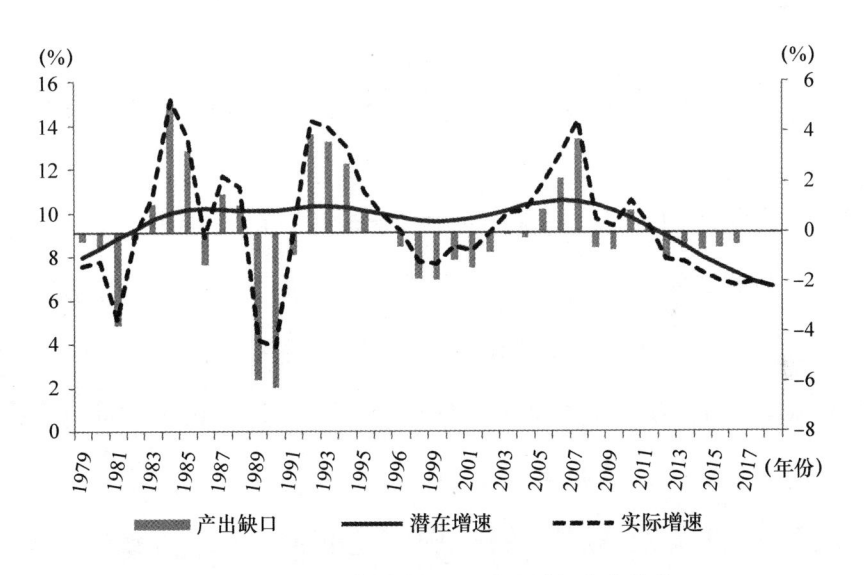

图42 中国经济潜在增速和产出缺口变化趋势

从中长期来看,在趋势性下滑和增速换挡过程中,中国经济发展还要完成以下任务:一是如何跨越"修昔底德陷阱",实现无战争的大国崛起,解决国内经济增长和国际关系协调问题,构建"人类命运共同体";二是如何跨越"中等收入陷阱",实现无民粹主义的大福利，解决进入高收入阶段面临的瓶颈问题；三是如何超越"明斯基时刻"，实现无危机的金融深化，解决金融发展和风险防范问题；四是如何破解"李约瑟之谜"，实现政府与市场协同下的大创新，解决科技进步和前沿创新问题；五是如何越过"环境库兹涅茨曲线"拐点，实现可持续发展的结构转型，解决人类发展与生态环境平衡问题。

◇◇（二）中国宏观经济运行的 5 大周期性因素

从周期性因素变化来看，当前中国经济正处于中美贸易摩擦全面爆发期、刚开启的世界经济周期新一轮下行期、投资周期底部波动期、金融调整下行期以及新一轮市场化去库存周期，这决定了 2019—2020 年的短周期定位总体处于下行状态，防止周期效应叠加是加强宏观政策逆周期调节的重点。

第一，世界经济周期的新一轮低迷期刚开启。直接的导火索是中美贸易摩擦。这不仅造成中美两大经济增长引擎受挫，也使得不确定性风险上扬和市场信心低迷，导致全球贸易品和投资品的全面收缩。在中美贸易摩擦全面加剧的引导下，2019 年以来，全球经济政策不确定性以及地缘政治风险纷纷大幅上扬到历史新高，加剧了世界范围内的投资品和耐用品消费下滑，导致全球制造业陷入集体性低迷期。因此，现阶段世界经济不仅趋势性下滑期没有结束，而且周期性的低迷期也才刚刚开始。全球经济长期停滞下的新一轮下行周期使世界经济又处于十字路口。

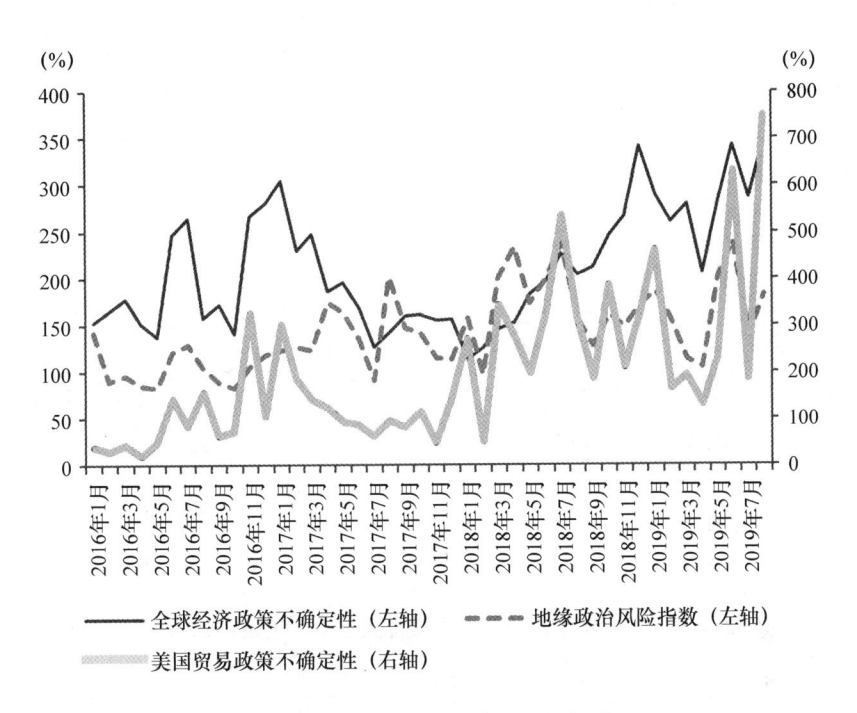

图43 全球不确定性指数大幅飙升

中美贸易摩擦必将全面改变中国外部环境，在近期成为中国经济下行压力的核心因素之一。

第二，中美之间的冲突具有长期性，但2020年是美国的大选年，中国可能会迎来一个相对稳定的外贸环境。原因在于，在中美贸易摩擦下，美国经济同样遭遇重创，并可能在2020年面临经济和金融市场的双重风险。2019年以来，美国经济下行压力加大，私人投资增速下滑，消费支出增速下滑，特别是耐用品

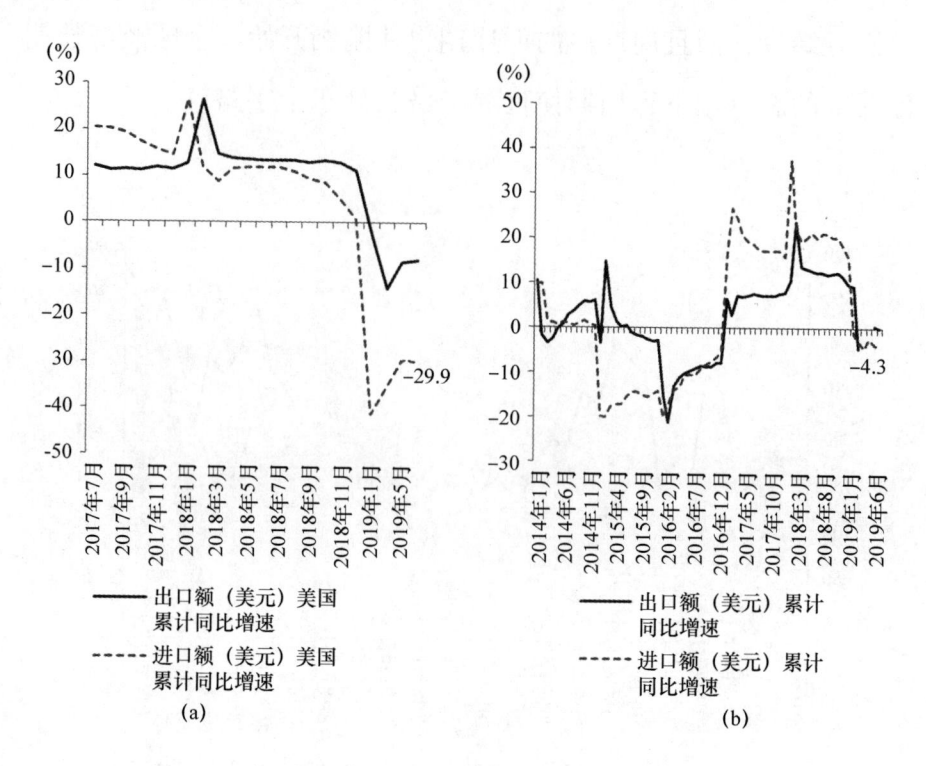

图 44　中国对美国进出口下滑幅度大于中国进出口总体情况

消费出现收缩。同时，美国金融参数发生变异，国债收益率期限倒挂。中小型对冲基金买入信用违约互换工具，押注美国经济衰退导致企业债券兑付违约的投资杠杆倍数已经超过 30 倍。与信贷指数相关的合成型担保债务凭证交易量在 2018 年逾 2000 亿美元的基础上又上涨约 40%，互换期权的日交易额达到 200 亿—250 亿美元。

第三，中国投资周期依然处于底部波动状态。中国固定资产投资名义增速目前仍处于持续放缓和探底的过程中，剔除价格因素的实际投资增速也刚开始摆脱极度低迷的状态。更为重要

三 中期视角下中国经济增长的性质和 2020 年运行模式 | 71

是，企业设备工器具投资和新建投资持续低迷，这表明各类企业主体还没有做好为下一轮经济繁荣进行投资和技术改造的准备。

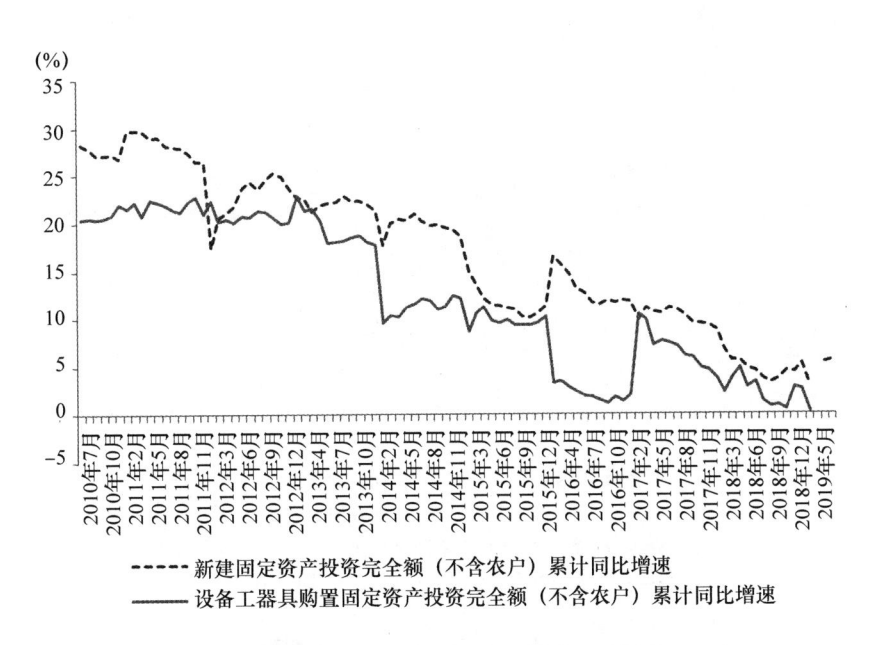

图 45 中国新建投资和设备工器具投资仍处于底部波动状态

第四，中国金融周期总体上已经见顶回落，不过 2019 年债务风险得到有效缓释，为 2020 年经济稳定提供了相对有利的融资环境。自 2017 年开始，中国金融周期下行期已经全面开启，金融供给侧结构性改革、宏观审慎监管以及监管政策的发力决定了中国金融下行周期的延长，各类金融周期指数也表明中国金融周期在 2017 年达到历史高点后开始持续回落。不过，从近期的金融市场形势来看，随着金融风险攻坚战取得阶段性胜利，特别是债务风险得到有效缓释，市场流动性处于稳健状态，为 2020

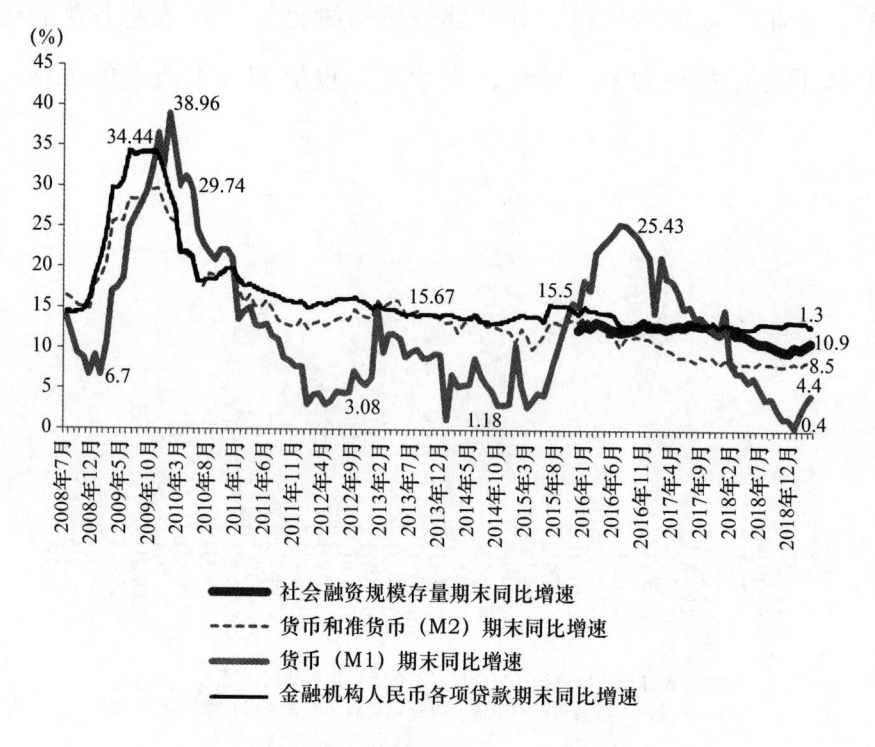

图 46 中国金融周期总体上已经见顶回落

年投融资和经济增长提供了较为有利的金融环境,对于提振市场信心也具有积极作用。

第五,2019年库存周期和房地产周期等其他短期因素趋于下行。首先,从库存周期来看,在悲观预期下,2019年企业过快去库存,目前已经接近周期性的底部,对2019年宏观经济运行产生了一定下行压力。随着2020年市场预期回暖,可能会出现补库存现象。

其次,从房地产周期来看,房地产市场不同指标间已经开始出现分化。近两年的房地产销售面积增速持续下滑,2019年开

三　中期视角下中国经济增长的性质和 2020 年运行模式　**73**

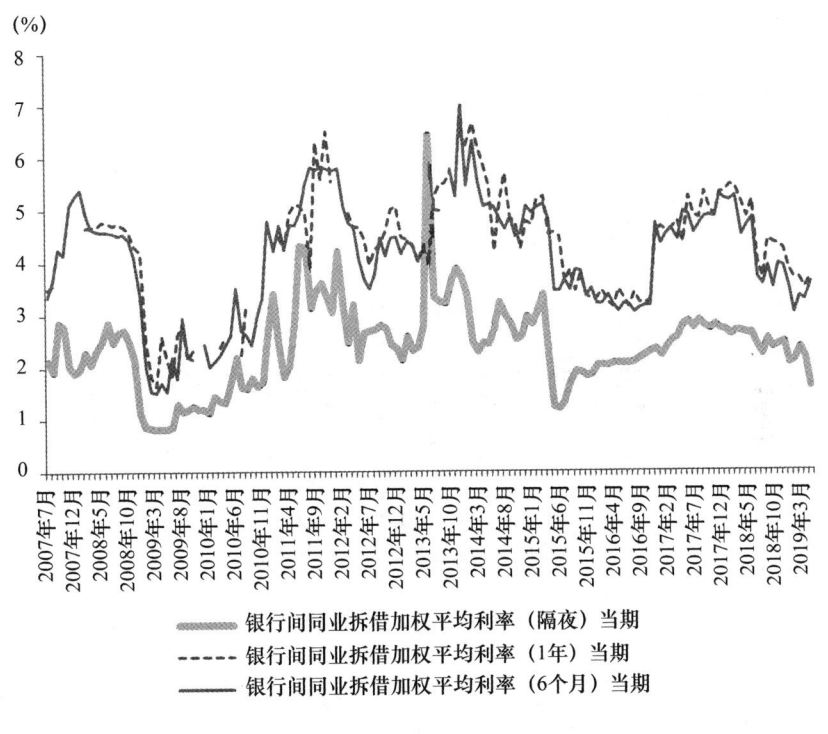

图 47　市场流动性处于稳健状态

始出现负增长，但房地产投资一直保持着 10% 左右的增速，似乎在有力支撑总投资增长。但是仔细分析发现，尽管前 3 个季度房地产新开工面积增长了 8.6%，但房地产竣工面积负增长 8.6%，两者缺口达到 17.2 个百分点，这一情形自 2018 年年初开始已经持续了近两年，2020 年可能会产生"有投资、无增长"的现象。

总体来看，在趋势性因素与周期性因素叠加、国际与国内不利因素强化的作用下，2020 年经济增速的回落还将会进一步持

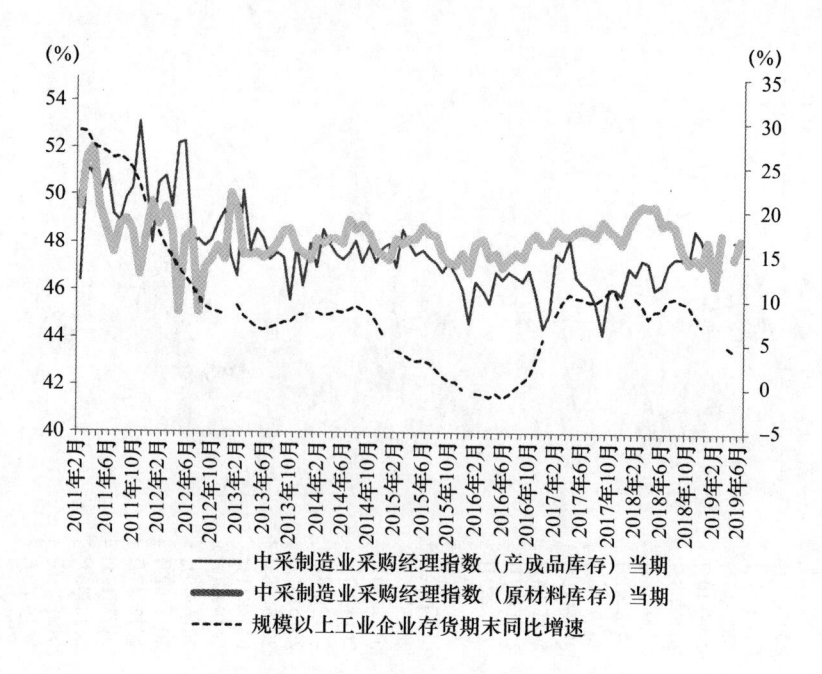

图 48 2019 年库存周期趋于下行

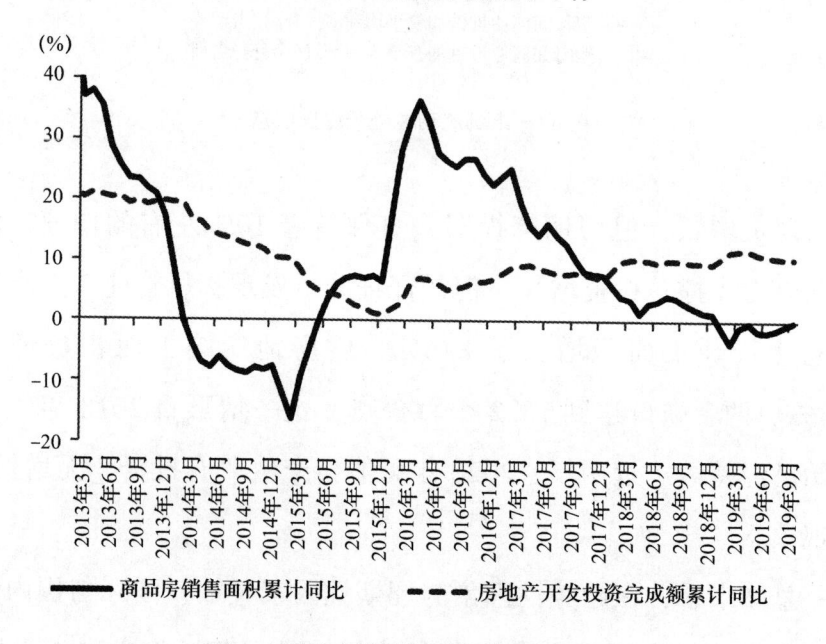

图 49 房地产销售和投资增速走势分化

三 中期视角下中国经济增长的性质和 2020 年运行模式 75

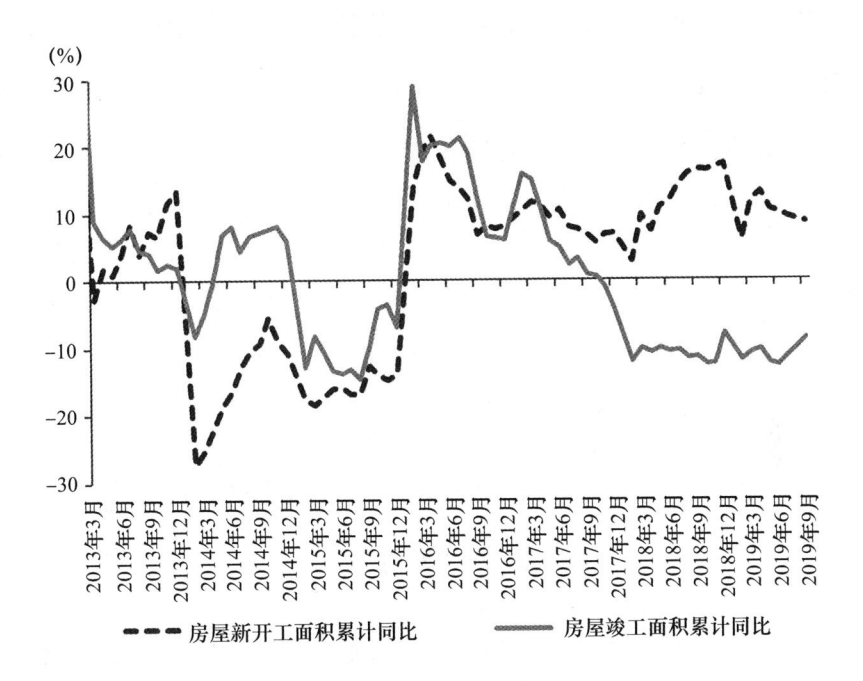

图50 房地产新开工和竣工面积增速走势分化

续。一方面，新常态的增速换挡期、动力转换期以及前期风险的释放期尚未结束，趋势性下滑力量仍然没有逆转。另一方面，国际和国内周期性波动加大，周期性力量与趋势性力量变化将在当前与未来一段时期出现叠加现象。过去 10 年间，中国经济增速平均每年下降 0.5 个百分点，按照这个趋势，2020 年经济增速的"下台阶效应"可能会持续显化。

但目前中国经济的制度性红利已经开始筑底回升，同时，近期金融风险的缓释和中美贸易摩擦的阶段性缓和将为 2020 年带来一个相对稳定的金融市场环境和外贸环境，这对于重建市场信心提供了非常有利的重要时点。新一轮信心构建将从 2019 年第四季度全面开始。同时，中期改革方案对十九届四中全会的快速跟进非常重要。十九届四中全会的精神和蓝图，需要尽快细化和落地，不能流于形式。特别是在十九届四中全会的基础上，对下阶段的收入分配制度和科技创新体系，要有中期规划和一揽子改革方案。

（三）2020年中国宏观经济运行的10大积极因素

基于对2019—2020年的趋势性因素和周期性因素的分析，悲观人士可能会认为，随着中国经济下行压力加大，2020年经济增速将会大幅回落。但是，我们通过对周期相位和各种经济参数进行测算分析发现，2020年部分周期性力量将出现反转，同时中国的制度红利将持续改善，宏观经济运行中存在10大积极因素，值得高度重视并加强培育和巩固。由此，2020年宏观经济下行将有所缓和，下行幅度将较2019年明显收窄。

一是随着吏治整顿的基本到位和十九届四中全会精神的全面落实，中国制度红利将全面上扬，TFP增速将明显改善。如前所述，我们测算发现，近两年的全要素生产率增速开始由负转正，且正处在逐步回升的阶段，说明过去一段时间的改革调整开始释放制度红利。一方面，吏治整顿目前已基本到位，改革浪潮中的新一代开始上马；同时，中央和省级的机构改革已经完成，正向县乡级深入。另一方面，社会各方对于新时代治理方式转变的适应期和磨合期基本完成，对新时代制度的适应性和对未来的信心提升。

如果按照十九届四中全会精神，2020年起抓紧部署和落实新一轮改革方案，将会加快培育和释放更多的制度红利。包括从所有制、分配制度和运行机制三个层面完善社会主义基本经济制度，全方位推进市场化、国际化、高标准的制度化开放，以及细化和落实对非公经济和非公经济人士的保护。

二是随着各类杠杆率的稳定、应付债务增速的下降、高风险机构的有序处置、金融机构资本金的补足、监管短板的完善使金融风险趋于收敛，化解金融风险的攻坚战取得了阶段性胜利，金融环境将得到明显改善。

(1) 近几年去杠杆成效显著，国有企业去杠杆接近完成，民企加杠杆开始相对稳定，大中型银行的风险抵御能力在增强。从杠杆率水平来看，在国有企业去杠杆、政策加大对民营企业融资支持力度的情况下，国有工业企业杠杆率稳中有降，私营工业企业杠杆率波动攀升，两者走势趋于收敛，截至2019年9月底，国有及国有控股工业企业资产负债率为58.4%，同期私营工业企业资产负债率为57.9%。(2) 事实上，自2013年以来的风险持续释放期，也开始步入尾声：P2P、股灾、民营企业的债券违约、中小银行的承压、几大金融控股集团出现的问题、各种跑路

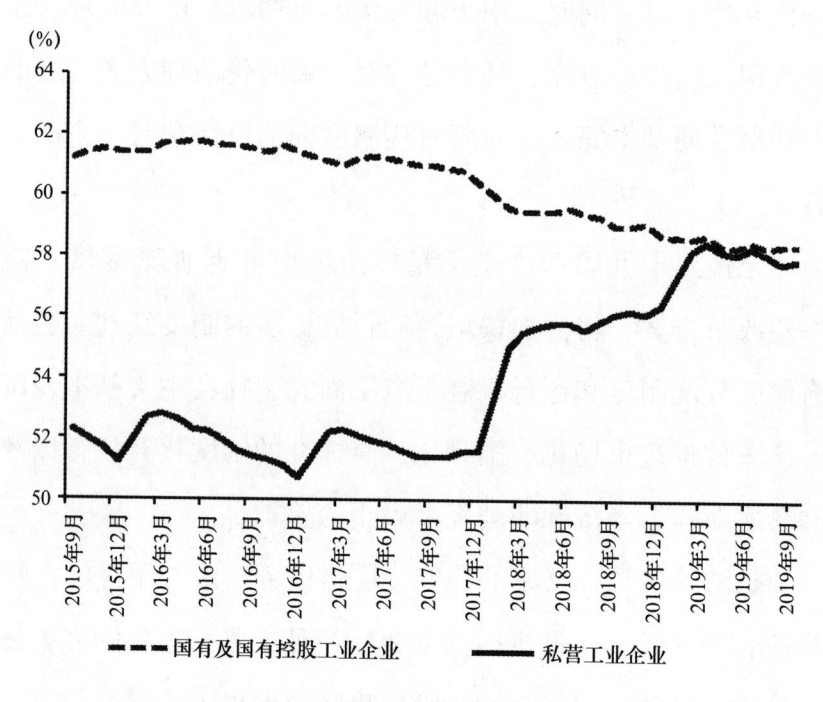

图51 国有及私营工业企业杠杆率趋于收敛

事件，目前都开始得到有效的控制。（3）2020年到期的偿债额增速有所下降，偿债压力减轻；同时，总体负债率过快上升的趋势得到有效逆转，为未来杠杆率的稳定和小幅回升提供了空间。

目前货币政策边际宽松的效果开始显现，企业资本金得到充实、经营性资金得到相对改善，这说明逐渐向好的调整过程已经开始。从现金流情况看，社融回暖，多数行业融资改善。从经营性现金流看，纺织服装、轻工制造等15个行业经营性现金流好转，企业数量占比高于2018年同期。从投资性现金流看，采掘、房地产、国防军工等18个行业投资性现金流好转,企业数量占比高于2018年同期。从筹资性现金流看,社融回暖背景下20个行业融资改善,筹资性现金流好转企业数量占比高于2018年同期,其中钢铁、有色金属、建筑材料等周期性行业改善较为明显。

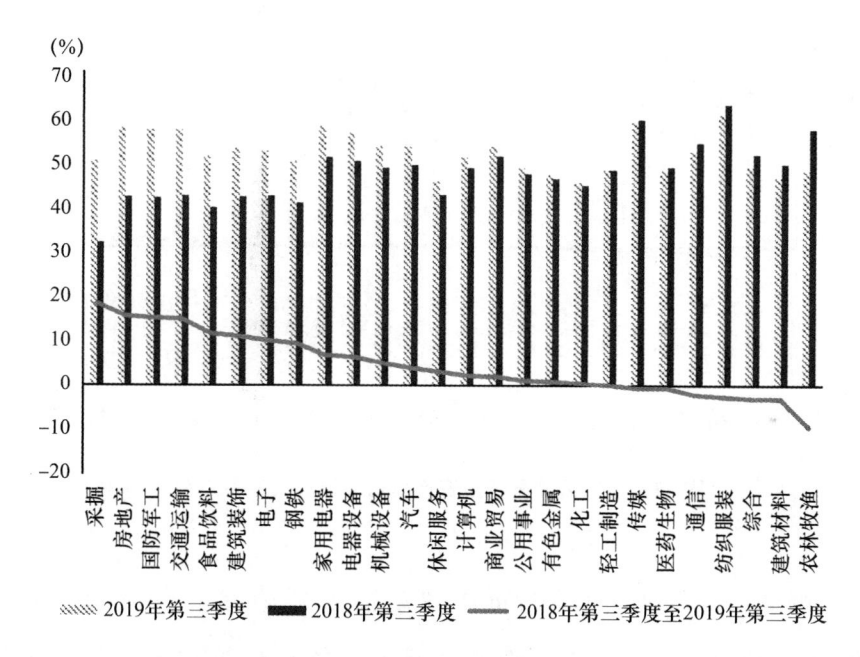

图52 上市公司分行业投资活动净现金流好转企业个数占比情况(剔除金融)

但是,目前企业的偿债能力还没有出现明显改观。在资产负债率方面,国防军工、休闲服务、建筑材料、钢铁等行业资产负债率有所回落,传媒、化工、有色金属等行业资产负债率上升。从短期偿债能力看,26个行业中仅交通运输、综合及传媒这3个行业短期偿债能力有所改善,货币资金/短期债务比值上升的企业数量占比较 2018 年同期增加，钢铁、汽车、国防军工、建筑材料等 22 个行业均较 2018 年同期恶化。

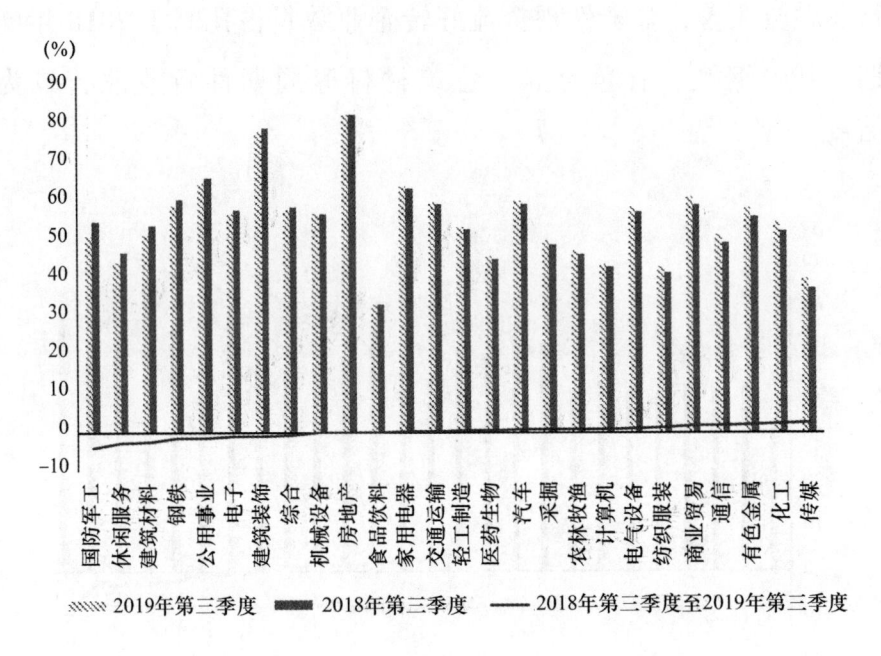

图 53　上市公司分行业资产负债率情况（剔除金融）

因此，2020 年稳健的货币政策需要新内涵。在流动性有所改善、偿债能力还没有改观的情况下，货币政策应该从数量工具转向侧重价格型工具，通过降息调节融资规模，稳定资产价格，降低还本付息压力。

三是企业库存周期触底反弹，前期过度地去库存为 2020 年企业补库存提供了较大的空间。近两年企业过度悲观，产生了库存超调现象，工业领域的产成品和库存量严重收缩，基本上已经接近前一轮工业萧条期的底部，2020 年触底回升将是大概率事件。因此，随着企业经营的正常化，2020年将加快回补库存，带来生产扩张效应。

四是对中美贸易摩擦的恐慌期已经过去，适应性调整基本到位，企业信心将得到明显回归。虽然中美贸易摩擦仍然面临不确定性，但是各类经济主体的预期和信心做出了重大调整，企业和各个阶层的恐慌期已经过去，进入相对从容和自信的适应调整期，即使中美贸易摩擦出现一定的反复，对于中国经济运行也不会产生过于剧烈的影响。同时，从国际政治的角度看，2020年中美冲突阶段性的缓和将是大概率事件。这说明过去两年我们应对中美贸易摩擦的方式得当，建议继续保持战略定力。

五是为应对外部冲击而启动的各类战略将有效提升相应部门的有效需求，特别是在关键技术、科技研发体系、国产替代、重要设备等方面启动的战略将产生很好的拉动效应。中美贸易摩擦使国家在战略上做出了重新调整，特别是在关键技术、科技研发体系、国产替代、重要设备等方面。新战略的短期效果目前已经在国防军工、计算机、机械设备、非银金融等行业领域显现。2019年以来中美贸易摩擦持续发酵，传统周期性行业生产经营情况仍未好转，但政策扶持下部分战略性新兴产业如国防军工、计算机、机械设备、医药生物产业等盈利改善，净利润同比增速均维持在20%以上的较高水平。此外，受金融监管政策红利密集出台影响，金融行业盈利情况逆势回暖，非银金融、银行营业收入、净利润增速均有回升，其中非银金融改善尤为明显。

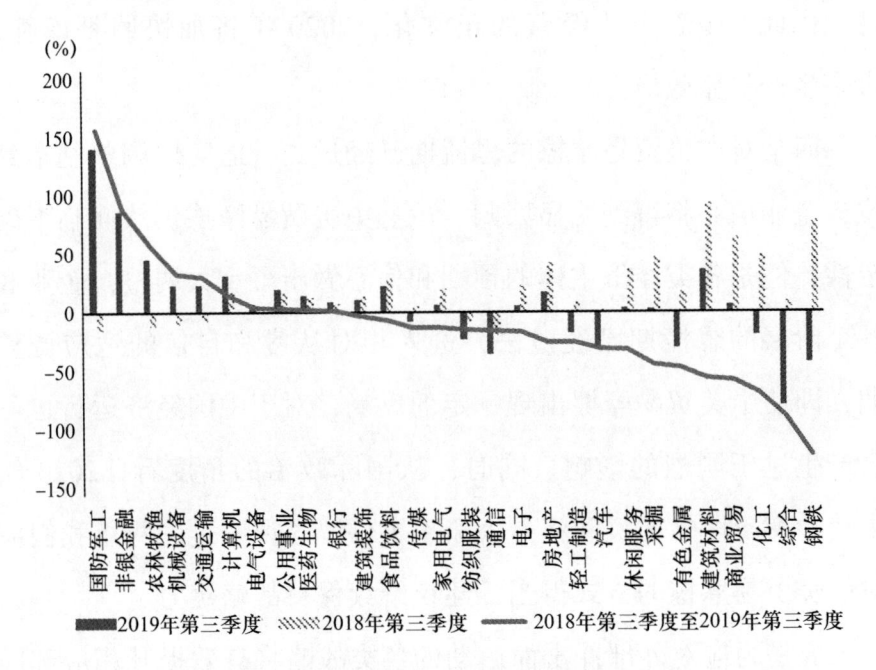

图54 上市公司分行业净利润同比增速情况

从扩大再生产来看，建筑材料、机械设备、国防军工等11个行业同比增速上升，企业扩大再生产能力较强；电子、商业贸易、计算机等中美贸易摩擦波及行业同比增速回落，企业扩大再生产能力受限；综合、家用电器、休闲服务、农林牧渔等行业总资产同比增速由正转负，企业再生产能力较弱。

六是随着全球汽车周期的反转，中国汽车市场可能企稳。2020年全球汽车周期可能出现见底回升，汽车贸易和汽车销售增速回暖，带动制造业改善。

七是猪周期反转，猪肉供求常态化，猪肉价格的大幅度下降将为宏观政策提供空间，改善民众的消费预期。按照当前的市场

三 中期视角下中国经济增长的性质和2020年运行模式 | 83

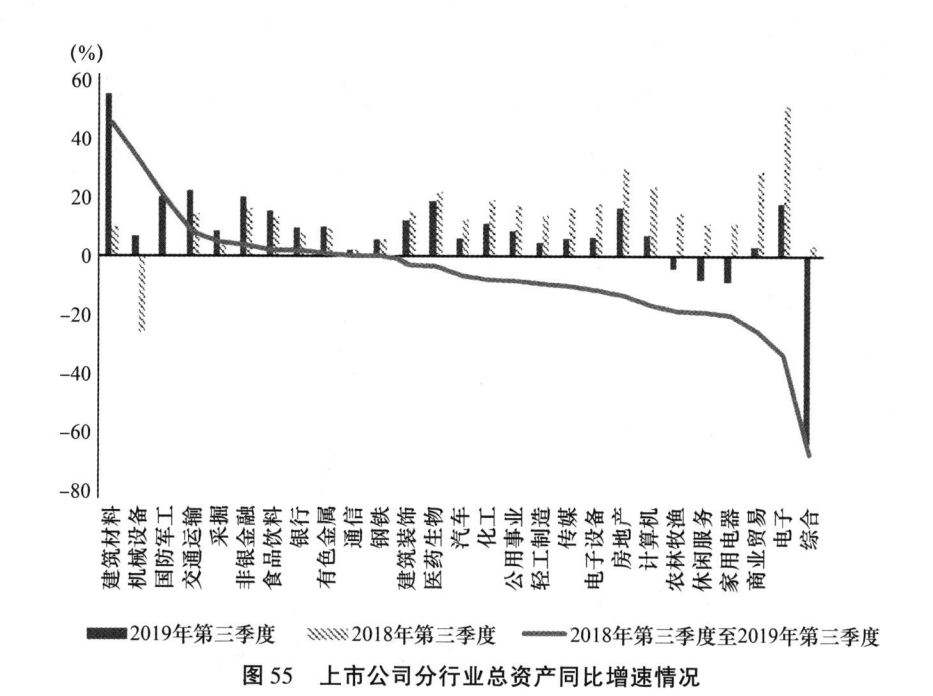

图55 上市公司分行业总资产同比增速情况

调整速度，预计猪肉生产将在2020年上半年全面改善，猪肉价格将在2020年下半年全面回落。随着猪肉价格见顶回落，对民生冲击和宏观政策的约束放松。

八是在基础设施投资持续改善、国有企业投资持续上升以及民营企业家预期改善的作用下，民营投资将在2020年摆脱底部徘徊的困局。（1）过去中国经济的低波动与国有企业的逆周期投资行为密切相关，但是近两年，在去库存、去杠杆和严审核作用下，国有企业投资在本轮逆周期调节中还没有发挥作用，反而在2018年出现了负增长，直到2019年下半年才开始发力。（2）更重要的是，国有企业投资对民营企业投资具有强烈的带动作用，是民营企业大型项目的来源、资金的来源，同时也是信心的来源。

因此，国有企业逆周期投资的恢复是本轮逆周期政策到位的关键。随着改革磨合期和适应期的基本完成，国有企业投资行为开始常态化，随着国有企业投资开始发力，总体投资形势有望好转。

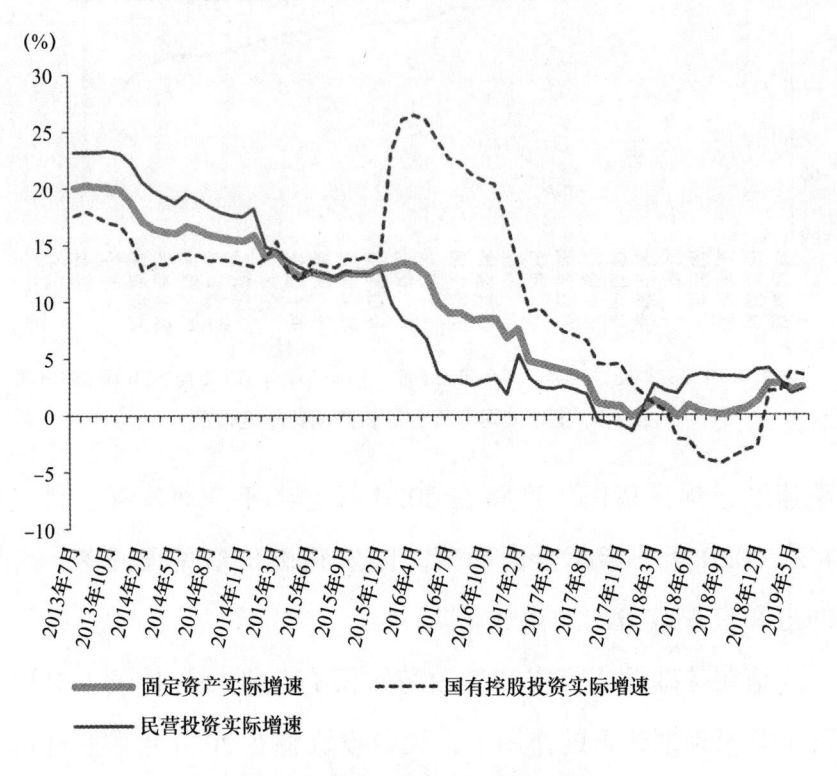

图 56　国企投资与民企投资关系

从扩大再生产来看，目前国有企业在建工程增长已加快，民营企业扩大再生产意愿还较弱。2019年第三季度，多数所有制企业总资产及在建工程同比增速较2018年同期出现下滑。从国有企业看，国有企业主要位于上游行业，受供给侧改革影响，总资产同比增速下滑，企业再生产能力受到一定影响，但在建工程同比增速较 2018 年同期回升，扩大再生产需求仍较强。从民营企业看，民营企业在下游占比更大，总资产及在建工程同比增速均较 2018 年同期下滑，企业再生产意愿较弱。从外资企业看，当前中国鼓励外商投资范围主要集中在现代农业、先进制造、高新技术、节能环保、现代服务业等轻资产型领域，2019 年第三季度外资企业总资产同比增速下滑明显，但受益于一系列促进外商投资政策红利的释放，外资企业在建工程规模提速扩容，企业扩大再生产意愿相对较强。

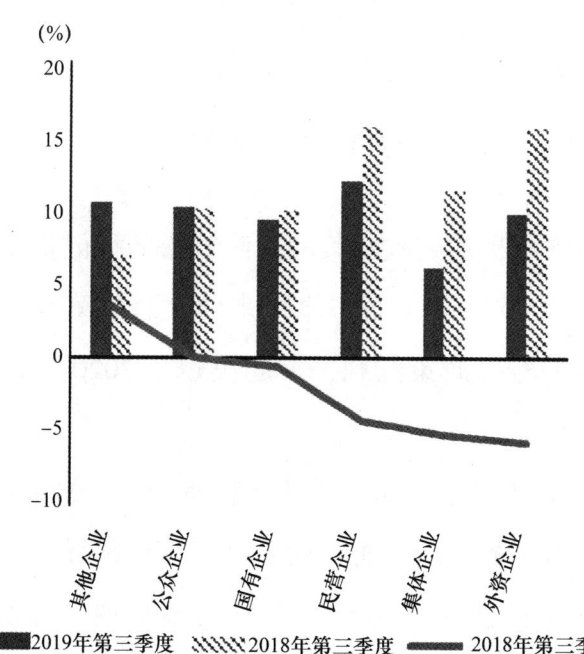

图 57 分所有制总资产同比增速情况

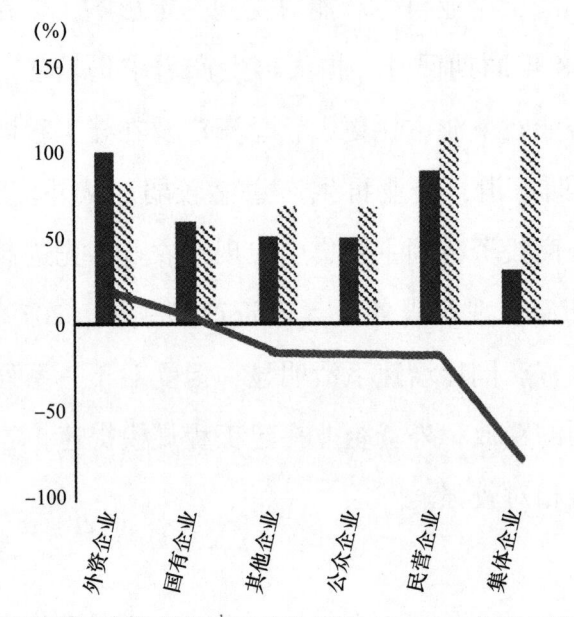

图 58　分所有制在建工程同比增速情况

九是新一轮更加积极的财政政策和边际宽松的稳健货币政策将进一步发力，这与 2020 年全面小康带来的社会政策红利以及全球同步宽松带来的全球政策红利，一起决定了 2020 年的政策红利大于前几个年份。

（1）减税降费的政策红利进一步显现。随着减税降费力度持续加大，企业微观基础不断改善，向宏观经济的传导仍存在一定的时滞，政策效果将会在 2020 年更为充分地显现。首先，运用充分考虑生产端和需求端企业异质性、同时识别生产函数和需求函数参数的结构模型，使用中国规模以上工业企业数据库中的

10个制造业行业数据，评估和模拟增值税减税效应发现：第一，增值税减税的短期实质效应相当可观。增值税减税后，产出会增长、就业会增加；增值税减税的幅度越大，产出和就业的增长效应就越强。以增值税减税3个百分点为例，制造业的总产出、总就业的增长率分别为4.30%、7.07%。第二，完善增值税的抵扣链条、提升企业进项税抵扣的便利，同样具有重要的降税政策效应。例如，若这些政策使得销项税率降低3个百分点、进项税率降低1.5个百分点，与基准结果相比产出增长率会提高3.81个百分点、就业增长率提高3.37个百分点。这表明区分销项税率和进项税率两条影响渠道确实能够提供丰富的额外信息。第三，增值税减税能够明显改善制造业的资源配置效率、提升宏观生产率。削减增值税税率后生产率越高的企业增长更快。其雇佣的劳动力增加更多、产出增长更快，从而市场份额增加。

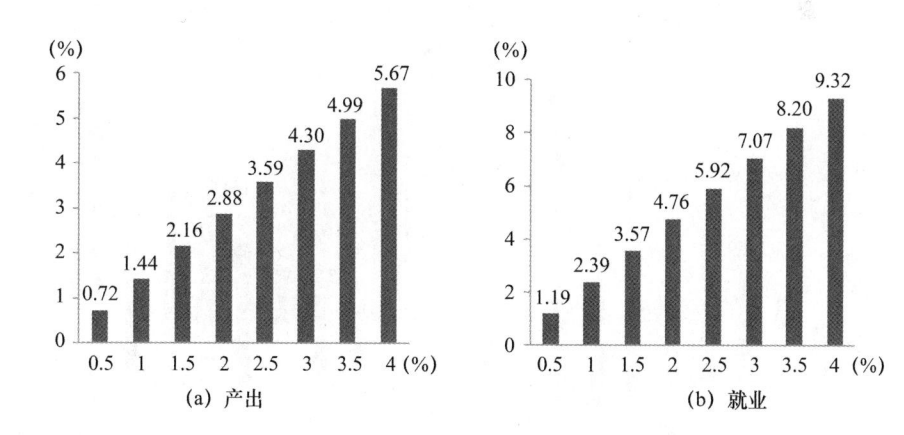

图59 制造业削减增值税税率的效应

其次，根据全国税收调查中的10个服务业行业数据，就服务业社会保险降费对产出、就业的影响进行了政策模拟发现：第一，服务业社会保险降费的产出效应和就业效应相当可观。服务业社会保险费率下调4个百分点，产出增长5.7个百分点。社保降费幅度与企业产出和劳动需求增长的程度基本呈现稳定关系，降费的就业效应是降费幅度的2倍，降费4.0个百分点，就业需求将增长近8个百分点。第二，服务业企业成本的变化更多体现为实质效应（产出和就业）而非传导至价格。面对劳动成本的下降，服务业企业更多地选择增加劳动雇佣量、提供更多服务，而不是削减服务价格。第三，降费能够明显改善服务业的资源配置效率、提升服务业整体全要素生产率。降费后生产率越高的企业增长更快、劳动需求增加更多，从而市场份额增加。第四，降费对小规模服务业企业的就业刺激效应更强。由于服务业中小规

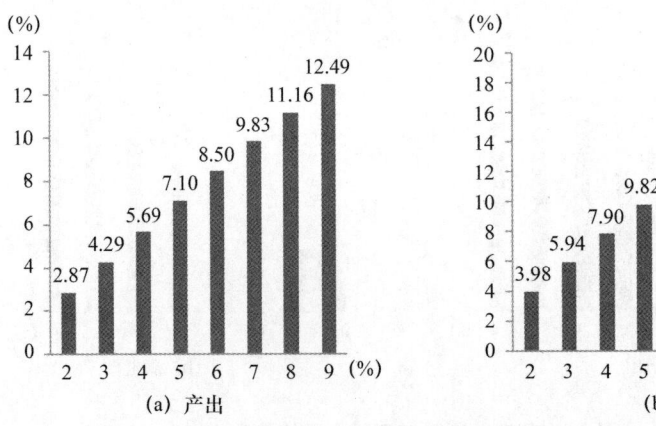

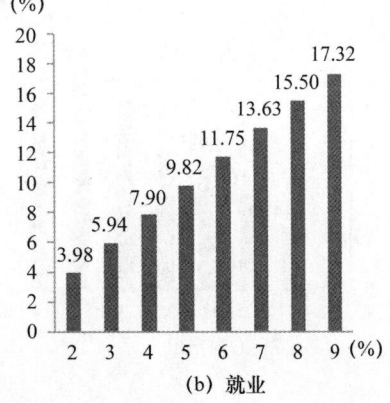

图60 服务业社会保险降费的政策效应模拟

模企业为数众多,降费对社会就业的促进作用确实不可小觑。同时,由于小规模服务业企业对劳动成本的变化更敏感,社会保险征费体制改革应该有实际性降费政策加以配合。

当前的财政政策效果已经显现,2020年需要坚持和巩固;同时,积极的财政政策需要更加积极有为,从生产端向消费端拓展。生产端的减税降费对降低企业成本具有明显成效,但如果老百姓不消费,政策传导效率就会下降;而如果消费起来了,生产自然就会跟上。虽然消费刺激容易形成跨期波动,但作为逆周期调节工具,效果立竿见影。最典型的就是降低汽车购置税。同时,可以考虑加大对中低收入群体补贴和转移支付力度,缓解猪价上涨和收入波动产生的民生冲击。

除了更加积极的财政政策进一步发力,2020年全面小康带来的社会政策红利以及全球政策同步宽松带来的全球政策红利,也一起决定了2020年的政策红利大于前几个年份。

(2) 全面建成小康社会的社会政策红利。2020年全面小康目标的实现,意味着中国进入减少相对贫困人口阶段,收入分配制度改革将作为十九届四中全会提出的改革重点而启动。

(3) 全球政策同步宽松的全球政策红利。这将带来国际政策的协同效应,全球经济形势持续恶化的局面有望得到边际改善。为促进经济的进一步复苏或者延长经济景气周期,全球开启了次贷危机以来的新一轮降息模式。与2019年年初相比,全球主要央行都下调了政策性利率水平,美联储2019年已经3次降息，联邦基金利率保持在1.50%—1.75%，全球短期基准利率下行。其中，日本、瑞士和瑞典都是负利率水平，欧元区利率为0，但存款便利利率为–0.5%。

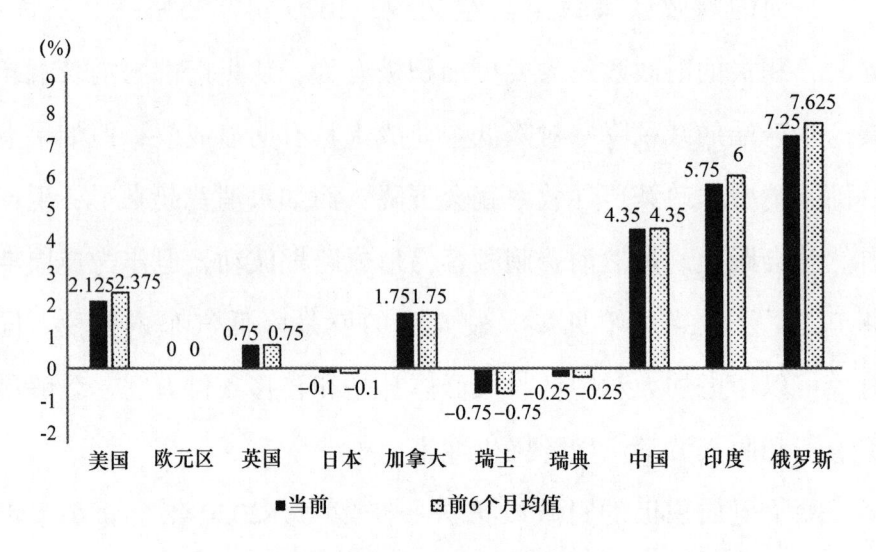

图61　全球主要发达经济体和新兴市场经济体的央行政策性利率水平

数据来源：BIS。

十是中国庞大的市场、多元化出口路径、齐全的产业、雄厚的人力资源、开始普及的创新意识和创新竞争、强大的政府及其控制能力决定了中国经济的韧性和弹性将在2020年进一步强化。2020年中国GDP总量将突破100万亿元，人均GDP超过1万美元，超大规模市场优势和中产消费潜力将得到进一步提升，强劲的结构变化意味着中国具有强大的发展后劲和动能。

（1）服务化孕育新机会和新问题。近年来，随着工业占GDP比重的持续回落，服务业占比持续上升，服务业发展成为

三 中期视角下中国经济增长的性质和 2020 年运行模式 | 91

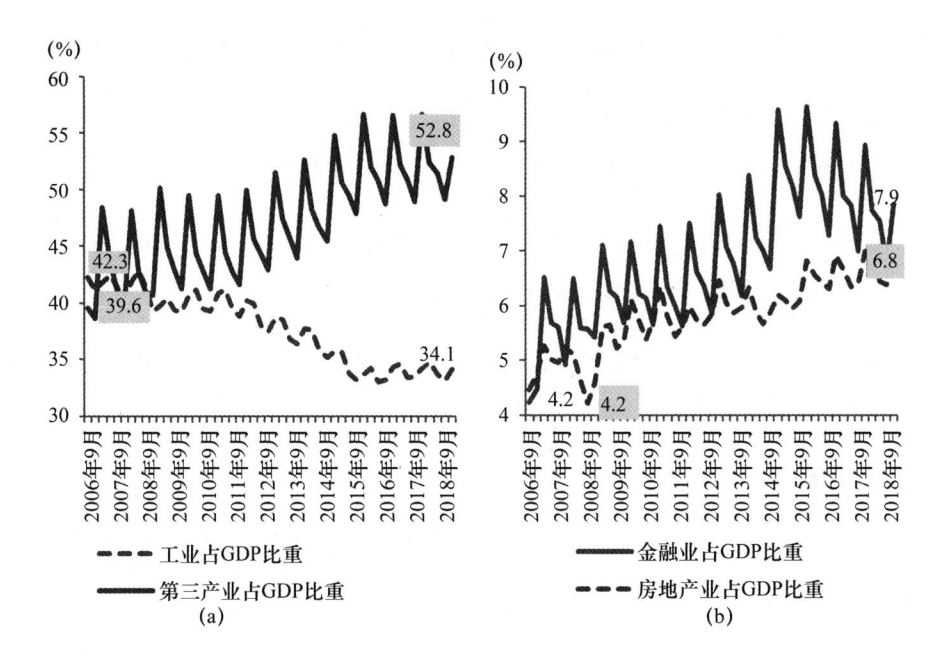

图 62 服务业发展拉动中国经济增长

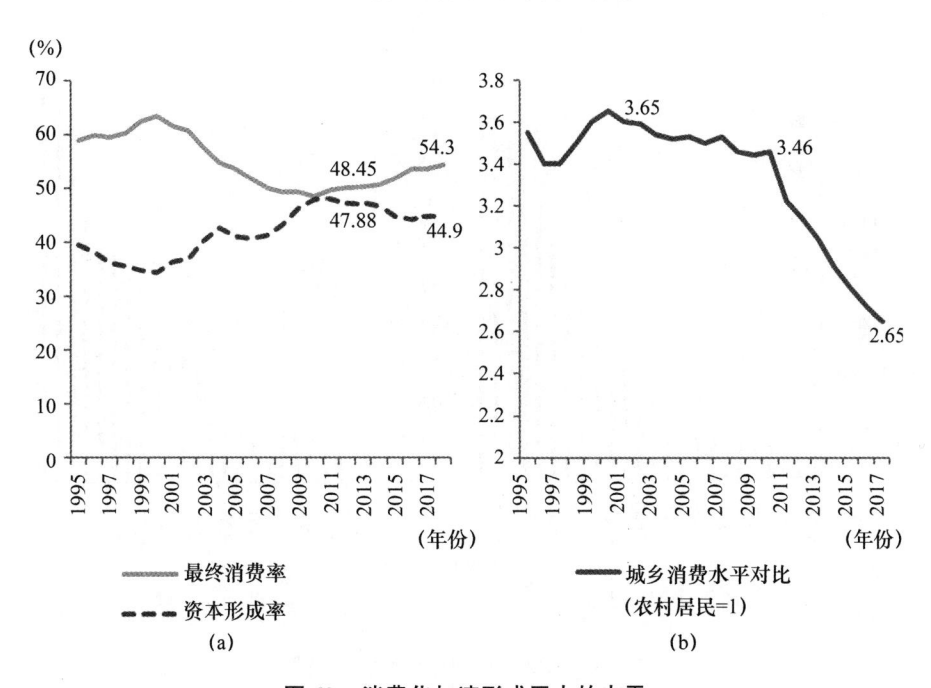

图 63 消费化加速形成巨大的内需

中国经济增长的主要驱动力。其中，金融业占 GDP 比重提升至 8% 左右，房地产业占 GDP 比重提升至 7% 左右。

（2）消费化加速形成巨大的内需。近年来，中国消费参数已经发生革命性变化：第一，恩格尔系数为 29.33%，达到联合国富裕水平的标准，进入发达国家行列，比 1978 年减少了 30 个百分点。第二，巨大的中国中等收入阶层意味着庞大的市场。根据第四次全国经济普查数据修订后的 2018 年中国人均 GDP 已经超过 1 万美元，接近世界人均 GDP 的 1.13 万美元。第三，物质消费和服务消费比例大幅度变化。服务消费支出占居民消费支出的比例在 2017 年超过 40%。第四，消费支出占居民可支配收入

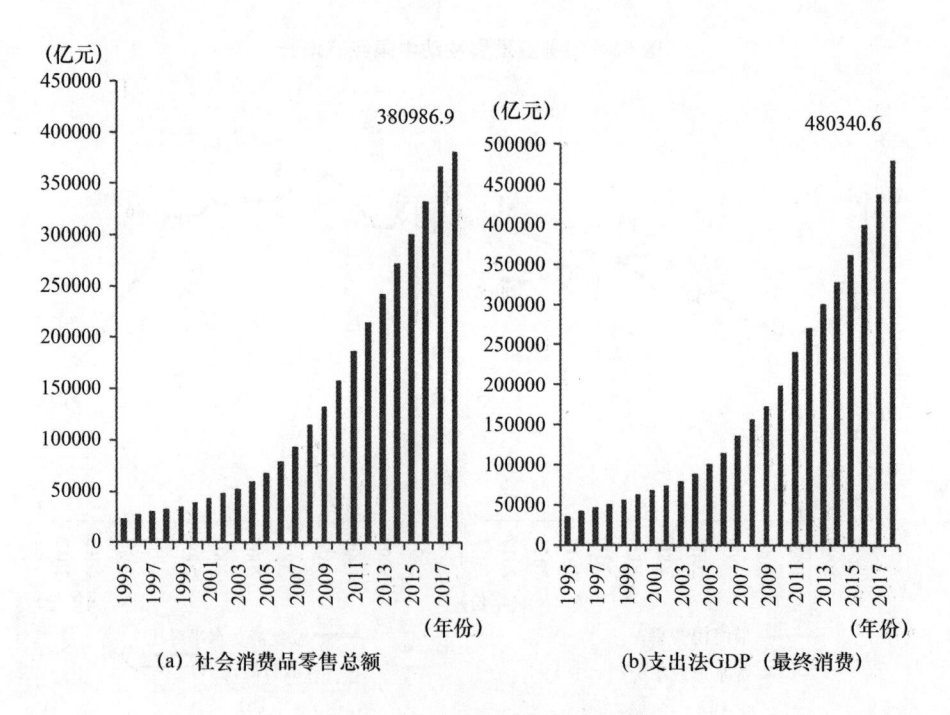

(a) 社会消费品零售总额　　(b) 支出法GDP（最终消费）

图 64　消费化加速形成巨大的内需

的比重为70.6%。第五国民储蓄率下降到46.4%，国民消费率在过去8年中提升了5个百分点。

（3）研发达到很高的高度。2018年中国研发支出占GDP比重达到2.2%，相比2008年提高了0.7个百分点；发明专利申请授权数达到43.2万件，是2008年的4.6倍。

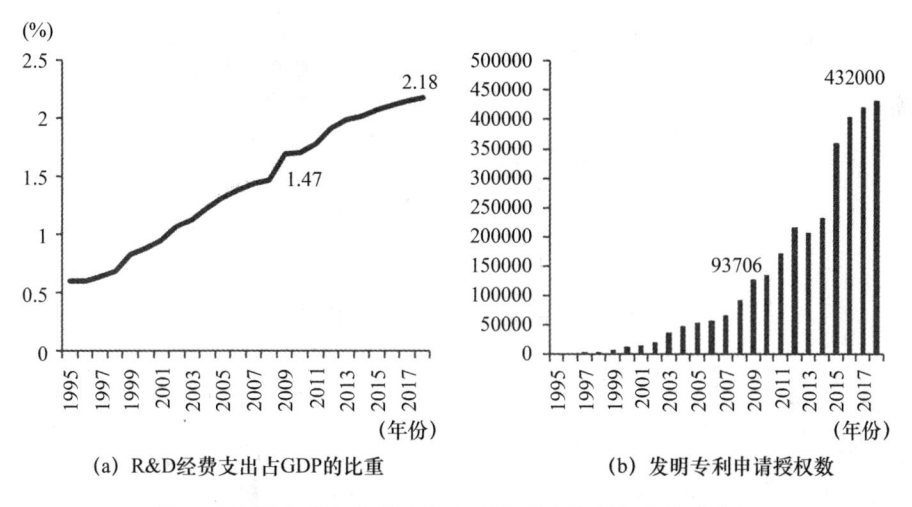

(a) R&D经费支出占GDP的比重

(b) 发明专利申请授权数

图65　中国研发经费支出和发明专利申请授权数快速上升

与美国相比，中国R&D支出的差距不断缩小，特别是试验发展研发支出规模已经超过美国。不过，从支出结构来看，中国研发主要是以试验发展阶段的投入为主，2016年占比达到84.2%，而基础研究投入则严重不足，占比仅有5.1%，基础研究以及应用研究投入占比合计为15.8%。相比之下，美国在基础研究领域的投入占比达到16.9%，基础研究以及应用研究投入占比合计达到36.4%。特别是在联邦政府层面，除了国防部，其他部门（包括能源部、NASA等）基本以资助基础研究与应用研究为主。

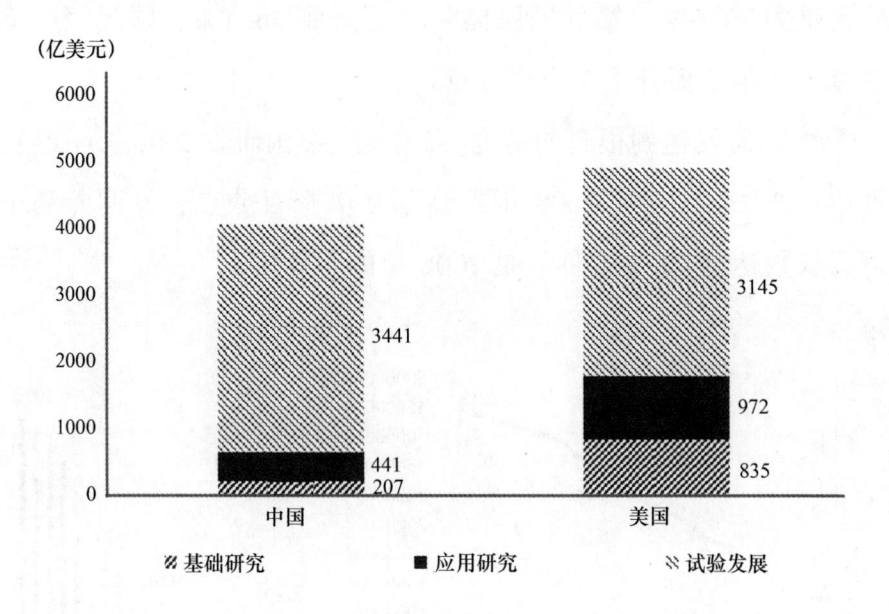

图 66 中国和美国研发支出结构对比

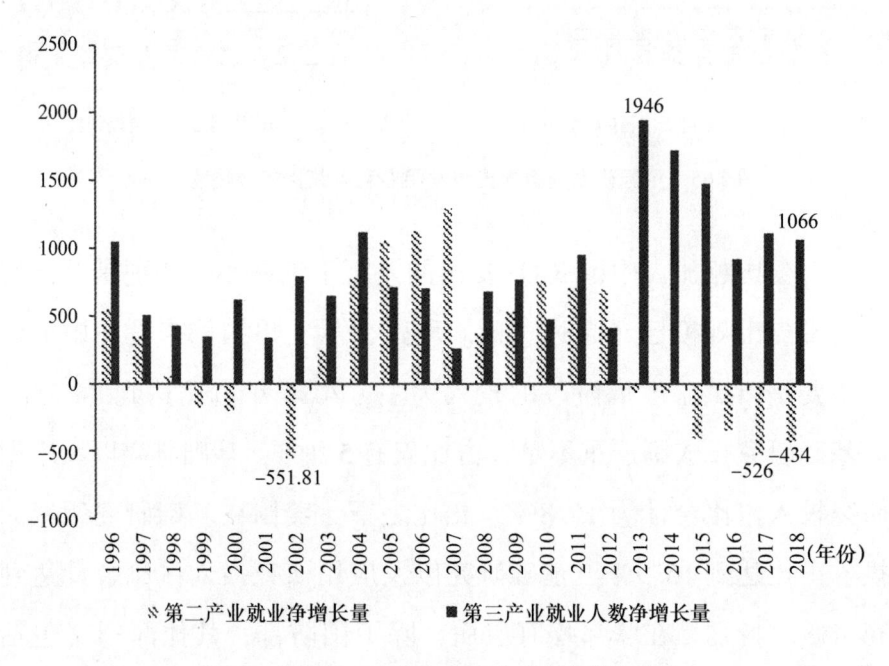

图 67 中国第二产业和第三产业就业增幅变化

（4）经济结构变化对就业产生格局性影响，使得在经济增速下降过程中就业却出现超预期的稳定。近年来，第二产业占GDP比重持续下降，第三产业占比则持续上升，就业加速从第二产业向第三产业转移，表现为第二产业就业人数开始出现负增长，但第三产业就业人数快速增长。在此背景下，同样的经济增速所能吸纳的就业人数增加。因此，在经济增速下降过程中，就业却出现超预期的稳定。

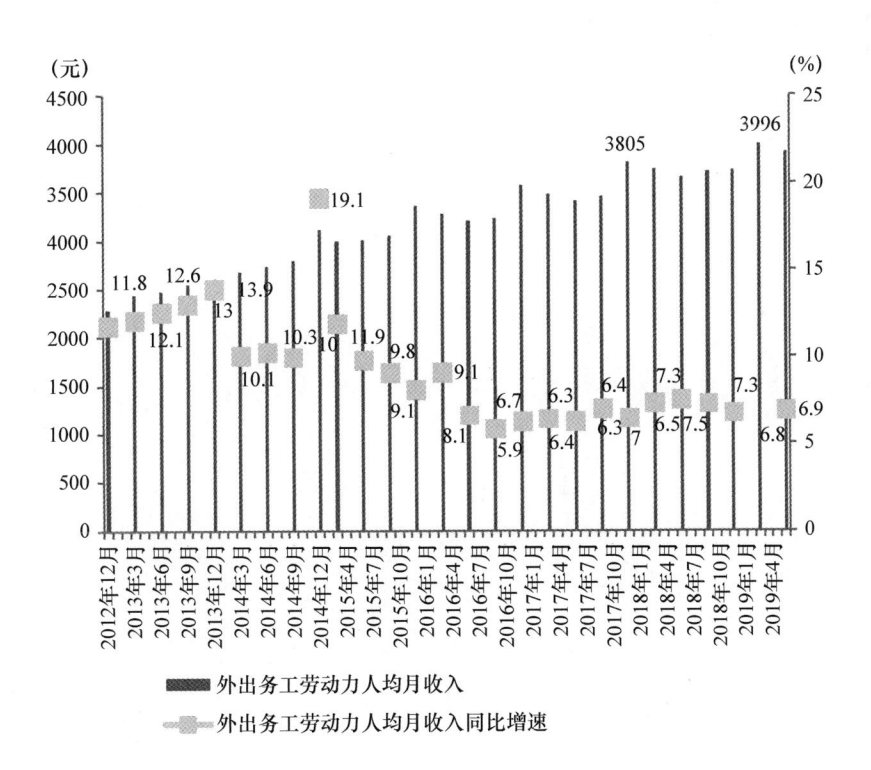

图 68 中国外出务工劳动力人均月收入及其增速变化趋势

除了城镇调查失业率总体平稳外，就业市场的稳定还体现在农民工收入的较快增长上。在各类就业群体中，农民工就业增长和工资增长最具弹性，也最能反映就业形势的变化。2019年上半年，农民工月收入达到近4000元，同比增长6.9%。

综上所述，在趋势性因素与周期性因素叠加、国际与国内不利因素强化的作用下，2020年经济增速还将进一步下行，但下滑幅度有望放缓。在此背景下，如何科学制定2020年经济增长目标，2020年宏观经济运行中又有哪些重大风险点，需要保持高度关注和采取前瞻性的应对举措。

四 2020年经济增长目标的确立和需要关注的风险点

2020年是全面建成小康社会的决胜之年,是第十三个五年规划的成果验收之年,对各项发展目标的约束收紧决定了2020年经济增长目标的下限。科学制定2020年增长目标的紧要之处在于目标下限约束与现实的增长潜力之间的空间大幅收窄。一方面,新常态的增速换挡期、动力转换期以及前期风险的释放期尚未结束,趋势性下滑力量仍然没有逆转。另一方面,国际、国内周期性波动加大,周期性力量与趋势性力量将在当前与未来一个时期出现叠加。在趋势性因素与周期性因素叠加、国际与国内不利因素强化的作用下,2020年经济增速的"下台阶效应"还将进一步显化。因此,必须强化底线意识,以底线思维制定和落实2020年经济社会发展的主要预期目标,加强巩固和培育积极因素,并对经济运行中可能出现的重大风险点保持高度关注和采取前瞻性的应对举措。

❖（一）2020年中国经济增长目标的确立

科学制定2020年经济增长目标，需要坚持三个基本原则：一是高质量发展；二是完成"两个一百年"目标的阶段性任务；三是保证社会就业基本稳定。与一些流行观点不同，经过反复测算发现，2020年增长目标不必拘泥于6%以上，保持在5.5%—6.0%，保守目标为5.8%左右，足以完成"两个一百年"目标的阶段性任务，也能够保证社会就业的基本稳定，同时也更有利于保持战略定力，按照既定方针推动经济高质量发展。

1. 坚持高质量发展原则，2020年GDP增长的区间管理目标宜设为5.5%—6.0%

按照既定方针推动中国经济高质量发展，要求2020年经济目标必须符合中国经济中长期发展趋势，并在此基础上加强宏观政策逆周期调节功能对冲周期性因素。2020年中国经济潜在增速仍处于下台阶阶段，当前经济增速换轨的4大力量中，除了制度性因素开始筑底回升外，其他3大趋势性因素仍然没有得到有效逆转，而且近期的TFP回升还没有承担起拉动中国经济常态化增长的重任。同时，国际、国内各种周期性因素的不利影响明显加大，可能会在2020年出现叠加，对此需要加强宏观政策逆周期调节功能进行有效对冲。

基于以上判断，2020年GDP增长目标宜设在5.5%—6.0%。原因在于，近10年来的GDP增速平均每年下降约0.5个百分点，2020年的潜在经济增速依然会出现明显回落。如果继续将2020年的GDP增长目标设在6.0%—6.5%，必须依靠强有力的财政刺激政策、宽松的货币政策以及放松房地产市场调控来刺激短期增长。但是，目前看这三个条件或不具备或不利于中长期的经济高质量发展。因此，从保持战略定力，按照既定方针推动经济高质量发展的角度来看，将2020年增长目标设在5.5%—6.0%进行区间管理较为适宜。

从中长期来看，在趋势性下滑和增速换挡过程中，中国经济发展还需要完成以下历史性任务，必须为2021年深化改革攻坚预留政策储备：一是跨越"修昔底德陷阱"，实现无战争的大国崛起，解决国内经济发展和国际关系协调问题，构建"人类命运共同体"；二是跨越"中等收入陷阱"，实现无民粹主义的大福利，解决进入高收入阶段面临的收入分配等瓶颈问题；三是超越"明斯基时刻"，实现无危机的金融深化，解决金融发展和风险防范问题；四是破解"李约瑟之谜"，实现政府与市场协同下的大创新，解决科技进步和前沿创新问题；五是越过"环境库兹涅茨曲线"拐点，实现可持续发展的结构转型，解决经济发展与生态环境再平衡问题。

2. 坚持实现"两个一百年"目标阶段性任务原则，2020年GDP增长目标宜保持在5%—6%，不必拘泥于6%以上

2020年GDP增长目标的下限面临完成"两个一百年"目标阶段性任务的紧约束。如果按照目前的统计口径，6%将是2020年GDP增长的目标下限。在2019年GDP增速为6.2%的假设下，要实现"2020年GDP比2010年翻一番"的目标，2020年的GDP增速需要达到6.0%；如果要实现"十三五时期年均增速在6.5%以上"的目标，2020年的GDP增速需要达到6.2%。

但是从历次经济普查数据调整的统计规律来看，要完成上述目标，2020年经济增长保持在4%—5%就已经足够。测算依据在于：第一次全国经济普查对1999—2004年经济数据调整后，增速平均每年提高了0.6个百分点；第二次全国经济普查对2005—2008年经济数据调整后，增速平均每年提高了0.5个百分点；第三次全国经济普查对2009—2013年经济数据调整后，增速平均每年提高0.56个百分点。因此，根据2018年年底开启的第四次全国经济普查进行数据调整后，2014—2018年的经济增速有望每年提高约0.5个百分点，5年累计提高2.0—2.5个百分点；即使第四次全国经济普查调整仅仅部分重现前3次的情况，按照每年仅提高0.2个百分点算，2020年增长5%也足够完成比2010年翻一番的目标。2019年11月22日，国家统计局发布了关于修订2018年国内生产总值数据的公告，将2018年GDP向上修订了2.1%，这意味着在2019年增长6.2%的基础上，2020年经济增速保持在4%—5%就已经足够实现比2010年翻一番的目标。

因此，2020年的经济增长目标不必为增速"破6"的关口过度紧张，在基于第四次全国经济普查数据进行调整后，2020年增速保持在5.5%—6.0%的目标区间，就能够实现"2020年GDP比2010年翻一番"的目标。

3. 坚持保证社会就业基本稳定原则，增速保持在5.5%—6.0%足以保证就业的基本稳定，5.8%是较理想的状态；5%是确保就业无虞的增长底线，但可能会牺牲就业质量

（1）根据我们的测算，5.5%—6.0%的增长目标可以保证就业的基本稳定。以2019年中国GDP增速为6.2%为基础，若2020年中国的经济增速为6.0%，那么非农就业增量预计为590万，与2018年相近，就业比较宽松；若2020年经济增速为5.8%，非农就业增量降至480万，比2019年略多，对标2019年的就业形势，2020年就业形势仍应无虞；若2020年经济增速为5.5%，非农就业增量为315万，比2019年少近百万，达到历史新低，就业形势会更加吃紧，但尚不会出现大面积的失业问题；若2020年中国经济增速降至5.0%，非农就业增量将降为0，这时才将真正考验中国之就业。基于此，5.0%是确保中国就业无虞所不能突破的增长底线，5.5%—6.0%可以保证就业的基本稳定，5.8%是较理想的状态。

（2）四种增长情形下中国就业的具体形势分析①如下所示。

测算的基本假设：①以2019年中国经济增速为6.2%为基础；②2020年三大产业的GDP占比按平滑方法分别为6.85%、33.23%、53.6%；③假设2020年中国经济增速有四种情形，分别为6.0%、5.8%、5.5%、5.0%。

情形1：若2020年中国经济增速为6.0%，非农就业增量将为590万，就业形势也将较为宽松。

若2020年中国经济增速为6.0%，非农就业增量将为590万，接近2018年的水平，因2018年的就业形势较好，对标之，2020年的就业形势也应较宽松。其中，工业部门减少劳动力960万，建筑业将增加劳动力220万，服务业将增加1330万，服务业中就业扩张最大的几个部门是批发和零售业（430万）、教育业（150万）、住宿餐饮业（130万）、租赁和商务服务业（120万）。

情形2：若2020年中国经济增速为5.8%，非农就业增量为480万，就业形势基本稳定。

---

① 人们在评判就业问题时喜欢用城镇新增就业指标，但这个指标并不好把握，也不严谨。城镇新增就业是人社部统计的，是城镇地区社区介绍了多少人找到工作，没有扣除退出的，一个人也可能重复计算，口径比较粗。非农就业增量是统计局发布的第二、第三产业就业人数的年度差值，是净增的概念。从本质上讲，城镇新增就业也是反映非农就业增长的情况，但由于有重复统计的偏差，还不如直接用非农就业增量指标更准确一些。

若2020年中国经济增速为5.8%，非农就业增量将为480万，比2019年的400万还要略强，因2019年中国就业虽较为吃紧，但还算稳定，对标之，2020年就业也算稳定。其中，工业部门减少劳动力980万，建筑业将增加劳动力200万，服务业将增加1260万，服务业中就业扩张最大的几个部门是批发和零售业（400万）、教育业（150万）、住宿餐饮业（120万）、租赁和商务服务业（115万）。

情形3：若2020年中国经济增速为5.5%，非农就业增量为315万，尚不会出现大面积失业问题。

若2020年中国经济增速为5.5%，非农就业增量为315万，比2019年的400万少近百万，因2019年中国就业比较吃紧，对标之，2020年就业形势应更加严峻，但与300多万的非农就业增量对应，尚不会出现大面积的失业问题。其中，工业部门将减少劳动力1020万，建筑业将增加劳动力190万，服务业将增加1150万，服务业中就业扩张最大的几个部门是批发和零售业（360万）、教育业（145万）、住宿餐饮业（115万）、租赁和商务服务业（105万）。

情形4：若2020年中国经济增速为5.0%，非农就业增量近乎为0，游走于失业风险的边缘。

若2020年中国经济增速为5.0%，非农就业将停止增长，中国就业将面临真正的考验。考虑到中国就业的实际情况，以16—70岁人口计，可能不足就业之需，游走于失业风险的边缘。

其中，工业部门减少劳动力1100万，建筑业将增加劳动力150万，服务业将增加960万，服务业中就业扩张最大的几个部门是批发和零售业（290万）、教育业（135万）、住宿餐饮业（100万）、租赁和商务服务业（90万）。

（3）基于上面四种测算结果，确保中国就业无虞的经济增长底线是5.0%，但可能会牺牲短期就业质量。从理论上来说，近年来中国劳动年龄人口呈绝对下降的趋势，即便非农就业岗位不增加，也足以满足就业的需要，但问题是，很多超龄人口仍在就业，他们若失业，既可能转而与年轻人抢工作机会，也会引起一定的社会问题，因此必须考虑到这部分人的失业问题。经测算发现，现在中国16—70岁人口正处于不增不减的阶段。要满足16—70岁人口的就业需要，至少非农就业岗位不能减少。从这个角度讲，5.0%是确保中国就业无虞的增长底线。此时，为保证就业不出问题，可能要以牺牲短期就业质量为代价。因为在这一过程中，带动就业的都是以批发和零售业、住宿餐饮业、租赁和商务服务业等为代表的低端服务业，劳动生产率低、工资低、就业质量低等矛盾突出。

综合考虑现阶段国际、国内的趋势性因素和周期性因素，坚持高质量发展原则、实现"两个一百年"目标阶段性任务原则、保证社会就业基本稳定原则，建议2020年中国经济增长的目标区间设为5.5%—6.0%，保守目标为5.8%左右。

◇◇（二）2020年宏观经济运行需要关注的风险点

第一，随着新一轮外部冲击的全面显现，2020年中国宏观经济面临较为严峻的外部挑战。作为开放性大型经济体，全球经济步入新的低迷期、大国博弈开启新征程、全球经济贸易政策不确定性达到新高度，不仅会通过贸易渠道给中国经济带来直接冲击，还会通过干扰中国经济的循环运行、恶化市场信心和未来预期等间接渠道，对中国经济产生更为深远的不利影响。

（1）全球经济步入新的低迷期，外部需求不足的冲击可能会在2020年进一步显化。2019年以来，全球经济增长发生系统性大幅下滑，个别主要经济体已经陷入经济衰退。目前，OECD、ECB、IMF、WB以及联合国贸易和发展会议、亚洲开发银行相继下调了2020年的增长预期。这就表明，中国经济的下滑不仅仅是内部因素导致的。2020年全球经济低迷期仍将持续。而是全球经济普遍面临的下行压力。首先，目前仍难以依靠新一轮的技术来带动世界经济走出低迷状况。进入21世纪以来，全球各种专利生产的增长速度持续下滑。各国的研发支出占GDP的比重，除了中国在上升外，其他地区全部在下降。特别是OECD国家，研发的比重在下降。其次，逆全球化的时间和深度可能比预期要长。在历史上，如果这种贸易摩擦根源于全球分工格局和世界政治格局大变化，那么贸易摩擦的深度和长度将会全面拉长，它的长度可能会达到20年。从2008年至今只有11年，仍处在逆全球化的低谷中。再次，全球不平等问题没有改善，还在一些局部问题上有所恶化。之所以会出现逆全球化，就是因为全球化带来了很多的不平等问题，部分群体的福利没有得到改善，所以出现民粹主义，进而出现保护主义，出现逆全球化的浪潮。可以说，逆全球化的背后不平等是很重要的一个问题。全球前1%的富人所占世界收入的比重，在20世纪80年代为16.3%，而2016年提升至20.4%；更重要的是，全球主要国家大都出现了这一问题。又次，债务率高企。2019年全球债务规模预计将超过255万亿美元，占全球GDP的比例将升至330%，债务问题已经到了一个新的临界点。最后，人口老龄化问题。目前全世界人口结构都在向老龄化转变，基本上劳动力人口占比都在下降，人口抚养比都在上升，这导致了全球经济增长速度下降。

（2）2020年全球制造业可能继续深陷集体性低迷期。2019年全球制成品投资、汽车商品、耐用品消费之所以急剧下降，除了全球贸易增速下滑所产生的直接影响外，更重要的是，对未来预期出现的极度不确定性，导致投资和耐用品消费下滑。如果2020年美国贸易政策不确定性、全球经济政策不确定性以及地缘政治风险继续攀升，世界范围内的投资和耐用品消费下滑还会进一步加剧，全球制造业将深陷集体性低迷期。

四　2020年经济增长目标的确立和需要关注的风险点

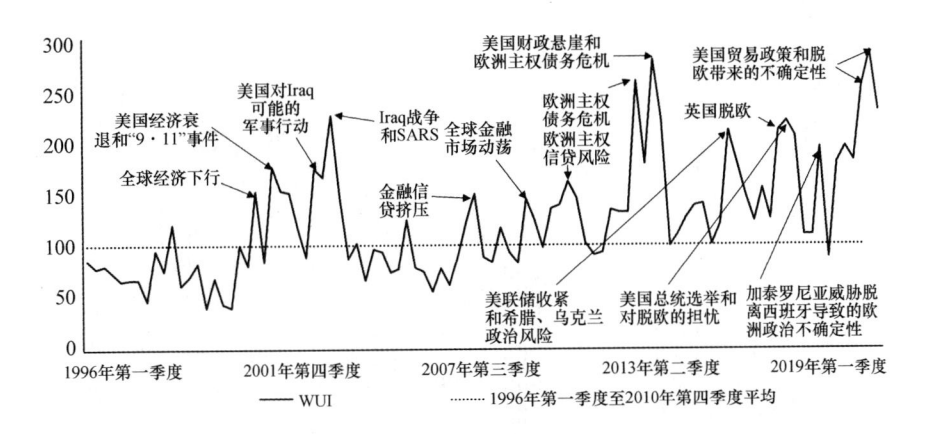

图69　世界不确定性指数（WUI）

数据来源：Policy Uncertainty.com, The use of the data and figure should be cited as: Ahir, H., N. Bloom, and D. Furceri (2018), "World Uncertainty Index", Stanford mimeo。

以汽车为例，全球乘用车销售量在2018年中期达到峰值后开始持续下降，2018年全年负增长3.4%，2019年上半年跌幅进一步扩大至8.3%，较2018年同期增速回落9.0个百分点。全球汽车销售和生产的下滑不仅导致汽车产业本身的萎靡，还会通过行业溢出效应和国际溢出效应，产生连锁反应。在此背景下，汽车产量占比高、汽车出口占比高的经济体所受到的冲击最大。从全球汽车市场份额来看，以德国为首的欧洲四国（德国、法国、意大利、西班牙）、墨西哥、日本不仅汽车产量占全球的比重较高，而且汽车出口量占全球的比重显著高于汽车产量占比，因此受到的经济冲击更为严重。目前，德国制造业已经陷入衰退，意大利经济陷入全面衰退，墨西哥经济也开始出现负增长。

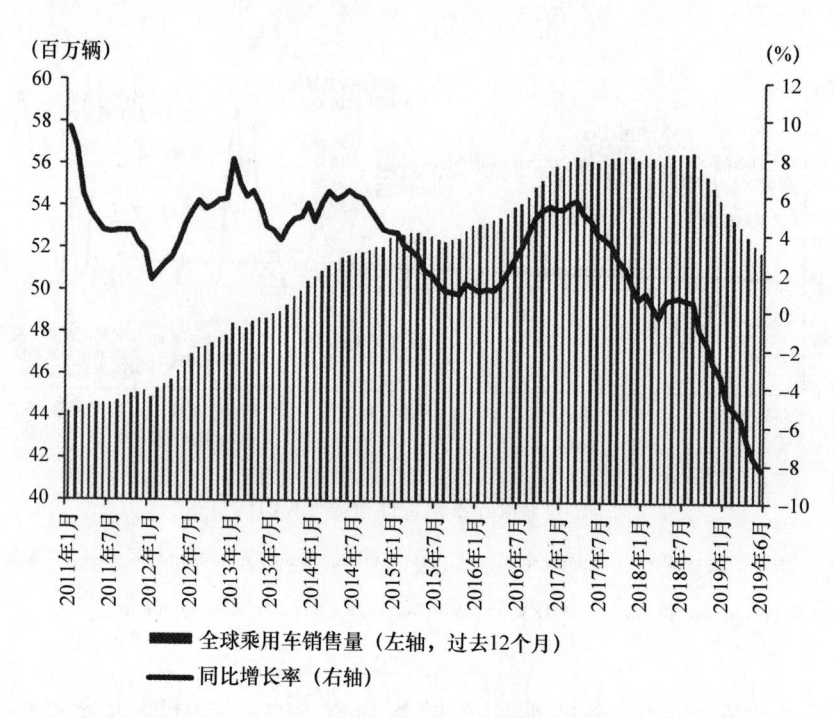

图 70　全球乘用车销售量及其增速变化趋势

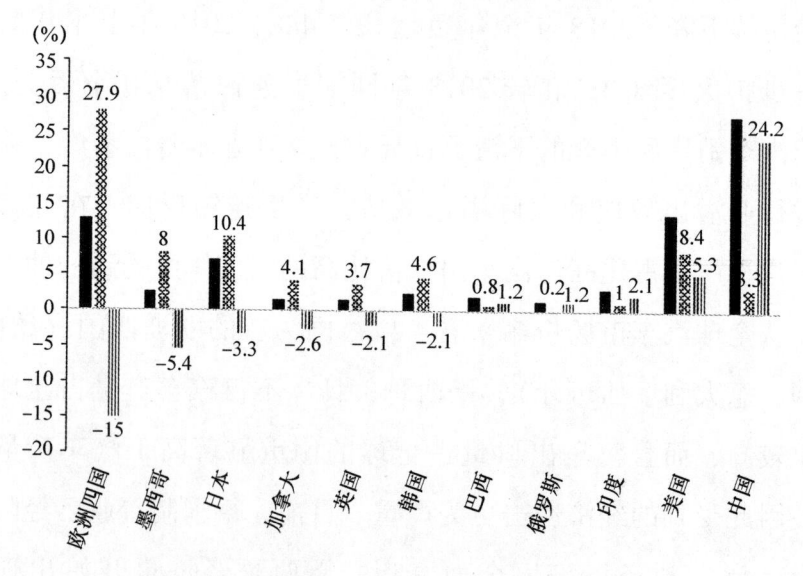

图 71　各国汽车产值和出口占全球的比重（2018 年）

具体地，以德国和美国为例，2019年前三个季度，由于德国乘用车出口增长率降至负增长12.0%，德国乘用车产量增长率降至负增长9.0%，尽管同期德国乘用车销量仍为正增长2.0%。作为对比，近年来美国汽车销售量持续负增长，2019年8月同比降幅达到13.4%，也导致美国汽车产量持续处于负增长区间，但由于出口依赖度低，且过去几年一直处于去库存过程，2019年美国汽车产量增长情况要好于汽车销量增长情况。但即使如此，2019年前8个月，由于美国汽车销售量负增长11.1%，汽车产量负增长6.5%，美国汽车的库存水平也开始回升。2019年第三季度，美国GDP增速下滑至2.0%，为2017年以来的最

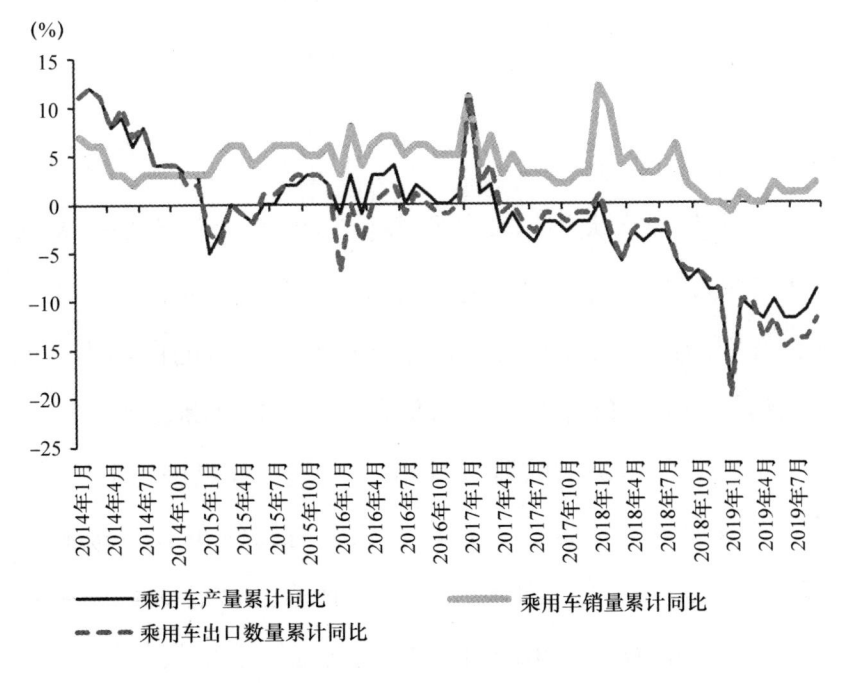

图72 德国乘用车产量、销量和出口增速变化趋势

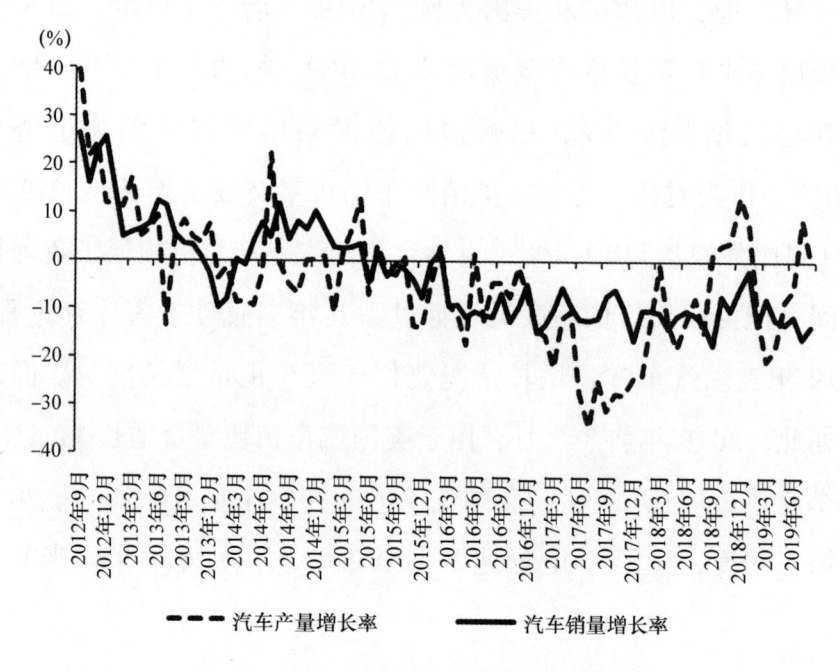

图73 美国汽车产量和销量增速变化趋势

低同比增速。

（3）中美开启大国博弈新征程，2020年美国大选以及地缘政治将带来高度不确定性。美国大选是否会进一步激化中美贸易摩擦，特别是由于特朗普的个性特征和两党斗争的白热化可能导致出现超预期事件的发生，所以仍存在高度的不确定性。

目前美国在加快与欧盟、日本、韩国、东盟进行双边谈判。除了形成国际战线同盟，未来可能还会有持续的技术战和人才战。2019年以来，美国对于一些关键技术、敏感领域的签证已经进行了全面的遏制。2020年汇率调整也可能引发争端。例如，2019年8月6日，人民币在岸价格跌破了"7"的关口，随即美国就宣布中国是汇率操纵国。但是,根据美国于2018年4月发布的最新《美国主要贸易伙伴外汇政策报告》,汇率操纵国的认定标准有三个:一是至少大于200亿美元的与美国的显著的双边贸易顺差;二是实质性经常项目顺差至少超过GDP的3%;三是长期单边干预外汇市场,在过去12个月内进行反复地外币净买入并且总额达GDP的2%。可以发现,中国可能只符合第一个标准,并不符合其他两个标准,然而,为了迎合政治需要,美国财政部把中国列为汇率操纵国。

总体而言,对未来预期的恶化和不确定性的上扬,加剧了世界范围内的投资品和耐用消费品的收缩,本轮中国经济下行具有全球性的基础性因素。因此,在分析研判2020年中国宏观经济形势时,需要高度关注全球经济的最新变化趋势,同时,2020年中国的宏观政策定位也必须明确国际化导向。

第二,内需增长的持续大幅下滑可能引发宏观经济加速性下滑的风险。2019年中国净出口实现了高速增长,但是内需增长出现了大幅下滑,从2018年的7.2%大幅回落至2019年前3个季度的5.0%,加剧了中国经济的脆弱性和对外需的依赖。特别是当企业不再扩大生产性投资,居民不再增加耐用品消费,不仅升级型的结构分化将会停滞,而且萧条型的结构分化也将加剧。短期内,仍需稳外贸以尽可能地争取时间。但是,从全球经济发展态势看,2020年中国继续保持净出口大幅增长的可能性极小。因此,在稳外贸的同时,更重要的是要在时间窗口关闭前,加大力度、加快速度、加强精准度地稳内需。

内需增长大幅下滑，加剧了中国经济的脆弱性。2019年不仅延续了2018年下半年以来总需求不足的局面，而且新一轮经济加速下行的紧缩机制产生了强烈的收缩效应。由此来看，中央在2018年年中就已经提出要做好"六稳"工作，具有前瞻性。2019年第一季度，中国实际GDP增长6.4%，与2018年第四季度持平，体现了"六稳"政策发力产生的企稳作用。但是，2019年第一季度宏观经济的超预期表现，掩盖了中国内需增长实际上已经出现大幅下滑的事实，这也导致后续宏观政策出现一定的反复。在第一季度6.4%的经济增速中，有高达1.5个百分点来自于净出口；扣除外需，内需（投资和消费）增长率只有4.9%，比2018年显著回落了2.3个百分点。当时有观点认为这可能是短期因素。但是，随着第二、第三季度数据的相继发布，已经可以确认2019年中国内需增长确实出现了大幅的下滑。如图74所示，2016年、2017年、2018年中国内需实际增长率分别为7.1%、6.3%、7.2%，即在7%左右波动，但是2019年前3个季度，中国内需增速显著下降为5.0%，回落幅度之大，值得高度关注。

从内需增长下滑的主要原因看，当前投资和消费两大需求拉动力都出现了较大幅度回落，共同导致了内需增长的显著下滑。其中，投资对GDP的拉动从2018年的2.1个百分点下降至1.2个百分点，回落0.9个百分点；消费对GDP的拉动从5.0个百

四 2020年经济增长目标的确立和需要关注的风险点

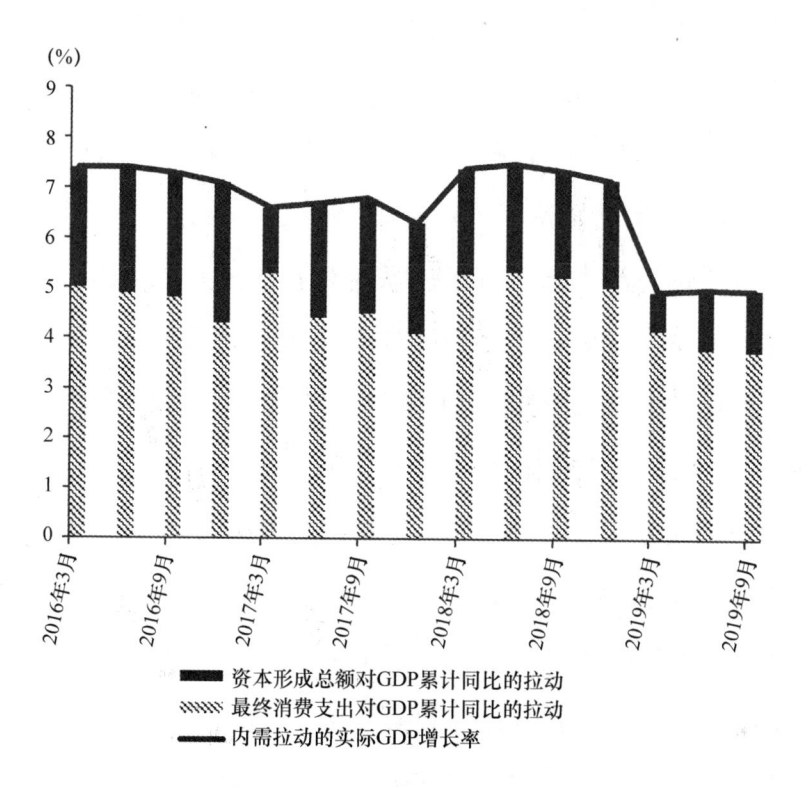

图 74 2019 中国内需增长出现大幅下滑

分点下滑至 3.8 个百分点，回落 1.2 个百分点。更重要的是，当前投资增速下滑不仅来源于总量放缓，也来源于结构恶化导致投资转化效率下降，产生了"有投资、无增长"现象。从总量上看，2019 年前 3 个季度，中国固定资产投资完成额名义增速为 5.4%，较 2018 年增速回落 0.5 个百分点。从结构上看，前 3 个季度，其他费用投资增长 12.1%，占比提高 0.9 个百分点，但设备工器具购置投资出现负增长 1.2%，占比下降 1.0 个百分点，导致固定资产投资向资本形成总额的转化效率下降。从行业方面看，近两年房地产开发投资一直保持10%左右的增速，2019年前3个季度房地产新开工面积增长8.6%，但房地产竣工面积负增长8.6%，两者缺口达到17.2个百分点，这一情形从2018年年初开始已经持续了近两年。

消费增速下滑来源于汽车、家居和服饰三大类耐用品消费出现集体性下滑，反映了居民在预期恶化下，大幅压减耐用品消费所产生的结构性紧缩效应。2019年前3个季度，消费同比增长8.2%，较2018年同期回落了1.1个百分点，主要是由于以下三大类商品消费不足：（1）汽车消费类。2019年前3个季度，汽车类消费负增长0.7%，其中9月负增长2.2%；石油及制品类增长1.7%，其中9月转为负增长0.4%。（2）家居消费类。前3个季度，家用电器和音像器材类、家具类、建筑及装潢材料类分别仅增长5.9%、5.9%、3.6%。（3）服饰消费类。前3个季度，服装鞋帽及针纺织品类、金银珠宝类分别仅增长3.3%和0.6%。除以上三大类商品外，其余商品消费和服务性消费目前依然保持较快增长。但以上三大类消费的集体性下滑，具有鲜明的缩减耐用品消费特征，反映了居民预期恶化所产生的结构性紧缩效应。

"衰退型顺差"加剧了未来经济的脆弱性。2019年前3个季度，中国出口和进口增速从2018年的两位数急剧回落至零增长和负增长，但净出口增速达到36.1%，拉动GDP增长1.2个百分点，贡献率达到19.6%，即净出口贡献了1/5的经济增长，创近10年最高纪录。随着全球经济增速出现新一轮全面放缓，"衰退型顺差"可能已达到极限。内需增长的大幅下滑，使得中国经济增长对净出口增长的依赖性显著提高，也加大了短期稳外贸工作的重要性，但是，从全球经济发展态势看，2020年中国继续保持净出口大幅增长的可能性极小。中国需要稳外贸以尽可能地争取时间，但更重要的是，要在时间窗口关闭前，加大力度、加快速度、加强精准度地稳内需。

第三，萧条性的结构分化加剧叠加升级性的结构分化停滞，可能带来总量性的紧缩效应；而增速下台阶反过来又可能引发结构性的短板效应显化，导致中小型企业、中小型银行进一步承压，进而诱发局部性的金融风险爆发；同时，也会导致一些经济结构脆弱的区域恶化，进而诱发失业风险。由此，结构性效应反过来会对总体经济造成新的冲击。

当前经济结构变动呈现新特征，升级性的结构变化趋缓，衰退性的结构变化加剧。从工业内部看，医药制造业、通用设备制造业、专用设备制造业等高新技术制造业增速放缓，而2019年新动能投资占制造业比重的高开低走趋势也反映了这一情况，截至9月底占比54.54%，较2018年同期和年初均有不同程度地回落；而黑色金属冶炼及压延加工业、有色金属冶炼及压延加工业、金属制品业等高耗能行业增长再度回升，这种变化意味着过去几年延续的工业结构调整趋势有所放缓。在服务业内部，信息传输、软件和信息技术服务、租赁和商业服务等细分行业的增速

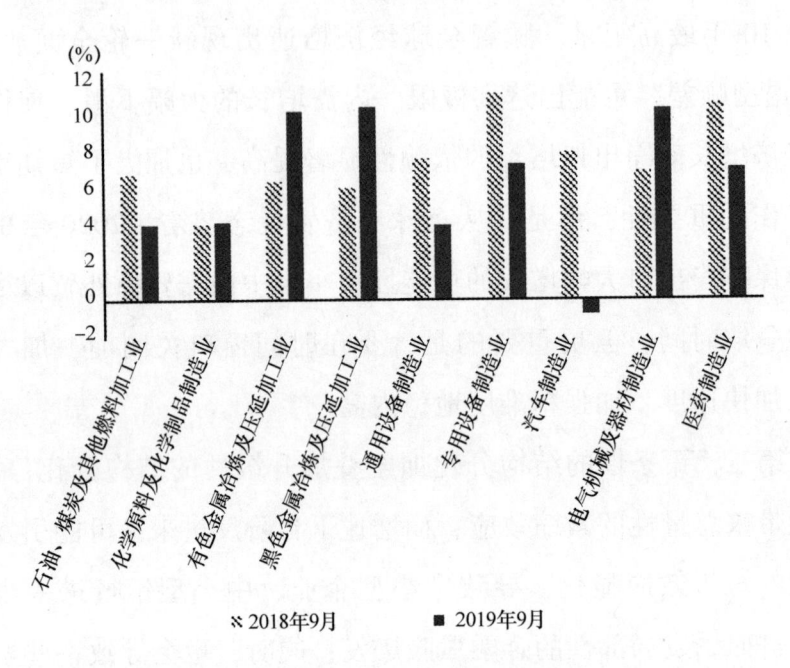

图 75 高新技术制造业增加值增速放缓和高耗能行业增速回升

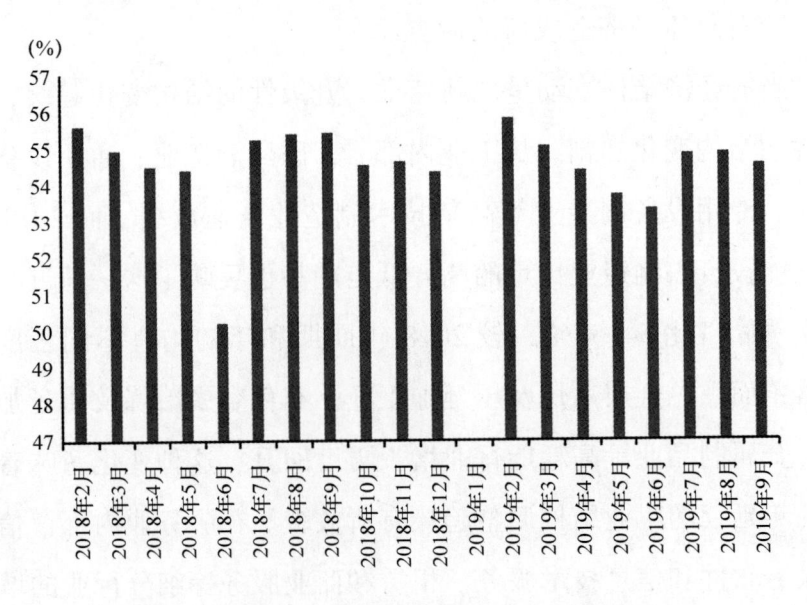

图 76 2019 年以来新动能占制造业投资比重高开低走

四　2020年经济增长目标的确立和需要关注的风险点 | 117

下降幅度明显大于服务业整体，而金融业的增速有所改善，这说明宽信用、结构性宽货币下的政策目标与政策效果之间还存在一定阻滞。

从区域维度分析，东部企业盈利承压，中部企业利润增长放缓明显，东北地区企业盈利能力恶化。在经济下行背景下，2019年第三季度全国四个地区（东北地区、东部地区、西部地区、中部地区）上市企业盈利能力均有所恶化，营业收入及净利润同比增速均放缓。其中，东北地区企业营业收入同比增速下滑明显，降幅超过10.0%，净利润同比增速由正转负，盈利能力大幅恶化；中部地区企业营业收入及净利润同比增速回落均超5.0%，净利润同比增速降幅最大；西部地区企业营业收入及净利润同比降幅均最小，盈利能力恶化程度相对较小。值得注意的

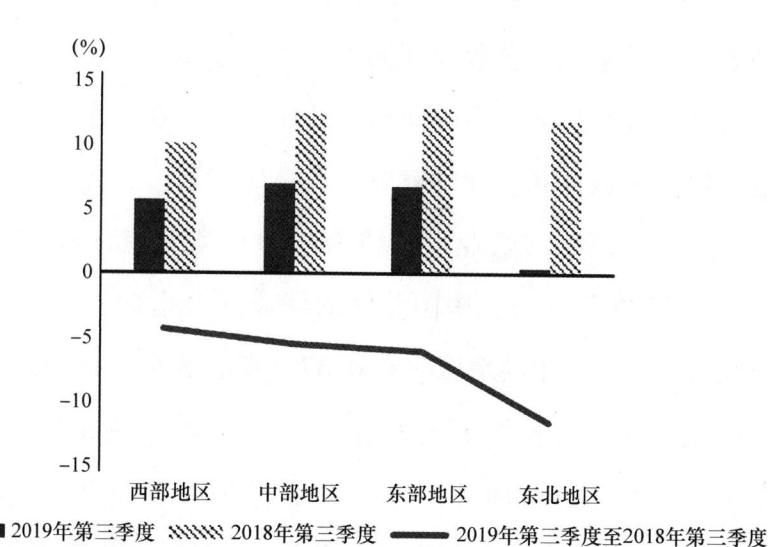

图77　分区域营业收入同比增速情

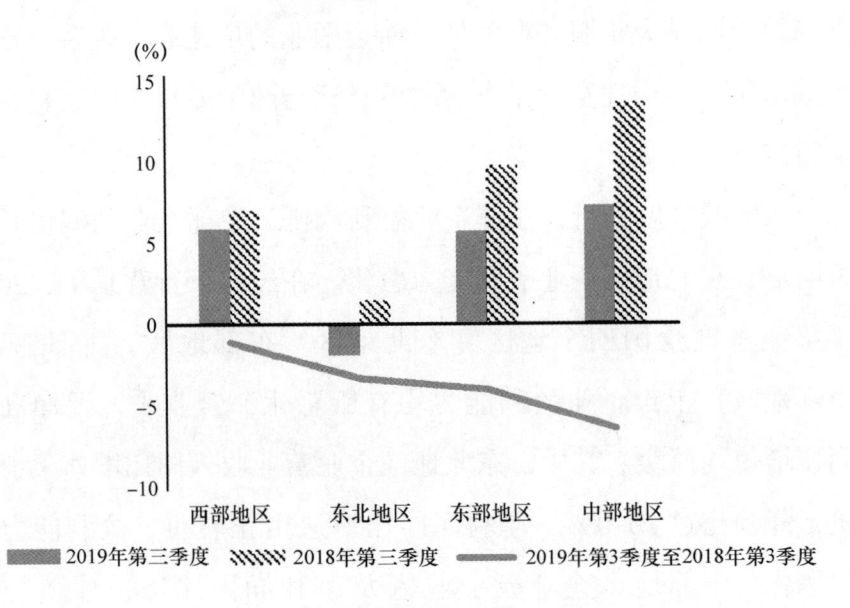

图 78　分区域净利润同比增速情况

是，受中美贸易摩擦影响，东部地区企业尤其是出口外向型企业盈利能力不断恶化，营收及利润增长持续放缓。

因此，虽然目前中国就业形势总体平稳，在总量上不存在大问题，但是区域性和行业性就业矛盾持续发酵。首先，分地区来看，东北、京津冀的就业形势没有根本改观，有的还在持续恶化。截至 2019 年 9 月，中国总体的就业景气指数为 1.92，东北地区只有 0.9，京津冀地区只有 0.87。东北和京津冀地区就业形势紧张主要源于地区经济发展的困境。东北地区经济形势整体差于全国。辽宁已有所回升，GDP 增速从 2017 年的 2% 左右回升至 2019 年第二季度的 5.8%，但吉林和黑龙江形势却更加严峻，特别是吉林持续下滑很严重，至 2019 年第二季度两地 GDP 增速分别跌至2%和4.3%，远低于全国6.3%的水平。在京津冀地区中，天津GDP增速只有4.6%。

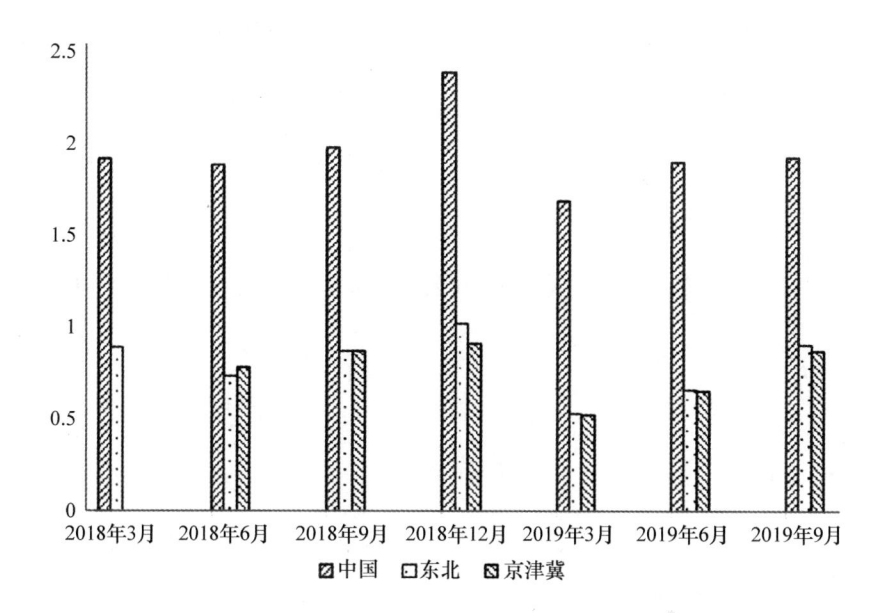

图79 分地区就业景气指数

数据来源：中国人民大学就业研究所和智联招聘联合发布的《2019年第三季度中国就业市场景气报告》。

分行业来看，汽车和手机等行业仍处于较为严重的下降通道，房地产、建筑业和信息服务业的收缩也比较明显，这些行业的销售和生产下行使其面临较大的就业压力。汽车行业从2018年开始步入困境，2019年1—9月汽车销量累计同比下降10.3%，行业萧条必然会引发失业压力。2018年年底汽车行业就业人数约450万，据此进行简单测算，2019年以来汽车行业的失业人数可能接近 50 万人。2018 年手机出货量同比下降达两位数以上，2019 年上半年以来在各种促销政策刺激下降幅有所收窄，4—5 月甚至由负转正，但是 9 月的同比降幅再次扩大到 7.1%。手机行业的困境必然会对上下游产业链的就业产生压力。受调控政策等因素的影响，房地产业持续萎靡，2019 年前 8 个月商品房销售面积同比下降 0.6%，9 月有所回升，但前 9 个月仍同比下降，商品房销售面积同比降幅为 0.1%。房地产业也有近 445 万就业人员，行业低迷会对就业造成较大影响。2019 年上半年，直接从事建筑业的生产经营人数比上年同期减少近 60 万人。2019 年前 8 个月建筑业固定资产投资累计同比减少达 20%。建筑业是农民工就业的一个重要产业，建筑业萎靡会对农民工就业产生很大影响。

未来一段时间，中美贸易摩擦也可能会演变为冲击中国就业的一个风险点，并可能在局部行业和局部地区率先爆发。中美经贸关系暂时缓和，但是相关的矛盾并没有得到解决。美国政府的关税行动只是推迟，并没有真正取消。迄今为止，美国已经实施的关税行动对中国就业的影响还没有完全显露出来。现有根据各行业销售利润率进行的测算表明，加征关税的幅度如果达到 21%—24% 这样的阈值，对就业的负面冲击将会迅速显露。此前所加征的 15% 的关税，对相关行业的影响暂时没有显露。如果关税进一步提高，通用设备制造业、电气机械和器材制造业、橡胶和塑料制品业以及金属制品业等行业可能会出现较大规模的失业。广东、浙江、江苏和山东等对美出口行业较为集中的省份可能会面临较大的失业压力。

第四，2020年中国经济出现新一轮通货紧缩的风险加大，需要保持高度关注和做好应对准备。尽管2019年第三季度以来以猪肉为代表的食品价格大幅上涨，带动消费者物价指数走高，但这绝不意味着2020年一定不会出现通货紧缩。相反，非食品CPI的持续下滑、PPI的连续下跌、GDP平减指数的回落，特别是本轮PPI下跌的节奏、涉及行业的广度和深度，都与前几轮通货紧缩的初期表现具有高度的相似性。需要密切关注2019年第四季度至2020年第二季度这一关键窗口期的PPI形势变化，并及时调整货币政策定位，构建货币政策稳健的新框架。

（1）当前价格走势高度分化，在关注食品上涨的同时，更应该高度关注已经出现的各种通缩迹象，未来两三个季度是关键的窗口期和政策反应期。2019年第三季度以来价格走势高度分化，对市场预期和宏观政策产生了很多影响。一方面，以猪肉为代表的食品价格大幅上涨，带动消费者物价指数走高，10月同比涨幅达到了3.8%；另一方面，生产价格指数持续下行并转为负增长，10月同比跌幅扩大到了1.6%。这种分化趋势还将延续至2020年第一季度。因此，对于价格形势的准确预判，成为确立2020年宏观调控总基调的关键。我们认为，当前的食品价格上涨并带动CPI冲高，是局部性、阶段性的，绝不意味2020年通缩风险不大。在上一轮通缩前夕，同样出现了食品价格的大幅上涨和CPI冲高。2011年6月，食品价格涨幅达到14.4%的峰值，带动CPI突破6.0%达到6.4%，但仅仅3个季度之后，就开启了一轮持续时间长达54个月的工业领域通缩。当前非食品CPI的不断下滑、PPI的持续下跌、GDP平减指数的显著回落、企业效益和市场预期的恶化，可能预示着新一轮的通缩正在形成。

（2）对比分析表明，当前价格走势与前三轮通货紧缩的前期表现，特别是与上一轮通货紧缩（2012年3月至2016年9月）具有高度的相似性。在本轮PPI下跌前，非食品CPI已从2018年第三季度的2.4%下滑至2019年6月的1.4%，截至2019年10月，非食品CPI进一步下滑至0.9%。由于当前非食品CPI的缓冲空间比上一轮更小，如果2020年出现新一轮通货紧缩，其严重程度可能不会低于上一轮。更重要的是，本轮PPI下滑的节奏、所涉及行业的广度和深度，都与前几轮通缩相似。2019年7月PPI开始出现负增长（-0.3%），10月跌幅已扩大至1.6%。对比上一轮通货紧缩，2012年3月PPI开始出现负增长（-0.3%），6月跌幅扩大至2.1%。2019年10月，在39个主要工业行业的出厂价格中，有15个行业价格出现下跌，其中6个行业的跌幅超过5%。对比上一轮通货紧缩初期，有11个行业价格出现下跌，其中4个行业跌幅超过5%。对比上上一轮通货紧缩（2008年12月至2009年11月）初期，有12个行业价格下跌，其中7个行业跌幅超过5%。对比更早一轮通货紧缩

(1997年6月至1999年12月）初期，有13个行业价格下跌，其中6个行业跌幅超过5%。

（3）本轮PPI的下行与工业企业效益的普遍恶化具有高度的一致性，表明主要由需求下滑而非效率提升所驱动。2019年工业企业利润总额出现了自2016年以来的首次负增长，前3个季度同比减少2.1%，特别是制造业同比减少了3.9%。分行业来看，在出现价格下跌的行业中，多数行业利润总额出现显著负增长或增速大幅下滑；在PPI涨幅已经低于1.0%的行业中，多数也出现了利润增速的下滑甚至负增长，处于即将步入价格下跌区间的边缘。

（4）除了总需求的持续回落带来需求拉动型的通缩压力，全球制造业低迷和国际大宗商品价格回落特别是原油价格进入下行通道，也将带来输入型的通缩压力，对2020年价格走势产生持续的下行压力。2020年的全球通胀预期和国际原油价格预期趋于下行。其中，发达经济体CPI预期从2018年的2.0%分别下滑至2019年的1.5%和2020年的1.8%。更重要的是，未来5年内全球原油价格都将处于下行区间。IMF预计，2019年国际原油价格下跌9.6%，2020年进一步下跌6.2%，2021年和2022年继续下跌4.6%和1.3%，直至2023年和2014年企稳。此外，2020年金属价格预计也将下跌6.2%。

因此，基于当前价格走势与前几轮通缩初期的对比，结合国内外宏观经济形势分析，2020年出现新一轮通货紧缩的风险较大，需要保持高度关注和做好应对准备。特别是2020年下半年可能出现全面通缩。当前工业领域的萧条已经出现，而且是全球性的，PPI持续回落将是大势所趋。未来总需求不足向价格领域的传递还会进一步持续，而且总需求本身的下行压力还会进一步加大。与此同时，全球范围内的制造业低迷和大宗商品价格下跌，使得外部输入型的通缩压力显著加大。内外价格预期低迷，在中期内将难以得到有效提振。2020年下半年，随着食品价格的翘尾因素回落，可能导致CPI出现明显下滑，届时GDP平减指数在2019年已经大幅回落的基础上，可能出现由正转负。

第五，2020年仍需高度关注猪肉等食品价格的结构性上涨和总需求不足可能带来的"双重风险"叠加困局。猪肉等食品价格飙升引发的价格结构性上涨将成为中期现象，对2020年民生和市场预期产生持续性冲击，并与总需求持续下滑产生叠加效应，不仅会使得当前的经济陷入困局，还会加剧市场主体对未来的悲观情绪，对2020年的宏观管理造成更为严重的问题。

猪肉等食品价格结构性上涨的局面在短期内难以扭转，将成为中期现象，且会通过直接效应和溢出效应向其他领域蔓延，在2020年对民生和市场预期产生持续性冲击。自2019年第三季度以来，猪肉价格的急速上涨受到了社会各界的广泛关注。猪肉价格飞涨引发的食品CPI与非食品CPI以及CPI与PPI等各种物价指数走势分化的局面进一步加剧，也使宏观政策困局上升到新高度。当前物价上涨因素主要是食品，食品价格上涨主要来自于猪肉，猪肉价格上涨主要来自于猪肉供给的大幅减少而非消费需求回升。值得注意的是，自2019年年初以来，食品价格出现轮番上涨：第一季度鲜菜价格大涨，第二季度鲜果价格大涨，进入第三季度，猪肉价格飙升，食品CPI涨幅持续走高。9月食品CPI涨幅达11.2%，较年初涨幅扩大9.3个百分点。但是不同于上半年的食品价格上涨，第三季度以来的猪肉价格上涨具有两大特征。

一是猪肉价格上涨的幅度更大，且带动了牛肉、羊肉、禽肉等替代品价格的较快上涨，所引发的民生和舆情风险更为严重。2019年9月，CPI猪肉价格同比上涨69.3%，带动牛肉、羊肉、禽肉价格同比上涨18.8%、15.9%、14.7%，畜肉类价格总体上涨46.9%。在猪肉价格的带动作用下，CPI同比涨幅持续走高，9月达到3.0%，预计第四季度会突破3.0%。截至10月11日，22个省份的平均猪肉价格已突破40元/公斤，达到42.3元/公斤，较之春节期间上涨了1倍，猪粮比价达到16倍，均创历史记录。猪肉占中国居民肉类消费的六成，猪肉价格飙升成为社会各界和媒体关注热点，民生和舆情风险上扬。

二是猪肉价格上涨的根源在供给端，且在短期内无法有效解决，将演化为中期现象，对宏观政策选择产生影响。本轮猪肉价格上涨主要是由非洲猪瘟和环保强化等因素叠加产生的供给剧烈收缩所导致的，短期内难以扭转。与近年来猪肉需求量走势相对平稳不同，近期生猪供给面的主要指标均发生系统性超常变动。

我们的判断是，尽管存量指标大幅下降已经引起市场主体的预期变化，但目前猪肉供应的底部实际上还没有到来。(1) 生猪存栏数继续大幅减少，显示中国生猪现实产能显著降低。继2019年8月生猪存栏数跌破2亿头，9月进一步下降至1.9亿头，相比2018年同期的3.3亿头，降幅达41.1%，较8月跌幅进一步扩大。(2) 能繁母猪存栏数继续大幅减少，预示未来一个时期生猪产能扩张将受到严重制约。继2019年8月能繁母猪存栏数跌破2000万头，9月进一步下降至1913万头，相比2018年同期的3136万头，降幅达38.9%，跌幅持续扩大，这意味着未来在扩张产能上面临制约。(3) 生猪出栏率大幅高于趋势值，显示当前猪肉生产已处于严重透支状态。2019年生猪出栏率出现大幅跳升，虽然在短期内增加了猪肉供给，使得生猪出栏数的降幅远小于存栏数降幅，但是生猪生产系统的超负荷运转已难以为继。自5月开始，生猪屠宰前平均重量已出现明显下降，自8月以来，生猪出栏率也开始呈现下滑迹象。(4) 猪肉进口大幅增长，但难以弥补巨大的国内供需缺口。中国猪肉年消费量约在5500万吨左右，占全球猪肉产量一半，猪肉进口的比例远不到5%，供给基本由国内产出决定。2019年1—8月，中国猪肉进口值大幅增长66.1%，预计全年在200万吨，对猪肉消费而言"杯水车薪"。综上所述，短期内猪肉价格上涨局面还将持续。

更为重要的是，价格结构性上涨与总需求加速性下滑产生的叠加效应，不仅会使得当前的经济陷入困局，还会加剧市场主体对未来的悲观情绪，对2020年的宏观管理造成更为严重的问题。

如前所述，在价格结构性上涨的同时，总需求不足的问题不仅没有得到缓解，反而进一步恶化，新一轮经济下行的内生性紧缩机制已经形成，引发宏观经济加速性下滑风险。特别是从中长期来看，当前宏观经济下行中最具有风险性的挑战是企业悲观预期和投资意愿不强，导致投资增速持续放缓，经济潜在增速可能出现变化。近两年的投资增速已经明显跌破合理区间，甚至低于同期美国的投资增速，存在较大的超调风险。作为对比，美国国内投资自2017年第二季度至2019年第二季度连续9个季度保持较快增长，投资增速平均值为6.6%。

更为重要的是，价格结构性上涨与总需求加速性下滑产生的叠加效应，不仅会使得当前的经济陷入困局，还会加剧市场主体对未来的悲观情绪，对2020年的宏观管理造成更为严重的问题。随着居民未来收入预期恶化和就业压力加大，对中等收入阶层的"双重积压"将会在2020年充分显化，加剧市场主体对政策的不信任和对未来的悲观情绪。2019年第二季度，城镇居民未来收入信心指数降至52.6%，为2016年年底以来的新低。与此同时，失业风险不断闪现，城镇调查失业率于2019年2月和7月两次攀上5.3%的高位。其他多项指标也发出走弱信号：（1）9月制造业和非制造业PMI从业人员指数下滑至47.0%和48.2%，为近年较低水平，这表明用工景气度处于紧缩区间；（2）领取失业保险的人数由降转增，上半年同比增加2.2%；（3）失业人员再就业数前7个月同比减少了8.6%;(4)"失业金领取条件"搜索指数比前几年飙升2—3倍。

在极限思维下,2020年中国经济和社会领域的收缩效应可能会比2019年还要严重,价格结构性上涨与总需求加速性下滑所引发的社会不安和动荡、中等收入群体的消费下滑、企业等市场主体预期的恶化,可能带来"预期型"的经济困局。当企业不再扩大生产性投资、居民不再增加耐用品消费、地方政府被沉重的债务负担所约束、新一轮的技术革命又遥遥无期,中国经济的韧性和超大规模市场优势将同时面临重大机遇和深刻考验。

第六,前期金融风险的缓释在2020年有出现反复的风险。一方面,尽管货币政策边际宽松,债务风险得到缓释,市场流动性也较为充裕,但金融机构贷款利率与企业资产利润率走势分化的局面仍未缓解,表明虽然金融回归初心,支持实体经济发展的趋势十分明显,但传递机制不畅的压力依然存在。另一方面,尽管2019年以来金融风险得到缓释,但未来一个时期仍将处于违约常态化阶段,特别是随着经济进一步下行调整,金融风险可能出现反复。金融风险的缓释和预防反复是2020年宏观审慎的核心。

(1)尽管货币政策边际宽松,债务风险得到缓释,市场流动性较为充裕,但金融机构贷款利率与企业资产利润率走势分化的局面仍未缓解,表明虽然金融回归初心,支持实体经济发展的趋势十分明显,但传递机制不畅的压力依然存在。

在经济下行压力加大的背景下，金融机构贷款利率一直居高不下，特别是随着PPI下行甚至由正转负，实际贷款利率不降反升。近年来，企业资产回报率持续下降，而贷款利率高企，特别是2018年以来资产回报率开始低于贷款利率，企业投资基本丧失经济意义，再投资意愿受到极大抑制。据我们测算，工业企业的息税前资产利润率从2011年的8.3%持续下滑至2015年的6.4%，随后在"去产能"提振作用下，小幅回升至2017年的6.7%，但2018年又急剧回落至5.8%，2019年上半年（折年率）进一步下滑至约5.2%。同期，金融机构人民币贷款一般贷款加权平均利率从2011年的7.8%持续回落至2016年的5.4%，但随着去杠杆政策的推进，金融条件不断收紧，贷款利率逐步提升至2018年的5.9%，2019年第一季度进一步上升至6.0%。由此，2018年首次出现了企业资产回报率低于贷款利率的情况，2019年上半年缺口进一步扩大。在企业资产回报率低于贷款利率的情况下，企业再投资意愿必然受到极大的抑制。特别地，上半年制造业利润总额首次出现负增长，降低了企业投资意愿和能力，导致制造业投资出现较大幅度下滑。上半年，制造业利润总额同比负增长4.1%，这是2019年以前从未出现过的新情况，2018年同期还是正增长14.3%。如果说此前制造业投资下滑更多是受市场空间收窄的影响，那么当前还进一步叠加了企业利润恶化的因素。

在企业盈利水平下降、实际贷款利率上升的背景下，企业贷

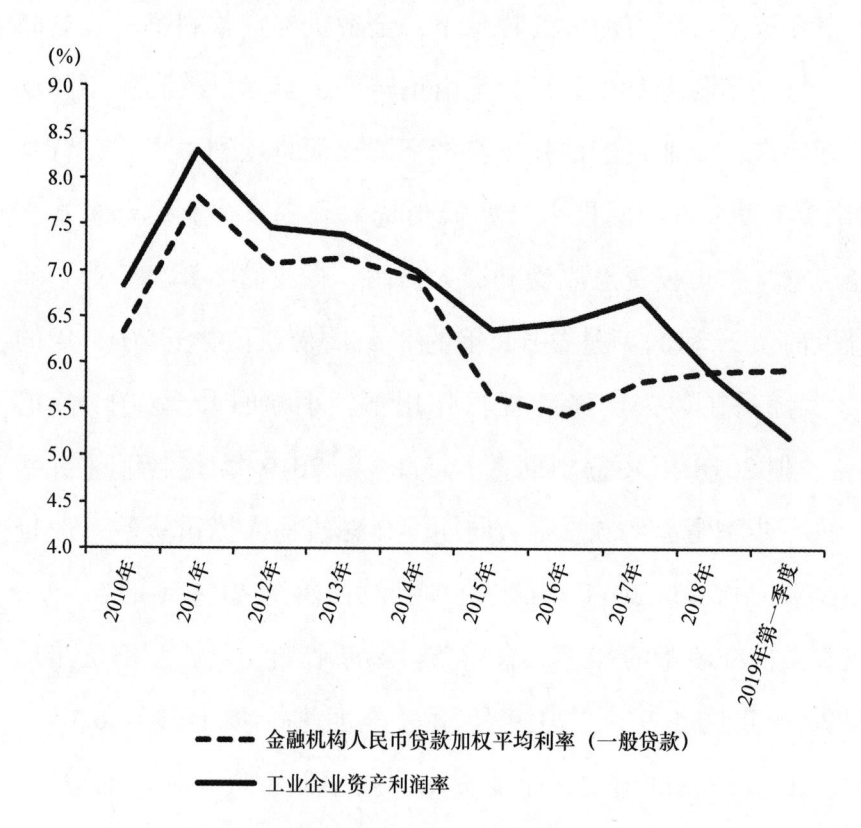

图 80　金融机构贷款利率与工业企业资产利润率走势分化

款需求出现明显回落，特别是大型企业和中型企业。2019 年第三季度，大型企业贷款需求指数下降至 54.4%，中型企业贷款需求指数下降至 57.2%，均为 2017 年年初以来的最低水平；相比之下，小型企业贷款需求仍处高位，第三季度为 70.2%，但也已连续 2 个季度下滑。

造成当前流动性传导不畅的因素很多，其中一点在于中国货币供给结构和供给渠道较前些年发生了较大变化，与新变化对应

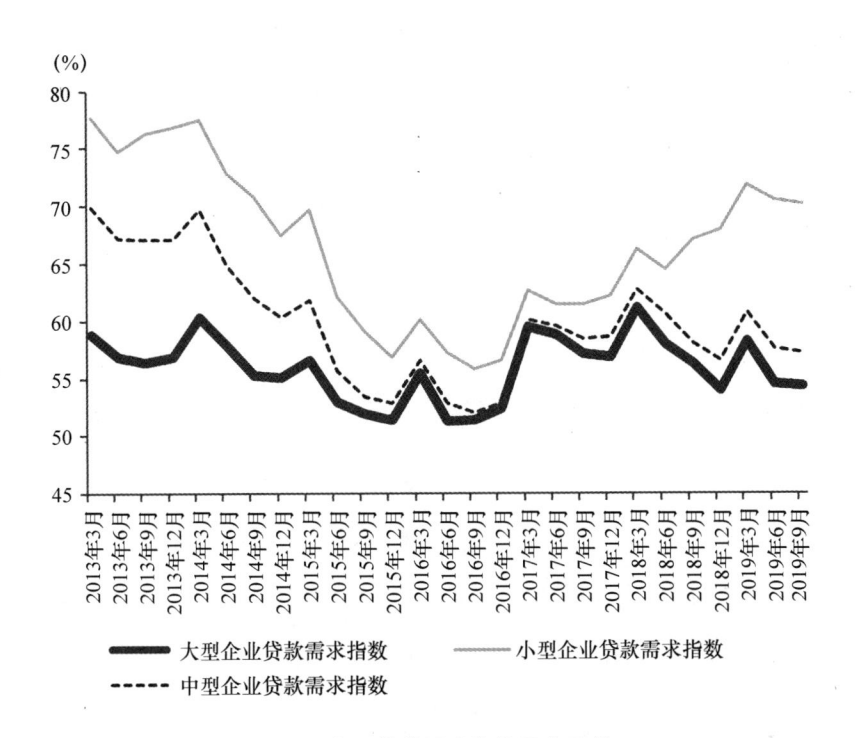

图 81 企业贷款需求指数显著回落

的改革还在进展中。在原有外汇占款投放渠道消失后，现有供给渠道存在较为严重的信息不对称问题，银行间市场利率波动性加大，导致商业银行等金融机构对流动性供给预期不稳定，更倾向于将资产投向利率债等低风险高流动性领域，以匹配负债端的波动性。这就导致了资金向实体传导不畅。同时，在金融去杠杆的大背景下，银行大幅收缩了表外业务。在有效地降低了金融风险的同时，也一定程度上导致企业的很多其他融资渠道受阻，包括产业投资基金等。在其他渠道受阻的情况下，企业只能依靠银行这一主体。由于不同企业有不同的融资需求，银行在定价中面对信息不确定性和自身的经营成本约束，只能采取相对平均的定价模式。这样难以有效降低企业的融资成本。所以必须要拓宽企业的融资渠道，用具有不同风险偏好和成本结构的金融主体满足企业的不同融资需求。这就需要在合规的基础上加大商业银行对其他金融主体的融资供给，通过各类金融主体的合力，将银行间市场的资金有效引导至实体经济，降低企业融资成本。需要以改革提高流动性供给渠道的透明性和效率。一方面，中央银行可以考虑适度增加交易商等措施扩大政策覆盖面；另一方面，商业银行也需要通过提升自身风控能力来将资金引导向实体经济。

鉴于中国原有的贷款市场报价利率机制市场化程度不高，未能及时反映市场利率变动情况，2019年10月，中国人民银行宣布改革完善LPR形成机制。改革后的LPR称之为贷款市场报价利率，在更名的同时扩大了报价行的范围，增加了城商行、农商行、外资行和民营银行，提高了报价的代表性。增加了5年期利率期限品种，丰富了利率期限结构。在这一系列操作中，最重要的是LPR"换锚"，即在公开市场操作利率（目前主要指中期借贷便利MLF）基础上加点形成。同时，刚性推广LPR报价在商业银行贷款利率形成中的应用，确定其基准利率地位。考虑到在过去十几年的利率市场化改革进程中，无论是出于自上而下的改革推动，还是自下而上的金融创新，商业银行负债端的构成已经出现了巨大的变化，同业资金、央行借款包括市场化定价的存款等项目，均已经与货币市场利率建立了清晰的联动关系，换言之，可以受到公开市场操作利率的有效引导。而正是由于这一点，LPR 与 MLF 利率挂钩，才能有效发挥从资金成本到贷款利率的传导作用。而 MLF 的引导作用是 LPR 效果发挥的关键起点。

因此，要想在短期内快速降低企业融资成本，还需直接对 LPR 中的基础定价，即 MLF 的利率进行直接调整。LPR 定价模式很难有效对冲银行最终贷款利率的加点问题。在改革后，银行新增贷款将在 LPR 之上再加点形成最终贷款利率。改革前 1 年期 LPR 为 4.31%，一般贷款的加权利率在 6% 左右，中间的点差实际体现了银行的风险溢价等因素。而在当前经济下行压力加大的情况下，商业银行风险偏好趋于谨慎符合其市场化经营的定位，风险溢价客观上是要上升的，也就是说加点部分实际还有上升的压力，因此在资金成本固定的情况下，贷款实际利率的下降幅度必然极为有限。当然，商业银行最终贷款的加点幅度还会受到金融市场一系列结构性因素的影响，包括企业融资渠道有限，商业银行的议价能力相对较强；企业的财务数据存在大量失真，社会信用建设还有待加强，导致银行的利差中隐藏了一部分反欺诈溢价等。这些结构性因素都是 LPR 改革无法解决的，需要其他改革措施的配套推进，特别是尽快降低 MLF 利率以对冲上行的风险溢价扩大因素。

（2）金融风险的缓释和预防反复是 2020 年宏观审慎管理的核心。尽管 2019 年以来金融风险得到缓释，但未来一个时期都处于违约常态化阶段，特别是随着经济进一步下行调整，金融风险可能出现反复。尽管2019年以来金融风险得到缓释,但截至11月中旬,仍有153只债券出现违约,规模达1187亿元,其中36家公司首次出现违约,未来一个时期都处于违约常态化阶段。

值得注意的是,当前结构性及区域性的金融风险仍较为突出。特别是在结构分化中,部分地方政府、部分行业、民营企业、中小银行不良率债务风险和金融风险较大,2020年可能承受较大压力。

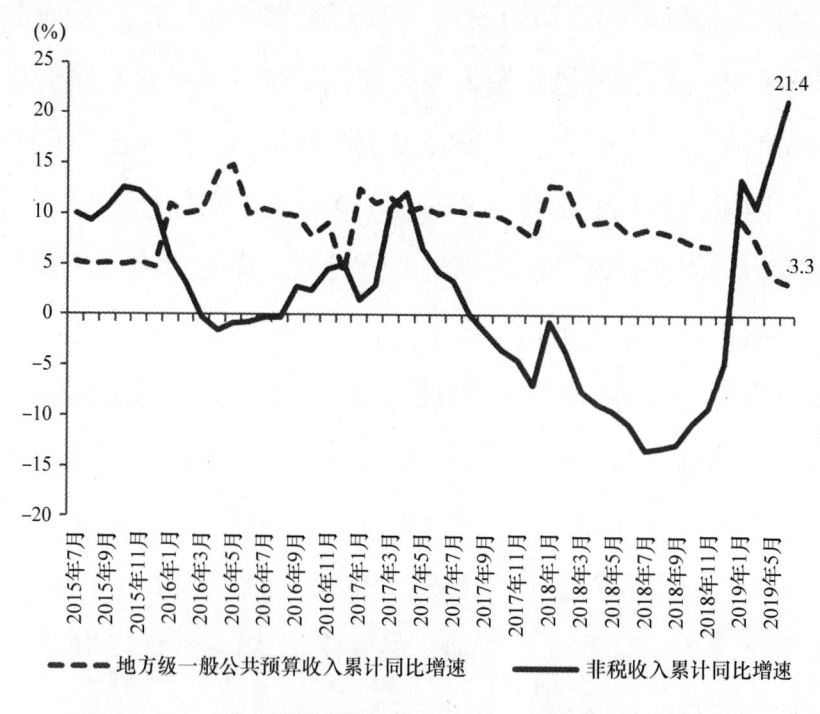

图82 地方政府财政收入增速大幅放缓、非税收入增速显著上升

首先,地方政府债务风险可能有所上扬。2019年在减税降费的过程中,地方政府公共财政收入增速大幅下滑,非税收入增

速大幅提高，反映了地方政府收入压力加大。与此同时，2019年地方政府债券发行额大幅提高，而且主要以新增债券的发行为主，置换债券和再融资债券所占比重较小，这与2017—2018年显著不同。2017年地方政府债券发行主要以置换债券和再融资债券为主，2018年新增债券与置换债券和再融资债券的占比相当，这使得地方政府的债务风险得到缓解。2019年地方政府债券发行以新增债券的发行为主，将使得2020年及以后的债务压力和风险有所上升。从政府债务率水平来看，贵州、青海、海南、内蒙古、陕西、甘肃、安徽、江西、黑龙江等地区的债务存量风险已经较高，债务的可持续性值得关注。

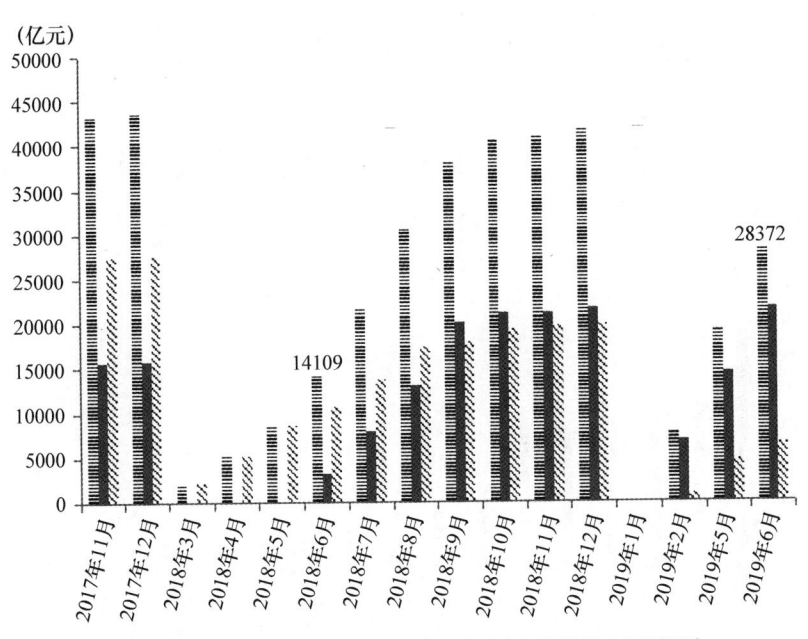

图83 地方政府债券发行情况

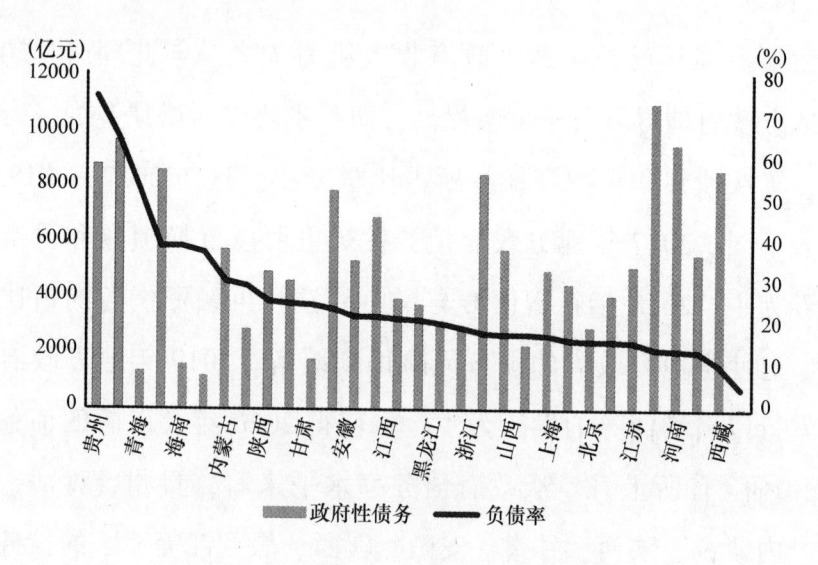

图 84　局部地区政府债务风险突出

其次，在经济结构分化中，部分地区的企业债务违约情况也呈现集中化的特征。山东、北京、上海、江苏、安徽、浙江、广东、河南、辽宁、黑龙江等地区，企业债券违约的情况较为严重。

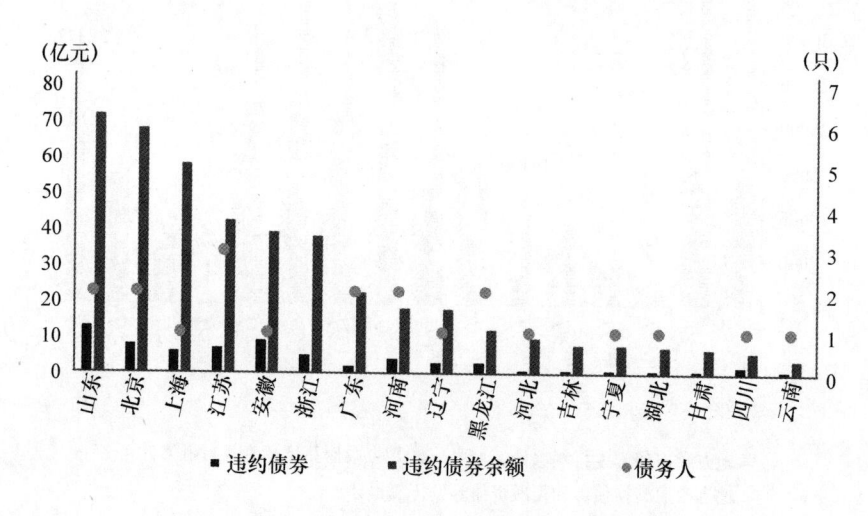

图 85　2019 年上半年违约债券在不同地区的分布情况

再次，部分行业和民营企业的债务违约情况也较为集中。从行业方面看，石油与天然气的炼制和销售、煤炭与消费用燃料、综合类行业、建筑与工程、多领域控股、食品加工与肉类、基础

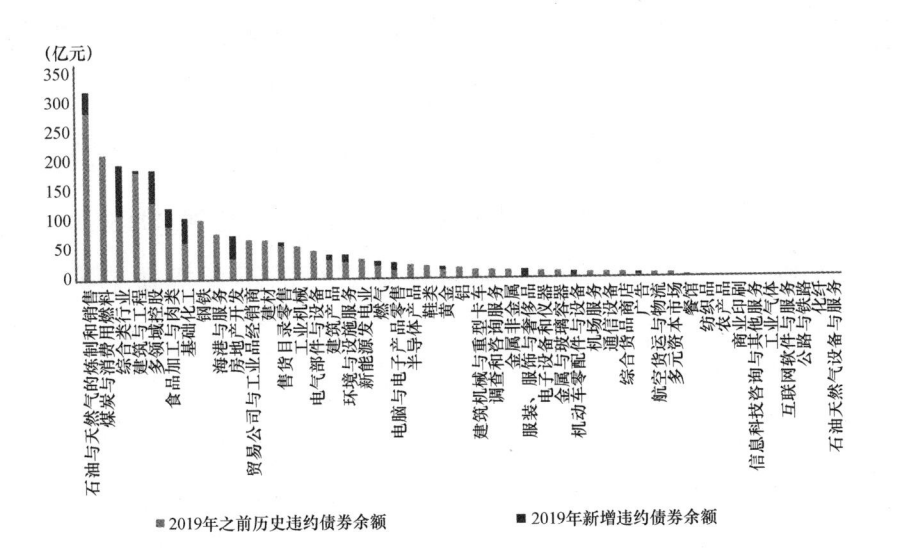

图86 2018年违约债券在不同行业的分布情况

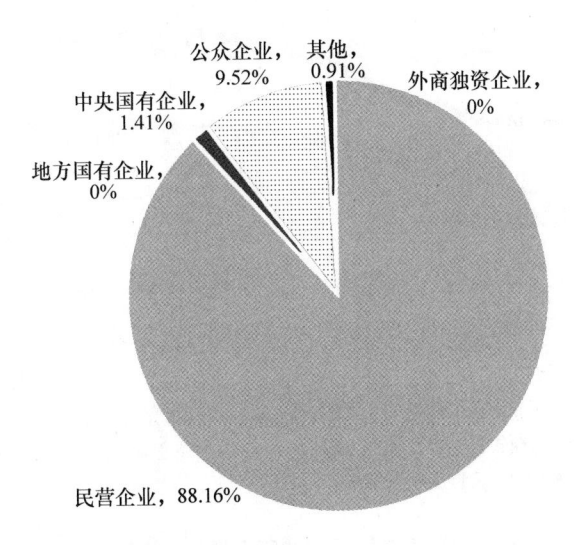

图87 2019年上半年违约债券余额在不同所有制企业的分布情况

化工、钢铁、海港与服务、房地产开发、贸易公司与工业品经销商、建材等行业，债券违约的分布较为集中。从所有制方面看，民营企业和公众企业的债务风险较大，在2019年上半年违约债务余额中，民营企业占比高达88.16%，其次为公众企业，占比达9.52%。

最后，从不同类型银行的稳健性来看，中小银行债务不良率和金融风险较大，2020年可能承受较大压力。其中，农村商业银行的不良贷款率从2013年年底的1.67%上升到2018年年底的3.96%，提高了1倍多，城市商业银行的不良贷款率也呈现较快上升趋势，值得高度关注。

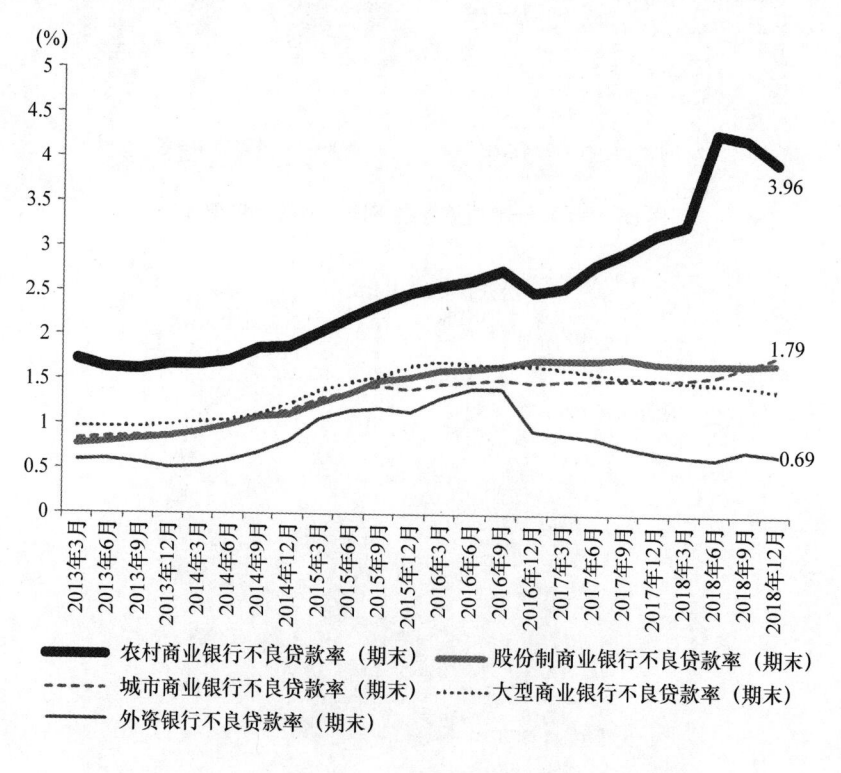

图88 不同类型银行的不良贷款率走势分化

五　结论与政策建议

在趋势性因素与周期性因素叠加、国际与国内不利因素强化的作用下，2019年中国经济增速明显趋缓。一方面，新常态的增速换挡期、动力转换期以及前期风险的释放期尚未结束，趋势性下滑力量仍然没有逆转。改革攻坚期决定了新一轮改革红利还没有完全出现，中美贸易摩擦和全球经济放缓决定了全球化红利处于快速下滑期，制造业比重的进一步下滑和第三产业的快速上升决定了工业化红利基本持续递减，人口老年化的加速决定了传统人口红利的衰竭。因此，中国经济趋势性力量当前并没有步入新的平台期，依然处于回落阶段，经济增速换挡的强化依然是今明两年结构调整攻坚期的特征之一。另一方面，国际、国内周期性波动加大，周期性力量与趋势性力量将在当前与未来一个时期出现叠加现象。中国经济正处于中美贸易摩擦全面爆发期、刚开启的世界经济周期新一轮下行期、投资周期底部波动期、金融调整下行期以及新一轮市场化去库存周期的拐点，这决定了今明两年的短周期定位总体处于下行状态，防止周期效应叠加是加强宏观政策逆周期调节的重点。

2020年是中国全面建成小康年，也是中国GDP增速持续回落的一年。中国宏观经济将在延续2019年基本运行模式的基础上出现重大的变化。一方面，2019年下行的趋势性力量和结构性力量将持续发力，导致2020年潜在GDP增速进一步回落；另一方面，2019年下行的很多周期性力量在2020年开始出现拐点性变化，宏观经济下行有所缓和，下行幅度将较2019年明显收窄。中国宏观经济运行需要高度关注六大风险挑战。一是随着全球经济步入新的低迷期、大国博弈开启新征程、全球经济贸易政策不确定性达到新高度，新一轮的外部冲击全面显现，不仅会通过贸易渠道对中国经济带来直接冲击，还会通过干扰中国经济的循环运行、恶化市场信心和未来预期等间接渠道，对中国经济产生更为深远的影响。二是萧条型的结构分化加剧叠加升级型的结构分化停滞，可能带来总量性的紧缩效应，并导致局部地区和行业的下行压力加大，就业问题集中化和局部金融风险上扬，必须引起重视和保持高度关注。三是非食品CPI的持续下滑、PPI的连续下跌、GDP平减指数的回落，意味着2020年中国经济出现新一轮通货紧缩的风险加大，需要保持高度关注和做好应对准备。四是内需增长的持续大幅下滑可能引发宏观经济加速性下滑的风险。特别是当企业不再扩大生产性投资、居民不再增加耐用品消费、地方政府被沉重的债务负担所约束、新一轮的技术革命又遥遥无期，中国经济的韧性和超大规模市场优势将同时面临重大机遇和深刻考验。五是食品价格结构性上涨与总需求加速性下滑产生叠加效应,不仅会使得当前的经济陷入困局,还会加剧市场主体对未来的悲观情绪,对2020年的宏观管理造成更为严重的问题。六是金融风险的缓释可能会出现反复。一方面,金融支持实体经济发展目前仍存在传递机制不畅问题,另一方面,未来一个时期仍将处于违约常态化阶段,随着经济进一步下行调整,结构性及区域性的金融风险上扬,进一步促进金融风险有序缓释和预防反复是2020年宏观审慎管理的核心。

结合中国宏观运行所处阶段特征和周期相位,针对2020年经济运行中的深层次问题和重大风险点,本报告提出以下八大方面的政策建议。

第一,科学制定2020年经济增长目标,建议目标区间为5.5%—6.0%。科学制定2020年增长目标的紧要之处在于目标下限约束与现实的增长潜力之间的空间大幅收窄。因此,必须强化底线意识,以底线思维制定和落实2020年经济社会发展的主要预期目标,需要坚持三个基本原则:一是高质量发展;二是完成"两个一百年"目标的阶段性任务;三是保证社会就业基本稳定。经过反复测算发现,2020年增长目标不必拘泥于6%以上,保持在5.5%—6.0%,足以完成"两个一百年"目标的阶段性任务,也能够保证社会就业的基本稳定,同时也更有利于保持战略定力,按照既定方针推动经济高质量发展。

(1) 坚持高质量发展原则,2020年GDP增长的区间管理目标宜设为5.5%—6.0%。按照既定方针推动中国经济高质量发展，要求2020年经济目标必须符合中国经济中长期发展趋势，并在此基础上加强宏观政策逆周期调节功能对冲周期性因素。2020年的经济增速已很难达到6.0%以上，如果继续将2020年的GDP增长目标设在6.0%—6.5%，必须依靠强有力的财政刺激政策、宽松的货币政策以及放松房地产市场调控来刺激短期增长。但是，目前看这三个条件或不具备或不利于中长期的经济高质量发展。因此，从保持战略定力，按照既定方针推动经济高质量发展的角度来看，2020年增长目标设在5.5%—6.0%进行区间管理较为适宜。从中长期来看，在趋势性下滑和增速换挡过程中，中国经济发展还需要完成以下历史性任务，必须为2021年深化改革攻坚预留政策储备。

（2）坚持实现"两个一百年"目标阶段性任务原则，2020年GDP增长目标宜保持在5%—6%，不必拘泥于6%以上。2020年GDP增长目标的下限面临完成"两个一百年"目标阶段性任务的紧约束。如果按照目前的统计口径，6%将是2020年GDP增长的目标下限。但是从历次根据全国经济普查数据调整的统计规律来看，在根据2018年年底开启的第四次全国经济普查进行数据调整后，2014—2018年的经济增速有望每年提高0.5个百分点，5年累计提高2.0—2.5个百分点。2019年11月22日，国家统计局发布了关于修订2018年国内生产总值数据的公告，将2018年GDP向上修订了2.1%，这意味着在2019年增长

6.2%的基础上,2020年经济增速保持在4%—5%就已经足够实现比2010年翻一番的目标。因此,2020年的经济增长目标不必为增速"破6"的关口过度紧张,2020年增速保持在5.5%—6.0%的目标区间,就能够实现"2020年GDP比2010年翻一番"的目标。

(3)坚持保证社会就业基本稳定原则,增速保持在5.5%—6.0%足以保证就业的基本稳定,5.8%是较理想的状态;5%是确保就业无虞的增长底线,但可能会牺牲就业质量。以2019年中国GDP增速为6.2%为基础,若2020年中国的经济增速为6%,那么非农就业增量预计为590万,与2018年相近,就业比较宽松;若2020年经济增速为5.8%,非农就业增量降至480万,比2019年略多,对标2019年的就业形势,2020年就业形势仍应无虞;若2020年经济增速为5.5%,非农就业增量为315万,比2019年少近百万,达到历史新低,就业形势会更加吃紧,但尚不会出现大面积的失业问题;若2020年中国经济增速降至5%,非农就业增量将降为0,这时才将真正考验中国之就业。因此,5%是确保中国就业无虞所不能突破的增长底线,5.5%—6.0%可以保证就业的基本稳定,5.8%是较理想的状态。

第二,将中期视角的"预期管理"作为各项宏观政策的统领和重要抓手。在内需增长出现大幅下滑和结构分化达到新的临界值的背景下,简单的预调、微调已经不足以应对宏观经济日益面临的加速性下滑风险,而必须借助于中期视角的"预期管理"。

（1）必须旗帜鲜明地稳定内需，引导市场主体形成一致预期，确保经济增速保持在合理区间。由于预期持续恶化，目前除了总量性的收缩，在投资领域和消费领域都已经出现了结构性的紧缩效应：企业不再扩大生产性的投资，居民不再增加耐用品的消费。如此持续下去，不仅升级型的结构分化将会停滞，而且萧条型的结构分化也将加剧，产生总量性的紧缩效应和局部性的风险恶化。

（2）新一轮的信心构建必须从2019年第四季度全面开始，以应对2020年经济增速"下台阶效应"的进一步显化。目前中国经济的制度性红利已经开始筑底回升，同时，近期金融风险的缓释和中美贸易摩擦的阶段性缓和将为2020年带来一个相对稳定的金融市场环境和外贸环境，这对于重建市场信心提供了非常有利的重要时点。

（3）对于猪肉等食品价格的结构性上涨和工业领域的通缩风险，同样要加强预期管理，采取"宏观政策＋分类施策"组合进行综合治理。针对猪肉等个别商品价格的大幅上涨，需在必要的"环保纠偏"的基础上，加强民生保障、舆情管理和市场预期引导。2019年年初以来，食品价格的"轮番上涨"已充分暴露了现有的"预调、微调"举措在应对当前局面上的缺陷，而以"预期管理"统领各项宏观政策，就不能就猪肉调猪肉，而是要基于未来价格走势和潜在转移路径的总体研判，通过前瞻性的指引，引导市场主体行为进行调整。在供给侧，主要防止环保督察与猪瘟疫情的进一步叠加，尽快恢复生猪生产。在需求侧，主要通过食品补贴或猪肉消费专项补贴，确保困难群众的基本生活。更重要的是，要加强舆情管理和市场预期引导：一方面应避免市场主体特别是中低收入家庭对未来产生悲观预期，要更加重视保就业政策，稳定居民未来收入预期；另一方面应避免借机宣扬全面通胀言论和制造噪音，干扰货币政策的制定和执行。对于工业领域的通缩风险，需要基于各类价格指数走势分化的准确判断，区别对待短期民生目标和中期宏观经济目标，采取"宏观政策+分类施策"组合进行综合治理，避免陷入政策方向选择上的困境。

第三，落实十九届四中全会精神，全面开启新一轮全方位改革开放和新一轮供给侧结构性改革来解决我们面临的深层次结构性与体制性问题。在经济结构转换的关键期和深层次问题的累积释放期，简单的宏观政策调节和行政管控，难以应对基础性利益冲突和制度扭曲所产生的问题，基础性、全局性改革依然是解决目前结构转型时期各类深层次问题的关键。必须以构建高标准市场经济体系为目标，推出新一轮改革开放和供给侧结构性改革。

（1）必须梳理各类问题的边界，区分短期波动问题与中长期增长问题之间的差别，区分外部冲击与内部冲击之间的差别，分类使用需求管理政策、结构性调整政策以及基础改革政策。防止用短期行政管控代替改革，用宏观调控来回避改革。一是必须对周期性波动进行宏观调控，防止经济波动过大导致改革环境的恶化；二是对于中长期增长问题要采取产业政策、区域政策，持续培育新增长点和新动能；三是对于资源配置性扭曲必须进行结构性改革，以减少市场摩擦，恢复市场功能；四是对于涉及基本利益冲突、大的制度扭曲从而导致各种短期需求管理政策、中期产业政策和区域政策出现严重失灵的问题，必须进行基础性改革。

（2）必须明确改革的核心不是出台政策或召开会议，而是要建立各类改革主体愿意改革、能够改革的激励相容的改革动力体系。新一轮改革必须从过去以责任、约束为主转向以激励相容、权责统一为主。要对不同层次的改革主体建立不同的第二轮改革红利的分享机制和改革成本的共担机制，全面激发三大精英阶层的改革积极性。要及时进行阶段性历史总结，甩开历史包袱，轻装上阵，强化产权保护，解决企业家原罪问题。要在关后门、堵旁门、取缔非法收入的原则上，正视各类灰色收入和影子活动的历史必然性和现实合理性，要寻找到灰色体系、影子体系规范化、阳光化的改革通道，而不是简单地进行取缔。要建立改革的容错机制，区分改革试错与违纪违法之间的本质差别。要重新界定顶层设计和基层创新的边界，一方面防止过多、过细的顶层设计完全约束了基层创新的空间和活力，另一方面也要防止过多的基层创新导致改革缺乏统一性和协调性，从而陷入碎片化改革困境之中。要充分认识到目前中国经济的历史方位和国际方位，充分利用国际问题倒逼中国的开放，用新一轮大开放来倒逼我们的深层次改革。

（3）在中期规划和设计新一轮基础性、引领性改革方案的基础上，全面总结4年来供给侧结构性改革的成就和经验，果断推出新一轮供给侧结构性改革。一是必须认识到第一阶段供给侧结构性改革的目标已经基本顺利完成，"三去一降一补"的内容、目标、手段都需要阶段性的大调整；二是第二轮供给侧结构性改革应当以"降成本、补短板"为重点；三是必须以市场化和法制化工具为主体，避免行政化实施带来的各种问题；四是解决各种供给侧问题的基本落脚点必须配合大改革的进行；五是不能割裂生产、流通、分配、消费以及所有制之间的相互关系，把结构性调整简单局限于生产端，而忽视其他环节在不同时段的核心作用。

（4）以改革的精神来全面梳理和定位中国2020年的宏观经济政策。一是要对短期宏观经济政策调控、中期经济增长政策、转型期结构性改革和基础性改革进行分类，防止各类政策在目标配置、工具选择上出现错配，避免出现市场工具行政化、总量政策结构化、行政举措长期化、宏观调控泛化等问题；二是宏观经济政策要定位于配合"大改革、新开放"，为新一轮改革开放创造必要的宏观经济环境，强化底线管理、全面缓和各种短期冲击；三是要正视改革疏导宏观经济政策传递机制、改革完善宏观经济政策体系需要一个过程，需要基础性改革的到位，因此在短期政策调整时必须前瞻性地考虑目前大改革、大调整带来的宏观经济政策效率弱化、外溢性以及合成谬误等问题，避免宏观调控在"过"与"不及"之间摇摆，进而成为加剧宏观经济波动的核心原因之一。

（5）2020年加强"六稳"的核心仍在于"稳预期"，"稳预期"的核心在于"稳信心"，必须认识到"稳信心"不在于某些宏观经济指标的短期稳定，不在于宏观经济政策随着市场情绪进行简单的宽松或定向性的帮扶，而在于市场主体对于长期战略问题有清晰、明确和科学的解决方案，在于我们在基础性问题上进行了真正的改革，为未来提供了一个可信的公平竞争环境。其一，市场情绪的动荡不仅在于中国市场存在问题，而在于政府过度干预、政府信用和类政府信用出现了过度膨胀，导致市场空间的挤压。其二，民营企业家信心的低迷不仅在于民营经济产权保护的不完善，更在于民营经济的生存和发展空间被严重挤压。因此，提振民营经济信心的核心关键不在于对于民营经济进行一次性的行政性帮扶，而是要通过系统性改革为民营经济提供一个公平、透明的竞争环境。其三，金融市场的忧虑不仅来源于市场的不完善和债务率的高企，更来源于我们解决债务问题的方法进一步加剧了资源配置的扭曲。其四，信心低迷不在于我们没有进行预期干预，而在于预期干预释放的信号十分混乱，干预行为反而成为信心下滑的原因。其五，市场情绪的变化往往具有前瞻性，我们在高度重视市场情绪变化的同时，必须认识到市场情绪往往会在信息不完全和不对称的情况下夸大实际问题的困难程度,科学分析市场情绪中的信息对于宏观经济"预调"和"微调"管理十分重要。

第四,构建货币政策新稳健的新框架,从哲学理念、目标体系、工具选择、审慎管理、汇率安排、预期管理和政策协调等方面,对新形势下的稳健货币政策的框架进行全面重构。

(1)稳健货币政策的哲学理念和目标体系需要重构。其一,货币政策在大转型期间需要更为积极的哲学理念。在新旧动能转换期,潜在GDP增速和产出缺口可能被低估,需要扬弃传统货币政策规则中关于潜在增速的理念。在哲学层面要有"非常之时需要非常之举"的理念,积极前瞻性地研究各类非常规货币政策的试点和实施策略。其二,在结构调整攻坚期和价格高度分化期,货币政策的目标必须从传统的CPI、实际GDP增速和就业数量转向以下几个方面:名义GDP增速、就业质量和GDP平减指数;流动性稳定和资产价格的异动;汇率预期以及套利性资本流动。货币政策不能简单地盯住实际GDP增速、CPI和就业数量,因为在中国当前的经济结构和统计体系中,这些传统的指标已经不能科学反映中国宏观经济运行的状况。

(2)在内生性回落加速和外部需求疲软全面扩展之时,稳健的货币政策需要明确新内涵和新举措。其一,稳健的货币政策要能够在必要时顺利地从"稳健定位"转向"适度宽松",以稳定市场预期,打破"债务—通缩"的恶性循环,扭转目前内生性回落的悲观情绪。其二，随着金融整顿和深化金融体制改革的持续推进，防范化解重大金融风险取得阶段性胜利，2020年将迎来一个相对稳定的金融市场环境，货币政策应当延续2019年的基本定位，但操作方式可以适度偏松：一是在内需持续回落、外需急剧疲软、金融风险得到缓释之时，货币政策应该避免过度从紧的取向，低利率政策依然是市场复苏的一个十分重要的基础，特别是实际贷款利率的下降仍是稳投资的一个关键。二是M2增速不宜设定过低，应为预防通货紧缩风险和各类金融指标内生性的收缩预留空间。当前非食品CPI的不断下滑、PPI的持续下跌、GDP平减指数的显著回落、企业效益和市场预期的恶化，可能预示着新一轮的通货紧缩正在形成，需要密切关注未来两三个季度的价格形势变化，及时调整货币政策定位。建议2020年M2增速应当高于名义GDP增速的水平，达到8.5%—9.0%；全社会融资总额增速不能过快回调，保持在11%左右符合金融整顿与强化监管的要求。

（3）稳健货币政策的工具箱和传导渠道需要重塑。其一，由于大改革与大转型期间的波动源具有多元性和叠加性，货币政策工具必须多元化，常规政策工具难以应对目前的格局。非常规货币政策甚至中国版QE需要进行系统研究，未来中国的政策篮子并不拒绝采取非常规宏观政策。其二，应当关注货币投放方式变化对于货币传导的冲击，2020年可以逐步降低金融机构的存款准备金率的方式完成货币投放。对内需要关注M0和M1增速的持续回落，丰富中国人民银行货币发行的渠道，加大银行准备金率降低的幅度，提高中国安全性资产的供给，加大货币市场的深度；对外需要高度关注美联储政策的调整以及美国金融市场的异变。其三，鉴于货币政策调控框架转型往往会带来基础货币供给节奏不稳定、供给工具不确定、供给对象不透明等问题，为防止市场流动性紧张时期引发市场紧张情绪，导致市场资金面和利率出现不必要的波动，货币政策除常用的公开市场操作工具外，应当通过常备借贷便利、中期借贷便利等一系列创新型工具向市场注入流动性，以强化引导市场预期。其四，在控制债务过度上涨的过程中，货币政策的工具选择十分重要，价格型工具对于高债务企业的调整更为有利，简单的数量宽松依然需要控制。因此，目前的宽松货币政策定位应当在数量型工具盯住流动性的基础上，以价格工具为主导。其五，在经济下行压力加大和不确定性上扬的背景下，需要 LPR 改革与其他改革举措配套推进，对商业银行的风险溢价加点进行有效对冲。近期中国人民银行通过贷款市场报价利率（LPR）改革，下调公开市场操作利率，引导 LPR 利率小幅下降。但是在经济下行压力加大和不确定性上扬的背景下，市场风险溢价客观上是趋于上升的，商业银行在 LPR 的基础上通过风险溢价加点，导致企业最终获得的一般贷款利率未必能够有效降低。因此，仍需要其他改革举措的配套推进，通过适度"降准"和大幅降低 MLF 利率进行有效对冲。其六，在价格形势高度分化下，特别是 CPI 与 PPI 走势分化，货币政策利率工具要考虑不同市场主体面临的实际利率差异。特别是在 PPI 为负的背景下，对于实际利率的跟踪，要分类采用与企业生产投资相对应的价格指数对名义利率进行调整。建议采用非对称降息工具。

（4）将预期管理作为货币政策的统领和重要抓手。其一，在改革继续推进、金融创新不断涌现、利率市场化尚未彻底完成的情况下，货币政策应注重加强预期管理，更加注重引导社会预期，以提高货币政策的有效性。其二，由于总需求不足问题已经显化，稳健的货币政策不宜保持以往模糊的稳健定位，必须旗帜鲜明地阐述新稳健的新内涵。包括汇率调整、存款准备金以及利率的调整应当更加明确其偏宽松的内涵，不宜过分含糊其辞，在货币政策定位上玩文字游戏。其三，货币政策要全面扭转市场悲观预期，就必须打破以往传统的"小步微调"调控节奏。要充分认识到过去两年中国货币政策在持续性"微调"中总是没有达到"预调"目标的核心原因在于市场主体对于"小步微调"并不认可，"微调"并没有改变其预期模式，更没有达到稳定信心和发挥"锚定效应"的功能。避免金融环境的收紧快于市场预期是货币政策预期管理的核心要点。其四，新一轮信心构建必须从 2019 年第四季度全面开始。目前中国经济的制度性红利已经开始筑底回升，同时，近期金融风险的缓释和中美贸易摩擦的阶段性缓和将为 2020 年带来一个相对稳定的金融市场环境和外贸环境，这为重建市场信心提供了非常有利的重要时点。即使在长端利率刚性、金融资源对于实体经济渗透力下滑的环境中，适度宽松的货币政策也具有必要性，依然是引导预期、防止过度收缩、配合积极财政政策的必要工具。其五，打破生产领域"通缩—高债务"的恶性循环，避免进入资产负债表衰退，货币政策必须抓住目前短暂的窗口期，将宽松的力度提升到一定水平，而不能采取事后追加的模式，失去引导预期的作用。一旦中国步入资产负债表衰退阶段，中国货币政策的效率也将随着中国经济出现断崖式下滑，从而带来巨额的调整成本。日本等国家的案例已经充分表明传统"微调"模式可能会贻误调控的契机，中国要避免进入资产负债表衰退，不仅要进行货币政策方向的全面转型，同时还必须将一次性宽松冲击达到一定的高度。

（5）以弹性汇率政策应对全球新一轮低迷期的挑战。其一，正确认识世界经济新一轮低迷期的开启及其引发的全球央行"降息潮"，特别是欧美重启降息和 QE 操作，2020 年主要国家货币政策宽松化操作将是常态。在此背景下，需要明确未来一个时期中国货币政策的国际化导向，货币政策宽松的节奏应与全球主要央行保持一致，实现汇率的基本稳定，作为应对 2020 年外部波动风险的核心。其二，内部经济稳定依然是基本出发点，汇率调整和资本项目开放的改革都必须服从这个目标。鉴于 2020 年各类因素叠加的不确定性，中国对外经济政策应当采取保守主义的策略，以稳固中国经济企稳的基础。其三，汇率市场化改革仍然是释放汇率机制以缓冲中国经济外部冲击作用的关键，是提高中国经济弹性和韧性的有效途径。从稳定金融市场的角度看，政府应该未雨绸缪，为应对人民币汇率和资本异常流动做好准备。

（6）逆周期宏观审慎需要适应结构调整攻坚期要求，加强政策的协同配合，避免产生新扭曲。其一，金融风险的缓释和预防反复是2020年宏观审慎的核心。尽管2019年以来金融风险得到缓释，但未来一个时期都处于违约常态化阶段。货币政策、宏观审慎监管、金融微观监管以及其他金融目标的一体化显得更为重要，货币金融当局的实体化、一体化、独立化和权力化也是制定科学货币政策的前提。其二，在结构调整期，逆周期宏观审慎需要强化货币投放、信贷投放、社会融资投放之间的关系，使货币政策与金融监管相互配合。建议采取"适度宽松货币政策+金融监管改革"的组合，以保证实体经济面临的货币条件指数的相对稳定。其三，"稳金融"应当以"不发生系统性金融风险"为底线，不宜过度定义，必须对于局部环节的金融问题和金融风险的暴露有一定的容忍度。特别是在大改革与大开放重启的时刻，局部风险的集中暴露有利于我们形成有效的改革路径。其四，不能简单地将"不发生系统性风险"等同于"金融指标的稳定"，大转型与大改革时期的各类金融指标必须做出调整，否则资源配置的方式和结构以及各种潜在的风险无法暴露。其五，宏观审慎监管必须从系统性金融风险的指标监管向一些结构性因素监管倾斜。经过2019年的风险缓释操作，未来两年对于重点城市、重点省份的债务可持续性风险的监控,对于部分行业和部分产品风险的监控显得尤其重要。其六,宽松货币政策必须辅之以"市场秩序建设"。金融市场缺陷的弥补和恢复金融市场配置资源的能力是适度宽松货币政策实施的一个重要前提。否则,"宽货币"下金融领域的泡沫很可能进一步诱发资金"脱实向虚",使得实体经济与虚拟经济的背离,导致"衰退性泡沫"的出现。其七,在高债务环境中,不仅要保持适度宽松的货币政策,同时还要对大量的"僵尸企业"进行出清、对高债务企业进行债务重组,对银行以及相关企业的资产负债表进行实质性的重构。存量调整是增量调整的基础,存量调整基础上的"积极财政政策+适度宽松货币政策+强监管"依然是我们走出困局的核心法宝。

第五,财政政策要精准,在更加积极的同时提高针对性,调动三个积极性。内需增长的大幅下滑,加剧了中国经济的脆弱性,2020年财政政策要更加积极有效,在时间窗口关闭前,加大力度、加快速度、加强精准度地稳内需。

(1)除继续落实好现有的减税降费政策外,进一步提高企业先进生产设备减税抵扣和研发费用税前加计扣除力度,调动企业扩大生产性投资和研发投资的积极性。可以进一步提高财政赤字率,考虑到内忧外困和大改革的特殊性,建议2020年财政赤字率可以提高到3.0%以上。目前,国家统计局根据第四次全国经济普查对2018年GDP数据进行了修订,将2018年GDP上调了 2.1%，从 900309 亿元增加 18972 亿元至 919281 亿元。GDP 总量的扩大意味着 2020 年的财政赤字空间有所提升，在维持赤字率不变的情况下，约能增加公共预算赤字 600 亿元，地方政府专项债 600 亿元，利用政府资金撬动社会资金的潜力提升。

（2）进一步明确财政纪律和市场规则，在此基础上充分发挥地方政府进行基础设施建设投资和公共事业投资的积极性，带动社会投资增速回升和稳定市场预期。虽然目前基础设施建设投资增速在企稳回升，但回升速度非常缓慢，仍在拖累总体投资增速，并对市场预期产生不利影响。2020 年财政支出应当从投资导向往民生导向转变，从补贴导向往福利导向转变，利用积极的财政政策加速广泛的大福利体系的构建，利用定向宽松的财政政策扩大养老产业、健康产业以及中高端服务业的发展，释放相应的需求。同时，2020 年地方政府专项债券规模的扩大不能搞"一刀切"，必须基于对地区债务风险评估的基础上"有保有压"，对于政府债务率已经较高的地区有所控制，并且以政府专项债的置换和再融资为主，促进债务风险的进一步缓释，而对于政府债务率较低的地区，可以适度鼓励新增债券的发行。

（3）关注局部区域财政收入崩塌的问题，特别是基层财政收入突变带来的各种民生问题。建议扩大财政平准基金的规模，设立过渡期基层财政救助体系；同时，适度弱化财政收入的目标，防止地方政府通过加大税收征收力度和非税收等方式，变相增加企业的负担。鉴于地方债市场容量的狭小和制度的不完善，建议2020年提高财政赤字水平的核心渠道是提高中央的财政赤字率，并积极利用国债发行规模的提高来增加政府支出能力，以加大改革推行的力度。

（4）减税降费从生产端向消费端和收入分配改革过渡，调动居民消费积极性。在储蓄率持续下滑的新时期，"稳消费"对于宏观经济稳定和健康发展具有基础性和引领性作用。必须高度重视目前消费增速下滑的内在原因，巩固和扩大中国居民的消费基础，发挥超大规模市场优势。其一，积极落实个税改革方案，减少工薪阶层的税收负担。其二，加大对公共服务均等化改革，提高公共服务的可获得性。其三，针对2020年猪肉价格波动和收入波动叠加风险，做好针对低收入阶层的消费补贴预案，防止宏观经济波动对低收入阶层的过度波动。其四，制定对中产阶层消费启动战略，特别是消费升级的促进战略：重视中产阶层家庭杠杆率的过快上升，尊重杠杆率的演化规律，通过建立相应的债务风险缓释机制，促进消费平稳增长；针对汽车等耐用品消费出台专项减税降费政策。例如，按照国际上人均汽车拥有量与人均可支配收入水平的拟合线，目前中国汽车拥有量仍有高达80%的增长空间。建议将汽车购置税率从10%下调至5%，释放汽车消费的增长空间。近10年的汽车消费经验表明，降低汽车购置税对促进汽车消费具有立竿见影的效果。2009—2010年以及2015—2016年，通过将汽车购置税率从10%下调至5%，大幅提高了汽车消费增长率；反之，近两年汽车消费的大幅下滑，在一定程度上与汽车购置税率从5%提高至10%有关。

第六，2020年稳增长的核心在于"稳投资"，但"稳投资"的政策方向和政策工具必须做出大幅度的调整，启动投资新举措需要有系统方案。同时，落实党的十九大提出的"发挥投资对优化供给结构的关键性作用"是一个中期任务，需要对中国投资结构优化提出一揽子改革方案，产业投资政策需要调整。

（1）启动民间投资是稳投资的关键，而民间投资启动的核心在于提高投资未来预期收益率，预期收益率的提升来源于产权的可保护性、资本投资的新空间、投资成本的降低以及投资产业需求的扩展等方面。因此，民间投资的启动不是任何单一政策和工具能够胜任的，必须采取系统性的政策方案和改革措施，必须从中期角度来系统展开，全面调整投资预期。必须认识到实体投资回报率过低不仅仅是一个周期性现象，更重要的是源自系列重大改革的缺位，启动民间资本的系统方案必须包含大量基础性的、中期导向的重大改革：一是政府必须从目前的投资型政府逐步转向民生型政府；二是国有企业投资体系和利润使用应当进行战略性重新定位改革，非主营业务投资必须严格限制；三是各类管制要重新梳理；四是事业单位和公共服务体系的市场化改革必须深化。必须看到以制造业为主的民间投资空间已经饱和，各类市场型和半公共服务领域的开放十分重要，放松这些行业的政府管制、减少政府在非公共领域的投资和全面收缩国有企业的非主营业务十分重要。

（2）加大对中小企业、民营企业和创新性企业投资需求的资金可获得性仍是投资启动的重要工作。"脱实向虚"的治理是提升实体经济投资增速的一个关键，但是，简单化、行政化的金融整顿和监管强化并不能达到稳投资的目标，特别是稳定民间投资的目标。因为在治理金融创新带来的风险和部分乱象的过程中行政化监管很容易扼杀金融创新，使大量金融资源过度依赖于传统体制内的路径进行融资，新型融资渠道出现全面收缩，大量中小企业、民营企业和创新性企业反而难以在治理整顿中获得融资，融资难、融资贵又成为这些企业投资的瓶颈问题。

（3）从短期来看，国家依然需要准备一些投资项目包，以防止固定资产投资增速过快下滑，2020年保持政府性投资增速和房地产增速的相对稳定依然较为重要。从中期来看，任何持续的扩张的政策性投资必定会通过资金挤占、产业空间挤占、政治疑虑等渠道带来大量的挤出效应，使市场性投资在扩展政策中不仅没有得到扩展，反而在中期出现萎缩，政府未来对于各类产业的投资和补贴不能进一步膨胀，需要适度容忍投资增速的回落。

第七，民生政策要托底，应对经济下行和民生冲击叠加带来的"双重风险"。民生冲击与总需求下滑叠加不仅会使得当前的经济陷入困局，还会加剧市场主体对未来的悲观情绪，对2020年的宏观管理造成更为严重的问题。面对"双重风险"，短期内既要加大民生保障支出，更要重视就业稳定政策，保就业的重要性大于保工资，通过提高工资弹性应对成本冲击。一是对中美贸易摩擦可能诱发失业风险的局部行业、局部地区，制定有针对性的干预措施或引导措施；二是对汽车、手机等近期面临较大困难的行业要研究专门的解决办法，结合产业政策、消费政策、税收政策、交管政策等进行；三是重视企业特别是民营、小微企业面临的经营困境，从多个维度为企业减负，扶持政策应结合就业目标进行；四是适当放宽对地摊经济、夜间经济的限制，扩大灵活就业的生存空间；五是通过就业补贴等工具引导企业的用工行为，同时更加注重对青年失业群体的就业引导；六是重构未来的就业政策体系，积极就业政策要更加积极，目标从充分就业转向高质量的充分就业，为提高就业质量做准备；消极就业政策要更完善，进一步健全社会安全网，做好托底准备。

第八，积极应对中美贸易摩擦，全新思考世界结构裂变期中国的战略选择。2020年世界经济可能发生超预期变化，对加强国际合作与政策协调的呼声将短暂压制贸易保护主义而达到一个小高潮，但一旦成效甚微，贸易保护主义将裹挟民粹主义发起更猛烈的反攻，世界经济结构与秩序将面临更加严重的破坏，必须从中期视角全面思考世界结构裂变期中国的战略选择。其一，要用深化改革和高水平开放来应对世界结构裂变带来的短期挑战，特别是在中美贸易摩擦中要以自由主义对抗新保护主义、用多边和双边主义对抗孤立主义、用新合作对抗新冷战。其二，在坚持以新开放应对挑战的同时，必须认识到裂变期世界经济的各种基本参数发生根本性变化决定了我们不可能重返过去的战略路径，必须重构新开放发展的实施路径。其三，全球产业链、供应链、价值链的重构必将发生，必须进行前瞻性研究和全面布局，尤其是对于美国可能采取的"经济铁幕"和"新冷战"要有深入研究。一是应当在战略上避免"新冷战"的快速出现，维护中国产业升级的良好国际环境，二是必须通过区域经济更高水平的一体化和自由化防止美国快速形成"经济铁幕"和"新冷战"的国际统一战线。其四，对于贸易战在其他领域的全面扩散必须要有充分的预案，特别是在技术战、人才战、汇率战以及安全领域等领域要有充分的研究和策略安排。其五，对于2020年可能出现的国际收支恶化和国际金融市场动荡冲击，做好短期安排和政策对冲的准备。其六，在应对中美贸易摩擦的过程中，需要避免几个陷阱：一是"以降促和"的陷阱；二是简单步入敌对状态的"修昔底德陷阱"；三是无技术外溢、高成本的军事竞赛陷阱；四是无贸易支撑和经济基础的政治联盟陷阱。

Chapter One   Overview and Forecast[*]

In 2019, under the effects of multiple factors, such as the intensification of Sino-US trade friction, the decline of global economy, the aggravation of domestic structural problems and the strengthening of cyclical downward forces, China's macroeconomy left the plateau of "stable but trending down" of 2016—2018. The decline of economic growth has increased, and economic structure has been significantly differentiated. However, the elasticity and resilience of China's macroeconomy have shown great strength under "six stability measures"[①]. China's economy is still operating within an expected and controllable range.

Firstly, noticeable declines of GDP deflator and demand-side parameters indicate that cyclical downward forces are still a core reason

---

[*] The manuscript was completed by the end of 2019. The outbreak of the novel coronavirus pneumonia is not considered in the prediction analysis in 2020. It is a reference for readers to analyze and compare the situation without the outbreak.

[①] Six stability: to keep employment, financial sector, foreign trade, foreign and domestic investments, and expectations stable.

for China's macroeconomic decline in 2019. First, after leaving a relatively high level in the third quarter of 2018, the inventory cycle of enterprises quickly entered a new downward phase. The combined effects of market-orientated destocking and policy-orientated destocking have brought about an accelerated contraction effect. Second, it's difficult for private investment to follow state-owned enterprise investment at the bottom of investment cycle, given the constraints of declining expected investment returns, weak confidence and limited investment opportunities. Third, due to enduring financial risks, the continued deleveraging of state-owned enterprises, and the exposure of risks to small and medium-sized financial institutions, solvency issues persist for many enterprises and China's financial cycle remains at the bottom. Fourth, under the influence of deglobalization movement and the spread of international conflicts, global uncertainties have risen sharply, the growth of international trade has fallen, and global demand for durable goods and investment goods has significantly contracted, leading to the resumption of global economic downturn.

Secondly, the weakness of supply side, the on-going changes to various basic economic parameters, and the inertia of potential GDP growth rate, indicate that the decline of trend forces and structural forces is still the main factor for the decline of GDP growth rate. First, the outbreak of Sino-US trade friction across the board and the resumption of global economic downturn have determined that the globalization dividend, one of the traditional drivers of China's economy, has not only failed to stabilize and recover, but has declined rapidly. Second, PPI's change from positive to negative, the persistent negative growth of industrial profits and the decline in the share of manufacturing industry show that the decline of industrialization dividend as a traditional driver of China's economy, has accelerated recently instead of stopping. Third, the accelerated aging rate of the population, the negative growth of floating population, and the continuous decline of saving rate indicate that the demographic dividend, which is another traditional driving force of China's economy, is still in a period of accelerated decline.

Thirdly, the outbreak of Sino-US trade friction across the board and soaring pork price are two of the most noteworthy macroeconomic events in 2019. The rising export tariffs on the United States and high uncertainty in Sino-US trade negotiations have brought about obvious marginal impact on China's external demand and the expectations of economic entities. The impact is a core reason why private investment has declined and other cyclical forces leading to economic downturn intensified. The surge in pork prices has not only had a significant impact on household consumption and consumer expectations, but has also had an evident impact on macroeconomic policy, which is one of the core reasons for the accelerated decline in China's consumption growth.

Fourthly, facing triple shocks of the weakening of short-term cyclical factors, the accelerated decrease of three major traditional dividends and two temporary emergencies, China's macroeconomy has fully demonstrated its elasticity and resilience. Under the effect of countercyclical policy with the "six stability measures" as the core and continued supply-side structural reform as a hedge, China's macroeconomy has successfully defended its bottom line and achieved its goals. First, employment is stable and there is no wave of unemployment, thus defending the bottom line. Second, financial situation is stable, ensuring that at least no systemic or regional financial risks has occurred. Third, the increase of institutional dividend has begun to accelerate, and resource allocation efficiency and TFP growth rates has begun to improve significantly.

Fifthly, however, it is worth noting that in the process of declining economic growth, the structural differentiation of the economy is serious. The upgrading type of structural adjustment slows down, while the depression-type structural adjustment continues to accelerate, leading to a difficult period for China's economic adjustment in 2019. First, although the growth rate of the tertiary industry is still higher than that of the secondary industry, the decline in growth rate of the tertiary industry is significantly larger than that of the secondary industry. Second, although the growth rate of many emerging and high-tech industries is still higher than that of traditional industries, the decline in the growth rate of emerging and high-tech industries has accelerated significantly and starts to converge with that of traditional industries. Third, industry differentiation, regional differentiation and performance differentiation among enterprises of different sizes are serious, leading to deteriorating performance of many industries, regions, and small and medium-sized enterprises.

In 2020, the mission of building a moderately prosperous society in all respects will be accomplished, even while GDP growth continues to fall. China's macroeconomy will undergo significant changes while still following the basic operation mode of 2019. On the one hand, trends and structural forces leading to the economic downturn in 2019 will continue, which will further reduce potential GDP growth rate in 2020. On the other hand, many cyclical forces that led to the economic downturn in 2019 will begin to reverse in 2020. Macroeconomic downturn will be eased, and the decline will be significantly narrower than that in 2019.

Firstly, the change in economic growth that is the "new normal" and the conversion of growth engine continue, while risks tend to linger. Forces that determine the globalization, industrialization, and demographic dividends have not shown signs of stabilizing. Therefore, China's potential GDP growth rate in 2020 will further decline, falling below 6% in 2020.

Secondly, 2020 is the year of the US presidential election and the

UK's exit from the European Union, when global geopolitical conflicts and uncertainties facing the world economy will increase. Thus, confidence will be low, investment will decline, and trade contraction will worsen. The external environment of China's macroeconomy will not improve in 2020.

Thirdly, the reversal of some cyclical forces and the improvement of China's institutional dividend will be the most noteworthy changes in 2020. First, with the reorganization of its bureaucracy and the full implementation of the guidelines of the fourth plenary session of the 19th CPC Central Committee, China's institutional dividend will increase and the growth rate of TFP will be significantly improved. Second, with the stability of leverage ratios, the decline in the growth rate of debts payable, the orderly closing of high-risk institutions, the replenishment of financial institutions' capital, and the improvement of regulatory deficiencies, financial risks tend to be restrained, and financial environment will be significantly improved. Third, the inventory cycle of enterprises will bottom out and rebound. Excessive destocking in the early stage will provide space for enterprises to replenish inventory in 2020. Fourth, the period of panic over Sino-US trade friction has passed, and adaptive adjustments are basically in place. As a result, business confidence will be restored. Fifth, various strategies launched to cope with external shocks will raise demand in several sectors, especially those launched in key technologies, science and technology, research and development, domestic substitution, and important equipment. Sixth, with the reversal of global auto market cycle, China's auto market may stabilize. Seventh, pig market cycle reverses and pork supply and demand return to normal. A sharp drop in pork prices will provide space for macro policies and improve consumer expectations. Eighth, with the upgrading of infrastructure investment, the increase of state-owned enterprise investment, and the improvement of expectations of private entrepreneurs, private enterprise investment will no longer lag the rest of the economy in 2020. Ninth, a new round of more proactive fiscal policy and a prudent monetary policy with marginal easing will further extend the policy impacts. These policies, together with the social policy dividend in 2020 brought about by a moderately prosperous society in all respects, and the global policy dividend from global monetary easing, suggest that the policy dividend in 2020 will be higher than those in previous years. Tenth, China's huge market, diversified exports, established industries, abundant human resources, growing acceptance of innovation and competition, and effective government oversight will strengthen the resilience and elasticity of China's economy in 2020.

Fourthly, 2020 will also be a year of uncertainty and risks. First, will the American presidential election further intensify Sino-US trade conflicts, especially because of Trump's personality and possible unexpected events caused by the heat of the battle between the two parties. Second, will the decline in pork prices follow a predictable path. Will there be deflation because of the pork price decline, or will the overall price level continue to rise due to spillover effects of rising pork prices. Third, will structural differentiation and further decline in GDP growth induce new risks to local industries, regions and small and medium-sized enterprises.

Considering domestic and international trends and cyclical factors at the current stage, the target range of China's economic growth for 2020 should be set from 5.5% to 6.0%, with a conservative target around 5.8%. This will not only enable the achievement of missions in this phase under "two centenary goals" and guarantee the basic stability of employment in the society, but also will be conducive for maintaining a strategic focus and promoting high-quality economic development in accordance with established policies.

Based on the above qualitative judgments, the report uses China's Macroeconomic Analysis and Forecasting Model of Renmin University of China (CMAFM) to forecast. Withoutconsideration of the adjustment to national economic accounting methods in 2019 and the revision of historical data by the fourth national economic census, it makes the following macroeconomic policy assumptions: (1) the nominal deficit to GDP ratio of the general public budget for 2019 and 2020 is 2.8% and 3.0%, respectively. (2) Average exchange rates of CNY against USD in 2019 and 2020 is 6.9 : 1 and 7.0 : 1, respectively. The core

Chapter One Overview and Forecast | **171**

macroeconomic indicators of China in 2019 and 2020 are predicted by year, and forecast results are shown in table 1.

Table 1   Forecast of core macroeconomic indicators for China in 2019—2020

Indicator	2016	2017	2018	2019*	2020*
1. GDP Growth Rate (%)	6.7	6.8	6.6	6.1	5.9
Primary Industry	3.3	4.0	3.5	3.2	3.3
Secondary Industry	6.3	5.9	5.8	5.5	5.3
Tertiary Industry	7.7	7.9	7.6	6.9	6.6
2. Investment Actually Completed in Fixed Assets (100 million CNY)	596,501	631,684	635,636	670,596	707,479
(Growth Rate,%)	8.1	7.2	5.9	5.5	5.5
Total Retail Sales of Consumer Goods (100 million CNY)	332,316	366,262	380,987	411,847	444,794
(Growth Rate,%)	10.4	10.2	9.0	8.1	8.0
3. Exports (100 million USD)	20,976	22,633	24,867	24,618	24,126
(Growth Rate,%)	-7.7	7.9	9.9	-1.0	-2.0
Imports (100 million USD)	15,879	18,438	21,357	20,289	20,492
(Growth Rate,%)	-5.5	16.1	15.8	-5.0	1.0
Net Exports (100 million USD)	5,097	4,196	3,509	4,329	3,634
(Growth Rate,%)	-14.2	-17.7	-16.4	23.4	-16.0
4. Consumer Price Index, Growth Rate (%)	2.0	1.6	2.1	2.7	2.3
Producer Price Index, Growth Rate (%)	-1.4	6.3	3.5	-0.5	-1.0
GDP Deflator, Growth Rate (%)	1.1	3.8	2.9	1.5	1.1
5. Money and Quasi-Money (M2) Supply, Growth Rate (%)	11.3	8.1	8.1	8.5	8.5
Money (M1) Supply, Growth Rate (%)	21.4	11.8	1.5	3.5	4.0
Social Financing Stock, Growth Rate (%)	12.8	13.4	9.9	10.9	10.5
Social Financing (100 million CNY)	178,022	223,969	192,584	235,446	240,000
6. Government Revenue (100 million CNY)	206,171	234,029	258,757	272,348	286,325

Continued

Indicator	2016	2017	2018	2019*	2020*
(Growth Rate,%)	6.0	13.5	10.6	5.3	5.1
Public Revenue (100 million CNY)	159,552	172,567	183,352	189,403	195,085
(Growth Rate,%)	4.5	7.4	6.2	3.3	3.0
Revenue of Government Funds (100 million CNY)	46,619	61,462	75,405	82,945	91,240
(Growth Rate,%)	11.9	34.8	22.6	10.0	10.0

Note: * represents predicted value.

Source: Wind, CMAFM.

Firstly, under the combined effects of cyclical forces and trends, such as the slowdown of global economic and trade growth, the intensification of Sino-US trade friction, and the fall of internal demand, China's macroeconomy in 2019 continued its weak trend since 2018, showing a sign of "continuous slowdown". Real GDP growth rate is forecasted at 6.1% for 2019, 0.5 percentage points lower than that in 2018, achieving the government's economic growth target of 6.0%—6.5%. At the same time, as the growth rate of GDP deflator index is expected to drop to 1.5%, the growth rate of nominal GDP will be 7.6%, 2.1 percentage points lower than that in 2018, thus increasing short-term downward pressure on the economy. Under the influence of both trends and cyclical factors, and the strengthening of international and domestic adverse factors, economic growth for 2020 is expected to further decline. However, with the effects of the "six stability" initiative, the impact of reform dividend, and the transformation of a series of short-term cyclical forces, the elasticity and resilience of China's economy will continue. It is expected that the real GDP growth rate in 2020 will be 5.9%, 0.2 percentage points lower than that in 2019. Meanwhile, as the growth rate of GDP deflator index is expected to drop to 1.1%, the growth rate of nominal GDP in 2020 will be 7%, 0.6 percentage points lower than that in 2019, a significantly smaller decline.

Secondly, from the perspective of supply side, under the impact of insufficient aggregate demand and sluggish global manufacturing, industrial growth is stable but trending down. Thanks to some hedging effects of the recovery of construction growth, the growth rate of the secondary industry declined slightly. The real growth rate of the secondary industry is expected to be 5.5% in 2019, which is 0.3 percentage points lower than that in 2018. However, the continuous decline in industrial growth has depressed the growth of producer services, leading to a slowdown in the growth momentum of the tertiary industry, which is expected to grow by 6.9% in 2019, 0.7 percentage points lower than in 2018. Growth in the primary industry is expected to slow to 3.2%, 0.3 percentage points lower than in 2018, due to factors such as the outbreak of swine fever. Under the influence of trend forces, the pattern of deepening economic restructuring in 2020 will continue, with the secondary industry expected to grow by 5.3% and the tertiary industry expected to grow by 6.6%, 0.2 and 0.3

percentage points lower compared with 2019 respectively.

Thirdly, three components of aggregate demand, namely consumption, investment and exports, have all declined to varying degrees. In 2019, the growth rate of durable goods consumption such as automobiles slowed down significantly under the impact of slowing personal income growth and deteriorating expectations. It is estimated that the total retail sales of consumer goods for 2019 will increase by 8.1%, 0.9 percentage points lower than that of 2018. After deducting price factors, actual growth will be 6.3%, 0.6 percentage points lower than that of 2018. The growth rate of infrastructure investment has gradually stabilized and picked up, but it is hardly enough to offset a significant decline in manufacturing investment. China's total investment in fixed assets has continued to slow down and is expected to grow at 5.5% in 2019, a further drop of 0.4 percentage points from 2018. Under the impact of global economic and trade slowdown and the intensification of Sino-US trade friction, China's export growth rate has dropped significantly in 2019, while its import growth rate dropped even more sharply, resulting in an obvious expansion of the scale of net exports. In 2019, dollar-denominated export is expected to grow by -1.0% and import by -5.0%. Net exports will be 432.9 billion USD, a sharp increase of 23.4% over 2018 and the first expansion in nearly three years. Due to the cyclical downturn in internal and external demand, investment and consumption growth will bottom out and stabilize, but it will be difficult to effectively recover in 2020. Investment is expected to grow by 5.5% and consumption by 8.0%. Exports is expected to grow by -2.0% and imports by 1.0%.

Fourthly, due to the outbreak of swine fever, a sharp rise in pork prices has led to a rise in food prices and broader CPI. CPI is expected to rise 2.7% in 2019, even though the shortfall in China's aggregate demand has worsened rather than eased. Non-food CPI and core CPI continue to fall, so do prices of major international commodities including crude oil, fell, resulting in a significant decline in prices of industrial goods. PPI is expected to decline by 0.5% in 2019, down 4.0 percentage points from 2018. On the whole, GDP deflator is expected to rise by 1.5%, 1.4 percentage points lower than that of 2018. The overall price level is stable, but the differentiation of price situation has reached a new high. In 2020, the structural inflation caused by the sharp rise in pork and other food prices will fall significantly in the second half of the year, and it is expected that annual CPI growth will fall to 2.3%. At the same time, under the influence of insufficient aggregate demand and imported deflation, the deflation risk in the industrial sector will rise in 2020, and estimated PPI will fall by 1.0%. Taken together, the growth of the GDP deflator index will further decline, and it is expected to fall back by 1.1%.

Fifthly, while striking a balance between ensuring stable growth and preventing risks, and maintaining prudent and neutral monetary policy in 2019, the process of reform has accelerated and thus has new connotations. M2 is expected to grow at 8.5% in 2019, up by 0.4 percentage points from 2018. Thanks to the easing of monetary policy margins and the reform of the Loan Prime Rate (LPR), total social financing has grown rapidly. The growth rate of total social financing stock is expected to be 10.9% in 2019, an increase of 1.0 percentage point over 2018. The positioning of monetary policy in 2020 will still be marginal easing. M2 is expected to grow at 8.5%, unchanged from 2019. But as pressure of endogenous economic contraction increasing, the growth rate of total social financing stock is expected to be 10.5% in 2020, slightly lower than that in 2019.

Sixthly, under the influence of the economic downturn and cutting taxes and fees, the growth rate of public revenue keeps falling. And the recession of land market has led to a sharp decline in the growth of revenue of government funds, thus resulting in an overall slowdown in the growth of government revenue. It is estimated that public revenue will grow at 3.3% to 18.9 trillion yuan in 2019, and revenue of government funds will grow at 10.0% to 8.3 trillion yuan in 2019. The combined revenue of these two sectors will reach 27.2 trillion yuan, an increase of 5.3%, 5.3 percentage points lower than the growth rate in 2018. The pressure on the government to balance the books will increase. As the macroeconomic fundamentals and proactive fiscal policies have not changed much, growth of public revenue and revenue of government funds in 2020 is expected to be basically the same as 2019, growing by 3.0% and 10.0% respectively, with a combined growth of 5.1%.

Chapter Two China's Macroeconomy under the Situation of Slowing Growth and Structural Differentiation

Global economic growth and trade both fell in 2019 to their lowest levels in nearly a decade. In this context, China's core macroeconomic indicators have also slowed somewhat, but by less than other major economies and better than market pessimism at the end of 2018. However, it is worth noting that the problem of insufficient aggregate demand in China's macroeconomy has intensified to some extent. Moreover, endogenous contractions from the economic downturn increase the risk of accelerated macroeconomic decline.

Table 2　　Basic data of China's macroeconomic indicators in 2019

Indicator	2015	2016	2017	2018	2019.1—6	2019.1—9
1. GDP Growth (%)	6.9	6.7	6.9	6.6	6.3	6.2
Primary Industry	3.9	3.3	3.9	3.5	3.0	2.9
Secondary Industry	6.2	6.1	6.1	5.8	5.8	5.6

Chapter Two China's Macroeconomy under the Situation of Slowing Growth and Structural Differentiation

Continued

Indicator	2015	2016	2017	2018	2019.1—6	2019.1—9
Tertiary Industry	8.2	7.8	8.0	7.6	7.0	7.0
2. Investment Actually Completed in Fixed Assets (100 million CNY)	551,590	596,501	631,684	645,675	299,100	461,204
(Growth Rate,%)	10.0	8.1	7.2	5.9	5.8	5.4
Total Retail Sales of Consumer Goods (100 million CNY)	300,931	332,316	366,261	380,987	195,210	296,674
(Growth Rate,%)	10.7	10.4	10.2	9.0	8.5	8.2
3. Exports (100 million USD)	22,735	20,976	22,633	24,867	11,711	18,251
(Growth Rate,%)	-2.9	-7.7	7.9	9.9 (7.1)	0.1 (6.1)	-0.1 (5.2)
Imports (100 million USD)	16,796	15,879	18,419	21,357	9,900	15,266
(Growth Rate,%)	-14.3	-5.5	16.0	15.8 (12.9)	-4.3 (1.4)	-5 (-0.1)
4. Money and Quasi-Money (M2) Supply, Growth Rate (%)	13.3	11.3	8.2	8.1	8.5	8.4
Money (M1) Supply, Growth Rate (%)	15.2	21.4	11.8	1.5	4.4	3.4
Social Financing (100 million CNY)	154,086	178,022	194,430	193,000	125,100	187,378
Social Financing Stock, Growth Rate (%)	12.4	12.8	12.0	9.8	10.9	10.8
5. Consumer Price Index, Growth Rate (%)	1.4	2.0	1.6	2.1	2.2	2.5
Producer Price Index, Growth Rate (%)	-5.2	-1.4	6.3	3.5	0.3	0
GDP Deflator, Growth Rate (%)	0.1	1.2	4.1	3.4	2.1	1.7
6. Government Revenue (100 million CNY)	194,547	206,171	234,029	258,757	139,627	203,841

Continued

Indicator	2015	2016	2017	2018	2019.1—6	2019.1—9
GrowthRate (%)	0.1	6.0	13.5	10.6	3.1	4.4
Public Revenue (100 million CNY)	152,217	159,552	172,567	183,352 (6.2)	107,846 (3.4)	150,678 (3.3)
Revenue of Government Funds (100 million CNY)	42,330	46,61,9	61,462	75,405 (22.6)	31,781 (1.7)	53,163 (7.7)

Note: growth rate in CNY is shown in parentheses.

Source: Wind, CMAFM.

◇ I. The global economy has entered a new phase of downturns, and China's economic growth has slowed significantly

Due to the intensification of Sino-US trade friction across the board, and the uncertainty of global economic and trade policies, geopolitical risks have surged to new highs. This has not only directly hampered the two engines of economic growth, China and the US, but also made global risks rise and market confidence fall, exacerbating the overall contraction in tradable goods, investment goods and consumer durables around the world. All of these have led to a downturn in global manufacturing and the start of a new downward cycle for the world economy.

Chapter Two China's Macroeconomy under the Situation of Slowing Growth and Structural Differentiation

Major international organizations have cut their economic and trade growth forecasts for 2019 in response to a general slowdown in the major economies and uncertainty over trade friction. According to the latest report of International Monetary Fund (IMF) in October, global economic growth is expected to decline to 3.0% in 2019, a sharp decline of 0.6 percentage points from 2018 and the lowest level since the end of the global financial crisis in 2010. Global trade growth is expected to decline to 1.1% in 2019, down 2.5 percentage points from 2018, a steeper decline than economic growth and the lowest level since 2010.

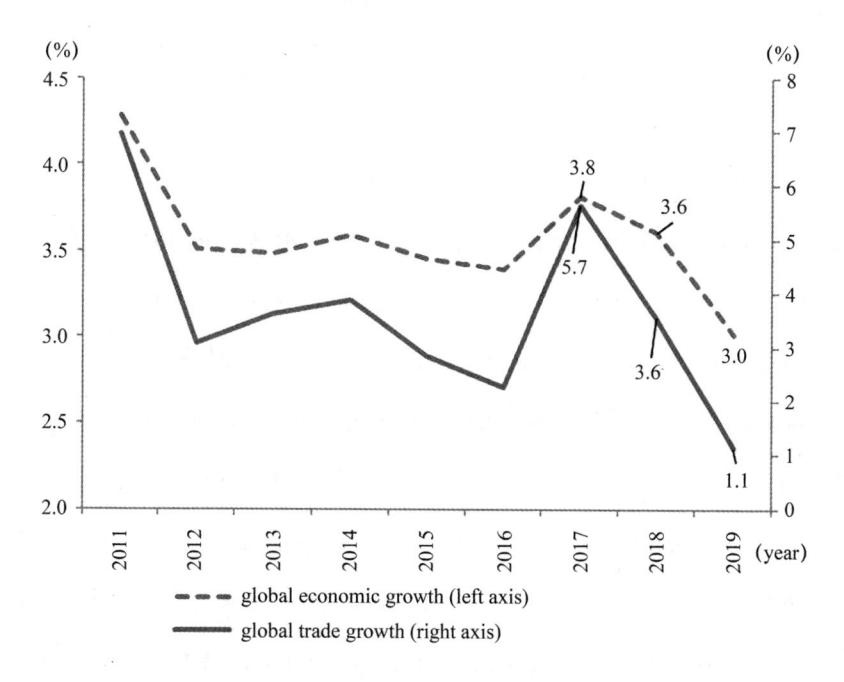

Figure 1 A sharp decline in global economic and trade growth

Because of the overall contraction in global tradable goods, investment goods and consumer durables, manufacturing around the world is in a downturn, and the divergence between manufacturing and services has reached a new historical level. Global manufacturing PMI has been on a downward trend since 2018 and has been below 50%, a range that indicates economic contraction, for five consecutive months since May of 2019. In September it fell to 49.7%. Meanwhile, services PMI also fell, but it is still in a range that indicates economic expansion. It was 51.6% in September, as its gap with manufacturing PMI continues to widen. The above situation is especially evident in the eurozone, and also emerges in Japan, the US and the UK. Since February, manufacturing PMI of the eurozone has fallen into the range that indicates economic contraction and has continued a deteriorating trend. As of October, manufacturing PMI had fallen to 45.7%, but services PMI remained in the range that indicates economic expansion, at 51.8% in October. Germany's manufacturing PMI fell into the range that indicates economic contraction since January, and fell to 41.9% in October, while its services PMI remained in the range that indicates economic expansion, at 51.2% in October. Japan's manufacturing PMI also fell into the range that indicates economic contraction since January, at 48.5% in October, while its services PMI remained in the economic expansion range, at 52.8% in September. Similarly, America's manufacturing PMI fell into the range that indicates economic

Chapter Two China's Macroeconomy under the Situation of Slowing Growth and Structural Differentiation | **183**

contraction since August, but at an even faster pace, at 47.8% in September, while its services PMI remained in the range that indicates economic expansion, at 52.6% in September. Manufacturing PMI of the UK fell into the range that indicates economic contraction since

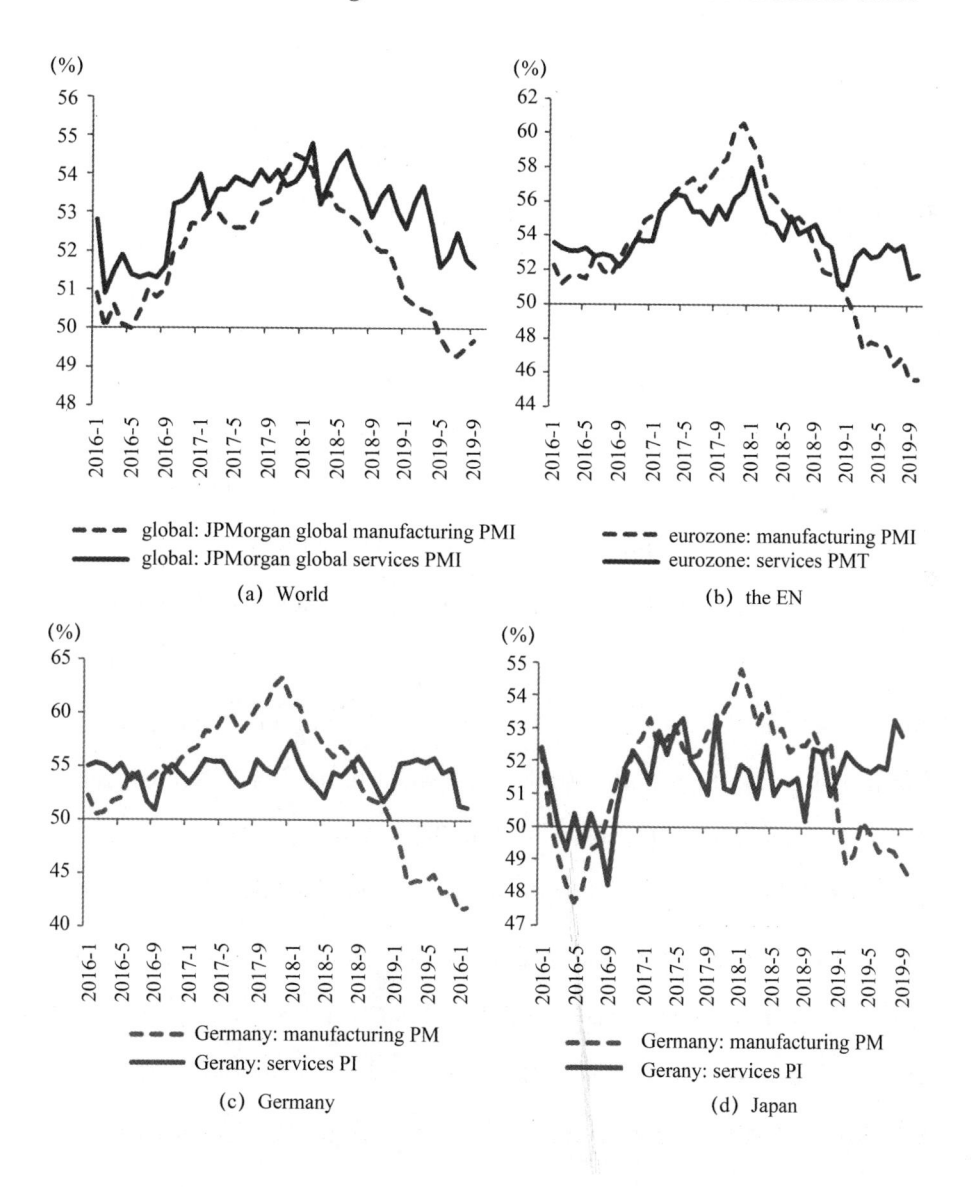

- - - global: JPMorgan global manufacturing PMI
——— global: JPMorgan global services PMI
(a) World

- - - eurozone: manufacturing PMI
——— eurozone: services PMT
(b) the EN

- - - Germany: manufacturing PM
——— Gerany: services PI
(c) Germany

- - - Germany: manufacturing PM
——— Gerany: services PI
(d) Japan

(%)
63
61
59
57
55
53
51
49
47
45

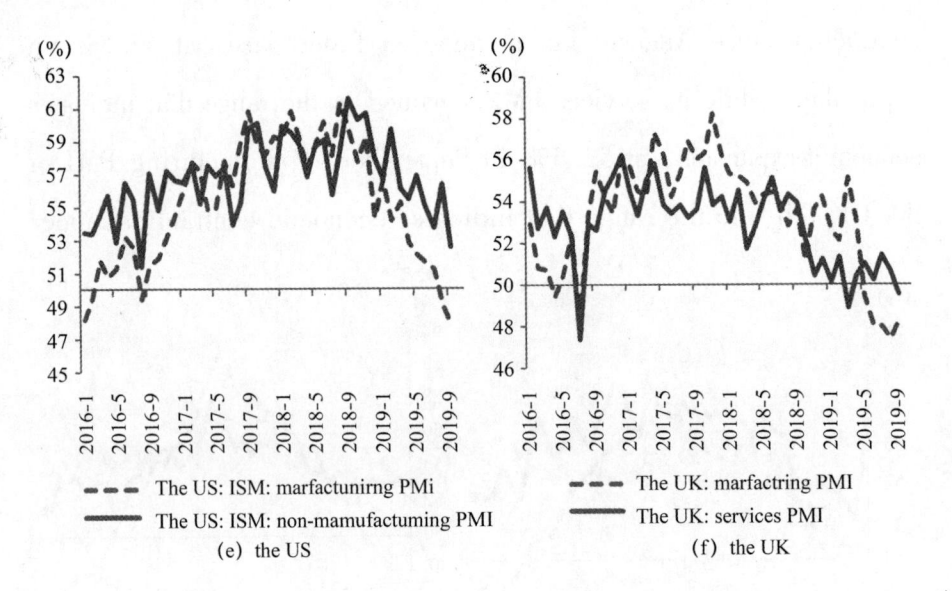

- - - The US: ISM: marfactunirng PMi
——— The US: ISM: non-mamufactuming PMI
(e) the US

(%)
60
58
56
54
52
50
48
46

- - - The UK: marfactring PMI
——— The UK: services PMI
(f) the UK

Figure 2　Manufacturing around the world in a downturn

May, at 48.3% in September, and its services PMI also fell into the economic contraction range, at 49.5% in September.

China's economic growth has continued to slow in 2019 due to a significant slowdown in global trade and economic growth. In the first three quarters, China's real GDP grew 6.2% cumulative year-on-year, down 0.4 percentage points from last year. The real GDP growth rate in the first, second and third quarters was 6.4%, 6.2% and 6.0% respectively, showing quarterly declines. Meanwhile, nominal GDP growth rate in the first three quarters was 7.9%, down 1.8 percentage points from a year earlier, as GDP deflator fell. Nominal GDP growth rates in the first quarter, second quarter and third quarter were 7.8%, 8.3% and 7.6% respectively, reflecting a fluctuating, downward trend.

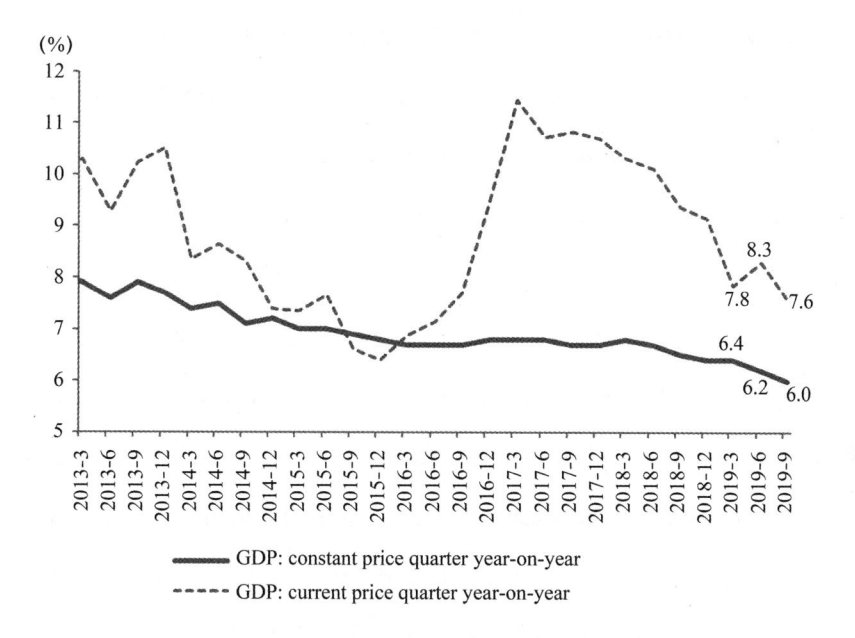

Chapter Two China's Macroeconomy under the Situation of Slowing Growth and Structural Differentiation

Figure 3 China's economic growth is slowing

Despite mounting downward pressure and slowing growth, China's economy remains steady and far ahead of the rest of the world's major economies. Global GDP growth rate has fallen by 0.6 percentage points in 2019. The United States and the eurozone have fallen by 0.6 and 0.7 percentage points respectively. India has fallen by more than 1.0 percentage point. Many countries have fallen into technical recession, while China has only fallen by 0.5 percentage points, ranking first among the world's major economies in terms of economic growth.

However, with the resumption of a new phase of global economic downturn, China's macroeconomy continues to face the same problem of insufficient aggregate demand that began in the second half of

2018. This has led to a relatively strong contraction effect.

First, consumption and investment demandhas fallen across the board, and the gap with output was mainly filled by a sharp reduction in imports; that is, a fragile balance has been achieved by relying on a large short-term increase in net exports. Second, the shortage of aggregate demand began to spread to the supply side at an accelerated pace. The growth of manufacturing and services has declined across the board, and business performance and market expectations deteriorated. Third, a decline in the growth of both manufacturing production and investment has been transmitted to producer services. Fourth, core CPI and PPI have both declined, and in turn, through the effect of price deflation, increased pessimism and reduced confidence in investment and consumption.

1. From the perspective of demand, the growth rate of consumption and investment continues to slow down

In the first three quarters of 2019, total retail sales of consumer goods grew by 8.2% cumulative year-on-year, down 1.1 percentage points from the same period in 2018. Growth in the third quarter was only 7.6%, down 1.0 percentage point from the second quarter. Deducting price factors, the total retail sales of consumer goods in the first three quarters grew by 6.4% year-on-year, 0.9 percentage points lower than the same period in 2018.

----- total retail sales of consumer: curulative year-on-year
——— total retail sales of consumer goods: cumulative year-on-year in real terms

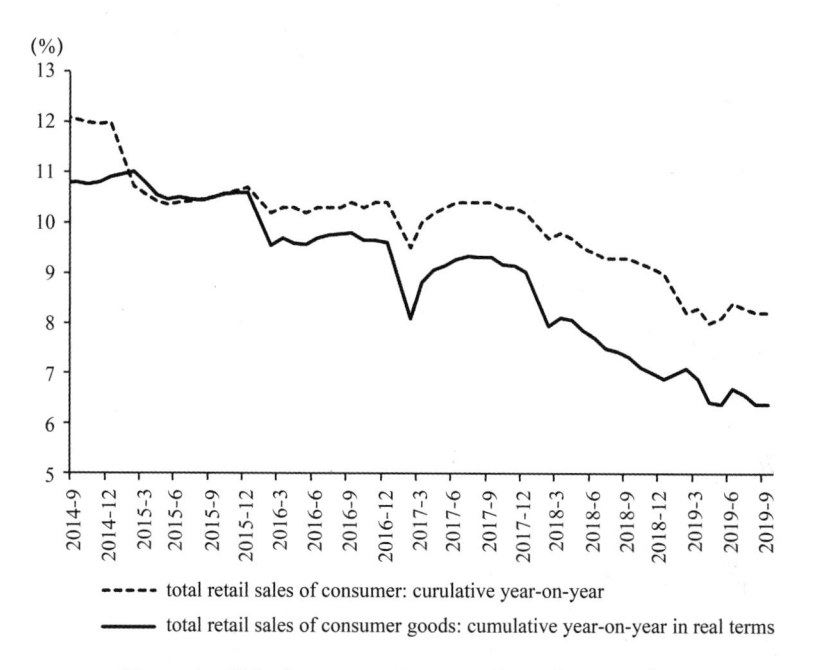

Figure 4　China's consumption growth continues to slow

Total investment in fixed assets grew 5.4% cumulative year-on-year in the first three quarters, falling back to the level of the same period in 2018. Specifically, private investment grew by 4.7% year-on-year, down 4.0 percentage points from the same period in 2018, showing a renewed accelerated decline; real estate investment rose by 10.5%, up 0.6 percentage points from the same period in 2018, providing some support to total investment.

2. On the supply side, the continuous shortage of aggregate demand has caused record lows of growth rate of industry and services

In the first three quartersin 2019, industrial added value above

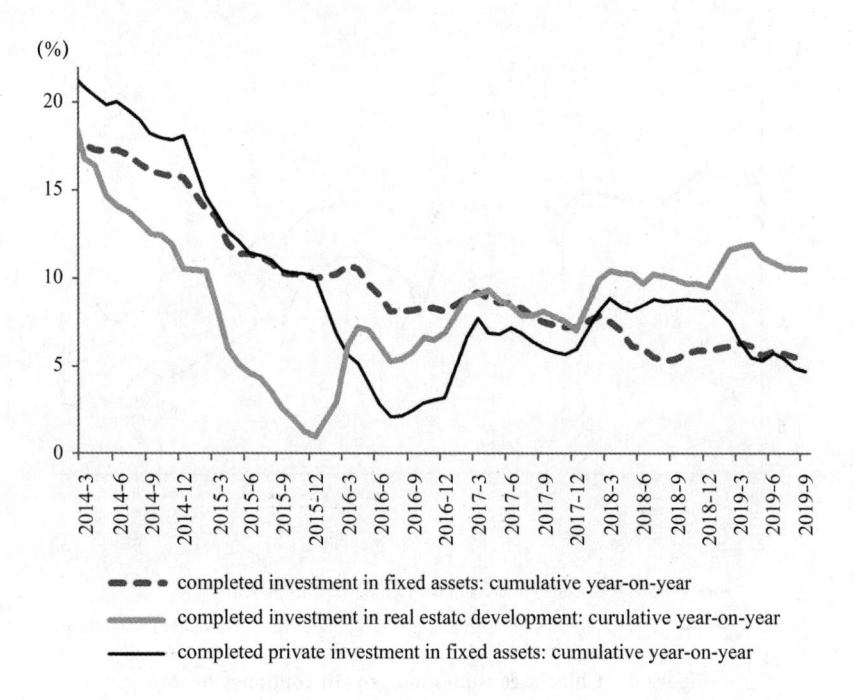

Figure 5 Increasing downward pressure on China's investment growth

(legend: completed investment in fixed assets: cumulative year-on-year; completed investment in real estate development: cumulative year-on-year; completed private investment in fixed assets: cumulative year-on-year)

designated size grew by 5.6% year-on-year, 0.8 percentage points lower than the same period in 2018. It has been declining continuously since the first quarter. Value-added of manufacturing rose by 5.9% year-on-year, also down 0.8 percentage points from the same period in 2018, and also on a downward trend since the first quarter.

Consistent with the slowdown in the growth rate of industrial value-added, the performance of industrial enterprises continues to deteriorate, manifested by a slowdown in the growth rate of operating income, the negative growth of total profits, and an expanding trend of losses. In the first three quarters of 2019, the operating income of

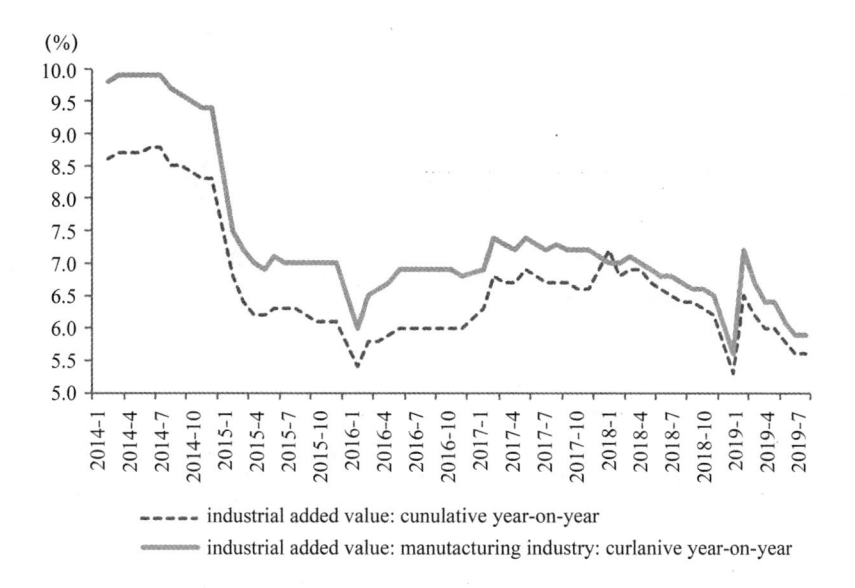

Chapter Two China's Macroeconomy under the Situation of Slowing Growth and Structural Differentiation

Figure 6 China's industrial growth continues to decline

industrial enterprises above designated size grew by 4.5% year-on-year, 5.1 percentage points lower than that of 2018. Total profits declined by 2.1% year-on-year, including 3.3% in the first quarter, 1.9% in the second quarter and 1.8% in the third quarter, showing quarterly declines. In the first three quarters, operating income margin was 5.9%, down 0.4 percentage points year-on-year. In terms of losses, in the first eight months of 2019, the number of loss-making enterprises increased by 5.7% year-on-year, 0.5 percentage points lower than the growth rate of 2018. However, the loss of loss-making enterprises increased by 11.6% year-on-year, 6.2 percentage points higher than the growth rate of 2018, indicating that there is a trend of loss concentration, and local industries and enterprises may face a critical point of operating risks.

(%)

—— industrial enterprise: total profits: cumulative year-on-year
----- industrial enterprise: number of loss-making enterprises: cumulative year-on-year
—— industrial cnterprise: amount of losses incurred by loss-making entemprises: cumulative year-on-year

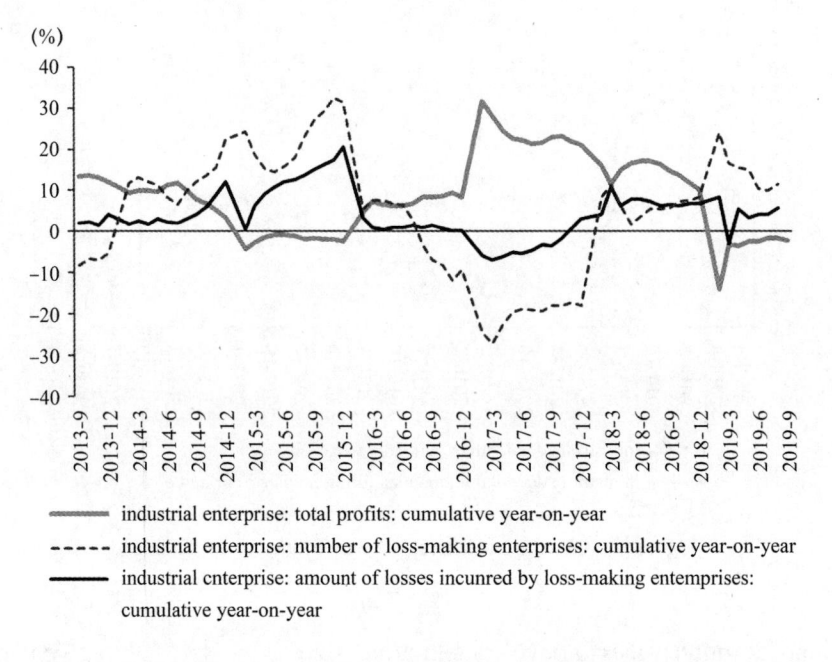

Figure 7　Performance of Chinese industrial enterprises has deteriorated

In line with the global manufacturing trend, China's manufacturing PMI has been declining since the middle of 2018 and has been in the range that indicates economic contraction for six months since May, at 49.3% in October. From the perspective of PMI sub-index, new orders, especially new export orders have brought a big drag. In October, PMI's new orders index slipped to 49.6%, and new export orders index fell to 47.0%, remaining in the range that indicates economic contraction for 17 consecutive months since June 2018, which is notable.

In the first three quarters of 2019, production in service sector remained within an appropriate range, but a trend of decline was obvious. During this period, value-added of the tertiary industry increased by 7.0%. Specifically, information transmission, computer services and software, leasing and business services, transportation, storage and post, and finance increased by 19.8%, 8.0%, 7.4% and 7.1% respectively, 12.8, 1.0, 0.4 and 0.1 percentage points higher than of the growth rate of the tertiary industry. In the first eight months of 2019, the operating revenue of service enterprises above designated size increased by 9.5% year-on-year, among which operating revenue of strategic emerging service industries, high-tech services, and science and technology service industries grew by 12.1%, 11.9% and 11.6%

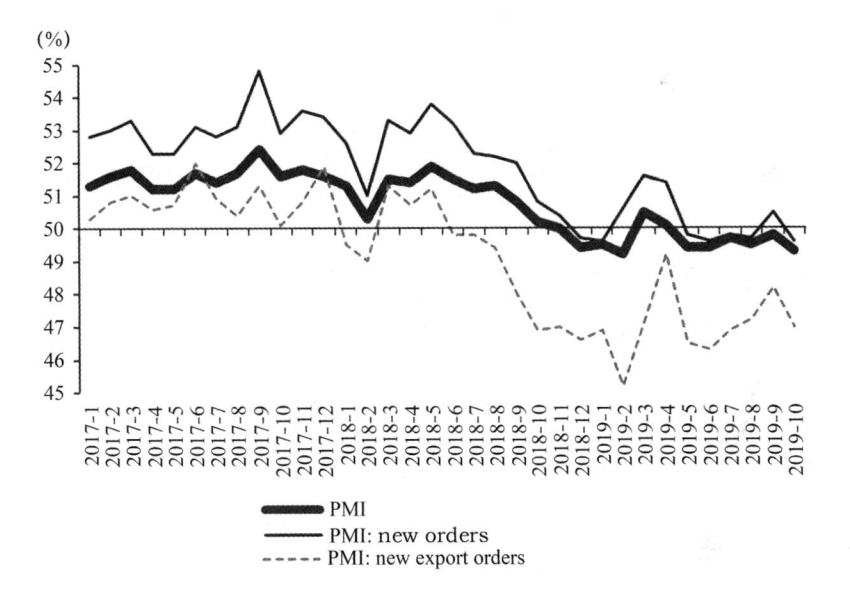

Figure 8 China's PMI of manufacturing sector remains in the range that indicates economic contraction

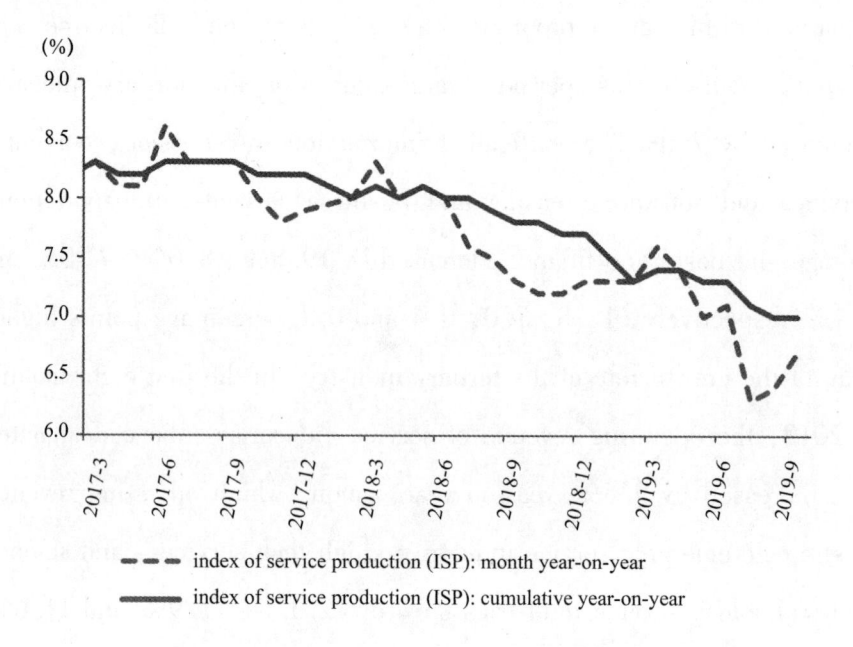

Figure 9 Downward pressure of China's index of service production increases

respectively, 2.6, 2.4 and 2.1 percentage points higher than that of all service industries enterprises above designated size.

The PMI of the service sector continues to run in the range that indicates economic expansion, showing an obvious divergence from the manufacturing sector. However, it is worth noting that as the manufacturing sector continues to weaken, the service sector, especially producer services, also faces considerable downward pressure. In the first three quarters of 2019, the index of service production grew by 7.0% year-on-year, 0.9 percentage points lower than the same period of 2018. In particular, the growth rate of the index of service production dropped to below 7.0% for the first time in the third quarter, that is, 6.3% in July, 6.4% in August and 6.7% in September. In October, the PMI index of service sector fell by 1.6 percentage points from September to 51.4%, indicating further downward pressure.

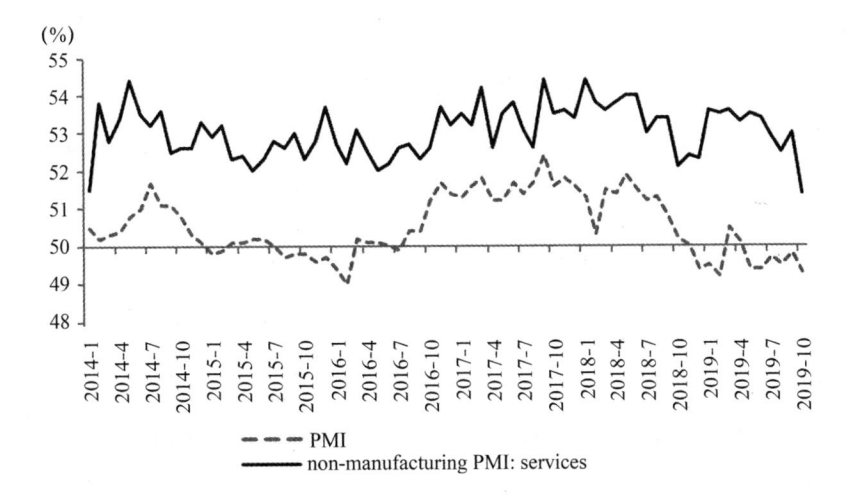

Figure 10 PMI for China's manufacturing and service sector

3. While food prices are rising, non-food CPI, core CPI and PPI continue to decline, reflecting accelerating downward pressure caused by insufficient aggregate demand

Since the beginning of 2019, food prices have been rising, especially in the third quarter when pork prices led to a large increase in food CPI, resulting in a sustained rise in CPI. In September, the food CPI rose by 11.2% and the CPI rose by 3.0% year-on-year. However, while food prices are rising rapidly, various price indexes corresponding to the macroeconomy continue to decline, reflecting the accelerated downward pressure of macroeconomy caused by insufficient aggregate demand and an endogenous mechanism of economic contraction. Since the beginning of 2019, non-food CPI, core CPI, PPI and other price indexes have continued to decline. The PPI, in particular, has fallen into the range that indicates deflation. Non-food CPI and core CPI growth fell to 1.0% and 1.5% respectively in September, down 0.7 and 0.4 percentage points from the start of the year. More importantly, there are some signs of deflation in the industrial sector. Since the beginning of 2019, PPI growth has fallen sharply from 3.5% in 2018 to nearly zero. Since the third quarter, it has turned from positive to negative, and the decline has been increasing. In September, the PPI declined by 1.2% year-on-year, 0.4 percentage points higher than that

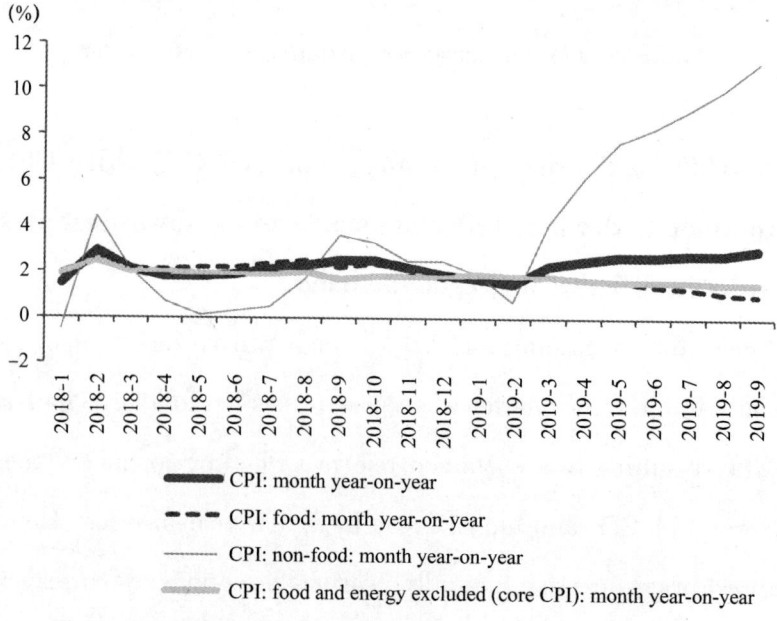

Figure 11 Differentiation of food CPI and non-food CPI in China

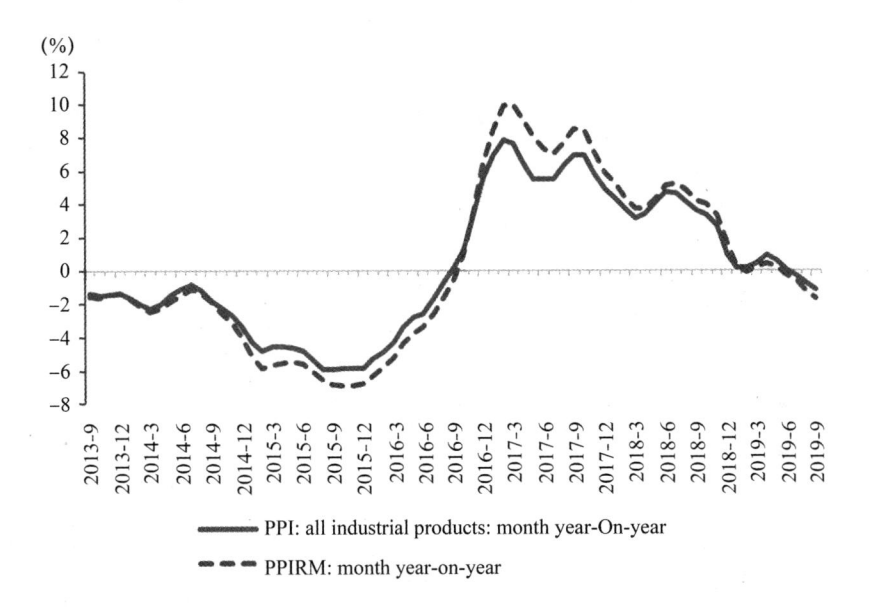

Chapter Two China's Macroeconomy under the Situation of Slowing Growth and Structural Differentiation

——— PPI: all industrial products: month year-On-year
--- PPIRM: month year-on-year

Figure 12 China's PPI index entered a negative range

of August.

4. With the increasing downward pressure on the economy, the expected income of urban residents has decreased, unemployment risk has increased, and market confidence remains relatively low

In recent years, the growth rate of urban residents' income continues to slow down and is significantly lower than the real GDP growth rate. In the first three quarters of 2019, per capita disposable income of urban residents grew by 5.4% in real terms, 0.3 percentage points lower than the same period last year and also lower than the real

GDP growth rate, which is 6.2%.

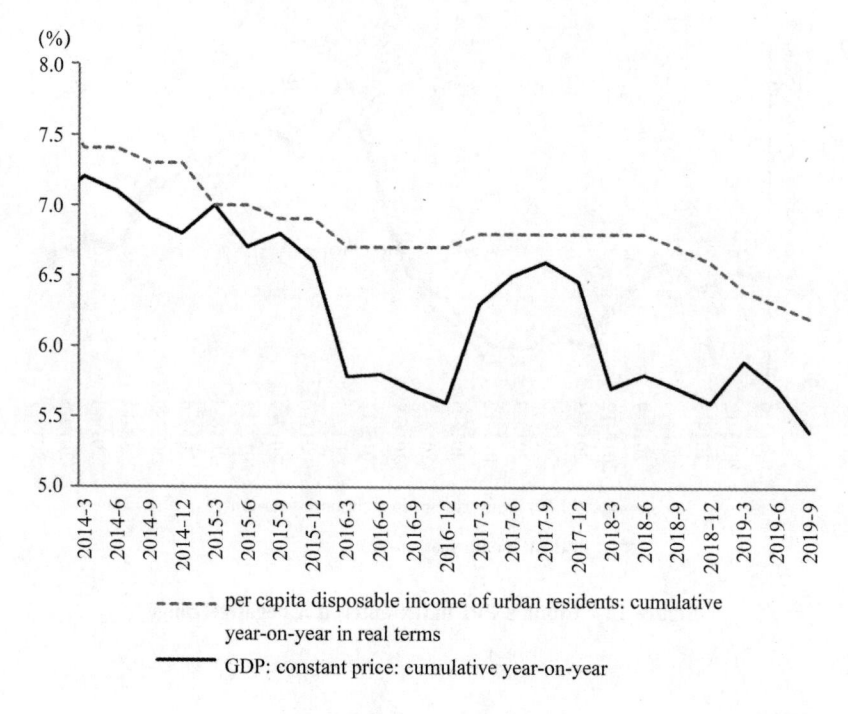

Figure 13　Growth of China's per capita disposable income of urban residents slows down

At the same time, the risk of urban unemployment continues, as the surveyed urban unemployment rate hit a high level of 5.3% in both February and July, an average 0.2 percentage points increase than 2018. In October, manufacturing and non-manufacturing PMI employment indices came in at 47.3% and 48.2% respectively, indicating a contraction in labor usage. In this context, the future income confidence index of urban residents fell to 52.6% in the second quarter, the lowest since the end of 2016.

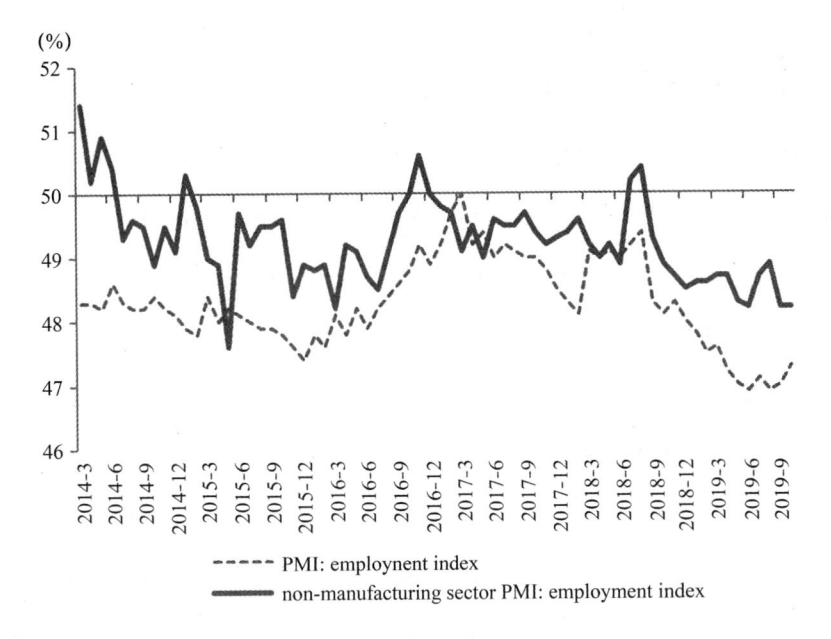

Figure 14 Downward pressure on China's employment prosperity is relatively high

II. Supported by the "six stability measures", the overall performance of China's economy has been better than pessimistic market expectations

Facing both internal and external economic pressure, China has actively responded with the "six stability" policy and strengthened counter-cyclical macro policies. It continues to introduce various reform measures to raise growth potential, ensuring a generally stable macroeconomic performance. Despite mounting downward pressure on China's economy and slowing economic growth, the "six stability measures" have achieved more than expected. The economy has withstood the downturn in the world economy in 2018 and the "squeeze" caused by Sino-US trade friction. This fully demonstrates the elasticity and resilience of China's economy.

Firstly, the "six stability" policy works. As early as July 2018, in a meeting of the political bureau of the CPC central committee, the central government proposed and deployed the "six stability" policy, calling for ensuring stability in employment, finance, foreign trade, foreign investment, domestic investment, and expectations. It reflects the central government's accurate and forward-looking judgments on the developing trends of the global economy, including Sino-US trade friction and the development law of China's economy in the critical period. It needs further readjustment and reorientation of macroeconomic policies, and more awareness of difficulties ahead. It requires working for the best but preparing for the worst. In line with the central committee's "six stability" initiative, various departments and regions have formulated and implemented a series of policies to ensure steady growth in a multi-pronged manner.

In terms of stabilizing foreign trade, at that time, China's trade maintained a double-digit growth rate, which was relatively high in the world. Still, the central government proposed to "stabilize foreign trade". The first aspect is trade diversification. Since 2013, the "Belt and Road" initiative has been put forward as a means to truly diversify China's export, import, trade and investment patterns. Second, while exporting on a large scale, China also needs to import on a large scale mainly through China International Import Expo (CIIE). And China needs to import high-quality commodities, so that they can be sold, produced, or even replaced domestically. The third aspect is a series of measures taken to hedge US taxes on Chinese exports. On the one hand, export tax rebate rate was further raised from 11% to 13%. On the other hand, China has cut taxes and fees at home and provided special support for some industries. In particular, improvement in business environment and foreign trade process has resulted in a substantial reduction in transaction costs, which is a comprehensive hedge against US trade protection.

In terms of fiscal policy, China has strengthened fiscal counter-cyclical regulation in 2019 by further reducing taxes and fees and stabilizing infrastructure investment. First, a plan of cutting taxes and fees worth more than 2 trillion yuan has been introduced in 2019, covering 12 tax categories such as value-added tax (VAT) and individual income taxe, as well as 19 fees such as pension insurance, to further reduce the burden on such market entities as enterprises and stimulate market vitality. Inclusive tax cuts for small and micro enterprises and individual income tax reductions have been implemented since January 1. Deepening VAT reform, including a 3 percentage point cut in value-added tax rate for manufacturing, has been implemented since April 1. A reduction in social security fees mainly based on reduction of enterprise pension insurance rates has been implemented since May 1. And from July 1, China has streamlined and regulated administrative fees and government funds. In the first three quarters of 2019, an additional total of 1,783.4 billion yuan was cut in taxes and fees, including 1,510.9 billion yuan in taxes and 272.5 billion yuan in social security fees. Among the new tax cuts, 703.5 billion yuan was from the VAT reform, 182.7 billion yuan from inclusive tax cuts for small and micro enterprises, and 442.6 billion yuan from a two-step reform of the individual income tax.

Secondly, in order to strengthen the counter-cyclical effects of fiscal policy, the growth rate of public financial expenditure reached 9.4% in the first three quarters, compared with a 3.3% growth rate of public financial revenue. Expenditure of government funds rose by 24.2% year-on-year, while the revenue of government funds rose by 7.7%. Therefore, in the first three quarters of 2019, the fiscal deficit to GDP ratio reached 4.0%, and the deficit ratio of government funds reached 1.2%. The combined deficit to GDP ratio of these two reached 5.2%, the highest level in recent years.

Finally, a proactive fiscal policy also includes promoting stabilization and recovery of infrastructure investment by increasing and

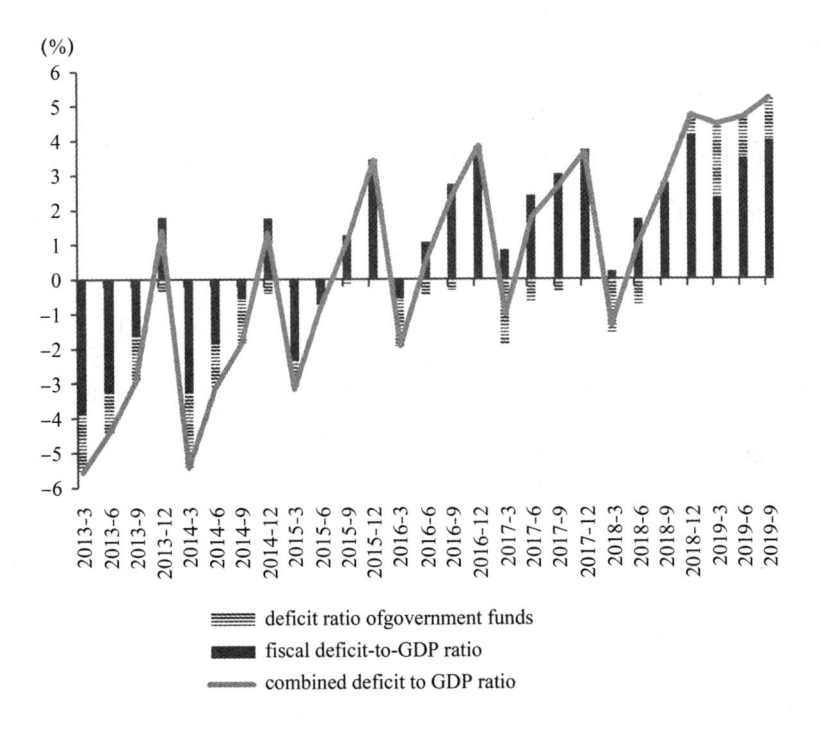

Figure 15 Fiscal deficit to GDP ratio and deficit ratio of government funds have increased significantly

accelerating the issuance of local government special bonds. In 2019, China has raised the ceiling for local government debt by 3,080 billion yuan, an increase of 900 billion yuan over last year, including 930 billion yuan for general debt and 2.15 trillion yuan for special debt, up 100 billion yuan and 800 billion yuan respectively over last year. At the same time, in the seventh session of the standing committee of the 13th National People's Congress (NPC), the state council was authorized to allocate the new quota for the next year in advance for each year after 2019, within 60% of the current year's new ceiling on local government debt. The authorization period is from January 1, 2019 to December 31, 2022. This means that in 2019, according to the actual needs of local projects, part of the new quota of special bonds has been allocated in advance, so as to ensure it's ready to use at the beginning of the year to boost effective investment and domestic demand. By the end of September, the new quota for new local government debt had been nearly used up, reaching 3,036.7 billion yuan, an increase of 1,025.4 billion yuan over the same period last year. This includes 907 billion yuan of general debt and 2,1297 trillion yuan of special debt.

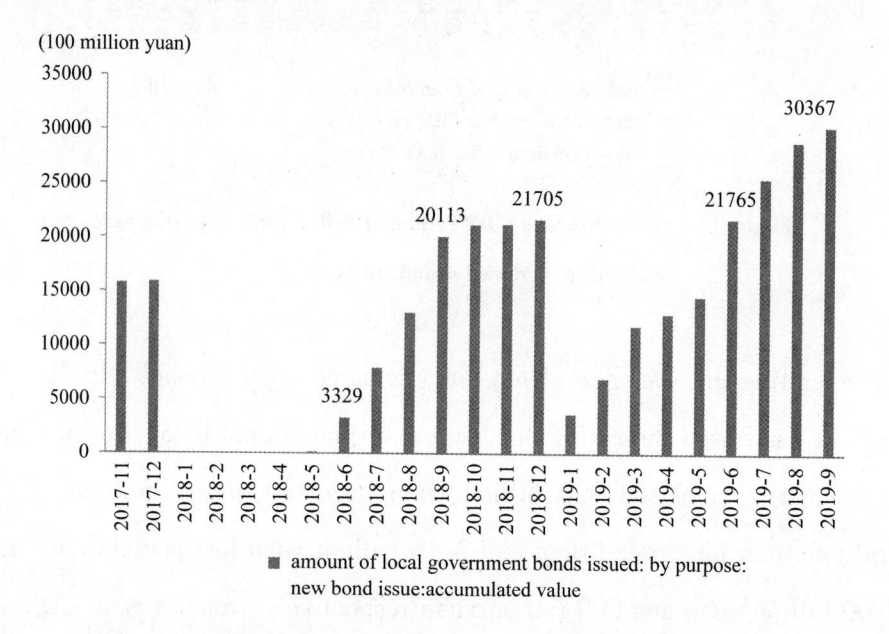

Figure 16　Increase of the amount of local government bonds issued and acceleration of issuance in 2019

In the first three quarters of 2019, infrastructure investment increased by 3.4% year-on-year, an increase of 3.2 percentage points over the same period last year. Excluding electricity, infrastructure investment rose by 4.5% year-on-year, up 1.2 percentage points from a year earlier. Although the growth rate of infrastructure investment has stabilized, infrastructure investment has picked up very slowly due to the strengthening of risk control on local government debt in recent years, especially the transformation of local government financing platforms. At present, the growth rate of infrastructure investment is still lower than the overall growth rate of investment, dragging down the recovery of investment.

However, with a new round of tax and fee cuts and continued regulation of the real estate market, both growth rates of fiscal revenue and revenue of government funds have dropped significantly in 2019. In the first three quarters of the year, public revenue grew by 3.3% year-on-year, down 5.4 percentage points from the same period of 2018. Specifically, tax revenue fell by 0.4%, down 13.1 percentage points from the same period last year. Revenue of China's government funds nationwide rose by 7.7% year-on-year, down 20.3 percentage points from the same period last year. Combined, these two revenues rose by 4.4% year-on-year, down 9.6 percentage points from the same period last year.

In 2019, monetary policy has remained prudent and neutral with marginal easing. In September, M2 grew by 8.4% year-on-year, a

— completed investment in fixed assets: infrastructure investment: cumulative year-on-year
■ ■ ■ completed investment in fixed assets: infrastructure investment (electricity excluded): cumulative year-on-year

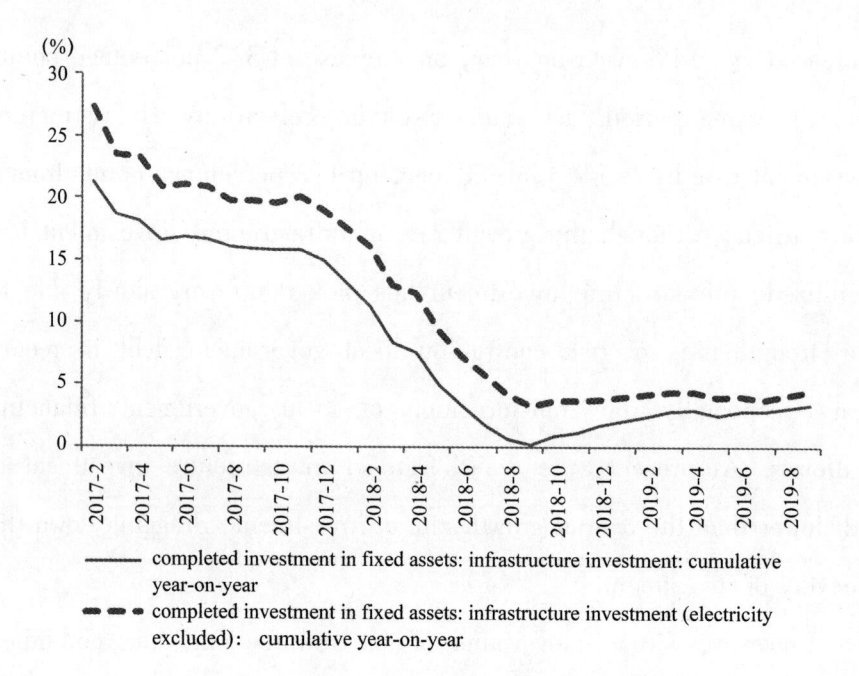

Figure 17 Infrastructure investment growth rate picks up slowly

■ ■ ■ tax revenue: cumulative year-on-year
— public revenue: cumulative year-on-year
▬▬ revenue of government ftunds: cumulative year-on-year

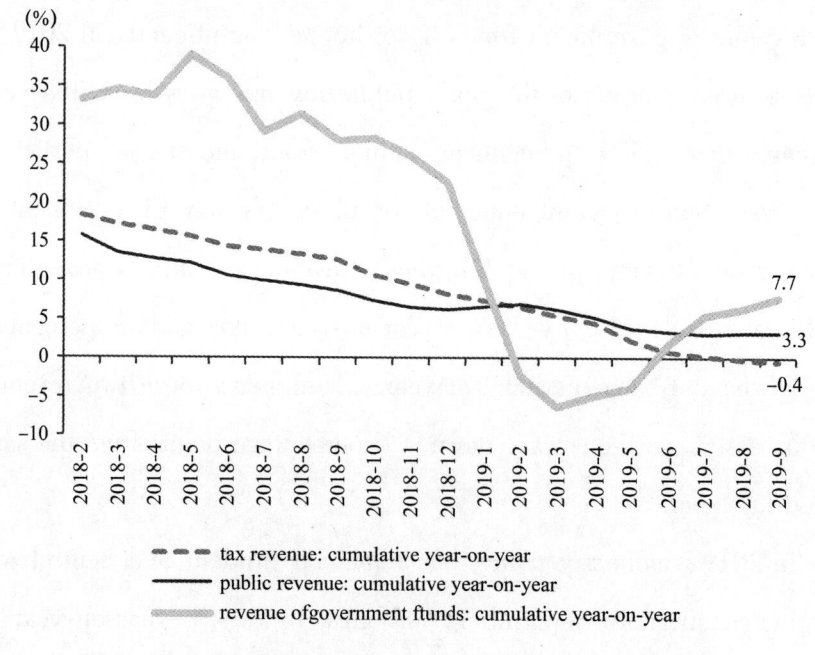

Figure 18 China's fiscal revenue growth rate slows significantly

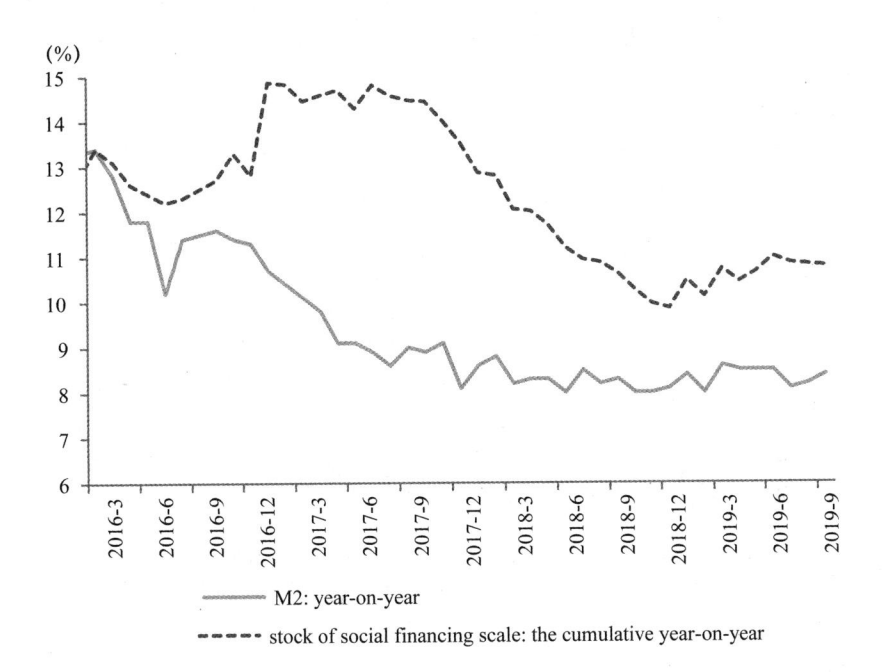

Chapter Two China's Macroeconomy under the Situation of Slowing Growth and Structural Differentiation

Figure 19 Marginal easing of monetary policy

slight increase of 0.1 percentage points over the same period last year. The stock of social financing increased by 10.8% year-on-year, slightly up 0.2 percentage points from the same period last year. M1, though, was up 3.4% year-on-year, down 0.6 percentage points from the same period last year. The year-on-year growth rate of social financing was 38% in the first quarter, 22% in the second quarter and 1% in the third quarter, showing a recovery trend, but also indicating that monetary policy has not shifted to comprehensive easing.

The marginal easing of monetary policy is reflected ina downward trend of market interest rates. The average issuing rate of various credit bonds in 2019 has decreased compared with the same period in 2018.

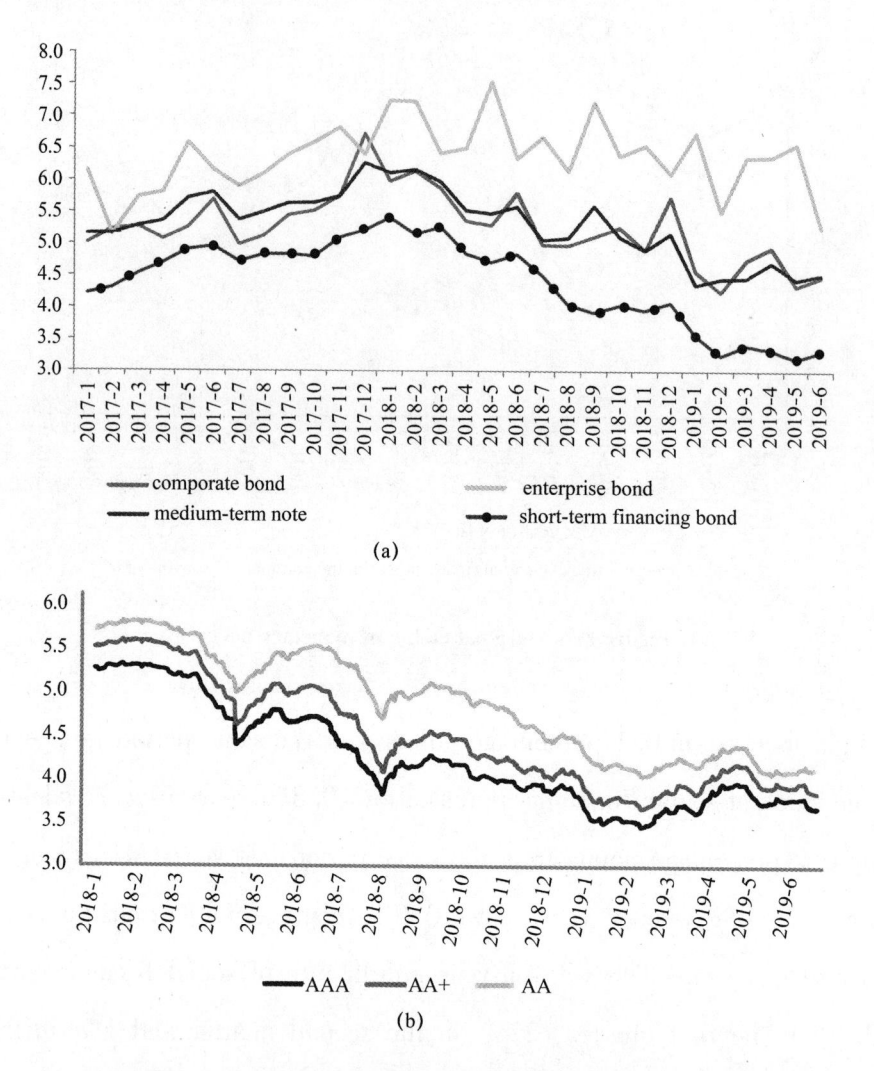

(a)

(b)

Figure 20　Issuing rate of credit bonds and profitability of 3 year medium-term note tend to decline

Since the middle of 2018, China has been implementing the "six stability" program, especially through cutting taxes and fees and

Chapter Two China's Macroeconomy under the Situation of Slowing Growth and Structural Differentiation

improving the business environment. The overall trend of China's economic development in 2019 is better than the pessimistic market expectation at the end of 2018. Faced with challenges of the world economic downturn and an unprecedented uncertain period caused by Sino-US trade friction, many forecasters made excessively pessimistic predictions concerning China's economy in 2018—2019.

Judging from the actual situation in 2019, China's economy has withstood the "squeeze" of the world economic downturn and Sino-US trade friction, and maintained relatively good development trend growth, thus the above pessimistic predictions turned out to be false. The reasons are discussed below.

First, high-tech Chinese companies have maintained good business performance and development trends. In 2019, the "three new economic patterns"① is still developing at a high speed. In the first three quarters of the year, profits of China's high-tech manufacturing and strategic emerging industries rose by 6.3% and 4.6% year-on-year respectively, better than overall industrial profitability. Value-added of information transmission, computer services and software rose by 19.8% year-on-year, 12.8 percentage points higher than the tertiary industry. In the 2019 "World Top 500 list", the number of Chinese

---

① Three new economic patterns: this term is short for new industries, new business formats and new business models, referring to economic patterns different from traditional ones. Three new economic patterns mainly include building economy, block economy and headquarters economy.

companies surpassed that of the US for the first time, reaching 129, 8 more than that of the US, which is of epoch-making significance. In the first quarter of 2019, 21 new unicorns were discovered in China, bringing the total number of unicorns to 202. In addition, according to the *National High-tech Zone Gazelle Enterprise Development Report 2018*, the number of gazelle enterprises in the high-tech zone reached 2,857. Meanwhile, as of October 31, according to lplytics, Chinese manufacturers have accounted for 36% of the 5G Standard Essential Patents (SEP), ahead of the US, South Korea and Finland. Huawei takes the lead in the 5G standard essential patents and technical contribution for 5G standards. The number of its 5G SEP is 2,160, accounting for 18%, ranking first among all manufacturers. On July 30, Huawei released its first-half results. In the first half, Huawei's revenue reached 401.3 billion yuan, up 23.2% year-on-year. Its net profit margin was 8.7%. Huawei shipped 118 million smartphones in the first half, up 24% year-on-year. Meanwhile, in this period, Huawei signed more than 30 international contracts for 5G. Therefore, predictions that some of China's biggest tech companies would soon collapse have come to nothing. Chinese companies are more resilient than pessimists think.

Second, the growth rate of trade has been positive, trade surplus has expanded, and the goal of "stable foreign trade" has been achieved. In the first three quarters of 2019, China's total imports and

Chapter Two China's Macroeconomy under the Situation of Slowing Growth and Structural Differentiation

exports grew by 2.8% year-on-year. Exports grew by 5.2% and imports by -0.1%. Trade surplus reached 2.0461 trillion yuan (US 298.4 billion), up 44.2% (36.1%) year-on-year. Despite a slight drop of 1.3 percentage points in export growth from the same period last year, China has made remarkable progress in stabilizing foreign trade in the context of the global economic downturn, especially given a sharp drop in global trade growth from 3.6% last year to 1.1%. In particular, thanks to concerted efforts of diversifying trade, cutting taxes and fees, and improving the business environment, China's foreign trade has made progress and maintained a good development trend. In the first half of 2019, imports and exports of goods between China and countries along the "Belt and Road" reached 4.2 trillion yuan, up

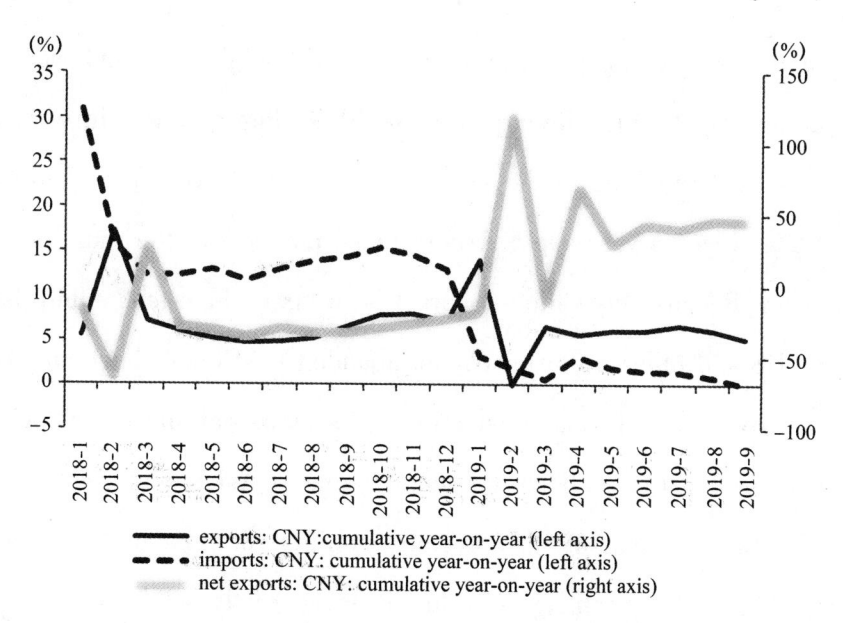

Figure 21 Trend of China's trade growth

9.7% year-on-year, 5.8 percentage points higher than the overall trade growth and accounting for 28.9% of China's total foreign trade.

Third, foreign direct investment and international reserves have undergone a significant reversal, and the goal of "stable foreign investment" has been achieved. In the first three quarters of 2019, foreign direct investment actually used in China increased by 6.5% year-on-year, 3.6 percentage points higher than the same period last year. In USD terms, foreign investment rose by 2.9% year-on-year, showing positive growth. Therefore, the so-called foreign capital withdrawal from China needs to be viewed objectively. According to our research, although some of China's low-end industries did relocate to Southeast Asia, the US—and especially Europe, Japan and South Korea—began to invest heavily in China's high-tech and service industries. In the first three quarters of 2019, foreign direct investment actually used in China in the service sector reached US 71.88 billion, up 9.2% year-on-year and 6.2 percentage points over the same period last year. Because the Chinese market is so large, high-tech enterprises in the US and other countries cannot abandon it. China's huge market, and the integrity and relative stability of its industrial and technological chains, are hard to replicate for some Southeast Asian countries.

In the context of the overall stability of foreign trade and investment, CNY exchange rate has been generally stable and foreign exchange reserves slightly recovered. The exchange rate of CNY against

Chapter Two China's Macroeconomy under the Situation of Slowing Growth and Structural Differentiation

—— foreign capital actually used: foreign direct investment cumulative year-on-year
▬▬ foreign capital actually used: foreign direct investment CNY: cumulative year-on-year
- - - serices: foreign capital actually used: cumulative year-on-year

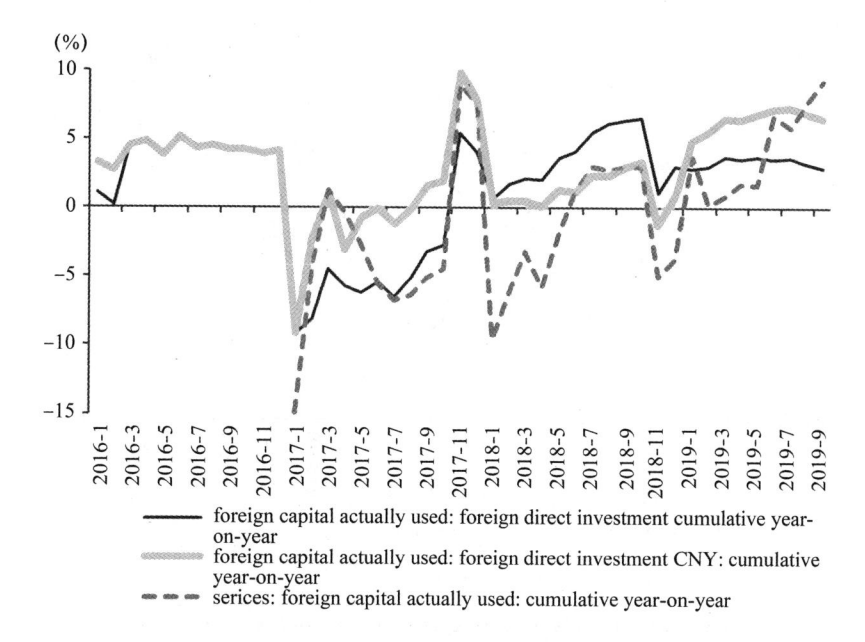

Figure 22　Foreign capital actually used by China has registered a stable performance with good momentum for growth

USD rose to 7.05 in October from 6.70 in January, but its overall performance has been stable compared with the ups and downs from 2016 to 2018. Meanwhile, official foreign exchange reserves edged up from US 3,087.9 billion to US 3,092.4 billion in October, also more stable than the past three years.

At the same time, China has won the critical battle against major financial risks. Various types of financial markets have remained stable, and debt risks have been alleviated. Default rates of various credit bonds have significantly decreased compared with the same period of 2018.

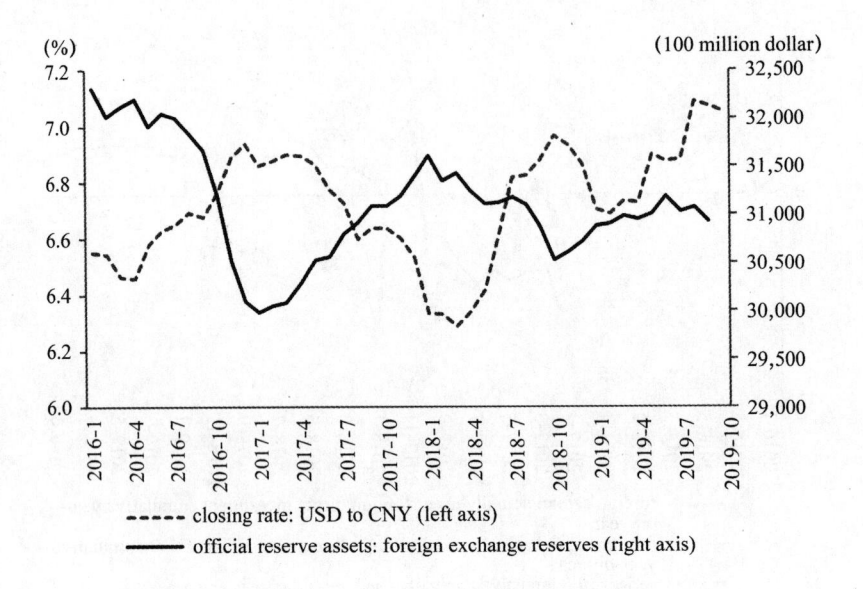

212 China's Macroeconomy in the Key Period of Structural Adjustment

Figure 23   Trends of CNY exchange rate and official foreign exchange reserves

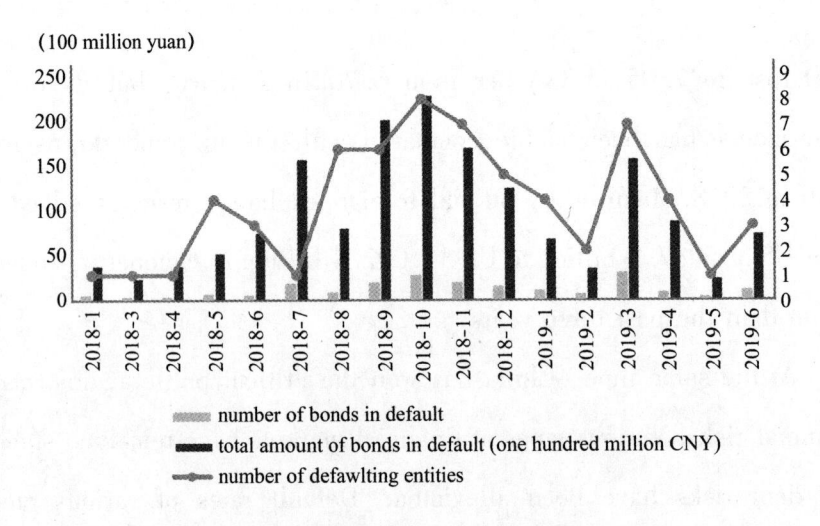

Figure 24   Default of credit bonds

Fourth, the business environment continues to improve, enthusiasm for entrepreneurship and innovation increases, employment in urban areas remains stable on the whole, and personal income maintains rapid growth. In the first three quarters of 2019, the number of newly registered market entities reached 17.66 million, with a daily average of 65,000, up 13.1% year-on-year. During this period, 10.97 million new urban jobs were added, basically meeting the target of 11 million new urban jobs for this year ahead of schedule. In September, the surveyed urban unemployment rate was 5.2%, and 4.6% for people aged 25 to 59, remaining within the target range of

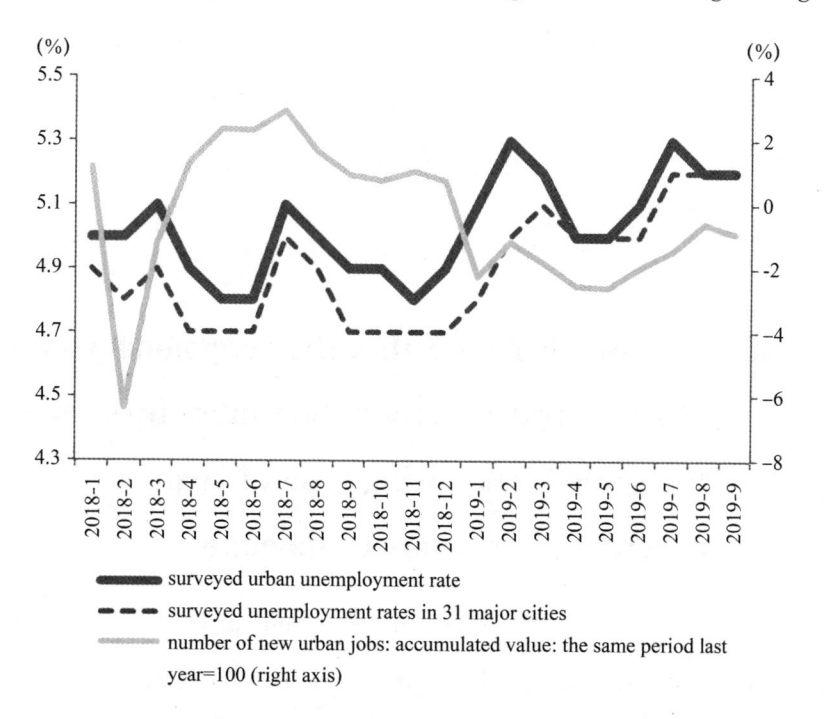

Figure 25 China's surveyed urban unemployment rate rose slightly

5.5%. In the first three quarters of this year, Chinese residents' per capita disposable income rose by 8.8% year-on-year, or by 6.1% in real terms.

To sum up, under the combined effects of internal and external factors, China's economy has not experienced the extreme situation expected by many foreigners and pessimists, which demonstrates the stability and risk resistance of China's economy. Moreover, compared with the performance of major global economies, China's economic growth still maintains its leading edge. It's estimated that global GDP growth will fall by 0.6 percentage points in 2019, growth in the US and the eurozone by 0.6 and 0.7 percentage points respectively, and India's growth will fall by more than 1.0 percentage point, while China's growth will fall by just 0.5 percentage points.

◇ III. It is worth noting that the recessionary type of structural differentiation intensifies, while the growth-enhancing type of structural differentiation tends to stagnate

Compared with the slowdown in economic growth, what is more noteworthy is that during the critical period of China's economic structural adjustment, the recessionary-type of structural differentiation intensifies, while the growth-enhancing type of structural differentiation tends to stagnate. In recent years, the structural differentiation of China's economy in different industries, regions, sizes and ownership has intensified. If neglected, it may reach a tipping point. Therefore, corresponding policies must be more detailed, more precise, and more forward-looking.

1. Structural differentiation of the flow of national savings

In 2019, while the effect of consumption on GDP growth has greatly weakened, structural changes in the flow of Chinese savings have taken place. The main result is a further decline in the effect of investment on GDP growth and a sharp rise in the effect of net exports on GDP growth. In other words, more of national savings are going abroad in the form of net exports than are staying home in the form of investment. In the first three quarters of 2019, the cumulative contribution of total capital formation to GDP year-on-year fell to 1.2 percentage points from 2.1 percentage points in the same period of last year, and its contribution to economic growth fell to 19.8% from 31.8% in the same period of last year. By contrast, net exports' cumulative contribution to GDP year-on-year rose to 1.2 percentage points from -0.7 percentage points in the same period last year, and its contribution to economic growth rose to 19.6% from -9.8% in the same period last year.

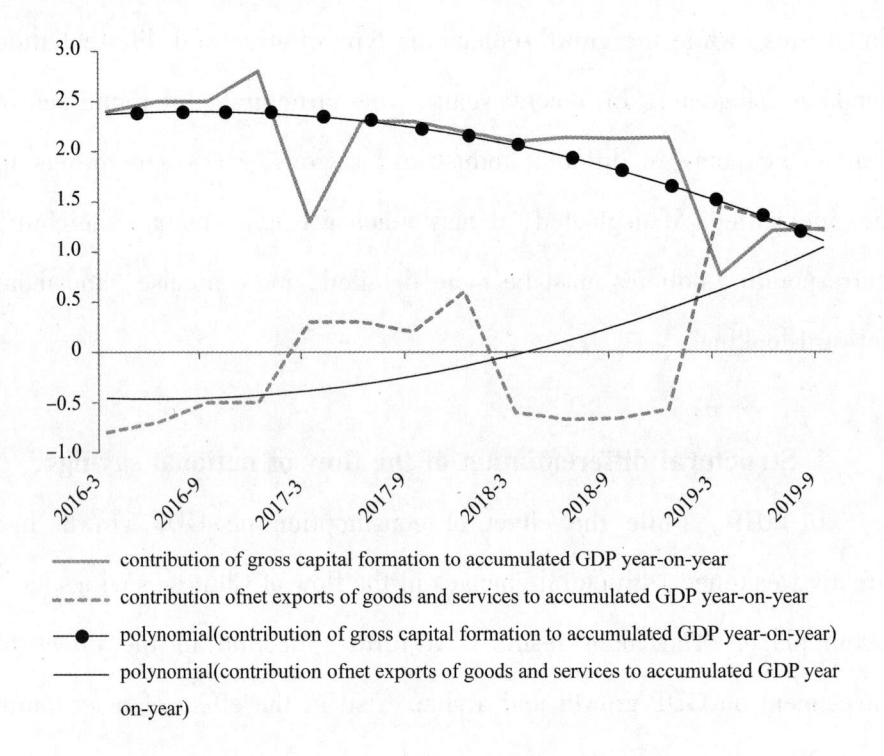

Figure 26 Differentiation of the driving effects of investment and net exports on economic growth

These changes are also reflected in the differentiation between the growth of China's total imports and exports and the growth of net exports in 2019. In the first three quarters of 2019, China's total imports and exports in USD terms fell by 2.4% year-on-year, 18.2 percentage points lower than the same period last year, but China's net exports rose by 36.1%, 60.5 percentage points higher than the same period last year. As a result, net exports contributed 1.2 percentage points to real GDP growth, accounting for 19.6%, up 1.9 percentage points and

Chapter Two China's Macroeconomy under the Situation of Slowing Growth and Structural Differentiation | **217**

29. 4 percentage points respectively, compared with the same period last year. In the context of slowing growth of domestic final consumption expenditure and total capital formation, net export has played a key role in supporting the growth of total demand. However, the differentiation between the growth of total imports and exports and the growth of net exports not only intensifies the dependence of China's economic growth on external demand, but also intensifies the vulnerability of China's economy due to the contraction of economic cycle.

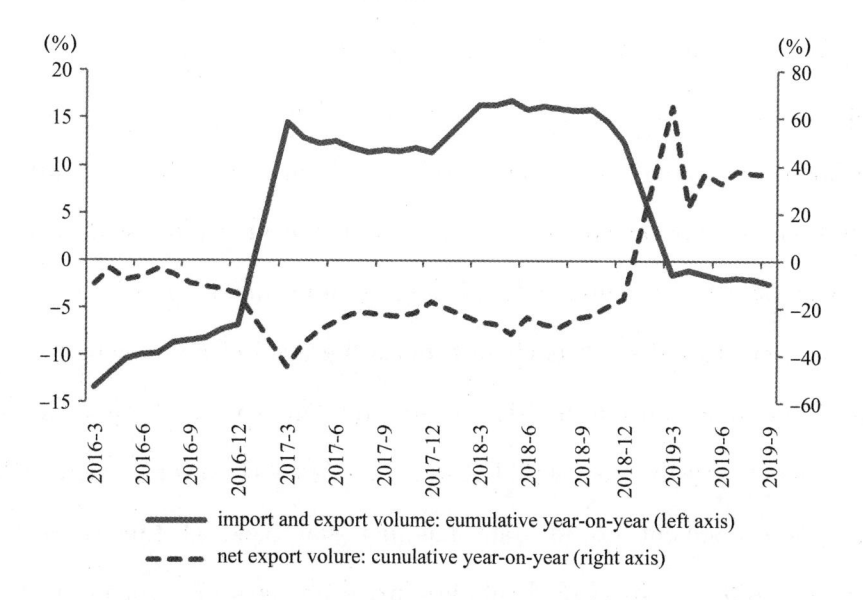

—— import and export volume: eumulative year-on-year (left axis)
- - - net export volure: cunulative year-on-year (right axis)

Figure 27 Trend differentiation between total import-export volume and trade surplus (denominated in USD)

From the medium-and long-term perspective, China's investment growth rate has declined rapidly. From 2003 to 2012, China's investment growth rate was stable above 20%, with an average growth rate of 25.3%. But as investment efficiency declined and debt ratios rose, the growth pattern driven by investment became unsustainable. Therefore, since 2013 China's economy has experienced an adjustment, with investment growth slowing down significantly from 20.3% in 2012 to 9.8% in 2015.

In theory, a certain degree of decline in investment growth rate is consistent with China's economic restructuring and high-quality development requirements. According to our calculation, it is appropriate to maintain an investment growth rate of 8.0% to 12.0% at this stage. The calculation basis is as follows. Suppose the rate of technological progress reaches 2.0%. Taking the negative growth of employment into consideration, the growth rate of capital stock should be about 8.0% to maintain 6.0% long-term economic growth. Because the current capital stock is about 6 times the level of investment, and if we set depreciation rate at 10%, currently China needs to maintain an investment growth rate of 8.0% to 12.0%. However, since 2016 China's investment growth rate has not stabilized at this level but plunged to 5.9% in 2018. Excluding price changes, real investment in 2018 increased by only 0.5%, and only 0.2% in the first three quarters before the "six stability" initiative played its role. The above level has obviously fallen below the reasonable range, even lower than that of the United States in the same period. As a comparison, the US maintained a steady growth of investment for 10 consecutive quarters from the first quarter of 2017 to the second quarter of 2019, with an average growth rate of 6.3%.

Even with the launch of the "six stability" policy and the implementation of the large-scale "tax cuts and fee reduction" policy, China's investment has showed no clear signs of recovery in 2019, with nominal growth of 5.4% in the first three quarters and real growth of 2.2%. At present, the growth rate of investment remains far below the desired level, mainly due to the weakening of the investment inclinations of enterprises. For example, investment in manufacturing industries has reversed the trend of gradual recovery and has become the main drag on current investment. Specifically, investment in "equipment, tools and instruments purchase" experienced negative growth for the first time in 2019, with a negative growth of 1.2% in the first three quarters, after three consecutive years of low-speed growth of 3.0%. After its first negative growth in 2017, investment in extension dropped by 7.2% in the first three quarters of 2019. Obviously, willingness of enterprises to undertake productive investment is weak, and therefore remains under great strain.

For China's future development trajectory, the above trends are not consistent with the requirements of the established development strategy. On the supply side, the supply structure is not in line with the people's growing demand for a better life. In order to solve this contradiction, enhancing productivity and adjusting the supply structure

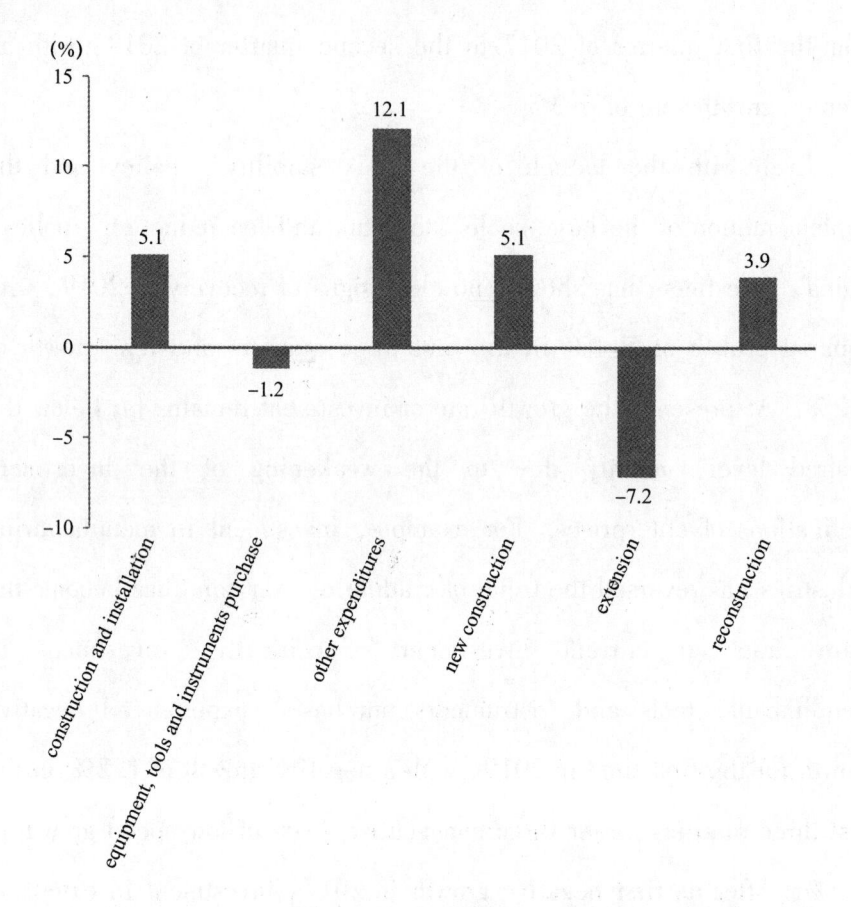

Figure 28 Structural differentiation of fixed asset investment (year-on-year growth rate in the first three quarters of 2019)

are important tasks at present and in the future. In this context, investment growth and capital formation should play a greater role. Comparing domestic and foreign demand, it is clear that China needs to reduce the economy's excessive dependence on net foreign demand. Economic rebalancing will be necessary in order to meet the increasing demand of the people for a better life and to achieve the internal

2. Regional economic differentiation

The pattern of regional economic differentiation has further increased. Regions experiencing rapid economic growth in the past few years have maintained their momentum in 2019, while regions with significant economic adjustments have continued to weaken.

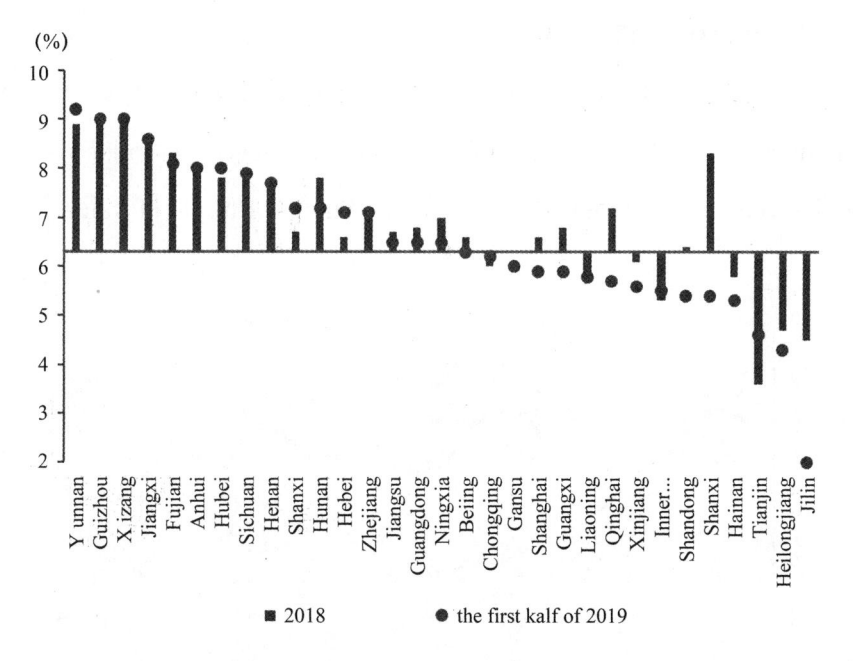

Figure 29 Differentiation of growth situation in different regions

The regional differentiation pattern is evident by looking at the growth situation of all regions in China. In the first half of 2019, provinces in the central and southwest regions continued to maintain a rapid growth rate of more than 7.0%, and the southeast coastal areas continued to maintain relatively stable growth despite the impact of Sino-US trade friction. However, in the northeast region, Inner Mongolia, the Beijing-Tianjin-Hebei region, Shandong, northwest region, Hainan and Guangxi, economic growth rates were basically below 6.0%. In Jilin, Heilongjiang and Tianjin, growth rates were 2.0%, 4.3% and 4.6% respectively, all lower than 5.0% and ranking last in China.

3. Industry differentiation

In 2019, under the influence of the overall downward trend of the manufacturing industry, the differentiation between the industrial and service sectors has reached a new high. First, in terms of value-added

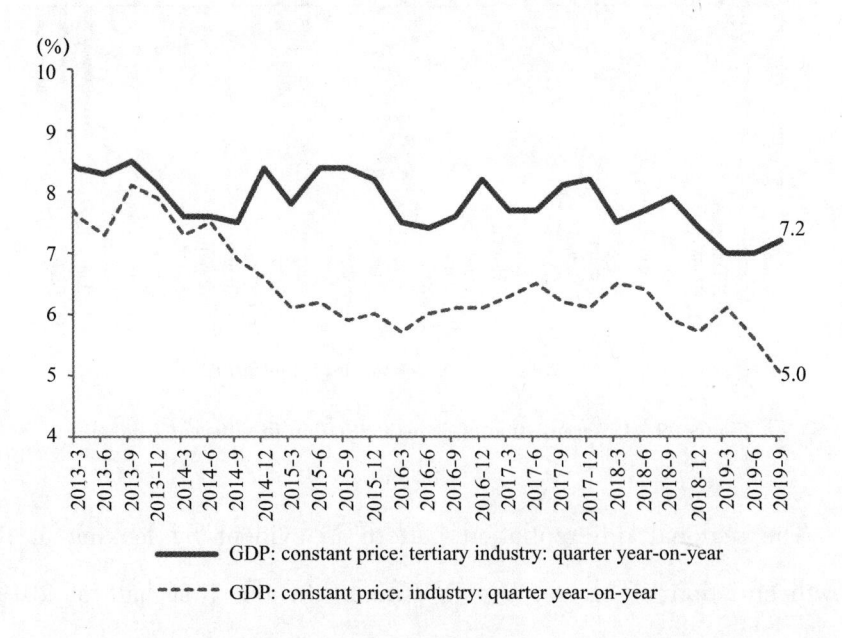

Figure 30 Trend differentiation of added value growth of industry and service industry

growth, the added value of service sector increased by 7.2% in the third quarter, while the growth of industrial value-added fell to 5.0%.

Second, the above differentiation trend is more apparent in investment. In the first three quarters, investment in the service sector increased by 7.2%, up 1.9 percentage points from the same period last year, while growth rate of investment in the secondary industry decreased to 2.0%, down 3.2 percentage points from the same period last year. The gap between the growth rates of investment in the secondary and tertiary industries reached 5.2 percentage points.

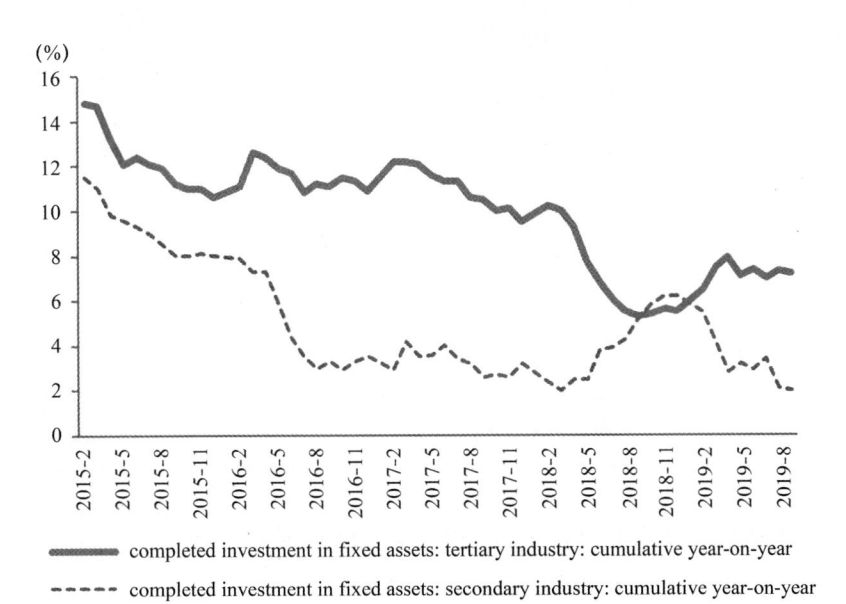

━━━ completed investment in fixed assets: tertiary industry: cumulative year-on-year
----- completed investment in fixed assets: secondary industry: cumulative year-on-year

Figure 31 Trend differentiation of investment growth rates of the secondary and tertiary industries

The divergence between the manufacturing and servicesectors is even more significant if we look at profit levels. In the first seven months of 2019, the accumulated operating profit of service sector enterprises above designated size increased by 9.2% year-on-year, but the total profit of industrial enterprises decreased by 1.7% year-on-year, with manufacturing enterprises decreasing by 3.4% year-on-year.

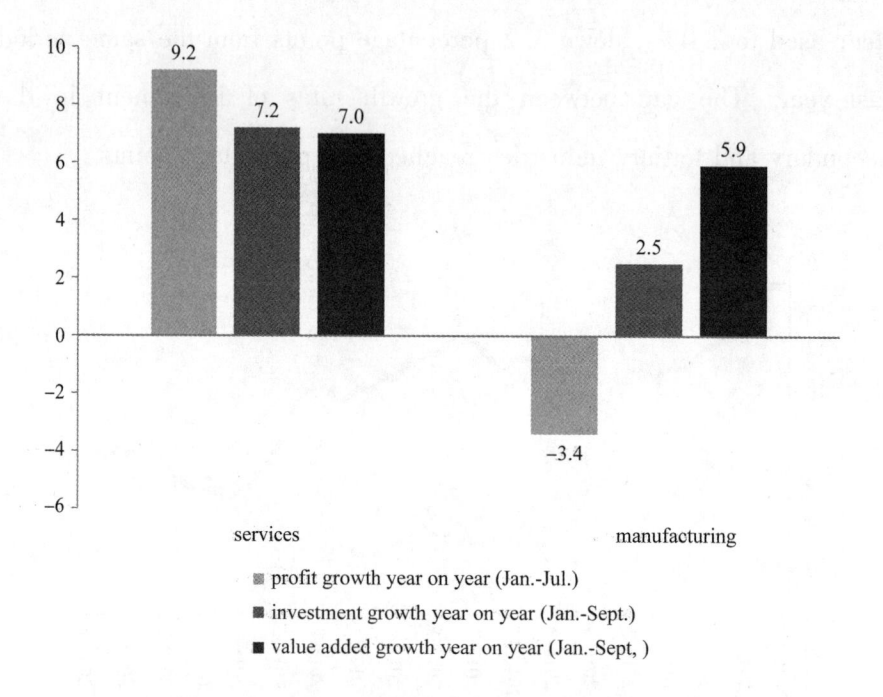

Figure 32 Comparison of year-on-year growth of service industry and manufacturing industry in 2019

In the manufacturing industry, differentiation of business performance is also distinct. In the first three quarters, we find: (1) negative growth in total profits of nine industries, including petroleum processing, coking and nuclear fuel processing, ferrous metal smelting and rolling processing, chemical fiber manufacturing, paper and paper products, automobile manufacturing, chemical raw materials and chemical products manufacturing, wood processing and wood, bamboo, rattan, palm, grass products, textile industry, clothing and fashion industry, with a decline of 53.5%, 41.8%, 29.1%, 20.2%, 16.6%, 13.0%, 4.4%, 4.3% and 1.6% respectively. (2) Eight industries achieved single-digit growth in total profits, including general equipment manufacturing, agricultural and sideline food processing, computer, communication and other electronic equipment manufacturing, instrument and meter manufacturing, non-ferrous metal smelting and rolling processing, printing industry and reproduction of recording media, leather, fur, feather and their products and footwear industry, and comprehensive utilization of waste resources. (3) Total profits of twelve industries achieved double-digit growth, including pharmaceutical manufacturing, metal products, food manufacturing, non-metal mineral products, culture and education, industry art, sports and entertainment products, rubber and plastic products, special equipment manufacturing, electrical machinery and equipment, wine, beverage and refined tea, furniture manufacturing, tobacco products, railway, ship, aerospace and other transportation equipment manufacturing.

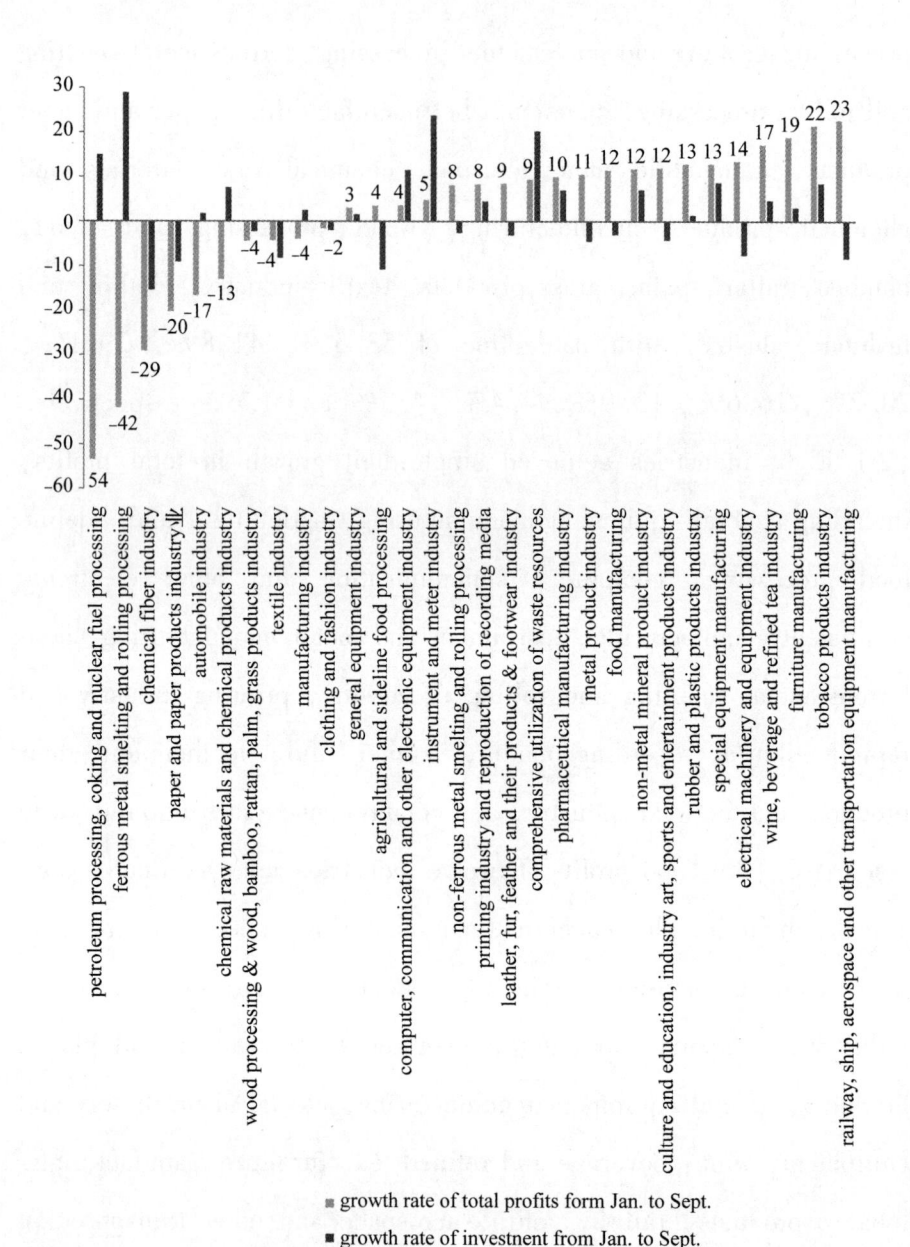

Figure 33 Differentiation of total profits and investment growth rate in different industries

4. Structural upgrading shows signs of slowing down

In particular, under the impact of multiple factors, such as the successive withdrawal of supporting policies, the adjustment of the industrial cycle, regional and industrial differentiation, Sino-US trade friction, and the decline of internal and external demand, the slowdown of China's "new drivers" of growth accelerated in the second half of 2019, putting downward pressure on the overall rate of economic growth. As the transformation of new and old economic drivers enters a difficult period, new ideas and policies are needed.

Development trends of the past three years indicate that the growth rate of new drivers has declined significantly, much faster than that of the traditional economy. Its growth rate is basically the same as that of the traditional economy. (1) The growth rate of industrial strategic emerging industries' value-added dropped by 4.3% from 11.0% in 2017 to 6.7% in the first quarter of 2019, while in the same period traditional industrial value-added growth dropped by 0.4%. The growth rate of strategic emerging industries' value-added was only 0.2 percentage points higher than that of all industries. (2) Value-added of high-tech manufacturing industry decreased from 13.4% in 2017 to 7.8% in the first quarter of 2019, down 5.6 percentage points, while strategic service industry decelerated from 17.3% to 13.0%, down 4.3 percentage points. (3) Investment in advanced technology dropped from 15.9% in 2017 to 11.4% in the first quarter of 2019, down 4.5 percentage points, while whole industries investment declined by only 1.1 percentage points in the same period. (4) The growth rate of online retail for the whole year decreased from 32.2% in 2017 to 17.8% from January to May in 2019, down 14.4 percentage points. The growth rate of total retail sales of consumer goods in the whole society fell by 2 percentage points over the same period.

From the perspective of the overall industrial structural adjustment, the internal structure of China's industrial and service sectors in 2019 has continued the adjustment trend in the past, but adjustment dynamics show signs of slowing down or even reversing. At the same time as the overall decline of economic growth, both manufacturing and high-end service industries have declined by larger margins, while the growth of construction and financial industries has rebounded significantly. Within the decline of the overall growth rate of service industry, growth rates of information transmission, software and information technology services, and leasing and business services have declined significantly more than the whole. Meanwhile, the financial industry has surged, which is not in line with China's policy goal of developing a high-end service industry, and it does not solve the problem of the "financial industry driving out the real economy".

From the perspective of the industrial sector's internal structural

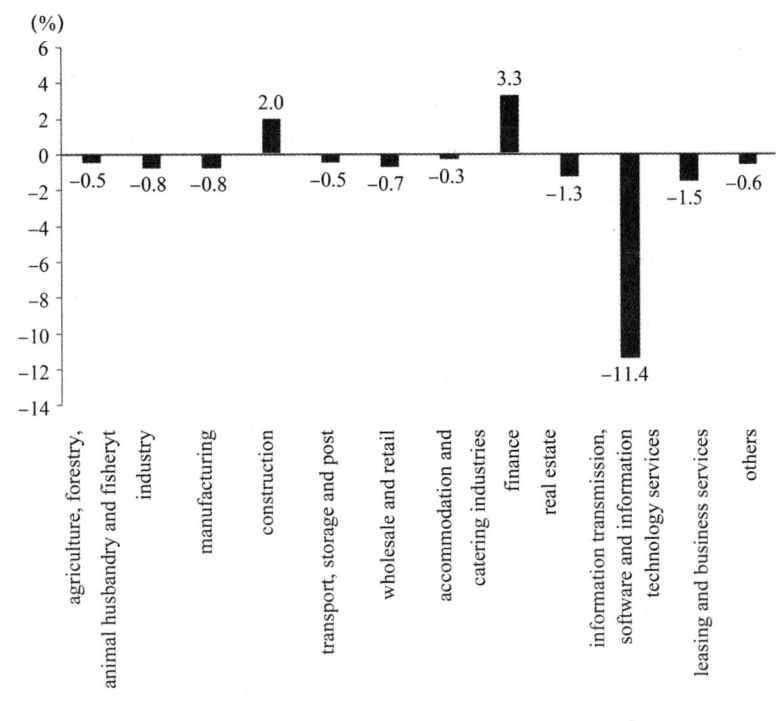

Chapter Two China's Macroeconomy under the Situation of Slowing Growth and Structural Differentiation

Figure 34 Signs of reversal in optimization and adjustment of service industry internal structure

(Bar chart values by sector)
- agriculture, forestry, animal husbandry and fishery: −0.5
- industry: −0.8
- manufacturing: −0.8
- construction: 2.0
- transport, storage and post: −0.5
- wholesale and retail: −0.7
- accommodation and catering industries: −0.3
- finance: 3.3
- real estate: −1.3
- information transmission, software and information technology services: −11.4
- leasing and business services: −1.5
- others: −0.6

■ decline of the growth rate in the first three quarters in 2019 from the same period in 2018 (%)

adjustment, the dynamics of structural optimization and adjustment also show signs of a reversal. Compared with the same period in 2018, for the first three quarters of 2019, the growth rate of added value of industries above designated size decreased by 0.4 percentage points. Breaking it down by industry, the decline in manufacturing was 0.8%, in high-tech 3.1%, pharmaceuticals 3.4%, general equipment manufacturing 3.5%, professional equipment manufacturing 3.7%, computer, communication and other electronic equipment manufacturing 4.3%, and in automobile manufacturing industry 8.5%. These figures provide further evidence that the impact of industrial restructuring has slowed down in the past few years.

From the perspective of investment, while fixed investment has achieved steady overall growth, the growth of the manufacturing industry's fixed investment has declined sharply, down 6.2 percentage points compared with the same period last year. Private investment growth dropped by 4 percentage points compared with last year and high-tech manufacturing industry's fixed investment growth of 2.3 percentage points. The growth rate of private investment has not been stable, and endogenous fixed investment growth in the whole society remains weak. The rapid expansion of the service industry coupled with a contracting manufacturing industry does not serve the goals of industrial development and adjustment in China. The decline of investment growth in the high-tech manufacturing industry especially does not meet the requirements for improving the overall strength and competitiveness of China's manufacturing industry.

From the perspective of consumption, the growth rate of the new driving forces of consumption has declined. Notably, online retail growth has decelerated faster than the whole retail industry compared with last year. In the first three quarters of 2019, nominal growth rate of total retail sales of consumer goods decreased by 1.1 percentage points compared with the same period last year, while growth rates of online retail sales of physical goods, and online goods and services decreased by 7.2 and 10.2 percentage points respectively, indicating that consumption upgrading in the past few years has slowed down. For example, although the proportion of online retail sales of physical goods in total retail sales of social consumer goods continued to increase by 2.0 percentage points compared with the same period last year, the increase was 1.5 percentage points lower than the same period last year.

retail sales of online goods and services: cumulative year-on-year
online retail sales of physical goods: cumulative year-on-year
share of online retail sales of physical goods in total retail sales of social consumer goods: accumulated value

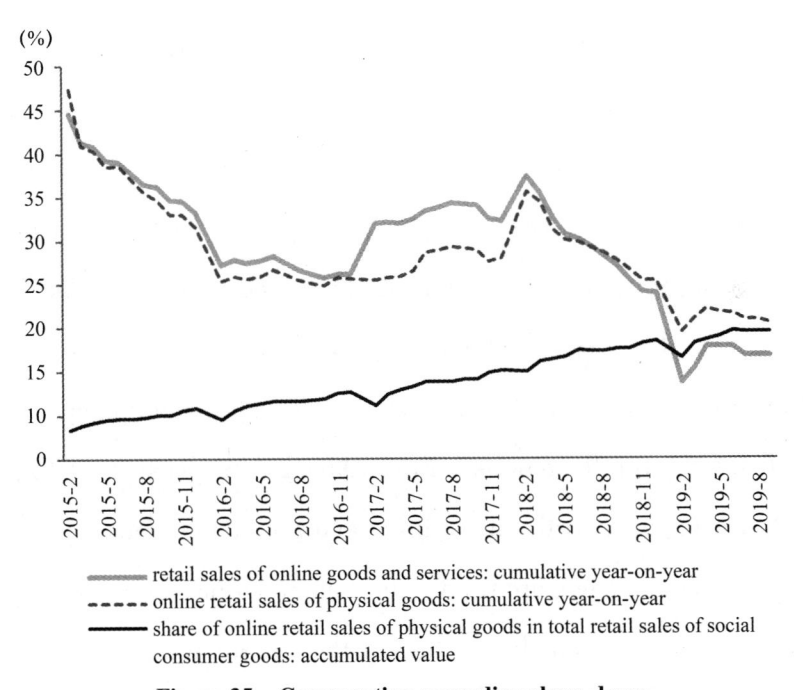

Figure 35　Consumption upgrading slows down

From the perspective of trade, the growth rate of trade of high-tech, mechanical, and electrical products has declined even more significantly. It is concerning that the growth rate of China's foreign trade in high-tech products and mechanical and electrical products has declined by a larger margin. From January to August 2019, the cumulative export growth rate of high-tech products decreased by 5.7 percentage points compared with the same period last year, far larger than the decline of the overall export growth rate. For example, the cumulative export growth rate of aerospace technology, biotechnology, material technology and computer and communication technology dropped by 36%, 19.6%, 15.3% and 10.9% respectively. The cumulative export growth rate of mechanical and electrical products was 1.4 percentage points lower than that of the same period last year, which was also significantly higher than the decline of the overall export growth rate. The cumulative export growth of means of transport, machinery, and equipment decreased by 13.9% and 5.2% respectively. The decline of import growth rate of high-tech products and mechanical and electrical products was also significantly higher than that of overall imports. From January to August 2019, the cumulative import growth rate of high-tech products decreased by 15.6 percentage points compared with the same period last year, again, significantly larger than the decline of the overall import growth rate. Meanwhile, the cumulative import growth of computer integrated manufacturing and electronic technology dropped by 42.9% and 19.1% respectively. The cumulative import growth rate of mechanical and electrical products was 15.7 percentage points lower than that of the same period last year, which is also significantly larger than the decline of the overall import growth rate. Finally, the cumulative import growth of mechanical equipment, electrical appliances and electronic products dropped by 20.8% and 18.2% respectively. In terms of product categories, foreign trade of high-tech products and mechanical and electrical products has declined by a larger margin. In terms of national classification, trade with the US has declined even more. A combination of these two reflects, to a certain extent, the deep-seated impact of Sino-US trade friction on China's foreign trade. This is not conducive to the further optimization of China's foreign trade product structure, nor to the upgrading of China's domestic manufacturing industry structure.

There are three main reasons for the slowdown of China's economic structural upgrading.

Firstly, due to the expiration of various strategic plans, the withdrawal of industrial support policies, and the expansion of financial subsidy gaps, the policy dividend will diminish, and many industries and enterprises that lack potential for development will face severe challenges.

In the past 10 years, the core reason for the rapid development of China's high-tech, strategic emerging industries and the "three new economic patterns" lies in the successive introduction of various strategies and the full policy dividend enjoyed by various industries. However, these policy dividends have quickly entered a declining period for the following reasons. (1) Many enterprises have exhausted the incubation and support period of preferential policies, for example, the 3—5 years of tax preferences and various subsidies enjoyed by enterprises in high-tech parks. (2) The planning period of a large number of strategic emerging industries will end in 2020, when various policy subsidies will begin to decline. For example, in accordance with the provisions of the *Strategic Action Plan for New Energy Development* (2014—2020), wind and coal power will be connected to the internet at a fair price by 2020. And in accordance with the provisions of the *Development Plan for Energy Saving and New Energy Vehicles* (2012—2020), new energy subsidies will be completely withdrawn in 2020. (3) Various industrial parks and industrial bases that are blooming everywhere have imposed heavy financial burdens on local economy. In 2019 and 2020, many subsidies for strategic industries and high-tech enterprises will be under political constraints and therefore unsustainable. For example, from 2009 to 2017, the Chinese government's subsidies for new energy vehicles totaled 200 billion yuan, and in the next three years, the subsidies are also planned to exceed 200 billion yuan. At the present time when the growth rate of financial revenue and the government's financing ability are declining, however, the gap of financial subsidies will be greatly widened. As a result, many enterprises and industries that depend on subsidies may not survive. By the end of 2017, cumulative renewable energy generation subsidy gap totaled 112.7 billion yuan, while the single-year subsidy gap in 2019 will expand to 120 billion yuan.

Secondly, as a result of misguided industrial projects, overbuilding, and market bubbles, China's previous economic energymay fade and possibly stagnate.

Under the influence of the new economy and competition in various parts of China, many ambitious projects have been launched, and many industrial parks opened. However, after 10 years of development, these administrative distortions will face the following market forces. (1) Many industrial parks and innovation bases without sufficient technical, industrial, human, and market foundations will be gradually shut down, since they will be unable to survive on their own after several years of administrative support. By the end of 2018, there were 2,5000 parks and more than 6,000 incubators in China, 70% of which are located in some third and fourth tier cities without any foundation. A large number of parks are finding it hard to break even and will shut down during 2019 to 2020. (2) Many industries still have no hematopoietic function, even with the policy of "blood transfusion" that sustained them for many years. After the "blood transfusion" is stopped, they will be eliminated by fierce market competition. For example, there are 169 new energy vehicle manufacturers in China, with an average market of less than 10,000 vehicles. A large number of them have found it difficult to reach the critical point of large-scale production in the past three years. Another example is that 28 provinces have chosen photovoltaics as their leading industry, and at least 280 prefecture level cities or industrial parks have proposed to build a 100 billion level new energy or photovoltaic industry base. The result has been serious overcapacity in many strategic emerging industries, and a large number of enterprises that are finding it difficult to survive. (3) Capital markets have largely contracted after the bursting of the economic bubble, resulting in a shortage of market funds in recent years. This is reflected in the collapse of the P2P, the Internet plus, and grassroots entrepreneurship. For example, in 2017, there were 1,011 Chinese artificial intelligence enterprises, with a total investment and financing amount of 27.7 billion US dollars, accounting for 70% of global raised funds. However, with the collapse of some science and technology success stories, many VC/PCs exited, with a year-on-year decline of 74.85% in raised funds in 2018.

Thirdly, trade friction between China and the United States will have a substantial impact on China's high-tech industry in the second half of 2019.

The US levied tariffs of 25% on US 200 billion in goods and signed an administrative order to ensure the security of its information and communication technology supply chain, which included Huawei and other companies on the list of export control entities. These measures have had a serious impact on the development of China's high-tech industry. These effects will fully manifest themselves in the near future. This is reflected in the following aspects. (1) The export growth rate of high-tech products fell from 19.5% in 2018 to 0 in the second quarter of 2019, while the import growth rate of high-tech products fell from 25.1% in 2018 to -9.6% in May 2019. The external demand and internal industrial chain were significantly impacted as a result. (2) The export restrictions on key technologies has led to a decline of the performance of some high-tech enterprises. Most notably, the US sanctions on Zhongxing Telecommunication Equipment Corporation (ZTE Corporation) led to a 252.88% drop in corporate profits in 2018. (3) Many enterprises began to plan for capacity and investment transfers due to concerns over the reconstruction of global value chains caused by trade and technology wars. This has had a serious impact on the investment of high-tech enterprises. For example, UBS conducted a survey of CFOs of multinational companies in North Asia and found that 82% of them planned to move or were in the process of moving due to trade friction between China and the United States in 2019. Many enterprises plan to move 20%—60% of their production capacity from mainland China during 2020 to 2021, of which 20% plan to move to the United

States, 25% to Vietnam and 22% to India.

Considering the above factors, China's economic growth in the fourth quarter of 2019 will still be stable, and the goals for the year can be achieved, but the key is 2020. GDP growth rate in the fourth quarter is expected to be stable at about 6.1%, and the annual economic growth rate around 6.1%—6.2%, remaining in the target range of 6.0%—6.5%. First, the tax and fee cuts are still working, and their effects will be most obvious at the end of 2019, when a large share of tax collection and deductions are most fully realized. Second, the investment and growth effects from the issuance of special bonds in the first three quarters have a certain lag, so the policy effect will be further reflected in the fourth quarter. Third, the recent easing of Sino-US trade friction provides support for short-term market optimism. But will the economic growth rate "break 6" in 2020? If not, what will be the basis for supporting economic growth? If it does "break 6", what will be the limit? Will it affect the realization of the "two centenary goals" and the stability of society and employment? This requires an in-depth analysis of the nature of China's economic growth at the current stage and its operation in 2020 from a medium-term perspective.

Chapter Three The Nature of China's Economic Growth in 2020 from a Midium-term Perspective

China's economic downturn in 2019 and 2020 stems from the decline of economic growth caused by trends and cyclical factors, and from the strengthening of international and domestic adverse factors. Among four trends, at present only institutional factors have begun to bottom out and recover. The reform dividend from this has promoted the improvement of TFP, but it has not yet resulted in normalized economic growth. Among five cyclical factors, the mitigation of financial risks and the gradual easing of Sino-US trade friction will bring a relatively stable financial and foreign trade environment for 2020, and contribute to a favorable rebuilding of market confidence. The reversal of some cyclical forces, and the continuous improvement of China's institutional dividend, will be the most noteworthy changes in 2020. With the consolidation and cultivation of ten positive factors, the macroeconomic downturn will be eased, and the downward range will be significantly narrower than that in 2019.

I. Four Trend Factors of China's Macroeconomic Operation

From the perspective of the following four trend factors, the forces affecting China's potential economic growth remain in a slowdown phase. In 2019 and 2020, this crucial period of reforms and adjustments will be characterized by a shift of economic gears.

Firstly, dividends from the new round of reforms have not yet materialized. TFP has improved recently, but it's still far from being the engine of sustained economic growth. With the last round of reform dividend fading, many current systems have become barriers to high-quality economic development.

TFP growth rate gradually fell from an average of 3.4% in 1992—2007 to -0.3% in 2008—2016, while its contribution to economic growth fell from 29.9% to -4.7%. Currently, a new wave of accelerated institutional bonus is improving TFP growth, which stabilized and rebounded from -0.5% in 2016 to 0.8% in 2017 and 1.3% in 2018, with its contribution to GDP growth rising from -7.3% to 11.0% and 19.5%.

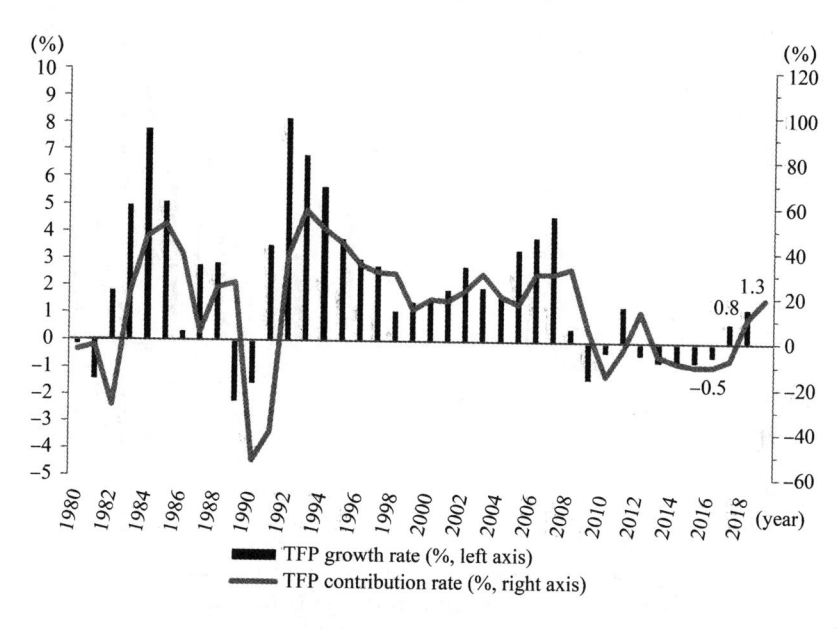

Figure 36 Trends of TFP growth rate and TFP contribution rate in China

Secondly, Sino-US trade friction along with a substantial slowdown of global economy has resulted in a sharp decline of globalization dividend. Even before the outbreak of Sino-US trade friction, the globalization dividend had declined sharply. The trade surplus of goods and services in China's GDP gradually fell from a peak of 8.6% in 2007 to 0.8% in 2018, among which the trade surplus of goods shrank while the trade deficit of services expanded. The recent intensification of trade friction between China and the US has further accelerated the decline of the globalization dividend, which may not improve in the medium-term.

As the growth rate of international trade has bottomed out since 2018, China's foreign trade sector enters yet another downturn. From

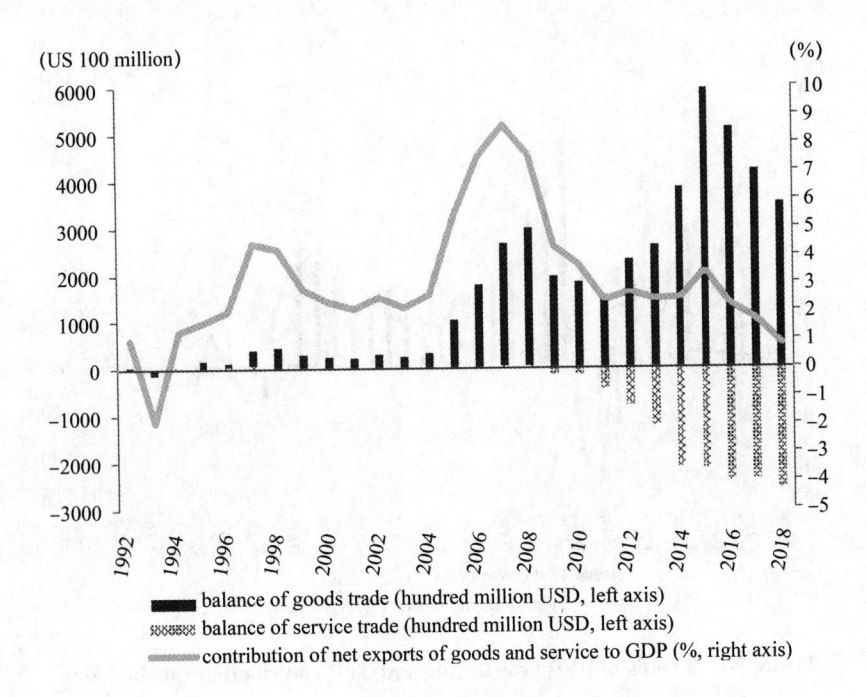

Figure 37 Trends of China's net export of goods and services

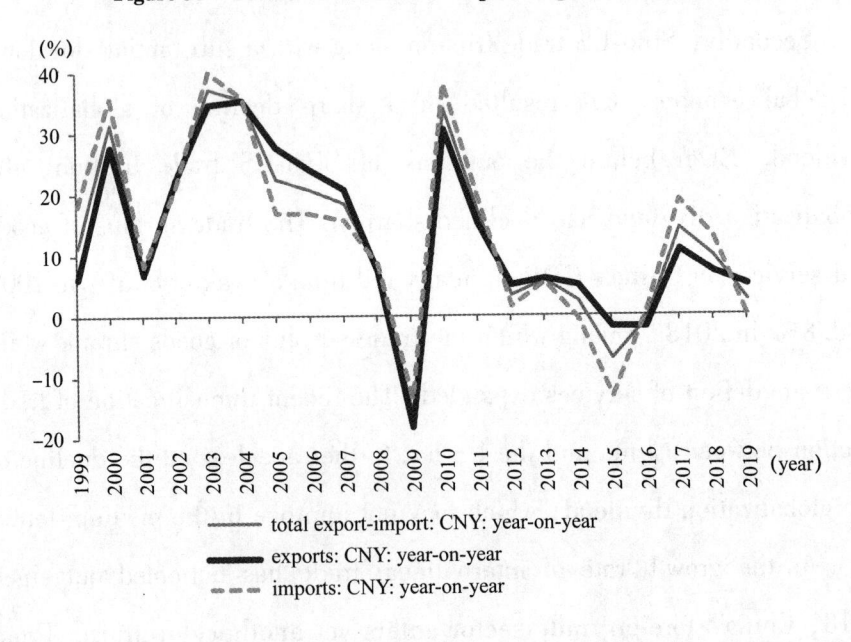

Figure 38 Trends of China's export and import

the perspective of the trade in goods, the growth rates of total export-import volume and exports and imports separately, decreased from 33.9%, 30.5% and 38.0% in 2010 to 9.7%, 7.1% and 12.9% in 2018, and further dropped to 2.4%, 4.9% and −0.4% in January to October 2019. Although a large-scale surplus of goods trade had been achieved in 2019, it has the characteristics of a "recessionary surplus". Additionally, the deficit of service trade continues to expand.

Thirdly, industrialization dividend starts to decrease. As the manufacturing industry's percentage in GDP declines and the proportion of the tertiary industry rapidly rises, the industrialization dividend necessarily falls. The proportion of China's industry to GDP remained stable at about 40% from 1978 to 2007, but it gradually declined from 41.3% in 2008 to 33.9% in 2018, an average annual decline of more than 0.7%. In the first three quarters of 2019, it further declined by 0.4% to 33.5%. As a result, the proportion of the tertiary industry to GDP exceeded that of industry for the first time in 2008, and it reached 54% in the first three quarters of 2019. At the same time, the proportion of the primary industry has dropped to 6.2%, and the growth effects from the transformation of traditional industries have been exhausted.

Fourthly, the acceleration of population aging results in a severe decline of the traditional demographic dividend. In 2013, China's national population aged 15—64 reached a peak of 1.01 billion, while

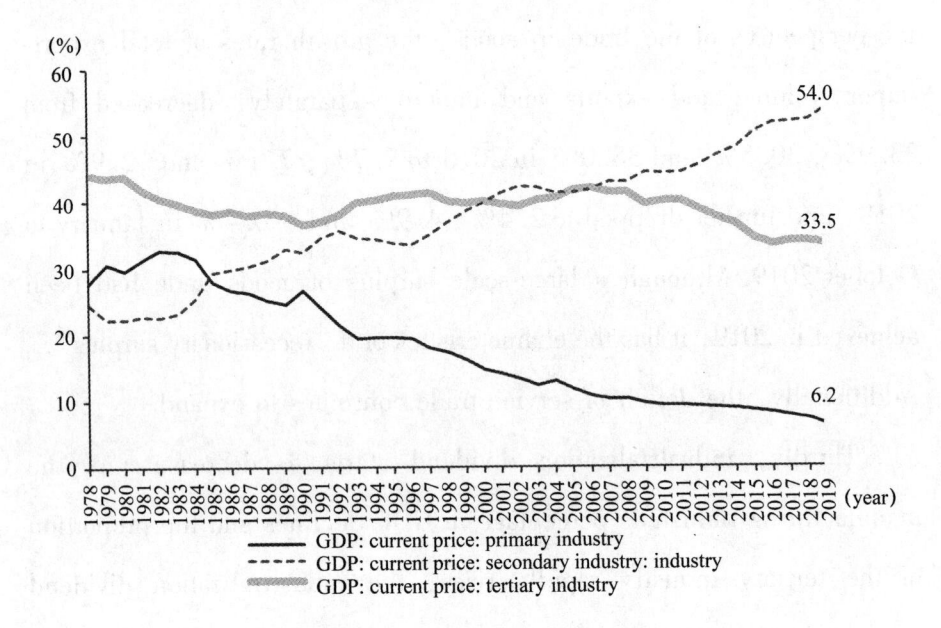

Figure 39 Industrialization dividend starts to decrease

its working age population aged 16—60 reached a peak of 920 million in 2012 and has continued to decline since then. The total dependency ratio began to rise and reached 40.4% in 2018 after its lowest point of 34.2% in 2010. These changes of the demographic structure have led China's national saving rate to continuously decline from its peak of 51.8% in 2010 to 45.3% in 2018.

At the same time, froma transitional view of the industry and urban-rural structures, the transfer speed of agricultural labor force has slowed down significantly, and the total number of floating population has reversed its previous upward trend. On a national scale it has continued to decline since 2014, indicating a subdued inclination for urban registration.

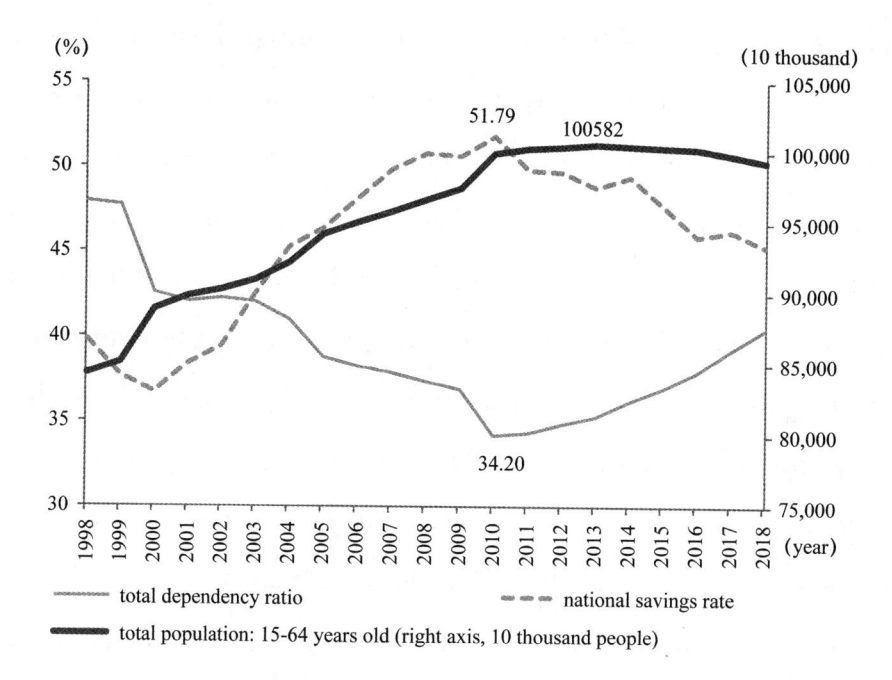

Figure 40 Trends of China's demographic structure and national saving rate

- total dependency ratio
- national savings rate
- total population: 15-64 years old (right axis, 10 thousand people)

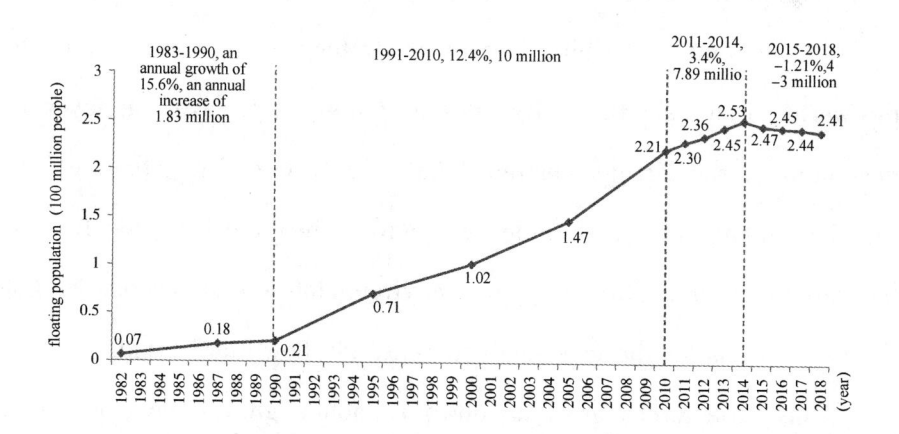

Figure 41 Trend of China's floating population

1983-1990, an annual growth of 15.6%, an annual increase of 1.83 million

1991-2010, 12.4%, 10 million

2011-2014, 3.4%, 7.89 million

2015-2018, -1.21%, -3 million

Apart from the above four traditional economic engines, it is worth emphasizingthat the deterioration of China's external environment is chronic. Factors putting the world economy on a medium-and long-term downhill slide have not faded. In addition, the Sino-US frade friction have triggered various structural changes. First, global technological progress is still in a downturn. Second, global income inequality has not improved. Third, international debt problems persist. According to a report released by the International Financial Association on November 15, global debt will exceed US 255 trillion in 2019, accounting for 330% of global GDP. Fourth, global population dividend is entering a downward period as a whole. Fifth, de-globalization may take longer and its effects may be deeper than expected. The conflict between China and the US is an inevitable outcome not only of the relationship between great powers in a world economic downturn, but also of the hegemonic cycle. Containment of China is a clear strategy of the US to dominate the world for a long time. By adding requirements layer on layer in negotiations, the US demonstrates that it only uses "negotiations" to practice unilateralism and trade hegemony. The Sino-US trade friction has directly altered China's external environment and has become one of the key reasons for the economy's increasingly downward trend.

Thus, the forces dragging down economic growth have not been effectively reversed. The deceleration of potential GDP is one of the core factors leading to the economic downturn. Among the four trend forces affecting China's potential economic growth, the institutional factor is the only one bottoming out and bringing TFP improvement, while the other major factors are declining. Following an average decline of 0.5 percentage points every year in the past 10 years, China's economic growth will continue to decline due to multiple internal and external strains in 2019 and 2020.

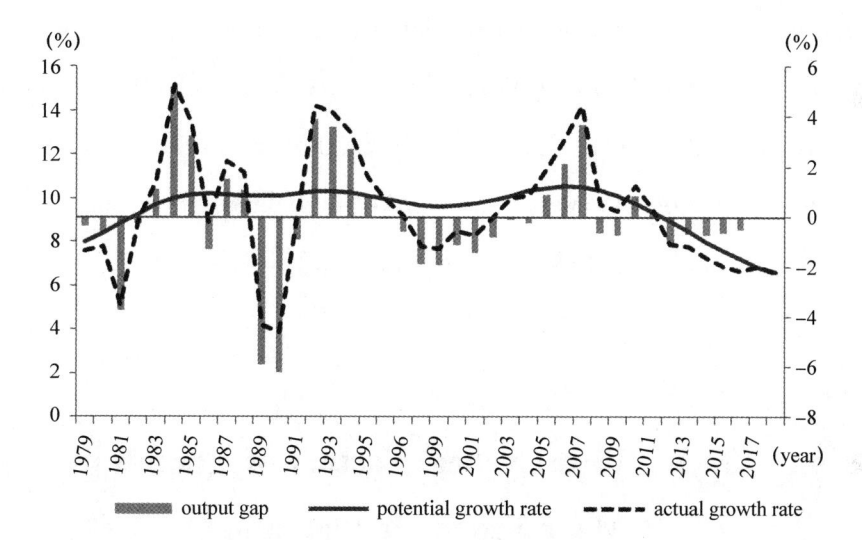

Figure 42 Trends of China's potential economic growth and output gap

In the medium-and long-term, China's economic development must complete the following tasks in order to shift the gears of economic growth.

First, avoid the "Thucydides trap". Pursue a peaceful rise, achieve coordination between domestic economic growth and international relations, and strive to build "a community with a shared future for mankind". Second, overcome the "middle-income trap". Improve general welfare without populism and remove the bottlenecks to entering a high-income stage. Third, transcend the "Minsky moment". Achieve a crisis-free financial environment that can finance development while preventing risks. Fourth, solve the "riddle of Needham". Promote innovation with the coordination of both government and markets, and solve the problems related to scientific and technological progress and frontier innovation. Fifth, cross the inflection point of "Environmental Kuznets Curve". Realize the structural transformation of sustainable development and strike a balance between human development and a healthy environment.

II. Five Cyclical Factors of China's Macroeconomic Operation

From the perspective of cyclical factors, China's economy is currently at a pointindicating that the short-term positioning of 2019 and 2020 is generally moving downward. The most relevant negative cyclical events include the intensification of Sino-US trade friction, a new global economic downturn, a bottoming of the investment cycle, financial market declines, and a new round of market-oriented destocking. Therefore, strong countercyclical macroeconomic policies are needed to offset and prevent these cycle effects.

Firstly, a new downturn in the world economic cycle has just begun. Its direct trigger is the Sino-US trade friction. This has not only stalled the two major economic growth engines, China and the US, but has also increased uncertainty and depressed market confidence, leading to the overall contraction of trade, investment, and consumption worldwide. As a result, the global manufacturing industry has fallen into a collective downturn, and this cyclical downturn is just a beginning. A new downward cycle combined with the long-term stagnation of the global economy has brought the world economy to a crossroad.

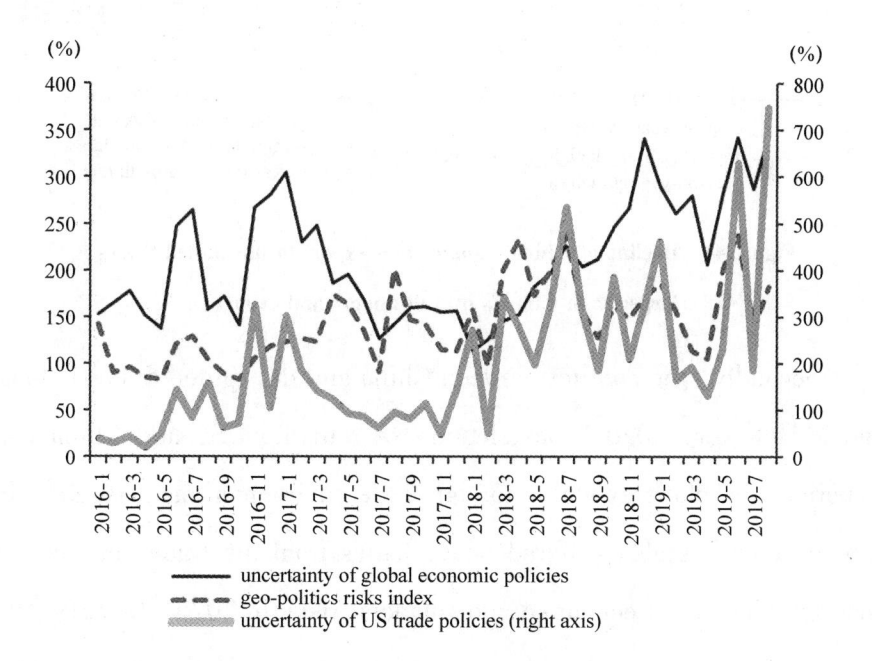

Figure 43 Global uncertainty index has surged

The Sino-US trade friction will comprehensively change China's external environment and become one of the core factors of China's economic downward pressure in the near future.

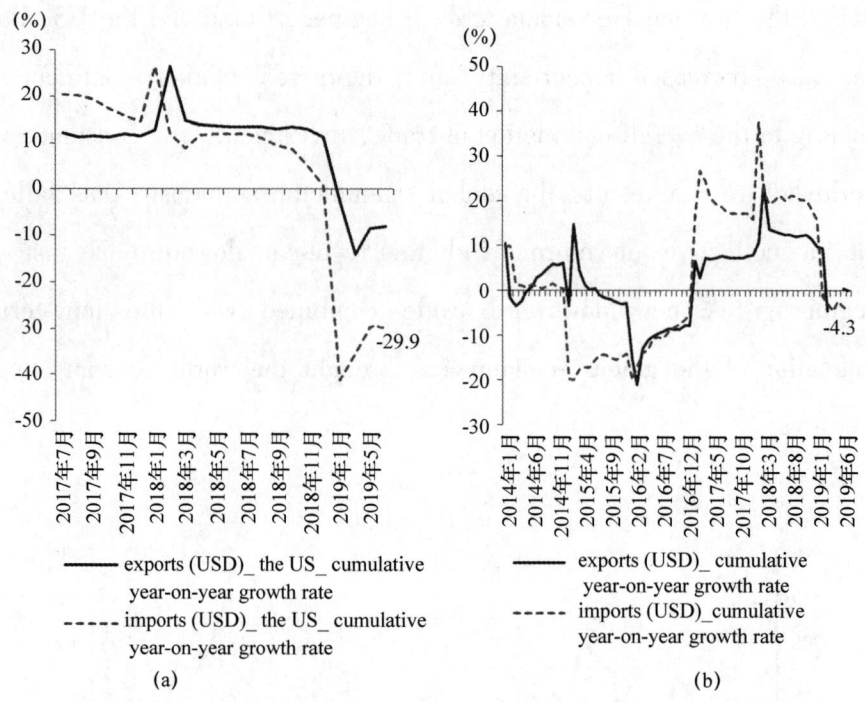

(a)

——— exports (USD)_ the US_ cumulative year-on-year growth rate
----- imports (USD)_ the US_ cumulative year-on-year growth rate

(b)

——— exports (USD)_ cumulative year-on-year growth rate
----- imports (USD)_ cumulative year-on-year growth rate

Figure 44　Decline of China's import and export to the United States is larger than China's overall import and export

Secondly, the conflict between China and the United States is long-term. However, 2020 is an election year in the US, and China may experience a relatively stable foreign trade environment as a result. The US economy has also suffered heavy losses from the trade conflict and may face increased economic and financial risks in 2020. In 2019, the downward pressure on the US economy has increased, the growth rate of private investment has declined at an accelerated rate and so does that of consumer spending. In particular, contraction of durable goods consumption has been noticed. At the same time, the financial parameters of the US have changed, for instance, there has been an inverted yield curve of American government bonds. Small-and medium-sized hedge funds have bought credit default swap instruments, betting that the current leverage ratio on corporate bonds greater than 30 signals default, especially in an economic downturn. The trading volume of synthetic guaranteed debt instruments related to the credit index has increased by about 40% from more than US 200 billion in 2018, and the daily trading volume of swap options has reached US 20 billion to US 25 billion.

Thirdly, China's investment cycle is still at its bottom. At present, the nominal growth rate of China's fixed asset investment is still slowing down. The actual investment growth rate excluding price factor is just beginning to move out of its extremely depressed state. What's more, the investment in equipment, tools, and new construction of enterprises, remains in the doldrums, indicating that all kinds of enterprises are not ready for investment and technological transformation for the next round of economic prosperity.

Fourthly, in general, China's financial cycle has peaked and fallen, but the debt risk in 2019 has been effectively mitigated, providing a relatively favorable financing environment for economic

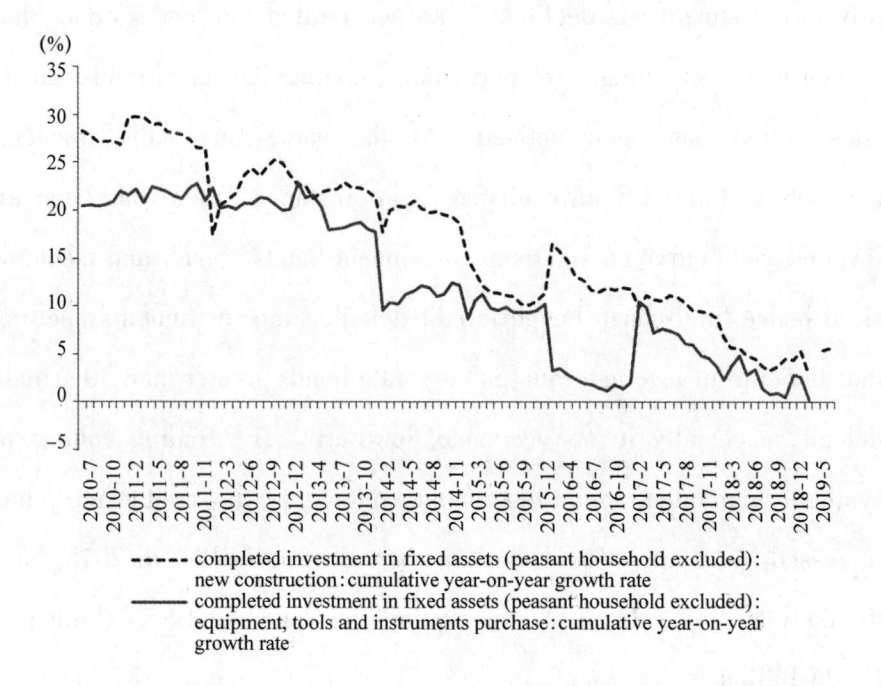

Figure 45 China's investment in new construction and purchase of equipment, tools and instruments hovers around bottom

- - - - - completed investment in fixed assets (peasant household excluded): new construction: cumulative year-on-year growth rate
———— completed investment in fixed assets (peasant household excluded): equipment, tools and instruments purchase: cumulative year-on-year growth rate

stability in 2020. Since 2017, China has experienced a downward period in its financial cycle. The strength of financial supply side structural reform, prudential macro supervision and regulatory policies have determined the extension of China's financial downturn. Various financial indexes also show that China's financial cycle began to fall after reaching a historical high in 2017. However, due to the stage success in containing financial risks, especially the effective mitigation of debt risk, market liquidity is in a stable state. This stability provides a more favorable environment for investment, finance, and economic growth in 2020, and also plays a positive role in boosting market confidence.

Fifthly, other short-term factors such as inventory cycle and real estate cycle have been on downward trends in 2019. First of all, from the perspective of the inventory cycle and under the most pessimistic scenario, enterprises have reduced inventory too rapidly, even though they were close to the bottom of the cycle. This has certainly exerted downward pressure on the macroeconomy in 2019. As the market is expected to pick up in 2020, replenishment may occur.

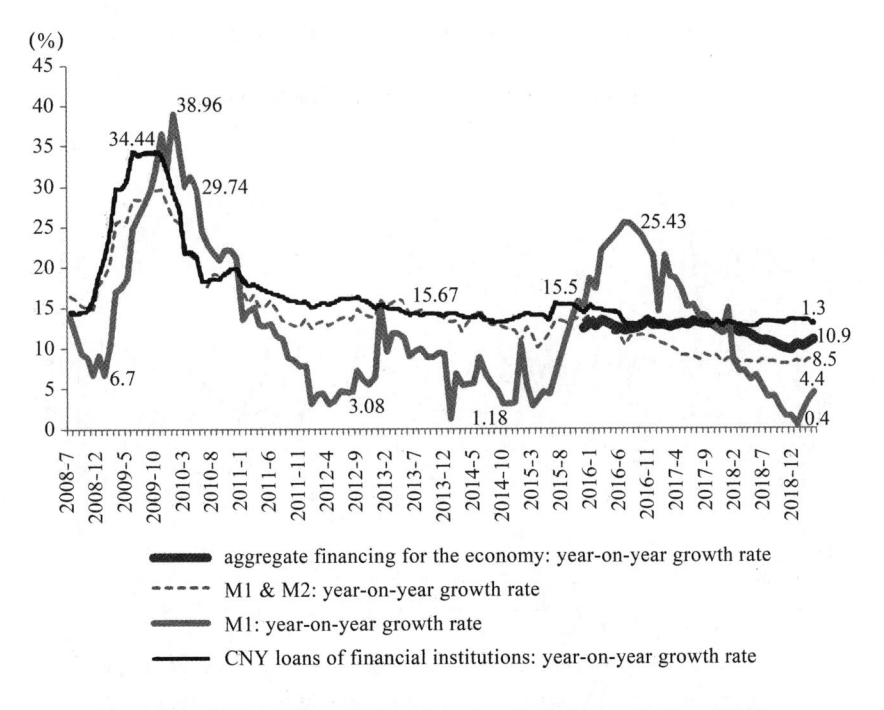

Figure 46　China's financial cycle as a whole has peaked and fallen

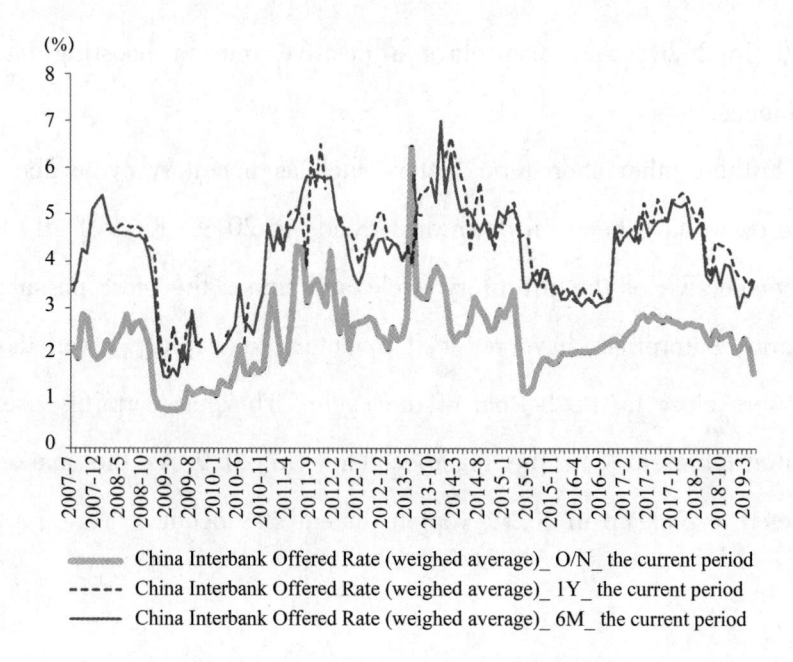

254 China's Macroeconomy in the Key Period of Structural Adjustment

— China Interbank Offered Rate (weighed average)_ O/N_ the current period
----- China Interbank Offered Rate (weighed average)_ 1Y_ the current period
— China Interbank Offered Rate (weighed average)_ 6M_ the current period

Figure 47　Market liquidity in a stable state

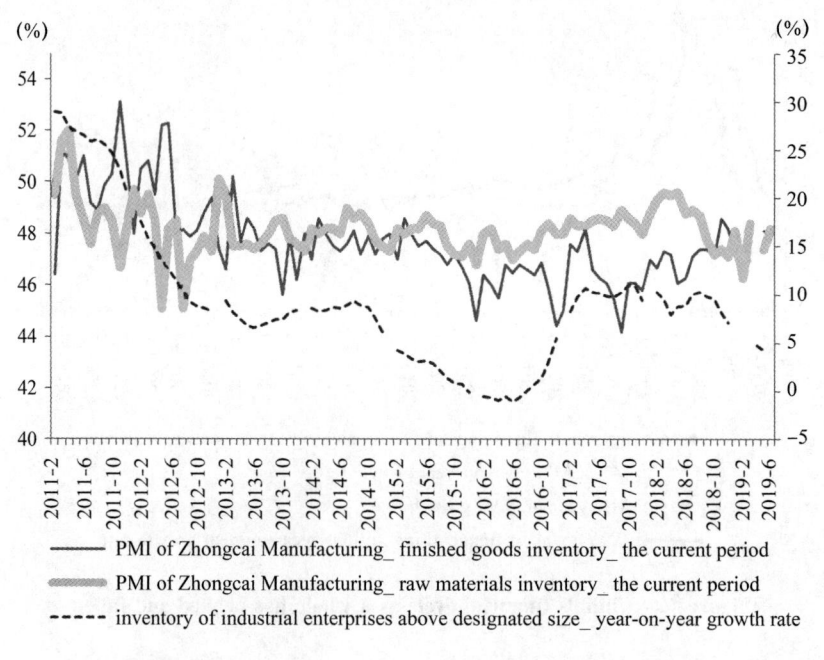

— PMI of Zhongcai Manufacturing_ finished goods inventory_ the current period
— PMI of Zhongcai Manufacturing_ raw materials inventory_ the current period
----- inventory of industrial enterprises above designated size_ year-on-year growth rate

Figure 48　Inventory cycle on a downward trend in 2019

Second, from the perspective of the real estate cycle, real estate market indicators have begun to diverge. In the past two years, the growth rate of real estate sales declined and turned negative in 2019. However, real estate investment has maintained a growth rate of about 10%, which seems to support the growth of total investment. Moreover, more detailed analysis finds thatconstruction starts in the first three quarters of 2019 increased by 8.6%, while the floor space of buildings completed increased by -8.6%—a gap of 17.2 percentage points. This situation has lasted for nearly two years since the beginning of 2018, and we may still face a phenomenon of "investment without growth" in 2020.

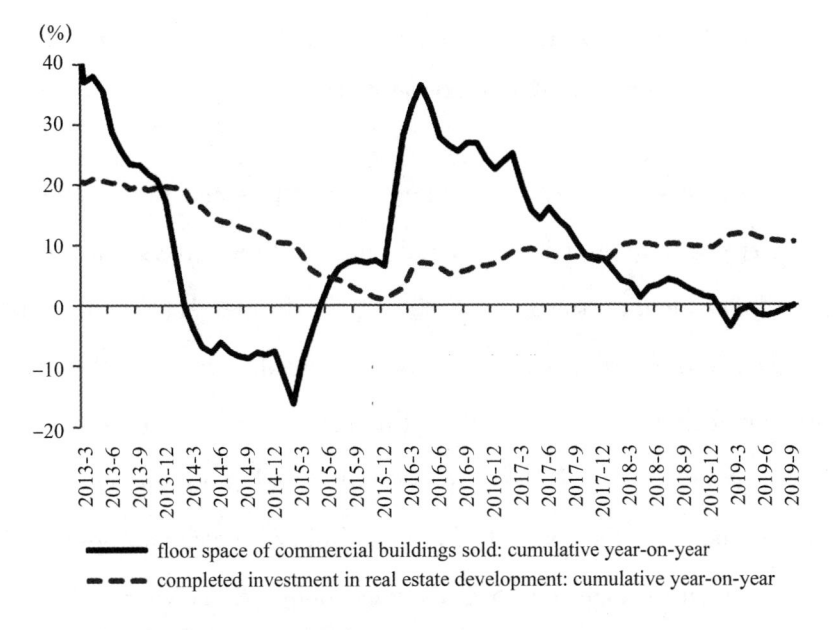

—— floor space of commercial buildings sold: cumulative year-on-year
--- completed investment in real estate development: cumulative year-on-year

Figure 49　Trend differentiation of growth rates of real estate sales and investment growth

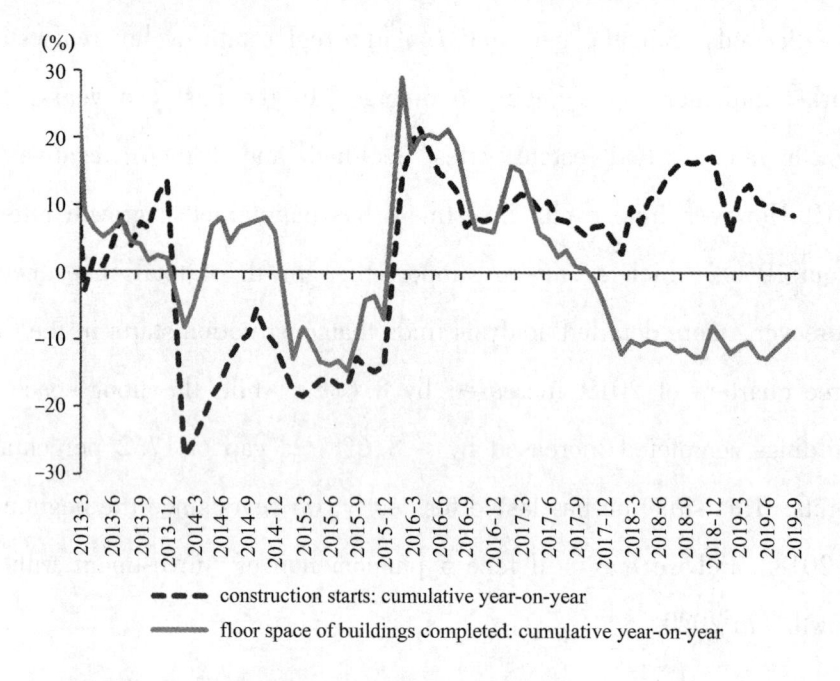

Figure 50 Trend differentiation of growth rates of construction starts and floor space of buildings completed

On the whole, under the influence of trends and cyclical factors, and the strengthening of international and domestic adverse factors, the decline of economic growth in 2020 will be further sustained. On the one hand, downward trends have not reversed. On the other hand, international and domestic cyclical fluctuations will increase, and the changes of cyclical and trend forces will overlap in the current and future period. In the past 10 years, China's economic growth has declined by an average of 0.5 percentage points every year.

But at present, the institutional dividend of China's economy has begun to recover. At the same time, the recent lowering of financial risks and the gradual easing of trade friction between China and the US will bring a relatively stable financial market and foreign trade environment for 2020, and contribute to the reconstruction of market confidence. A new round of confidence building will start in the fourth quarter of 2019. Moreover, a medium-term reform plan is very important for the rapid follow-up of the fourth plenary session of the 19th CPC Central Committee. The guidelines and blueprint of the fourth plenary session needs to be refined and implemented as soon as possible. In particular, there should be a medium-term plan and a package of reform programs for the next stage focused on income distribution and scientific and technological innovation.

◇ III. Top 10 positive factors of China's macroeconomic operation in 2020

Based on the analysis of the trends and cyclical factors in 2019—2020, pessimists may believe that the increasing downward pressure on China's economy means that economic growth will fall sharply in 2020. However, our research and analysis find that in 2020 part of the cyclical forces will be reversed, and China's institutional dividend will continue to improve. Moreover, we identify 10 positive factors in the operation of the macroeconomy that should be recognized and strengthened.

Therefore, the macroeconomic downturn in 2020 will be eased, and the downward range will be significantly narrower than that in 2019.

Firstly, with the reorganization of its bureaucracy the full implementation of the principles of the fourth plenary session of the 19th CPC Central Committee, China's system dividend will rise, and TFP growth rate will significantly improve. As mentioned above, we find that the growth rate of TFP in the past two years has changed from negative to positive and is in gradual recovery, indicating that the reforms and adjustments of the past period are beginning to bear fruit. A new wave of reforms has begun: the institutional reforms at the central and provincial levels have already been completed and are deepening at the county and township levels. Therefore, the adaptation period for the transformation of governance is basically completed, and confidence in the future is getting stronger.

In accordance with the spirit of thefourth plenary session of the 19th CPC Central Committee, the positive impacts of the institutional dividend can be enhanced if we implement a new round of reform programs for 2020. The reforms should focus on perfecting the socialist economic system from the three aspects of ownership, distribution, and operations, and should also promote the opening of markets, internationalization, high standards, and more effective protection of the private economy.

Secondly, with the stability of leverage ratios, the decline of the growth rate of debt, the orderly closing of high-risk institutions, the supplement of capital of financial institutions, and the improvement of regulations, financial risks are reduced, and the financial environment will be significantly improved.

(1) The leverage ratio of state-owned industrial enterprises has steadily declined, while the leverage ratio of private industrial enterprises has been rising. These two trends are converging. As of the end of September, the asset liability ratio of state-owned and state-owned holding industrial enterprises was 58.4%, and the asset liability ratio of private industrial enterprises was 57.9% in the same period. (2) In fact, the period of high risks evident since 2013 has come to an end: P2P, stock disasters, bond defaults of private enterprises, pressure on small and medium-sized banks, and the problems of several financial holding groups are all under effective control. (3) The growth rate of the debt service due next year has declined and debt service pressure has been reduced. At the same time, the trend of rapidly rising debt ratios has been effectively reversed, which provides space for the stability and slight recovery of leverage ratios in the future.

At present, the effects of marginal easing of monetary policy are beginning to show. Enterprise capital has been replenished, indicating that a gradual adjustment process has begun. From the perspective of cash flow, social financing has recovered and financing in most industries has improved. From the perspective of operating cash flow,

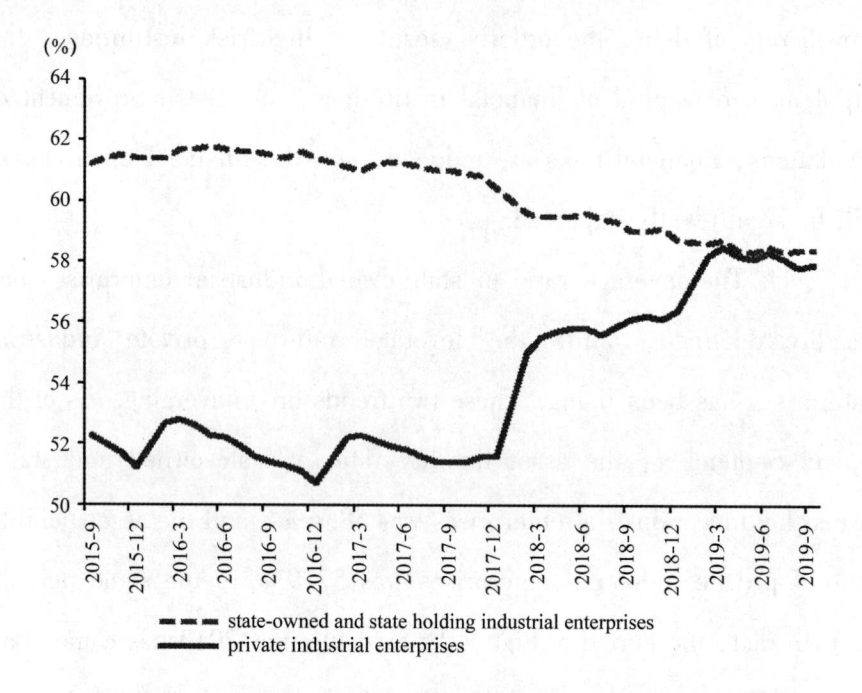

Figure 51 Leverage ratios of state-owned and private industrial
enterprises tend to converge

the proportion of enterprises with improved operating cash flow across 15 industries—such as textile and garment, and light industry manufacturing—is higher than in the same period last year. From the perspective of investment cash flow, the proportion of 18 enterprises with improved investment cash flow in mining, real estate, national defense and military industries is higher than that in the same period last year. From the perspective of financing cash flow, financing of 20 industries has improved, and the proportion of enterprises with improved financing cash flow is higher than that of the same period last year, among which cyclical industries such as steel, non-ferrous metals, building materials have improved significantly.

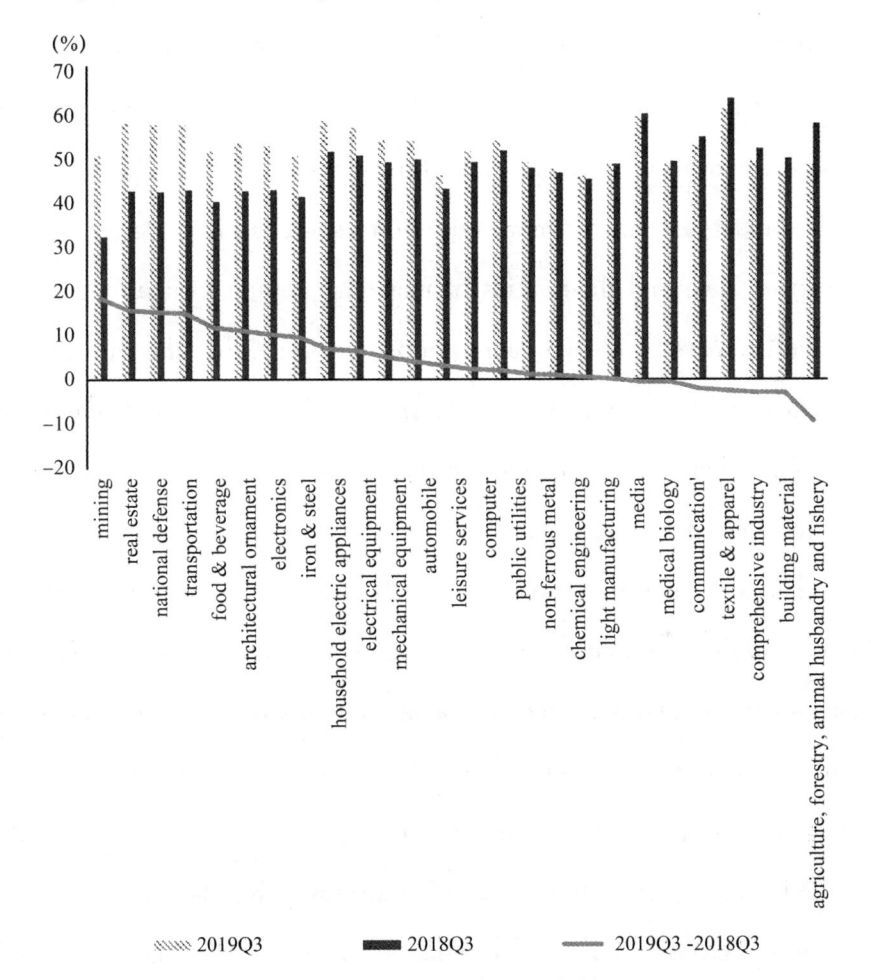

Figure 52 Proportion of enterprises with improved net cash flow from investment activities in different industries of listed companies (excluding finance)

However, at present, the solvency of enterprises has not changed significantly. The asset liability ratios of industries such as national defense and military industry, leisure service, building materials, iron and steel have declined, while the asset liability ratios of media, chemical industry, non-ferrous metals and other industries have increased. From the perspective of short-term solvency, among the 26 industries shown in Fig. 53, only transportation, comprehensive and media industries have improved their short-term solvency. More enterprises have had their ratios of monetary capital to short-term debt increase compared with the same period last year, but the ratios of 22 industries including iron and steel, automobile, national defense and military industry, and construction materials have decreased compared with the same period last year.

Therefore, monetary policy for 2020 should adopt a new approach. When liquidity has improved but solvency has not changed, monetary policy should shift from quantitative instruments to price instruments—cutting interest rates to adjust financing scale, stabilize asset prices, and reduce the pressure of debt service.

Thirdly, the inventory cycle of enterprises has bottomed out and rebounded. Excessive inventory reduction in the early stage provides a large space for enterprises to replenish inventory in 2020. In the past two years, enterprises have been excessively pessimistic, resulting in the phenomenon of inventory overshoot. Inventory levels in the industrial sector have shrunk significantly and are close to the lowest levels of the previous industrial depression. There is a high probability

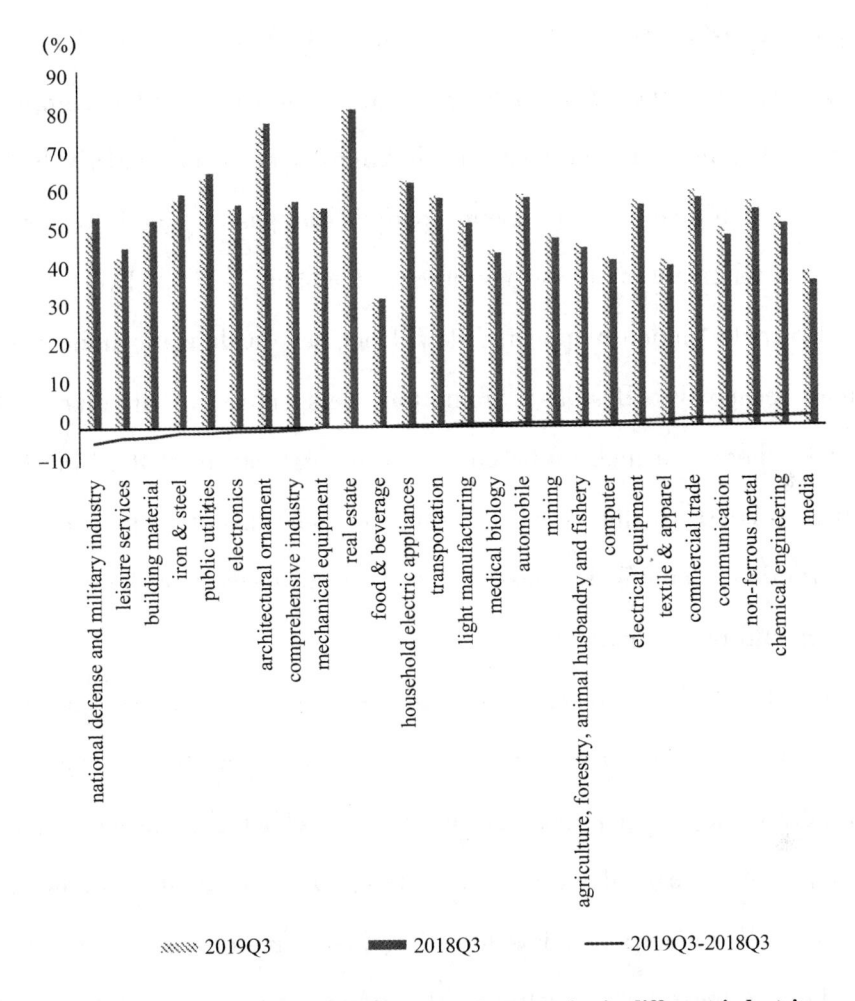

Figure 53 Asset liability ratios of listed companies in different industries (excluding finance)

of recovery in 2020. Therefore, with the normalization of business operations and the replenishment of inventories in 2020, production will expand.

Fourthly, the panic period of Sino-US trade friction has passed, adaptive adjustments have been made, and enterprise confidence should return. Although the future of Sino-US trade friction is still uncertain, the expectations and confidence of all kinds of economic entities have improved significantly. The panic period has passed, and we have entered a relatively calm and confident adjustment period. Even if the Sino-US trade friction reappears, it will not have a dramatic impact on China's economy. Besides, from the perspective of international politics, there is a high probability of a gradual easing of the Sino-US friction in 2020. In the past two years, we have handled the Sino-US trade friction in an effective manner, and it's suggested that the strategic focus should be maintained.

Fifthly, various strategies launched in response to external shocks will effectively enhance the effective demand of corresponding departments, especially in key technologies, scientific and technological research and development system, domestic substitutes, and important equipment. The Sino-US trade friction has forced China to readjust its strategies, especially in these key industries. At present, the short-term effects of the new strategies have appeared in the fields of national defense, military industry, computers, mechanical equipment and non-bank finance. On the other hand, in 2019, trade friction between China and the US have continued to ferment, and the production and operation of traditional cyclical industries have not improved. However, with supportive policies, some strategic emerging industries such as national defense and military industry, computers, mechanical equipment, biological industry, new material industry, have maintained net profit growth of over 20% year-on-year. In addition, due to the impact of financial regulatory policy, the profitability of the financial industry has

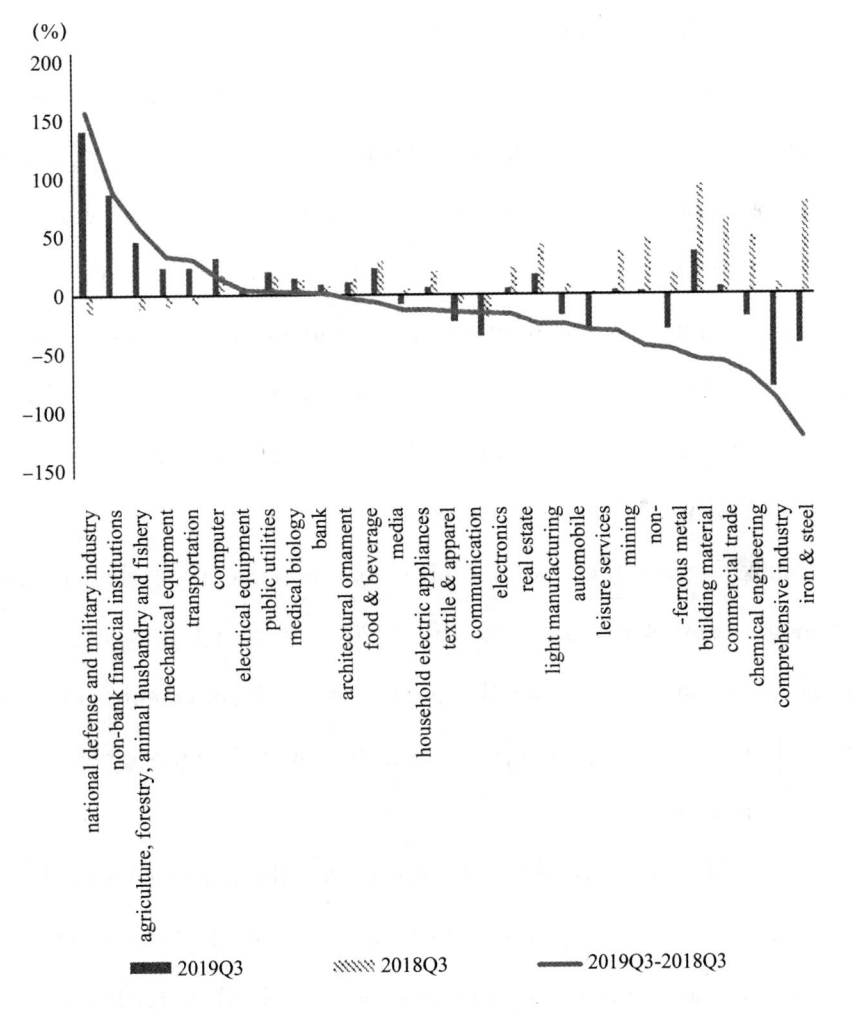

Figure 54 Year-on-year growth rates of net profits of branches of listed companies

rebounded, especially in the growth rates of the operating revenue and net profits of non-bank finance and banks.

From the perspective of expanding reproduction, 11 industries—including building materials, machinery and equipment, national defense and military industry—have increased their year-on-year growth rates, indicating that these enterprises have strong capacity to expand reproduction. Trade-sensitive industries, such as electronics, commerce, and computers have declining year-on-year growth rates, demonstrating limited capacities to expand reproduction. The year-on-year growth rates of the total assets in industries such as household appliances, leisure services, agriculture, forestry, animal husbandry and fishing, and textile and apparel have gone from positive to negative, displaying weak reproduction capacities.

Sixthly, with the reversal of global automobile cycle, Chinese automobile market may stabilize. In 2020, the global automobile cycle is likely to bottom out, and the growth rates of automobile trade and automobile sales will pick up, driving the overall improvement of the manufacturing industry.

Seventhly, the reversal of the pig cycle, the normalization of pork supply and demand, and the substantial decline of pork prices, will provide room for expansionary macro policies and will improve consumer expectations. According to current market adjustment speeds, pork production is expected to improve in the first half of 2020, and pork

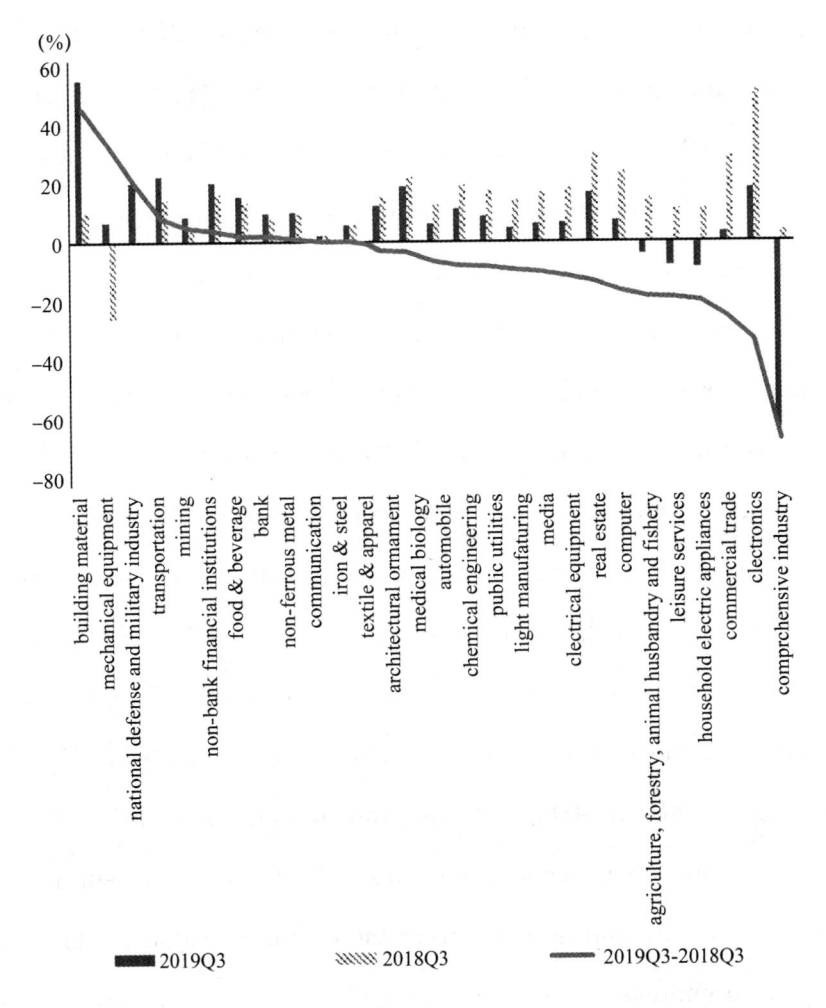

Chapter Three The Nature of China's Economic Growth in 2020 from a Midium-term Perspective | **267**

Figure 55 Year-on-year growth rates of total assets of branches of listed companies

prices will fall in the second half of 2020. Declining pork prices will positively impact people's livelihood and will allow for relaxing the constraints on macro policies.

Eightly, with the increase of infrastructure and state-owned enterprise investment, and the improved expectations of private entrepreneurs, private investment will no longer lag the rest of the economy in 2020. In the past, the low volatility of China's economy was closely related to the countercyclical investment behavior of state-owned enterprises. However, in the past two years, because of de-stocking, de-leveraging, and strict auditing, state-owned enterprise investment has not played its traditional countercyclical role. On the contrary, there was a negative growth in 2018 that lasted until the second half of 2019. More importantly, the investment of state-owned enterprises has a strong driving effect on the investment of private enterprises. It is the source of large-scale projects, investment funds and business confidence. Therefore, the recovery of state-owned enterprises' investment is the key to the implementation of countercyclical policy. With the completion of the reforms, the investment behavior of state-owned enterprises has begun to normalize. With the investment of state-owned enterprises starting to recover, the overall investment situation is expected to improve.

From the perspective of expanding reproduction, at present, the growth ofconstruction by state-owned enterprises has accelerated, but the willingness of private enterprises to expand reproduction is still weak. In the third quarter of 2019, the year-on-year growth rates of total assets and construction in progress of most enterprises decreased compared with the same period last year. Since state-owned enterprises

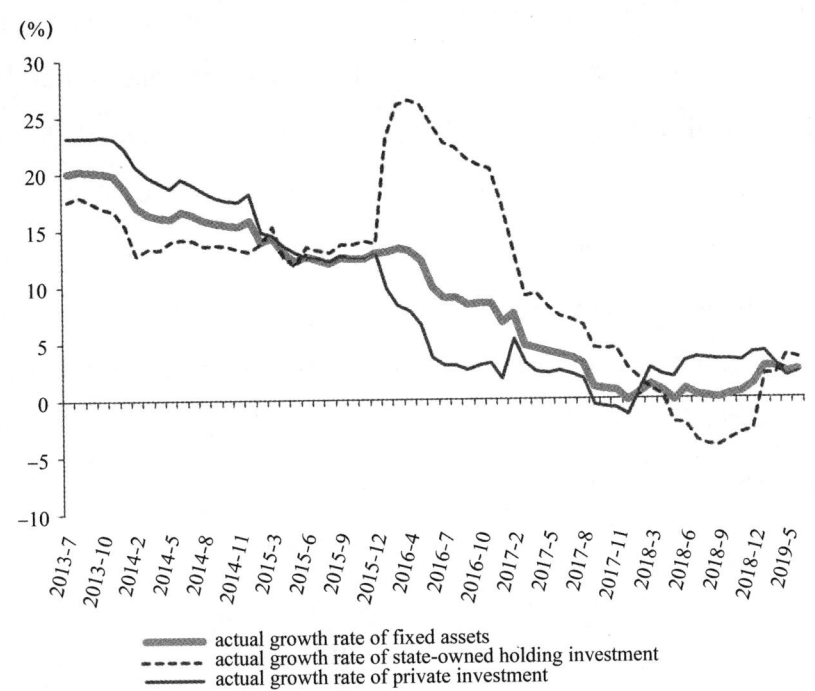

Figure 56 Investment relationship between state-owned enterprises and private enterprises

— actual growth rate of fixed assets
----- actual growth rate of state-owned holding investment
— actual growth rate of private investment

are mainly located in upstream industries and are affected by the supply side reform, the year-on-year growth rate of total assets has declined, and their reproduction capacities have been affected to some extent. However, the year-on-year growth rate of construction in progress has picked up compared with the same period last year, and the demand for expanding reproduction is still strong. Conversely, since the proportion of private enterprises in the downstream is larger, their year-on-year growth rates of total assets and projects under construction have been lower than that of the same period last year, and the willingness of enterprises to reproduce is weak. At present, the scope of foreign investment in China is mainly concentrated in modern agriculture, advanced manufacturing, high technology, energy conservation and environmental protection, modern service industry, and other light asset fields. In the third quarter, the growth rate of the total assets of foreign-funded enterprises declined significantly year-on-year. But they have benefited from the release of a series of foreign investment policy dividends, and as a result, the scale of projects under construction of foreign-funded enterprises has increased and expanded, and the willingness of these enterprises is relatively strong.

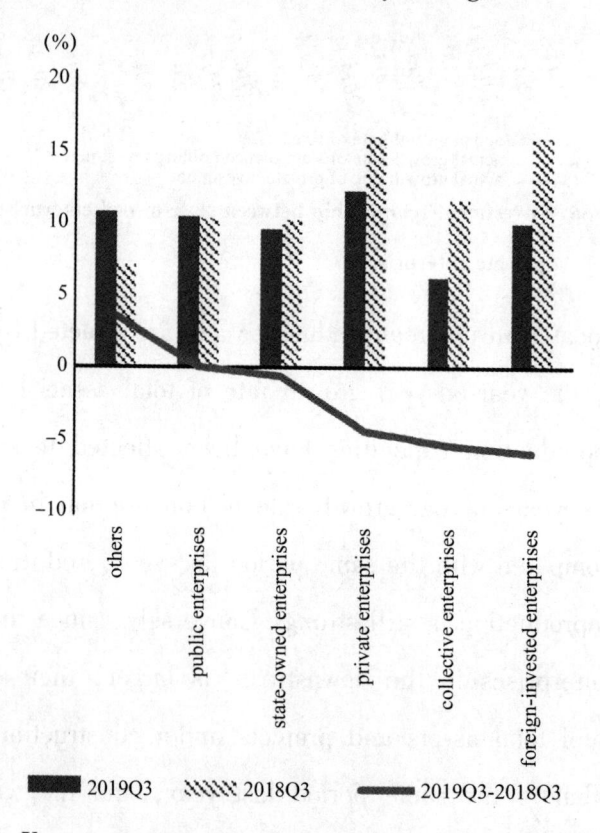

Figure 57 Year-on-year growth rates of total assets under separate ownership

Chapter Three The Nature of China's Economic Growth in 2020 from a Midium-term Perspective **271**

Ninethly, a new round of more active fiscal policy and a stable monetary policy of marginal easing will make positive impacts. Together with the social policy dividend from a moderately well-off society in all aspects and a global policy dividend from global monetary easing, the policy dividend in 2020 will be greater than previous years.

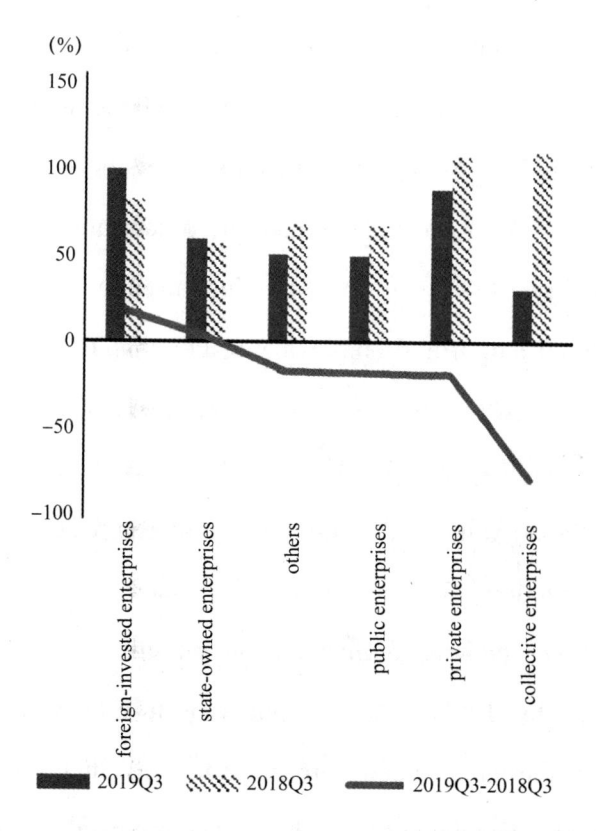

Figure 58 Year-on-year growth rates of construction in progress under separate ownership

(1) The policy dividend of taxcuts and fee reduction will be fully realized. While tax cuts and fee reduction deepen and then improve the

micro foundation of enterprises, there remain delays in the transmission to the macroeconomy. Therefore, the policy effects will be more fully apparent in 2020. To illustrate, we develop a structural model that fully considers the heterogeneity of production and demand and identifies the parameters of the production function and demand function at the same time. Using 10 manufacturing industries in the database of industrial enterprises above the scale of China, we evaluate and simulate the effect of the VAT reduction. First, the short-term effects of the VAT reduction are considerable. After the VAT reduction, output and employment will increase; the larger the range of VAT reduction, the stronger the growth effects will be on output and employment. For example, for a 3% VAT reduction, the growth rates of total output and total employment of manufacturing industry are 4.30% and 7.07% respectively. Second, improving both the value-added tax deduction chain and the enterprise input tax deduction also result in significant policy effects. For example, if these policies reduce the output tax rate by 3% and the input tax rate by 1.5%, the output growth rate will increase by 3.81%, and the employment growth rate will increase by 3.37% compared with benchmark results. These results confirm that distinguishing output and input tax rates provide considerable additional information. Third, a VAT reduction can significantly improve the efficiency of resource allocation in manufacturing industries and enhance macro productivity. With higher rates of production, enterprises grow faster, their market share increases, and they employ more labor and raise output.

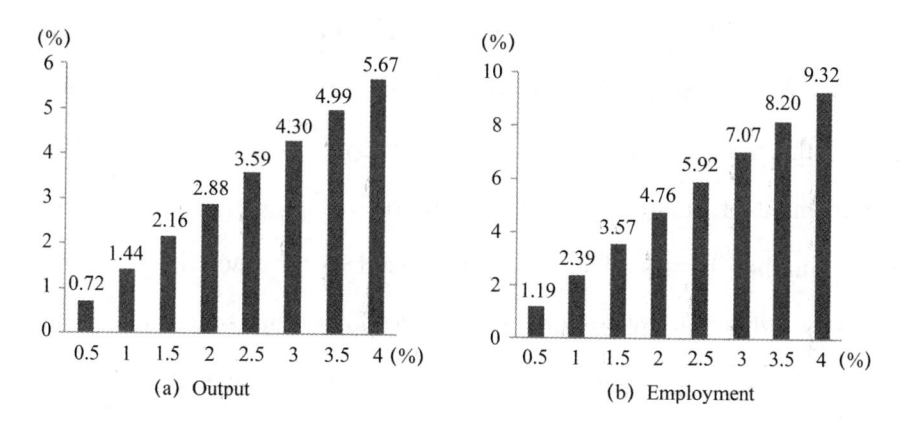

Figure 59　Effects of reducing VAT rate in manufacturing industry

Furthermore, according to the data of 10 service industries in a national tax survey, the policy simulation of the impacts of social insurance reductions on output and employment in service industries shows that, first, the output and employment effects are considerable. When the social insurance rate of the service industry is cut by 4%, output will increase by 5.7%. It turns out that the relationship between the range of social security reduction and the growth of enterprise output and labor demand is stable: the employment effect of the reduction is twice the range of the reduction. For example, if the reduction is 4%, employment demand will increase by nearly 8%. Second, the change of service enterprise cost is reflected more in real effects (output and employment) than in price transmission. In the face of declining labor costs, service enterprises have chosen to increase employment and provide more services rather than reduce prices. Third, the reduction of fees can significantly improve the efficiency of resource allocation and the overall TFP of the service industry. The higher the production rate, the faster the growth of enterprises, the more the labor demand, and the higher the market share. Fouth, the incentive effect of reducing fees on employment of small-scale service enterprises is stronger. Due to the large number of small and medium-sized enterprises in the service industry, the role of reducing fees in promoting social employment cannot be underestimated. At the same time, because small-scale service enterprises are more sensitive to the change of labor cost, the reform of social insurance levy system should be coordinated with the actual policy of reducing fees.

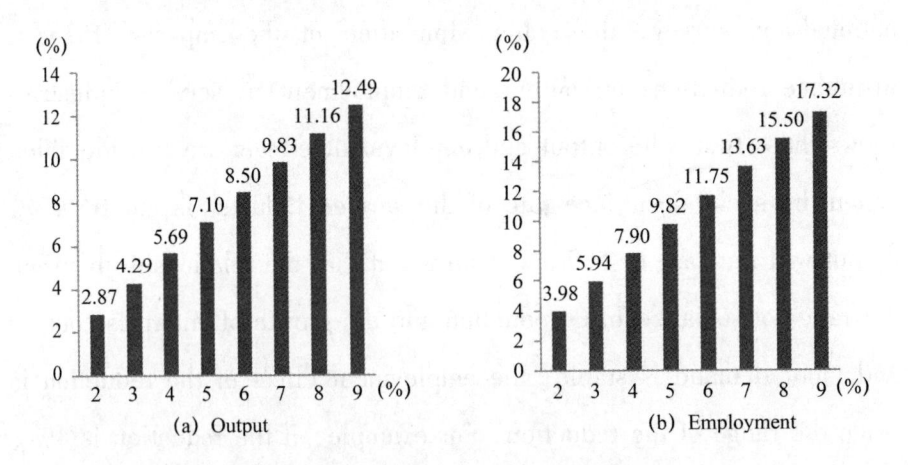

Figure 60　Simulation of policy effect of social insurance fee reduction in service industry

Effects of the current fiscal policy are evident, and therefore should be extended to 2020. At the same time, a proactive fiscal policy should shift focus from production to consumption. Tax reductions aimed at production have clear effects on reducing the cost of enterprises. But if consumption lags, the efficiency of policy transmission will decline. Additionally, the effects of using consumption stimulus as a counter cycle adjustment tool are immediate. The most typical case is a reduction of the car purchase tax. Besides, we can consider increasing subsidies and transfer payments to low-income groups to alleviate the impact of rising pig prices and income fluctuations on people's livelihood.

In addition to a more active fiscal policy, the social policy dividend brought about by amoderately well-off society in all aspects in 2020, and the global policy dividend brought about by global monetary easing, also determine that the policy dividend in 2020 will be greater than that in previous years.

(2) A social policy dividend will derive from building a moderately prosperous and all-inclusive society. The realization of this goal in 2020 requires that China reduced relative poverty and reformed income distribution, the latter being the focus of the reforms proposed at the fourth plenary session of the CPC Central Committee.

(3) Global policies are consistent with an enhanced global policy dividend. This will bring about a synergy effect of international policies, as the global economic situation is expected to marginally

improve. In order to further promote economic recovery, central banks worldwide have embarked on a new round of interest rate reductions. The US Federal Reserve has cut interest rates three times in 2019, with the federal funds rate remaining in the range of 1.50%—1.75%. The global short-term benchmark interest rate has also declined. Japan, Switzerland and Sweden are all at negative interest rates. The interest rate in the euro area is 0, but its deposit facility rate is -0.5%.

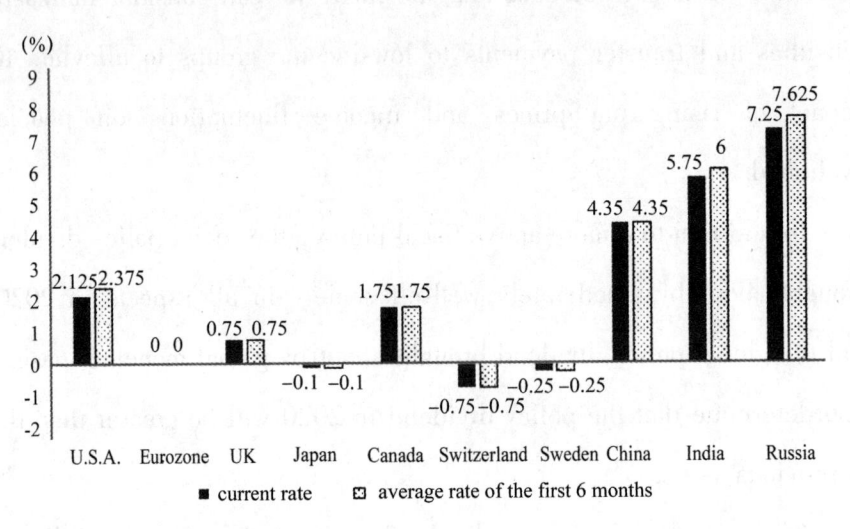

Figure 61 Central bank policy interest rates in major developed and emerging market economies

Source: BIS.

Tenthly, as a result of China's huge market, diversified exports, established industries, abundant human resources, enhanced and expanding innovation and competition, and strong and effective government, the resilience and flexibility of China's economy will be

Chapter Three The Nature of China's Economic Growth in 2020 from a Midium-term Perspective | **277**

further strengthened in 2020. Next year, China's GDP will exceed 100 trillion yuan, with a per capita GDP of more than 10,000 US dollars. The large-scale market advantage and middle-class consumption potential will be further improved. Strong structural changes mean that China has strong development potential and momentum.

(1) Service Industries breed new opportunities as well as new problems. In recent years, with the continuous decline of the proportion of industry to GDP, the proportion of the service industry continues to rise, and the development of the service industry has become the main driving force of China's economic growth. The proportion of financial industry to GDP has increased to about 8%, and the proportion of real

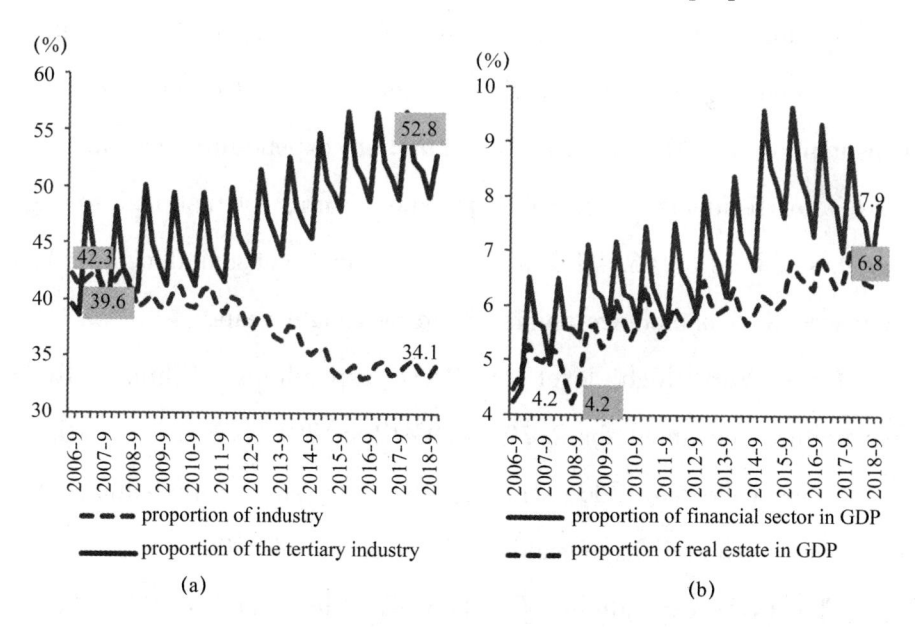

Figure 62 Development of service industry drives China's economic growth

estate industry to GDP has increased to about 7%.

(2) Accelerated consumerization has boosted huge domestic demand. In recent years, China's consumption parameters have undergone revolutionary changes, with the following implications. First, Engel's coefficient is currently 29.33%, reaching the United Nations' standard of affluence and entering the ranks of developed countries, 30 percentage points lower than that in 1978. Secon, the huge middle-income class in China means a huge market. According to the revised data of the fourth national economic census, China's per capita GDP in 2018 exceeded US 10,000, which is close to the average world per capita GDP of US 11,300. Third, the proportions of material consumption and service consumption have changed substantially. Service consumption accounted for more than 40% of household consumption in 2017. Fourth, consumption expenditure accounts for 70.6% of residents' disposable income. Fifth, the national savings rate has fallen to 46.4%, and the national consumption rate has increased by 5 percentage points in the past eight years.

(3) Very high level of R&D expenditure. China's R&D expenditure accounted for 2.2% of GDP in 2018, with a growth of 0.7% compared to 2008. The number of patent applications for invention reached 432 thousand, 4.6 times that of 2008.

The R&D expenditure gap between China and the US keeps declining, andin particular China's scale of R&D expenditure for experimental development has exceeded that of the US. China's R&D

Chapter Three The Nature of China's Economic Growth in 2020 from a Midium-term Perspective | **279**

expenditure is mainly allocated to investment in the experimental development stage, which reached 84.2% of the total expenditure in 2016. Yet, the expenditure for fundamental research is seriously insufficient, only accounting for 5.1% of the total expenditure. Fundamental research and applied research investment combined is 15.8% in total. In contrast, the proportion of fundamental research in the US reaches 16.9%, and the proportion of fundamental and applied research investment reaches 36.4% in total. In particular, departments at the federal government level (including the Department of Energy and NASA but excluding the Department of Defense) allocate the majority of their investment to fundamental and applied research.

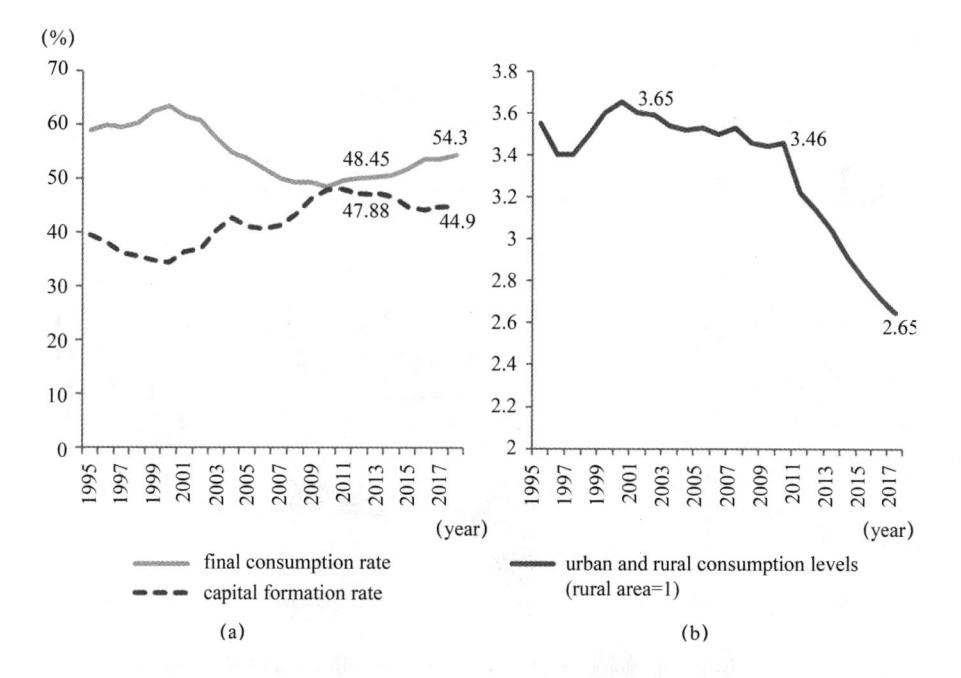

Figure 63 Accelerated consumerization leads to huge domestic demand

(a) Total retail sales of consumer goods

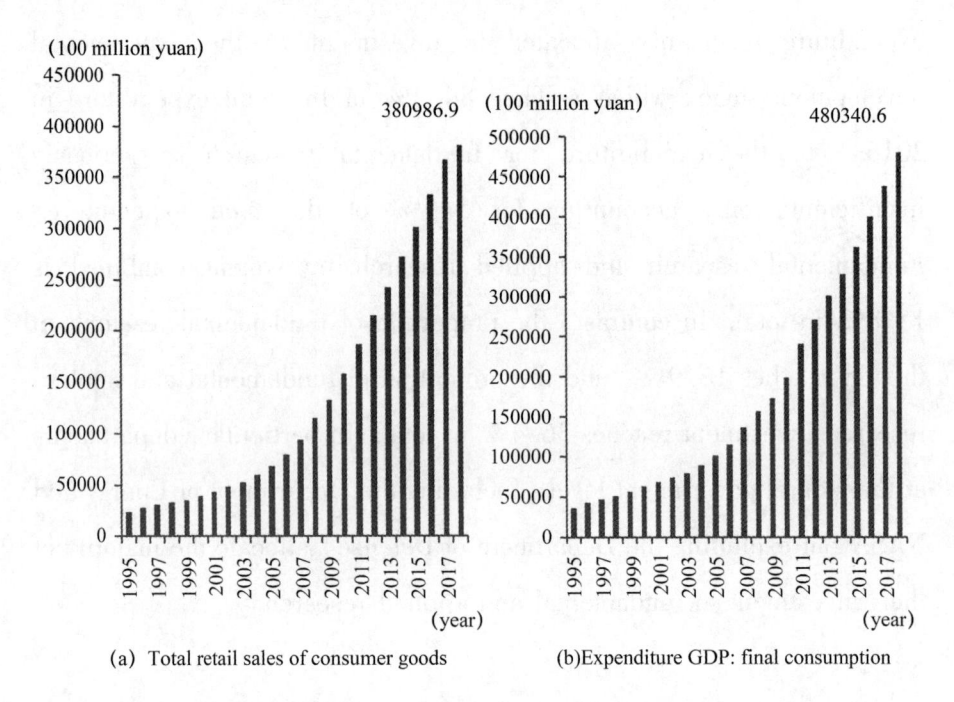

(b) Expenditure GDP: final consumption

Figure 64 Accelerated consumerization leads to huge domestic demand

(a) R&D expenditure as a proportion of GDP

(b) The number of patent applcations

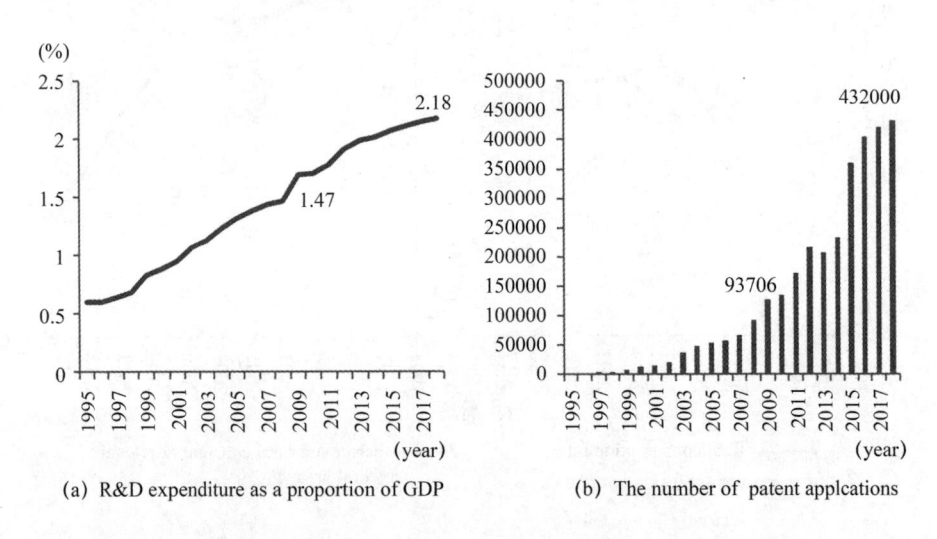

Figure 65 Rapid increase in China's R&D expenditure and the number of patent applications

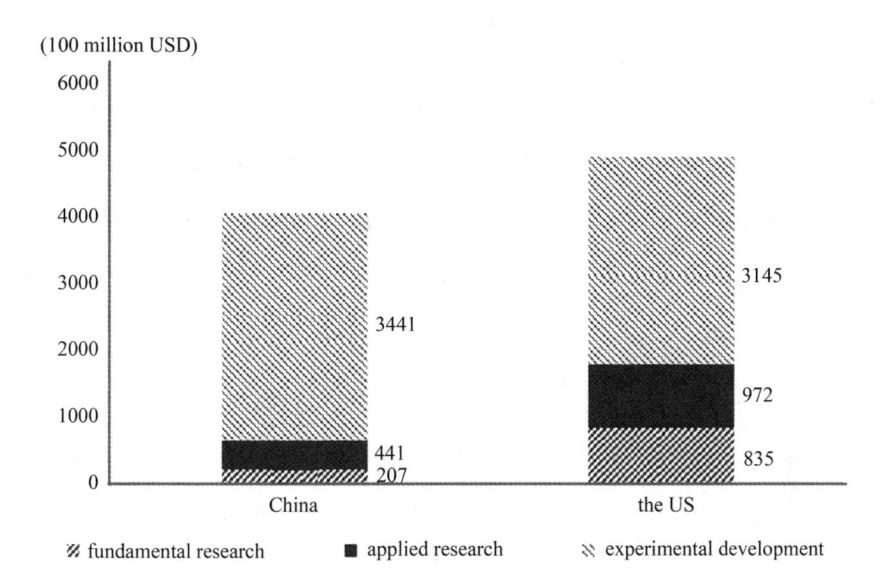

Chapter Three The Nature of China's Economic Growth in 2020 from a Midium-term Perspective **281**

Figure 66 Comparison of R&D expenditure structures in China and the US

(100 million USD)

China: fundamental research 207, applied research 441, experimental development 3441

the US: fundamental research 835, applied research 972, experimental development 3145

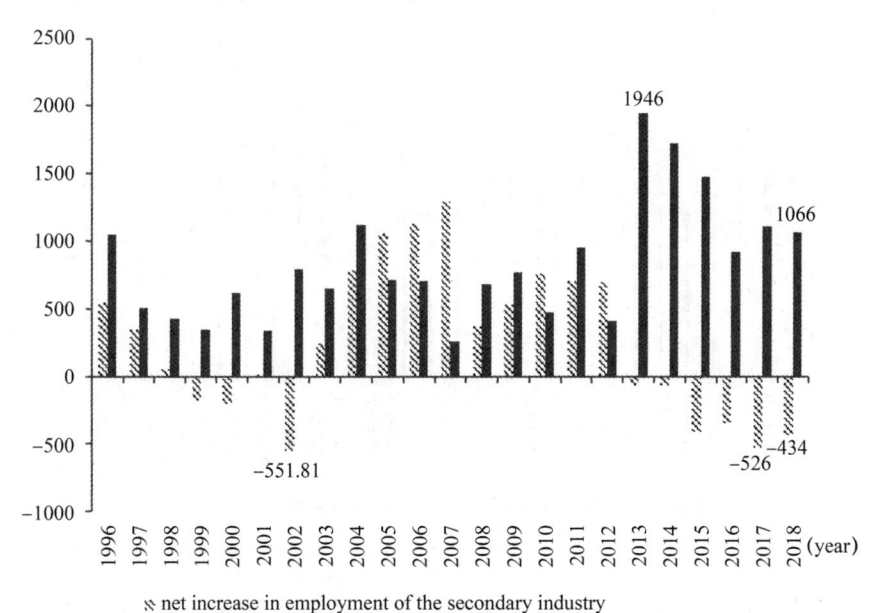

Figure 67 Changes in employment growth for the secondary and tertiary industries in China

net increase in employment of the secondary industry

net increase in employment of the tertiary industry

Key values: 1946 (2013), 1066 (2018), −551.81, −526, −434

(4) The changing economic structure makes employment appear more stable than would be expected from the decline of economic growth. The proportion of the secondary industry in GDP continues to decline, while the proportion of the tertiary industry continues to rise. The acceleration of an employment transfer from the secondary to the tertiary industry can be seen through the fact that the level of employment in the secondary industry has begun to decline while employment in the tertiary industry has increased rapidly. In this context, the same economic growth can absorb more jobs. Therefore, in

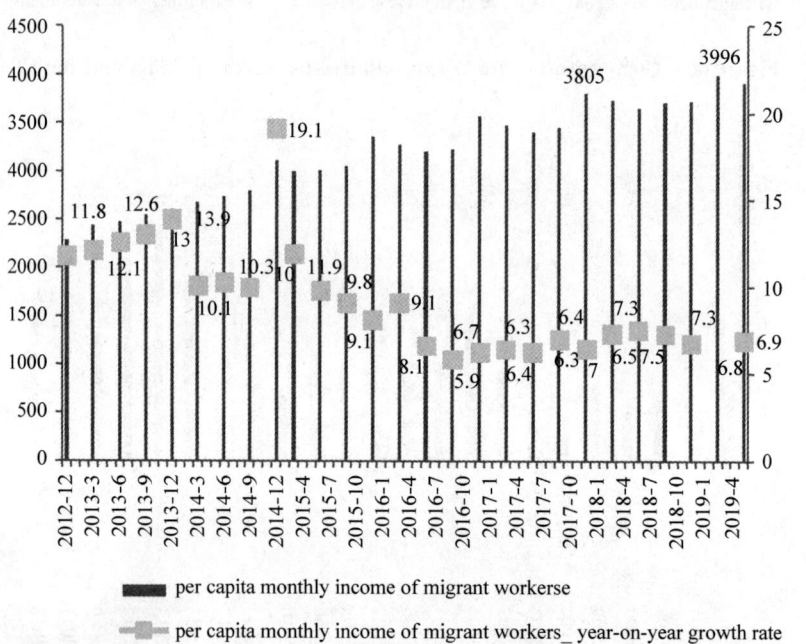

Figure 68 Per capita monthly income of migrant workers and its growth rate in China

the case of declining economic growth, employment is more stable than expected.

In addition to the overall stability of thesurveyed urban unemployment rate, the stability of the labor market is also reflected in the rapid growth of migrant workers' income. Among all categories of workers, the employment and wage growth of migrant workers are the most flexible and most indicative of the changing employment situation. In the first half of 2019, the monthly income of migrant workers reached nearly 4,000 yuan, a year-on-year increase of 6.9%.

In summary, with trends and cyclical factors combining with unfavorable international and domestic factors, economic growth is expected to slow further in 2020. But the decline is expected to be at a slower pace. How to scientifically formulate the economic growth target for 2020 in this context? What are the major risks in the operation of the macroeconomy in 2020? What forward-looking measures are needed?

Chapter Four The Establishment of an Economic Growth Target for 2020 Considering Possible Risks

2020 is the decisive year for building a moderately prosperous society in all aspects, and the year for checking the results of the 13th Five-Year Plan. The lower bound of the economic growth target in 2020 is determined by tightening the constraints on all development goals. The urgency of setting a scientific growth target for 2020 lies in the sharp narrowing of the space between the lower bound of the target and the realistic growth potential. As we have seen, the reduction of the growth rate, changing momentum, and the continued risks that mark the "new normal" period have not ended, and the downward forces have not been reversed. International and domestic cyclical fluctuations will also be of great concern in both current and future periods. Consequently, it's expected that these downward trends be reflected in

2020's economic growth rate. Thus, China must formulate and strive for its main targets for economic and social development in 2020 while preparing for the worst. More effort should be exerted to foster and consolidate and favorable factors, and closer attention should be paid to major risks that may arise in the course of economic operations, for which proactive measures should be taken.

◇ I . The establishment of economic growth target for 2020

To set the 2020 economic growth target scientifically, China needs to adhere to three basic principles: pursue high-quality development, accomplish the missions in this phase under the "two centenary goals", and ensure the basic stability of employment. Contrary to popular belief, after repeated calculations, we have found that 2020's growth target needs not be stuck at more than 6%: 5.5%—6.0%, or even a conservative target of around 5.8% is enough to achieve the missions under the "two centenary goals". It can also ensure the basic stability of social employment, and it is more conducive to maintaining strategic focus and promoting high-quality economic development in accordance with established policies.

1. Adhering to the principle of high-quality development, the target interval for GDP growth in 2020 should be set at 5.5%—6.0%

To promote high-quality economic development in accordance with established guidelines, it is required that the 2020 economic target be in line with the medium-and long-term development trend of China's economy. This means that countercyclical macro policies need to be strengthened in order to hedge against the downward cyclical factors. China's potential growth rate in 2020 will still be at a lowering stage. Among the four forces that have changed the course of economic growth, only the institutional factors have been effectively reversed. In addition, the recent recovery in TFP has yet to assume the responsibility of driving China's economic growth on a regular basis. Meanwhile, the unfavorable effects of various domestic and international cyclical factors have increased significantly and may continue into next year. Therefore, the countercyclical adjustment function of macro policies needs to be strengthened to effectively hedge against this.

Based on the above judgment, the GDP growth target for 2020 should be set at 5.5%—6.0%. The reasons are that GDP growth has declined by about 0.5 percentage points per year on average over the past decade, and the potential economic growth rate in 2020 will still decline significantly. If target GDP growth is still set at 6%—6.5% in

2020, China must rely on strong fiscal stimulus, loose monetary policy and easing of the real estate market to stimulate short-term growth. However, at present, these three conditions may not exist or may be not conducive to medium-and long-term high-quality economic development. Therefore, it is appropriate to set the target for 2020 growth at a range of 5.5%—6.0% in order to maintain strategic focus and promote high-quality economic development in accordance with established policies.

In the medium-and long-term, China's economic development still needs to complete the following historic tasks, so to as provide room for policies when deepening reforms in 2021. First, China should overcome the "Thucydides trap": realize the rise of a great power without war, coordinate domestic economic development with international relations, and build "a community with a shared future for mankind". Second, China should avoid the "middle income trap": improve social and economic welfare without populism and solve the bottleneck problems of income distribution in the high-income stage. Third, China should surpass the "Minsky moment": realize crisis-free financial deepening and solve the problems of financial development and risk prevention. Fourth, China should solve the "Needham puzzle", that is, to realize great innovation under the coordination of both government and market, and to solve the problems of scientific and technological progress and frontier innovation. Fifth, China should cross the inflection point of "Environmental Kuznets Curve": realize the structural transformation of sustainable development and seek a balance between economic development and environmental quality.

2. Adhere to the principle of the "two centenary goals" by keeping the GDP growth target for 2020 at 5%—6%, rather than above 6%

The lower bound of the GDP growth target for 2020 faces the task of achieving the "two centenary goals". If we follow the current statistical standard, 6% will be the target lower bound of GDP growth in 2020. Under the assumption that the GDP growth rate in 2019 is 6.2%, the GDP growth rate in 2020 needs to reach 6.0% to achieve the goal of "doubling the GDP in 2020 compared with that in 2010". If China wants to achieve the goal of "an average annual growth rate of over 6.5% in the 13th Five Year Plan period", the GDP growth rate in 2020 needs to reach 6.2%.

However, according to previous economic censuses, to achieve the above target, economic growth of 4%—5% in 2020 will besufficient. The calculation is as follows. After the first national economic census adjusted the economic data from 1999 to 2004, the growth rate increased by an average of 0.6 percentage points every year. After the second national economic census adjusted the economic data from 2005 to 2008, the growth rate increased by 0.5 percentage points on average every year. After the third national economic census adjusted the economic data from 2009 to 2013, the growth rate increased by an average of 0.56 percentage points every year. Therefore, according to the data adjusted after the fourth national economic census, which was launched at the end of 2018, the economic growth rate is expected to have increased by about 0.5 percentage points annually from 2014 to 2018, with a cumulative increase of 2.0—2.5 percentage points over these five years. Even if the fourth census adjustment only partially reproduced the situation of the first three, with an annual increase of, say, 0.2%, an increase of 5% in 2020 will be enough to achieve the goal of doubling the 2010 figure. On November 22, 2019, the National Bureau of Statistics issued a notice on revising the 2018 GDP data, which revised the 2018 GDP up by 2.1%. This means a growth rate of 4%—5% in 2020, on top of 6.2% in 2019, would be enough to double the 2010 figure.

Therefore, 2020's economic growth target does not need to be over the "6" threshold of growth. After adjustment based on the data of the fourth census, if the growth rate in 2020 remains in the target range of 5.5%—6.0%, the goal of "doubling the GDP in 2020 compared with that in 2010" can be achieved.

3. Adhering to the principle of ensuring basic stability in employment, the growth rate of 5.5%—6.0% is sufficient, with 5.8% being the ideal level. 5% is the lowest level for employment growth, but that level may sacrifice the quality of employment

(1) According to our calculations, a growth target of 5.5%—6.0% will ensure the basic stability of employment. Based on China's

GDP growth rate of 6.2% in 2019, if China's economic growth rate is 6% in 2020, the increase in non-agricultural employment is expected to be 5.9 million, similar to that in 2018, with relatively loose employment. If the economic growth rate is 5.8% in 2020, the increase of non-agricultural employment will be reduced to 4.8 million, slightly more than that in 2019. In comparison with the employment situation in 2019, the employment situation in 2020 will remain stable. If the economic growth in 2020 is 5.5% and the increase in non-agricultural employment is 3.15 million, nearly one million less than that in 2019 and a record low, the employment situation will be even tighter, but there will not be widespread unemployment. The real test for China's employment will come when growth slows to 5% in 2020 and non-farm payroll growth falls to zero. Based on this, 5% is the bottom growth threshold that cannot be broken to ensure that China's employment is secure. In sum, 5.5%—6.0% can ensure the basic stability of employment, while 5.8% is ideal.

(2) Analysis of the specific situation of employment in China in four growth scenarios[①].

[①] People like to use the new urban employment index when examining the employment problem, but this index is not easy to grasp, nor is it rigorous. New urban employment is calculated by the Ministry of Human Resources and Social Security. It's the number of people who have entered urban communities to find a job, but the number does not exclude those who quit. One person may also be double counted, so the figures are not very accurate. The increment of non-agricultural employment is the annual difference between the number of people employed in the secondary and tertiary industries (issued by the Bureau of Statistics), which measures net increase. In essence, urban new employment also reflects the growth of non-agricultural employment, but due to the deviation of repeated statistics, it is not as accurate as using the indicators of non-agricultural employment increase directly.

Chapter Four The Establishment of an Economic Growth Target for 2020 Considering Possible Risks | **291**

Basic assumptions are as follows. The first assumption is to base the measurement on 6.2% economic growth in 2019. The second is that the proportions of GDP of the three industries in 2020 are 6.85%, 33.23% and 53.6% respectively by using a smoothing method. The third is to suppose that there are four scenarios for China's economic growth in 2020, namely 6.0%, 5.8%, 5.5% and 5.0%.

Scenario 1: If China's economy grows by 6% in 2020, the increase of non-agricultural employment will be 5.9 million, and the employment situation will be more relaxed.

If China's economic growth rate is 6% in 2020, the increase of non-agricultural employment will be 5.9 million, which is close to the level of 2018. As the employment situation in 2018 is considered relatively good, the employment in 2020 should also be relatively strong. Specifically, 9.6 million jobs will be eliminated in the industrial sector, 2.2 million jobs will be added in the construction industry, and 13.3 million will be added in the service industry. The biggest employment expansion in the service industry will be in wholesale and retail (4.3 million), education (1.5 million), accommodation and catering (1.3 million), leasing and business services (1.2 million).

Scenario 2: If China's economy grows by 5.8% in 2020, non-agricultural employment will increase by 4.8 million, and the employment situation will be basically stable.

If China's economic growth rate is 5.8% in 2020, the increase of non-agricultural employment will be 4.8 million, which is slightly more than the 4 million in 2019. As China's employment in 2019 has been relatively tight but stable, employment will also be stable in 2020. Specifically, 9.8 million jobs will be eliminated in the industrial sector, the construction industry will add 2 million jobs, and employment in the service industry will increase by 12.6 million. The biggest employment expansion in the service industry will be in wholesale and retail (4 million), education (1.5 million), accommodation and catering (1.2 million), leasing and business service (1.15 million).

Scenario 3: If China's economy grows by 5.5% in 2020, non-agricultural employment will increase by 3.15 million, and there will not be large-scale unemployment.

If China's economic growth is 5.5% in 2020, the non-agricultural employment will increase by 3.15 million, nearly one million less than the 4 million in 2019. As China's employment has been tight in 2019, the employment situation in 2020 should be even more severe. However, there will not be large-scale unemployment given the non-agricultural employment increase of more than 3 million. The industrial sector will shed 10.2 million jobs, the construction industry will increase by 1.9 million jobs, and the service industry will add 11.5 million jobs. The biggest employment expansion sectors in the service industry will be wholesale and retail (3.6 million), education (1.45

million), accommodation and catering (1.15 million), leasing and business service (1.05 million).

Scenario 4: If China's economy grows by 5% in 2020, non-agricultural employment will not increase, and the economy will be faced with increasing risks of unemployment.

If China's economic growth rate is 5% in 2020, non-agricultural employment will stop growing, and China's employment will face a real test. Considering the actual employment situation in China, much of the population aged between 16 and 70 will face the risk of unemployment. In this scenario, 11 million jobs will be lost in the industrial sector, while 1.5 million jobs will be added in the construction industry and 9.6 million will be added in the service industry. The biggest employment expansion sectors in the service industry are wholesale and retail (2.9 million), education (1.35 million), accommodation and catering (1 million), leasing and business service (0.9 million).

(3) Based on these four scenarios, the lowest economic growth rate for ensuring employment in China is 5%, but the quality of short-term employment may be sacrificed. Theoretically, in recent years, the working age population shows an absolute downward trend in China. Even if non-agricultural employment does not increase, it will still be enough to meet the overall need of employment. Yet, the problem is that many overage people are still working. If they lose their jobs, they may compete with young people, which will also cause certain social

problems. Therefore, the unemployment of older people must be considered. Currently, the population aged 16—70 in China is neither growing nor declining. To meet the employment need of the 16—70 year old, non-agricultural employment cannot be reduced. In this sense, 5% growth is the lowest level for securing employment in China, when the quality of short-term employment may have to be sacrificed to ensure that employment does not fall. This is because the driving force for employment is in low-end service industries, such as wholesale and retail, accommodation and catering, leasing and business services. The result is a sharp contradiction between increasing employment and low labor productivity, low wages and low employment quality.

Considering both international and domestic trends and cyclical factors at the present stage, and adhering to the principle of high-quality development, the principle of achieving the "two centenary goals", and the principle of ensuring basic stability in employment, it's suggested that the target interval for China's economic growth in 2020 be set at 5.5%—6.0%, and the conservative target be set at 5.8%.

◇ II. Risks in the operation of the macroeconomy in 2020

Firstly, with the emergence of a new round of external shocks,

China's macroeconomy will face relatively severe external challenges in 2020. The global economy has entered a new downturn, the game between big powers has entered a new chapter, and the uncertainty of global economic and trade policies has reached a new height. All of these will not only have a direct impact on China's economy through trade channels, but will also have profound impacts through indirect channels, such as interfering with the operation of China's economy, deteriorating market confidence, and depressing future expectations.

(1) As the global economy enters a new downturn, the impact of insufficient external demand may be further manifested in 2020. Global economic growth has experienced a systematic and significant decline since 2019, and some major economies have fallen into recession. At present, OECD, ECB, IMF, WB, UNCTAD and ADB have all lowered their growth projections for 2020. This suggests that China's economic downturn is not only due to internal factors, but also from downward pressure on the global economy in general. The global economic downturn will continue in 2020. First, it is clear that there won't be a new round of technological innovation to pull the world economy out of the downturn. Since the beginning of the new century, the growth rate of global patent production has been declining. R&D spending as a share of GDP is falling everywhere except in China, where it is rising. In OECD countries, in particular, the share of R&D is falling. In addition, anti-globalization may last longer, and its impact may be

stronger than expected. Historically, if trade conflicts were rooted in major changes in the global division of labor and world politics, the depth and length of trade conflicts would be extended, possibly reaching 20 years. Only 11 years have passed since 2008, and the world is still facing a wave of anti-globalization. Moreover, global inequality has worsened. The reason for the emergence of anti-globalization is that globalization has brought about increasing inequality and declining welfare for many. Therefore, populism, protectionism and the wave of anti-globalization have emerged in response. The share of world income accounted for by the top 1% rose from 16.3% in the 1980s to 20.4% in 2016. More importantly, the problem is present in most of the world's major countries. What's more, debt levels are high. In 2019, the scale of global debt is expected to exceed US 255 trillion, accounting for 330% of global GDP. The debt problem has reached a critical point. Finally, the population is aging. At present, the population structure of the world is getting older. Basically, the proportion of the population in the labor force is declining and the dependency ratio is rising, which leads to a slowdown of global economic growth.

(2) The global manufacturing industry is likely to remain in a collective downturn in 2020. In 2019, the direct impact of the decline in global trade growth, and more importantly, the extreme uncertainty of future expectations, has led to declines in investment and durable goods consumption. If the uncertainties of US trade relations, global economic

policies and geopolitical risks continue to rise in 2020, the decline of global investment and durable goods consumption will be further intensified, and the global manufacturing industry will fall into a collective downturn.

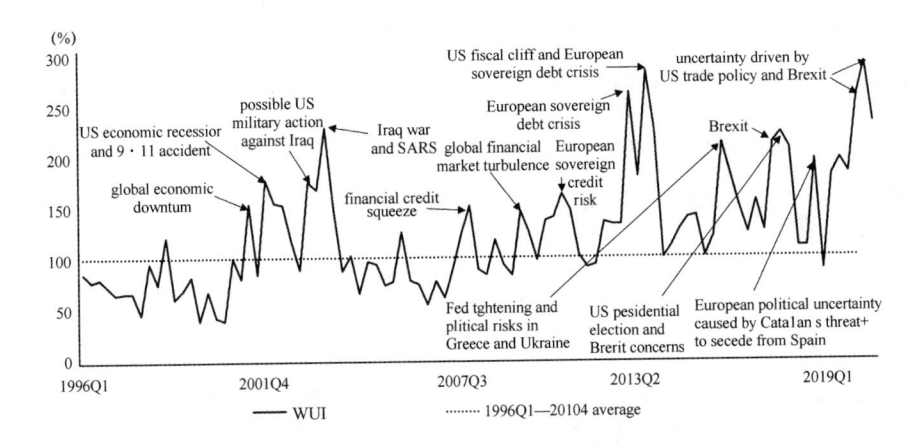

Figure 69 World Uncertainty Index (WUI)

Source: PolicyUncertainty.com, The use of the data and figure should be cited as: Ahir, H, N Bloom, and D Furceri (2018), "World Uncertainty Index", Stanford mimeo.

Taking automobiles as an example, global vehicle sales started to decline after peaking in the middle of 2018, with a growth rate of -3.4% for the whole of 2018 and a further decline of 8.3% in the first half of 2019, which is 9.0 percentage points lower than the growth rate in the same period of 2018. The decline of global automobile sales and production not only leads to the decline of automobile industry itself, but also has a chain reaction through industry and international spillover effects. In this context, economies with a high proportion of automobile output and high proportion of automobile exports experience the greatest impact. In terms of global market share, four European countries led by Germany (Germany, France, Italy, Spain) and Mexico and Japan account for a higher proportion of global automobile production and a significantly higher proportion of global automobile exports, so the economic impact on them is more serious. Germany's manufacturing sector is already in recession. Italy is in a full-blown recession and Mexico is starting to see negative growth.

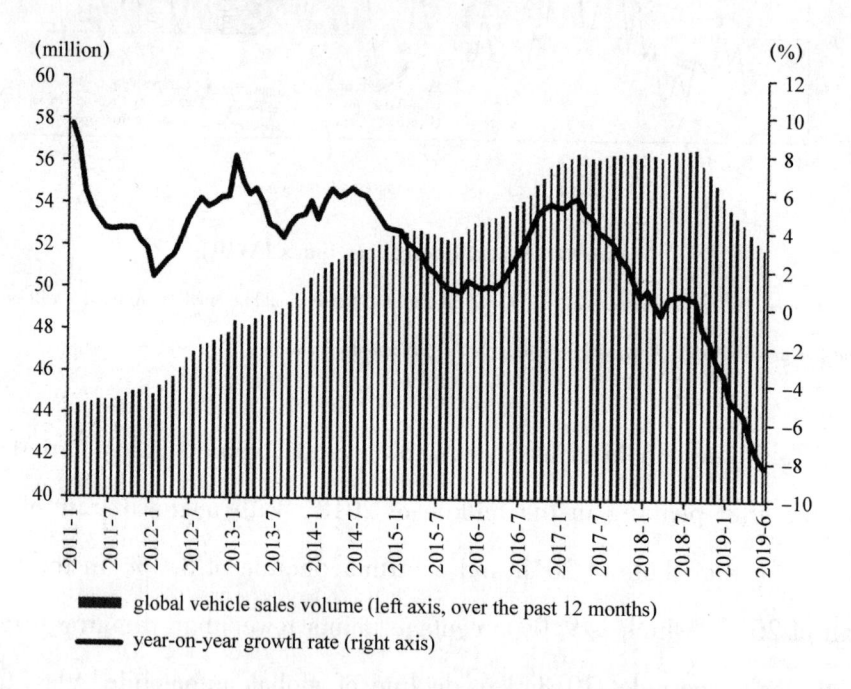

Figure 70 Global vehicle sales volume and its growth rate

Specifically, in Germany for example, in the first three quarters of 2019, the growth rate of its car exports dropped to −12.0%, and the

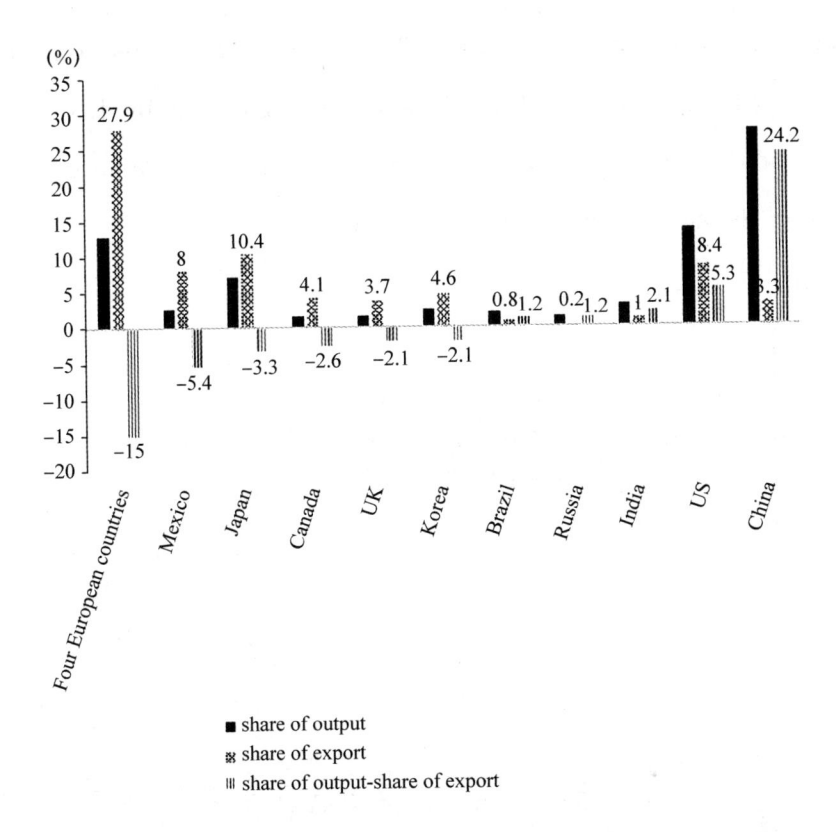

Chapter Four　The Establishment of an Economic Growth Target for 2020 Considering Possible Risks

(figure: bar chart showing share of output, share of export, and share of output-share of export by country)

- share of output
- share of export
- share of output-share of export

Figure 71　Share of vehicle output and exports in the world by country (2018)

growth rate of its car production dropped to −9.0%, although German car sales in the same period was still up 2.0%. In comparison, in recent years, US automobile sales volume has kept declining, with a year-on-year decline of 13.4% in August, which also corresponds to the decline in the US automobile production. But due to low export dependence and inventory destocking in the past few years, US automobile production growth in 2019 has been higher than its sales growth. Even so, however, US vehicle inventory level started to recover in the first eight months of 2019 as US car sales fell by 1.1% and production fell by 6.5%. US GDP growth slowed to 2.0% in the third quarter, the slowest year-on-year rate since 2017.

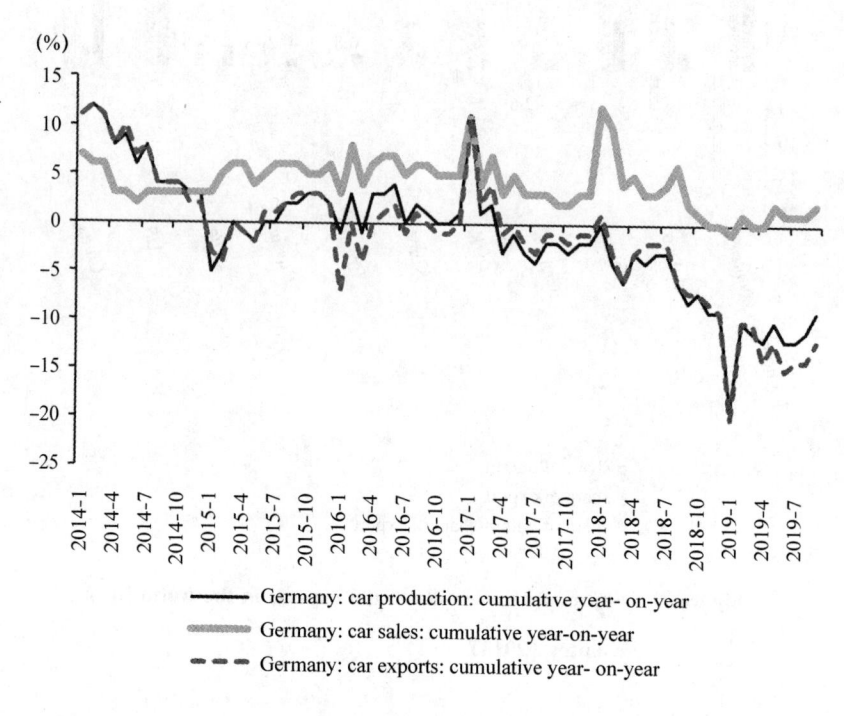

——— Germany: car production: cumulative year-on-year
━━━ Germany: car sales: cumulative year-on-year
- - - Germany: car exports: cumulative year-on-year

Figure 72　Growth rates of Germany's car production, sales and export

(3) China and the US have entered a new chapter of the great power game. The US election in 2020 brings a high degree of uncertainty to trade relations and geopolitics.

The US is accelerating bilateral negotiations with the European Union, Japan, South Korea and ASEAN, possibly forming an international alliance. There is also likely to be a continuing struggle

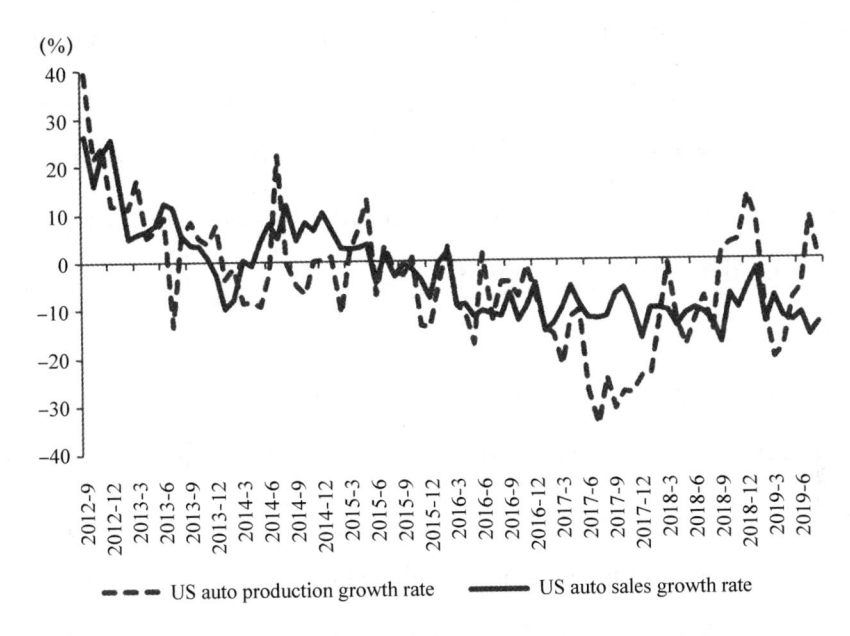

Chapter Four The Establishment of an Economic Growth Target for 2020 Considering Possible Risks | **301**

Figure 73 Growth rates of US auto production and sales

over technology and human resources in the future. The US has carried out a comprehensive containment of visas in key technologies and sensitive areas since the beginning of 2019. Currency adjustments in 2020 are also likely to spark disputes. On August 6 in 2019, for example, the US declared China a currency manipulator shortly after the onshore price of RMB fell below the "7" threshold. However, according to the latest *Macroeconomic and Foreign Exchange Policies of Major Trading Partners of the United States* issued by the US in April 2018, there are three criteria for identifying exchange rate manipulators: first, a significant bilateral trade surplus with the US of at least US 20 billion; second, a substantial current account surplus of at least 3% of GDP; third, a long-term unilateral intervention in the foreign exchange market, with repeated net purchases of foreign currencies amounting to 2% of GDP over the past 12 months. It can be seen that China may only meet the first criterion and not the other two, yet the US Treasury has labelled China a currency manipulator to meet political needs.

Overall, the deterioration of future expectations and the rise in uncertainty have exacerbated the worldwide contraction in investment goods and consumer durables. Therefore, when analyzing and judging China's macroeconomic situation in the coming year, we need to pay close attention to latest trends in the global economy. At the same time, China's macroeconomic policy orientation in the coming year must also be clearly internationalized.

Secondly, the sharp decline of domestic demand growth may lead to an accelerated macroeconomic decline. In 2019, China's net exports has achieved high-speed growth, but the growth of domestic demand has fallen sharply, from 7.2% in 2018 to 5.0% in the first three quarters of this year, which has increased China's economic vulnerability and dependence on foreign demand. Especially when enterprises no longer expand productive investment and residents no longer increase durable goods consumption, the upgrading forms of structural adjustment will stagnate and depression structural differentiation intensify. In the short term, foreign trade still needs to be stabilized, but global economic trends suggest that China is unlikely to sustain substantial net export growth in 2020. Therefore, it is more important to step up efforts, increase speed, and sharpen precision to stabilize domestic demand before the time window closes.

Domestic demand growth has fallen sharply, adding to the fragility of the economy. 2019 has not only continued the problem of insufficient aggregate demand since the second half of 2018, but also created a strong contraction effect of an accelerated economic downturn. From this point of view, the "six stability" framework proposed by the Central Committee in the middle of 2018 is forward-looking. In the first quarter of 2019, China's real GDP grew by 6.4%, the same as in the fourth quarter of last year, reflecting the stabilizing effect of the "six stability" policy. However, the higher than expected performance of the macroeconomy in the first quarter masked the fact that the growth of domestic demand in China had actually declined sharply, which led to certain setbacks in subsequent macro policies. Net exports accounted for as much as 1.5 percentage points of the 6.4% growth in the first quarter. Excluding foreign demand, domestic demand (investment and consumption) grew by just 4.9%, 2.3 percentage points lower than that in 2018. It was thought at the time that this might be a short-term phenomenon. But with the release of data for the second and third quarters, it has been confirmed that the growth of domestic demand in China has indeed experienced a sharp decline in 2019. As shown in

Figure 74, the actual growth rates of domestic demand in China in 2016, 2017 and 2018 were 7.1%, 6.3% and 7.2% respectively, all of which fluctuated around 7%. However, in the first three quarters of 2019, the growth rate of domestic demand in China dropped significantly to 5.0%, which is of great concern.

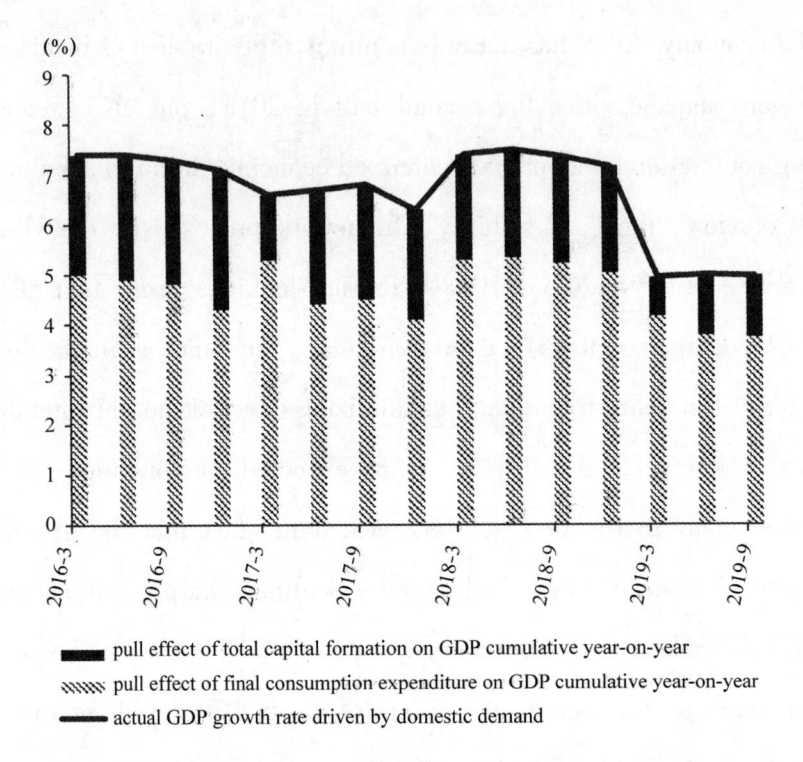

■ pull effect of total capital formation on GDP cumulative year-on-year
▧ pull effect of final consumption expenditure on GDP cumulative year-on-year
— actual GDP growth rate driven by domestic demand

Figure 74 China's domestic demand growth drops sharply in 2019

Both investment and consumption, the main drivers of demand, have dropped, leading to a significant decline in the growth of domestic demand. The contribution of investment to GDP has dropped from 2.1 percentage points in 2018 to 1.2 percentage points, a decline of

0.9. The contribution of consumption to GDP has fallen from 5.0 percentage points to 3.8 percentage points, down 1.2%. More importantly, the current decline in investment growth is not only due to the slowdown in the total, but also due to the deterioration of investment efficiency, resulting in the phenomenon of "investment without growth". In terms of the total level of investment, in the first three quarters, the nominal growth rate of China's fixed asset investment completed was 5.4%, 0.5 percentage points lower than last year's growth rate. In terms of the structural efficiency of investment, in the first three quarters of 2019, investment in "other expenses" increased by 12.1%, accounting for an increase of 0.9 percentage points, but investment in "purchase of equipment and instruments" decreased by 1.2%, a decrease of 1.0 percentage point, which indicates a decline in the transform efficiency of fixed asset investment into total capital formation. In terms of the industries, investment in real estate development has maintained a growth rate of about 10% in the past two years. In the first three quarters of 2019, construction starts increased by 8.6%, but floor space of buildings completed decreased by 8.6%, leaving a gap of 17.2 percentage points. This situation has lasted for nearly two years since the beginning of 2018.

The decline of consumption growth is due to the collective decline of durable goods consumption in three categories: automobile, household and apparel. In the first three quarters, consumption increased by 8.2% year-on-year, a decrease of 1.1% compared with the same period of 2018, mainly due to insufficient consumption of the following three categories of goods. First, automotive consumption. In the first three quarters, automotive consumption decreased by 7%, including a decline of 2.2% in September; consumption of oil and products increased by 1.7%, but it turned to decrease by 0.4% in September. Second, household consumption. In the first three quarters, consumption of household appliances and audiovisual equipment, furniture, and construction and decoration materials increased by only 5.9%, 5.9%, and 3.6% respectively. Third, clothing consumption. In the first three quarters, consumption of clothing, footwear, needle textiles, and gold and silver jewelry increased by only 3.3% and 0.6% respectively. With the exception of the above three categories, the consumption of other goods and services still maintains rapid growth. However, the collective decline in the above categories has a distinct feature of reducing the overall consumption of durable goods, reflecting a structural tightening caused by deteriorating expectations of consumers.

The "recessionary surplus" exacerbates the vulnerability of the future economy. In the first three quarters of 2019, China's export and import growth rates dropped sharply from double digits last year to zero and negative respectively. But the growth rate of net exports reached 36.1%, increasing overall GDP growth by 1.2 percentage points. The contribution of net exports to GDP reached 19.6%, which means that it contributed to one-fifth of economic growth, the highest level in nearly 10 years. With the latest slowdown in global economic growth, the "recessionary surplus" may have reached its limit. The sharp decline in domestic demand growth has significantly increased the dependence of China's economic growth on the growth of net exports, and also increased the importance of stabilizing foreign trade in the short term. However, from the perspective of global economic development, it is extremely unlikely that China will maintain the substantial growth of net exports in 2020. China needs to stabilize its foreign trade, but more importantly, it needs to stabilize domestic demand with greater intensity, speed and precision.

Thirdly, the structural differentiation of the slowdown intensifies the effects of stagnation. In turn, the downward trend of growth reveals structural weaknesses, which will put further pressure on small and medium-sized enterprises and banks, thus triggering localized financial risks. At the same time, it will also lead to the deterioration of some regions with fragile economic structures, and thus induce unemployment risks. As a result, structural effects will in turn cause new shocks to the overall economy.

The current changes in the economic structure are showing new characteristics: the upgrading structural changes are slowing down, while the declining structural changes are intensifying. From an industrial perspective, the growth rates of high-tech manufacturing industries such as pharmaceutical, general equipment and professional equipment have slowed down. This is also reflected in the rising and falling share of new kinetic energy investment in manufacturing in 2019, which accounted for 54.54% by the end of September, down to different degrees from the same period last year and the beginning of this year. However, the growth of ferrous metal smelting and processing industries, non-ferrous metal smelting and processing industries, and metal products and other energy-intensive industries, has picked up again. These changes indicate that the industrial restructuring in the past few years has slowed down. Within the service sector, the growth rates of information transmission, software and information technology

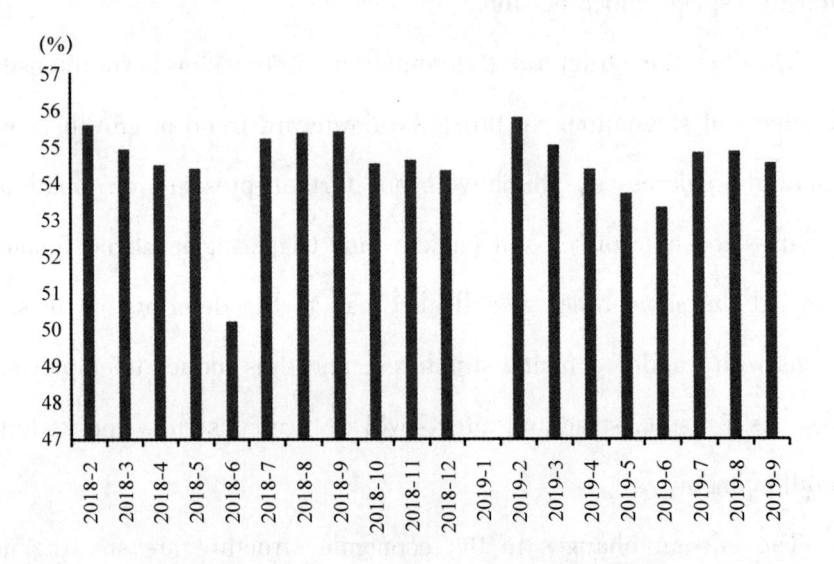

Figure 76 The proportion of new kinetic energy investment in manufacturing investment has been rising and falling since 2019

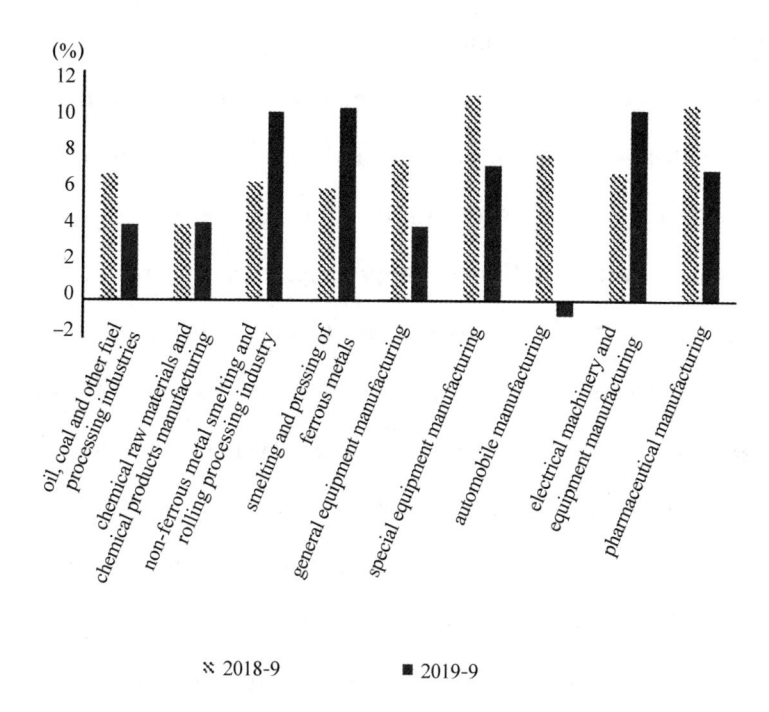

Figure 75 Slowdown in value-added growth of high-tech manufacturing industries and rebound of energy-consuming industries

services, and leasing and commercial services have declined by more than that of the service sector as a whole, while the growth rate of the financial sector has improved. This indicates that there is still some blockage between the policy objectives and policy effects under the conditions of loose credit and a expansionary monetary policy.

From a regional perspective, the profitability of eastern enterprises is under pressure, the profit growth of enterprises in central China has slowed down significantly, and the profitability of enterprises in the northeast has deteriorated. In the context of the economic downturn, the profitability of listed companies in the four regions of China (Northeast, Eastern, Western, and Central China) all deteriorated in the third quarter, with their operating income and net profit growth slowing year-on-year. The year-on-year growth rate of operating revenue of enterprises in Northeast China dropped significantly, with a decline of more than 10%. The year-on-year growth rate of net profit turned from positive to negative, leaving profitability deteriorate significantly. The year-on-year growth rates of operating revenue and net profit of enterprises in the central region both fell by more than 5%, with the largest year-on-year decline in net profit growth among the four regions. In Western China, the year-on-year decline of operating income and net profit was the smallest, and the deterioration of profitability was

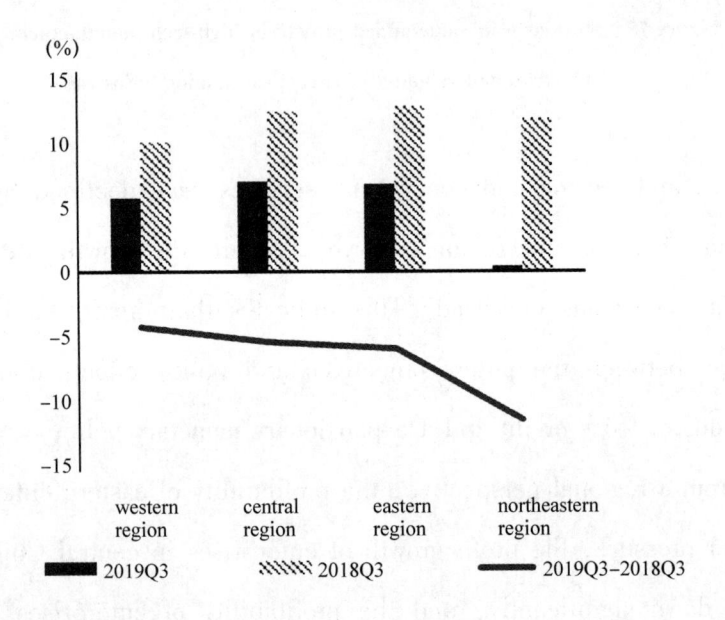

Figure 77 Year-on-year growth rates of operating revenue in different regions

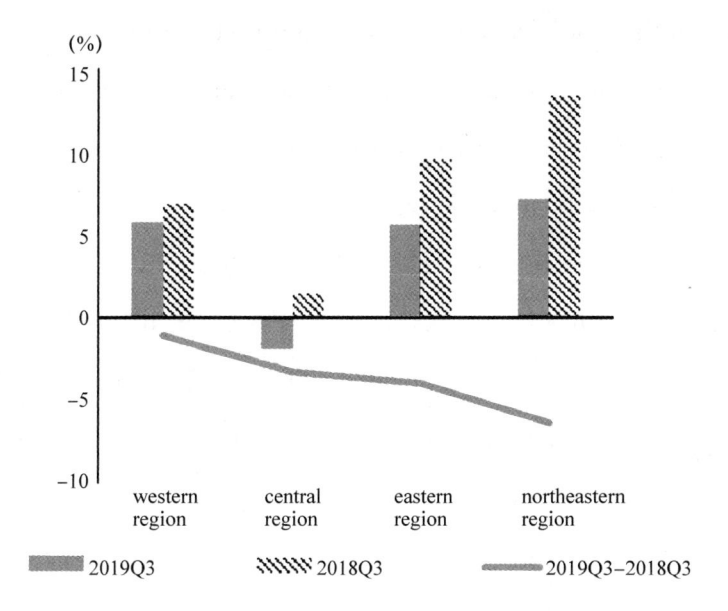

Figure 78 Year-on-year growth of net profits in different regions

relatively weak. It is worth noting that due to the impact of the trade war between China and the US, the profitability of enterprises in the eastern region, especially export-oriented enterprises, has been deteriorating, with the growth of revenue and profit continuously slowing down.

Therefore, although the current employment in China is generally stable, regional and industrial employment problems continue. In particular, the employment situation in Northeast China and the Beijing-Tianjin-Hebei region has not fundamentally improved, and in some cases continues to deteriorate. As of September 2019, China's overall employment prosperity index was 1.92, but only 0.9 in the Northeast and 0.87 in the Beijing-Tianjin-Hebei region. The tense employment situation in the Northeast and Beijing-Tianjin-Hebei region mainly stems from the plight of regional economic development. The overall economic situation in Northeast China is worse than the whole country. Liaoning has rebounded, with its GDP growth rate rising from about 2% in 2017 to 5.8% in the second quarter of 2019. However, the situation in Jilin and Heilongjiang has become even more severe. In particular, Jilin has witnessed a serious continued decline. Their GDP growth rates dropped to 2% and 4.3% respectively in the second quarter, far below the national level of 6.3%. In the Beijing-Tianjin-Hebei region, Tianjin's GDP growth rate was only 4.6%.

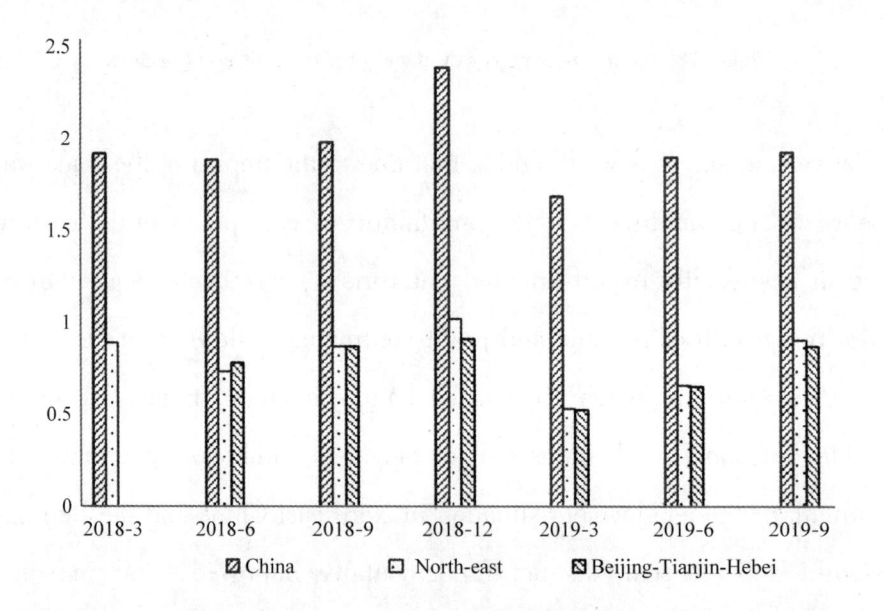

Figure 79 Employment prosperity index by region

Source: the *Report on the Prosperity of China's Employment Market in the Third Quarter of* 2019 jointly released by the Employment Research Institute of Renmin University of China and Zhilian Recruitment.

In terms of different industries, the automobile and mobile phone industries are still in a serious decline, and the real estate, construction and information service industries have also contracted significantly. The downward sales and production in these industries mean they face greater employment pressure. The auto industry has been in trouble since 2018, and the accumulative sales volume of automobiles in the first nine months of 2019 dropped by 10.3% year-on-year. This industry depression will inevitably lead to unemployment pressure. At the end of 2018, about 4.5 million people were employed in the automobile industry. Based on a simple calculation, the number of unemployed people in the automobile industry may be close to 500,000 in 2019. In 2018, the year-on-year decline of mobile phone shipments reached more than double digits. Since the first half of 2019, thanks to various promotion policies, the decline has been narrowed and even changed from negative to positive in April and May. But the year-on-year decline in September of 2019 widened again to 7.1%. The plight of the mobile phone industry will inevitably put pressure on the employment of the upstream and downstream industries. Due to the impact of regulatory policies and other factors, the real estate industry has continued to be sluggish. In the first eight months of 2019, sales of commercial housing declined by 0.6% year-on-year. Although it picked up a bit in September, it still declined by 0.1% year-on-year in the first nine months. The real estate industry employs nearly 4.45 million people, so its downturn will have a big impact on employment. In the first half of 2019, the number of people directly engaged in the construction industry fell by nearly 600,000 compared with the same period last year. In the first eight months of 2019, the cumulative investment in fixed assets in the construction industry decreased by 20% year-on-year. The construction industry is important for migrant workers seeking employment. Therefore, the sluggish construction industry will have a great impact on the employment of migrant workers.

In the near future, trade friction between China and the US may evolve to a point where it impacts China's employment levels. If so, the effects will likely be first seen in local industries and regions. Sino-US trade friction has temporarily eased, but relevant contradictions have not been resolved. The US government's tariff action has been delayed, not actually lifted. So far, the full impact of tariffs already in place by the United States on Chinese jobs has yet to be determined. Calculations based on profit margins on sales across industries suggest that a tariff threshold of between 21% and 24% would quickly have a negative impact on employment. The 15% tariff imposed previously has not yet had an impact on related industries. General equipment manufacturing, electrical machinery and equipment manufacturing, rubber and plastic products, and metal products may see large-scale job losses if tariffs are further raised. Provinces such as Guangdong, Zhejiang, Jiangsu and Shandong, where exports to the US are concentrated, could face higher unemployment.

Fourthly, the risk of a new round of deflation in China's economy will increase in 2020, which requires close attention and full preparation. Although food prices, notably pork price, have risen sharply since the third quarter, driving up the consumer price index, this in no way means that deflation will not occur in 2020. On the contrary, the continuous decline of non-food CPI, the PPI, and GDP deflator—especially the pace of the PPI decline and the breadth and depth of the industries involved—all bear a high degree of similarity with previous rounds of deflation. Close attention should be paid to the change in the PPI situation especially from the fourth quarter of 2019 to the second quarter of 2020, and monetary policy should be adjusted to build a new framework for price stability.

(1) The current price trend is highly uneven. While focusing on food inflation, close attention should be paid to various signs of deflation. The next two or three quarters will be the key period for a policy response. Since the third quarter of 2019, price trends have been highly divergent, generating a lot of noise for market expectations and macro policies. On the one hand, a sharp rise in food prices, notably pork price, has driven up the CPI, which rose by 3.8% in October from a year earlier. On the other hand, the producer price index has continued to decline and turned negative, with the year-on-year decline widening to 1.6% in October. This divergence will continue into the

first quarter of 2020. Therefore, an accurate forecast of the price situation is key to setting the general tone of macro policy next year. We believe that the current increases in food prices and CPI inflation are local and phased, which does not mean that deflation risks will be low next year. On the eve of the last bout of deflation, there was also a sharp rise in food prices and a CPI spike. In June 2011, the increase of food prices reached a peak of 14.4%, which led the CPI to break through 6.0% and reach 6.4%. However, only three quarters later, a round of industrial deflation started and ended up lasting for 54 months. At present, the declines of non-food CPI, PPI, GDP deflator, corporate efficiency, and market expectations may indicate the formation of a new round of deflation.

(2) An comparative analysis shows that the current price trend is highly similar to the previous three rounds of deflation, especially the last round from March 2012 to September 2016. Prior to the latest round of PPI decline, non-food CPI declined from 2.4% in the third quarter of 2018 to 1.4% in June of 2019. As of October, non-food CPI had further declined to 0.9%. Since the gap of current non-food CPI is smaller than that of the previous round, deflation in 2020 may not be any less severe than the previous round. More importantly, the pace, breadth, and depth of this PPI decline are similar to previous episodes. This year, the PPI started to show a negative growth of 0.3% in July, which widened to 1.6% in October. In the previous round of deflation,

the PPI started to show a negative growth of 0.3% in March 2012, which widened to 2.1% in June. In October of 2019, EXW prices fell in 15 of the 39 main industrial sectors, with six falling by more than 5%. In the early stage of the previous round of deflation, 11 industries experienced price declines, four of which fell by more than 5%. In the early stage of the earlier case (December 2008 to November 2009), there were 12 industries whose prices fell, 7 of which fell by more than 5%, while in the period from June 1997 to December 1999, there were 13 industries whose prices fell, six of which fell by more than 5%.

(3) The current downward trend of the PPI is consistent with the general deterioration of industrial enterprises' profits, indicating that it is mainly driven by the decline of demand rather than the improvement of efficiency. In 2019, the total profits of industrial enterprises showed the first decline since 2016, with a year-on-year decrease of 2.1% in the first three quarters, especially in the manufacturing industry, with a year-on-year decrease of 3.9%. In industries with falling prices, the majority have seen a significant decline in total profits and the growth rate of total profits. In industries with PPI growth rate lower than 1.0%, most have also seen declining or negative profit growth.

(4) In addition to demand-led deflationary pressure, the downturn in global manufacturing and the decline in international commodity prices (especially crude oil) will exert additional sustained downward pressure on prices in 2020. Global inflation expectations and

international crude oil price expectations for next year tend to decline. In developed economies, the CPI is expected to fall from 2.0% in 2018 to 1.5% in 2019 and 1.8% in 2020. More importantly, global crude oil prices will be in a downward range for the next five years. The IMF forecasts that international crude oil prices will fall by 9.6% in 2019, 6.2% in 2020, and 4.6% and 1.3% in 2021 and 2022 respectively until they stabilize in 2023 and 2024. In addition, metal prices are also expected to fall by 6.2% in 2020.

Therefore, based on the comparison between the current price trend andthose at the early stages of previous rounds of deflation, combined with the analysis of the domestic and international macroeconomic situation, the risk of a new round of deflation in 2020 is relatively high, requiring a high degree of attention and preparation. In particular, there may be full deflation in the second half of 2020. At present, the depression in the industrial sectors is global. It is the general trend that PPI will continue to fall. In the future, the transmission of insufficient aggregate demand to prices will continue. At the same time, the global manufacturing downturn and the fall of commodity prices have significantly increased the pressure of external input-oriented deflation. Domestic and foreign prices are expected to be low, which will make it difficult to get an effective boost in the medium-term. In the second half of 2020, as food prices fall, the CPI may decline significantly, when on the basis of a sharp fall in 2019, the

GDP deflator may turn from positive to negative.

Fifthly, in 2020, China must pay close attention to the "double risks" caused by the structural rise of pork and food prices and insufficient aggregate demand. The price increases caused by the soaring price of food, especially pork, will be a medium-term phenomenon, which will have a negative impact on people's livelihood, total demand, and expectations next year. This dilemma of the multiple effects of changing prices will create serious challenges for macro management in 2020.

The structural rise of pork price and other food prices is difficult to reverse in the short term. It will become a medium-term phenomenon and spread to other areas through both direct and spillover effects, which will have a sustained impact on people's livelihood and market expectations in 2020. Since the third quarter, the rapid rise of pork prices has been a concern. The divergence of various price indexes, such as the food CPI and non-food CPI, CPI and PPI, caused by the soaring price of pork, further aggravates the situation, and creates a dilemma for macro policy. At present, the rising price of food comes mainly from pork. Rising pork prices are primarily the result of the sharp decrease of pork supply rather than the rise of consumer demand. It is worth noting that since the beginning of 2019, food prices have been rising in turns: the price of fresh vegetables soared in the first quarter, the price of fresh fruits soared in the second quarter, and the price of pork soared in the third quarter. The food CPI rose 11.2% in September, up 9.3 percentage points from the beginning of 2019. But unlike food inflation in the first half of the year, pork inflation since the third quarter has two main features.

First, the price of pork has risen sharply, which has driven up the prices of its substitutes such as beef, mutton and poultry, driving down people's standard of living and public opinion. In September, the CPI for pork rose by 69.3% year-on-year, driving up the prices of beef, mutton and poultry by 18.8%, 15.9% and 14.7% year-on-year. The prices of livestock meat rose by 46.9% in total. Driven by pork prices, year-on-year CPI inflation continued to rise, reaching 3.0% in September and is expected to break through 3.0% in the fourth quarter. As of Oct. 11th, the average price of pork in 22 provinces and cities had exceeded 40 yuan/kg, reaching 42.3 yuan/kg—a doubling over the Spring Festival period, while the price of pig grain reached 16 times, both record highs. Pork accounts for 60% of China's meat consumption, so the soaring price of pork has become a focus of attention for all sectors of society and the media.

Second, the root cause of the increase in pork prices lies on the supply sideand is a medium-term phenomenon. It cannot be effectively solved in the short term. Currently, increasing pork prices are mainly caused by the combination of African swine fever, strengthened environmental protection, and other factors causing a sharp contraction of supply. It is difficult to reverse in the short term. In contrast to the relatively stable trend of pork demand in recent years, the main factors determining pig supply have undergone systematic abnormal changes. Our judgment is that while the sharp decline in stock indicators has caused a change in market participants' expectations, the worst has not actually arrived yet for pork supply, for the following reasons. (1) The number of live pigs continues to decrease significantly, indicating a substantial reduction in the actual production capacity of live pigs in China. Pig stocks fell further to 190 million in September after falling below 200 million in August, down 41.1% from 330 million in the same period last year and a further decline from August. (2) The number of breeding sows continues to decrease significantly, indicating that the expansion of pig production capacity will be severely restricted in the coming period. After dropping below 20 million in August, the stock of breeding sows fell further to 19.13 million in September, a 38.9% decline from 31.36 million in the same period last year, a decline that continues to grow, suggesting constraints on future capacity expansion. (3) The pig yield rate is significantly higher than the trend value, indicating that the current pork production has been seriously overdrawn. In 2019, the pig breeding rate has jumped sharply. Although the pork supply increased in a short period of time, enabling the decrease of the pig breeding number much less than the decrease of stock number, still the overload operation of the pig production system was unsustainable. Since May, the average weight of pigs before slaughter has declined significantly, and since August, pig clearance rates have begun to show signs of decline. (4) Pork imports have increased sharply, but it is difficult to make up the huge gap between domestic supply and demand. China's annual consumption of pork is about 55 million tons, accounting for half of global pork production. The proportion of pork imports is far less than 5%. From January to August, China's pork imports surged by 66.1%. The pork imports for 2019 is expected to reach 2 million tons, a drop in the bucket for pork consumption. To sum up, pork prices will continue to rise in the short term.

More importantly, the combined effect of structural price increases and an accelerated decline in aggregate demand will create a dilemma for macro management in 2020.

As mentioned above, while prices are rising structurally, the problem of insufficient aggregate demand continues to worsen, leading to an increased risk of accelerated macroeconomic decline. Particularly, in the medium-and long-term, the biggest challenge in the current macroeconomic downturn is that pessimistic expectations and weak investment will lead to a sustained slowdown in investment growth and possibly a reduction in potential growth. In the past two years, the growth rate of investment has even fallen below that of the US in the same period. By contrast, domestic investment in the US has maintained rapid growth for nine consecutive quarters, from the second quarter of 2017 to the second quarter of 2019, with an average growth rate of 6.6%.

With the deterioration of residents' future income expectations and increasing employment pressure, the "double backlog" for the middle class will be fully felt in 2020, which will increase their distrust of policies and add to their pessimism about the future. In the second quarter, the index of urban residents' confidence in their future income fell to 52.6%, the lowest since the end of 2016. At the same time, signs of unemployment risks continued to flash, with the surveyed urban unemployment rate climbing to 5.3% in February and July. A number of other indicators also signal weakness: (1) the manufacturing and non-manufacturing PMI employment indices fell to 47.0% and 48.2% in September, the lowest levels in recent years. (2) the number of people receiving unemployment insurance turned from a decline to a year-on-year increase of 2.2% in the first half of 2019. (3) the number of unemployed workers re-employed in the first seven months decreased by 8.6% year-on-year. (4) the search index for "criteria for unemployment benefits" has soared two to three times higher than in previous years.

The effects of contraction on China's economy and society may be even more serious in 2020. The social unrest and turbulence caused by structural price increases, the accelerated decline of total demand, the declining consumption of middle-income groups, and the deterioration of expectations may bring about an "expected" economic dilemma. When enterprises no longer expand productive investment, residents no longer increase durable goods consumption, local governments are constrained by heavy debt, and technological innovation lags, China's economic resilience and large-scale market advantage will face both major opportunities and profound tests at the same time.

Sixthly, in 2020, there will be challenges to financial risk mitigation. On the one hand, although monetary policy is accommodating, debt risks are largely mitigated, and market liquidity is relatively abundant, the divergence between the interest rates of financial institutions and the profit rates of corporate assets continues. On the other hand, although financial risks have been mitigated in 2019, defaults may happen a lot in the coming period, and the financial risks may manifest themselves again. Therefore, the mitigation and prevention of financial risks needs to be the core of a prudent macro policy next year.

(1) Although healthy returns to the financial sector are supposed to support the development of the real economy, there is apparently a poor transmission mechanism.

Against the background of increasing downward pressure on the economy, the interest rates on loans provided by financial institutions have remained high. Indeed, as the PPI has turned negative, real interest rates have risen. In recent years, the return on assets of enterprises has continued to decline, while interest rates remain high—especially since 2018, when the return on assets started to fall below the loan interest rate. As a result, the investment of enterprises has basically lost its economic significance, and the willingness to reinvest has been greatly inhibited. According to our calculation, the profit margin before interests and taxes of industrial enterprises continued to decline from 8.3% in 2011 to 6.4% in 2015, then recovered slightly to 6.7% in 2017 with the boost of "cutting capacity", but it plunged to 5.8% in 2018 and further to about 5.2% in the first half of 2019 (annualized rate). In the same period, the weighted average interest rate of general CNY loans by financial institutions continuously fell from 7.8% in 2011 to 5.4% in 2016. However, with the promotion of the deleveraging policy and the continuous tightening of financial conditions, the loan interest rate gradually increased to 5.9% in 2018 and further increased to 6.0% in the first quarter of 2019. Thus, for the first time in 2018, the return on corporate assets was lower than the lending rate, and the gap further widened in the first half of 2019. When the return on enterprise assets is lower than the loan interest rate, the willingness of enterprises to reinvest will inevitably be greatly inhibited. In particular, the total profit of the manufacturing industry in the first half of 2019 showed negative growth for the first time, which reduced enterprises' willingness and ability to invest and led to a relatively large decline in manufacturing investment. In the first half of 2019, total manufacturing profits declined by 4.1% year-on-year, a level not seen before 2019, compared with a positive growth of 14.3% in the same period last year. If the decline in manufacturing investment had been driven originally by a narrowing market, it is now compounded by a further deterioration in corporate profits.

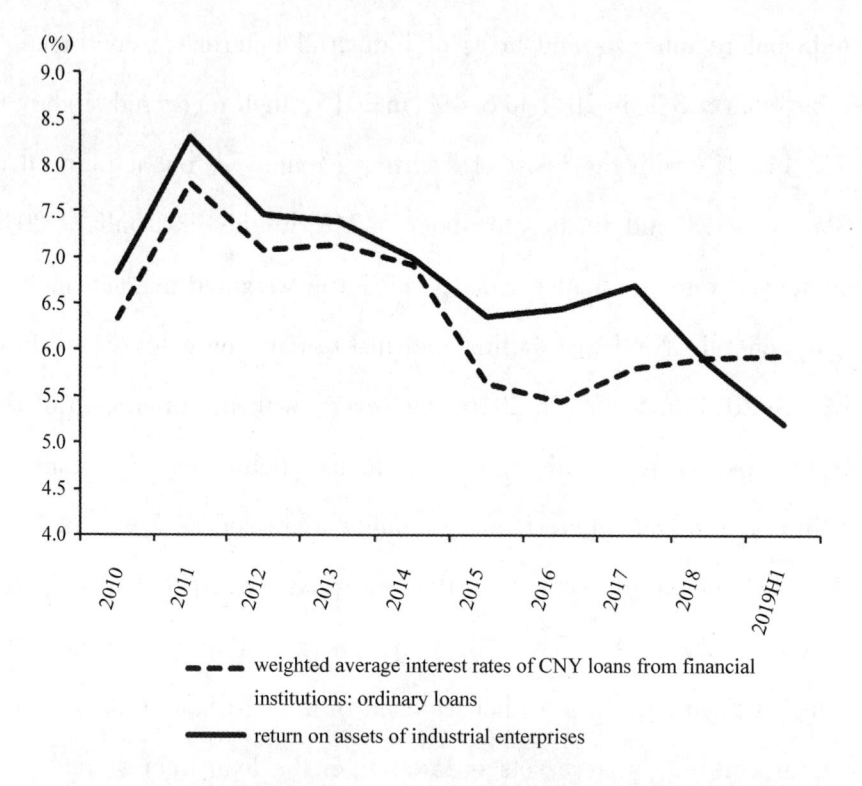

Figure 80 Differentiating Trends of interest rates of loans from financial institutions and industrial enterprises' profit margins

Against the backdrop of declining corporate profitability and rising real interestrates, loan demand of enterprises has declined significantly, especially for large and medium-sized enterprises. In the third quarter, the loan demand index for large enterprises fell to 54.4%, and for medium-sized enterprises it fell to 57.2%, both being the lowest levels since the beginning of 2017. The loan demand for small enterprises was relatively high at 70.2%, but it had also declined for two consecutive quarters.

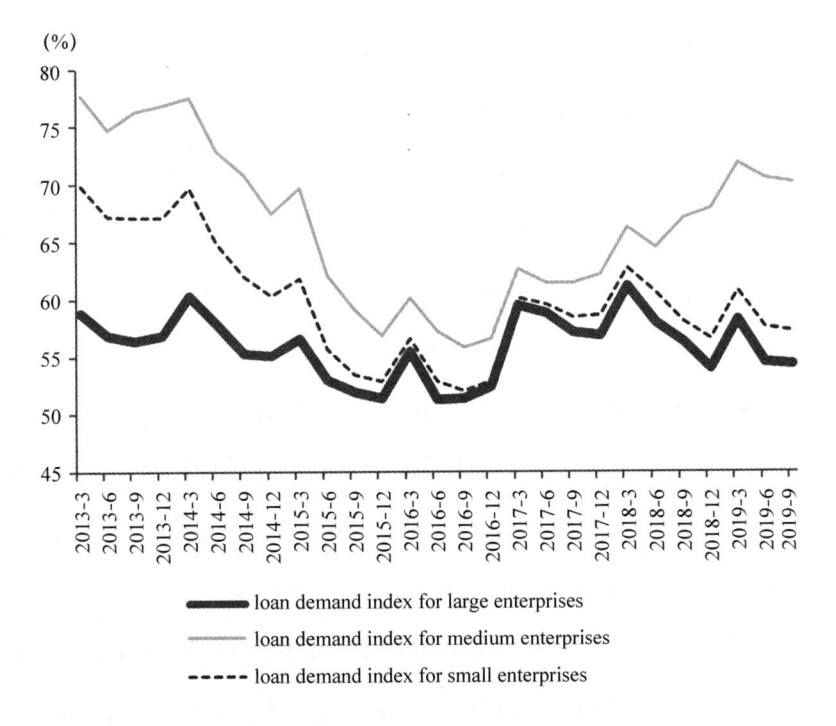

Figure 81 Significant decline corporate loan demand indexes for enterprises

There are many factors responsible for the current inefficient liquidity. One is that China's money supply structure and supply channels have changed significantly from previous years, and reforms corresponding to new changes are still in progress. After the disappearance of the original foreign exchange payment channel, the existing supply channel has more serious information asymmetry problems. This hascaused increased interest rate volatility in the interbank market and instability of liquidity supply expectations of financial institutions like commercial banks. As a result, these financial institutions are more inclined to invest in low-risk and high-liquidity areas, such as interest rate bonds, to match the volatility of the liability end, rather than loaning to enterprises. At the same time, due to financial deleveraging, banks have significantly reduced their off-balance sheet business. While this effectively reduces financial risks, it also blocks alternative financing channels for enterprises, such as industrial investment funds. When other channels are blocked, companies can only rely on bank financing. Facing information uncertainty, operating cost constraints, and diverse financing needs of different enterprises, banks necessarily adopt an average pricing model. This makes it difficult to effectively reduce the financing costs of enterprises. Therefore, it is necessary to broaden the financing channels available to enterprises, and use a variety of financial options with different risk preferences and cost structures to meet the full range of financing needs of enterprises. This also requires broadening the financial connections between commercial banks and other financial entities. Through the joint efforts of various financial entities, the funds in the interbank market can be effectively guided to the real economy and corporate financing costs can be reduced. Reforms are needed to improve the transparency and efficiency of liquidity supply channels. For one thing, the central bank can consider measures such as appropriately increasing dealers to expand policy coverage. For another, commercial banks also need to increase their risk control capabilities to guide funds to the real economy.

In view of the fact that China's original loan market quoted interest rate mechanism was not market-oriented enough and failed to reflect changes in market interest rates in a timely manner, in October 2019, the People's Bank of China (PBC) announced a reform and improvement of the LPR mechanism. The reformed LPR is called the loan market quoted interest rate. In addition to changing its name, the PBC also expanded the range of quoted banks—including city and rural commercial banks, foreign banks, and private banks—and increased the representativeness of quotes. Meanwhile, five-year interest rate maturity varieties have been added to enrich the term structure of interest rates. In this series of operations, the most important is the "anchor swap" of LPR, which is based on the open market operation interest rate, or the medium-term lending facility (MLF). At the same time, the PBC will rigidly promote the application of LPR quotes in the formation of commercial bank loan interest rates and determine their benchmark interest rate status. During the interest rate marketization reform process in the past ten years—whether driven by top-down reforms or bottom-up financial innovations—the composition of the liability end of commercial banks has undergone tremendous changes. Interbank funds, central bank borrowings and market-priced deposits have all established clear linkages with money market interest rates. In other words, they can be effectively guided by open market operation interest rates. It is precisely for this reason that LPR is linked to MLF interest rates in order to provide an effective transmission from the cost of funds to loan interest rates. The guiding role of MLF is the key starting point for the effectiveness of the LPR mechanism.

Therefore, in order to quickly reduce corporate financing costs in the short term, it is also necessary to directly adjust the basic pricing in LPR, that is, the interest rate of MLF. It is difficult for the LPR pricing model to effectively hedge the increase of the bank's final loan interest rate. After the reform, the final loan interest rate will be the LPR plus points. The one-year LPR before the reform was 4.31%, and the weighted interest rate of general loans was around 6%. The spread actually reflected the bank's risk premium and other factors. Under the current downward pressure on the economy, commercial banks tend to be more cautious, which increases the risk premium and puts upward pressure on rates. With a fixed cost of capital, the decline in the real interest rate of a loan is bound to be extremely limited. Of course, the margin of adding points in the final loan of commercial banks will also be affected by a series of structural factors in the financial market, including limited corporate financing channels, the relatively strong bargaining power of commercial banks, distortions in corporate financial data, and problems with social credit construction, which have led to some anti-fraud premiums hidden in the spreads of banks. These structural factors cannot be solved by LPR reform. Other supporting measures are needed, especially to reduce the MLF interest rate as soon as possible to hedge the rising risk premium.

(2) Financial risk mitigation and prevention is the core of macro-prudential management in 2020. Although financial risks have been mitigated, a period of defaults will continue, especially with a further downward adjustment of the economy. As of mid-November in 2019, 153 bonds have defaulted, reaching 118.7 billion yuan, and 36 companies have defaulted for the first time.

It is worth noting that structural and regional financial risks are still prominent. Some local governments, industries, private enterprises, and small and medium-sized banks have high levels of non-performing debt and other financial risks, andthey may face even greater pressure in 2020 as discussed below.

First, the risk of local government debt may rise. In the process of cutting taxes and fees in 2019, the growth rate of local government financial revenue has fallen sharply, while the growth rate of non-tax revenue has increased significantly, reflecting the increasing pressure on local government revenue. At the same time, the issuance of local government bonds has increased in 2019, mainly based on the issuance of new bonds, with a relatively small proportion of replacement and refinancing bonds, which is notably different from 2017—2018. The issuance of local government bonds in 2017 primarily consisted of replacement and refinancing bonds, while in 2018 the proportions of new bonds and replacement and financing bonds were roughly the same, easing the debt risk of local governments. In cont rast, local government bonds issued in 2019 have been predominantly composed of new bonds, which will increase debt pressure and risks in 2020 and beyond. Judging from the level of government debt, debt risks in regions such as

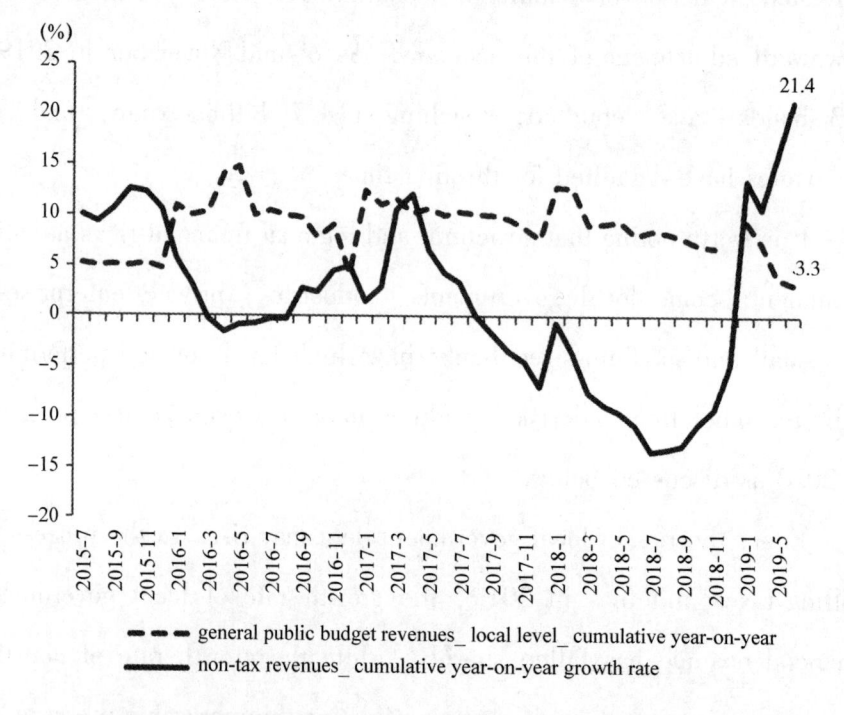

Figure 82 Substantial slowdown in local government fiscal revenue growth and significantly increased non-tax revenue growth

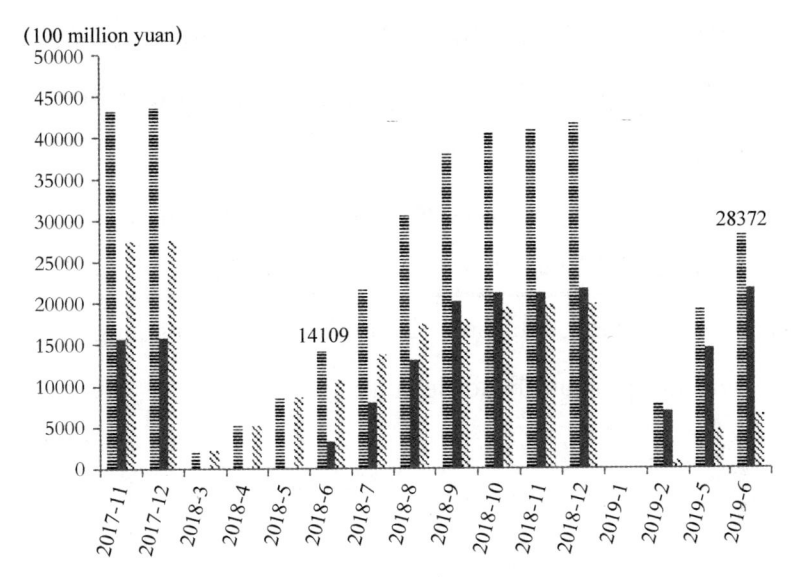

Chapter Four   The Establishment of an Economic Growth Target for 2020 Considering Possible Risks | **333**

≡ Local Government Bond Issuance: Cumulant
■ Local Government Bond Issuance: Additional Bonds Cumulant
⩘ Local Government Bond Issuance: Replacing and Refinancing Bonds: Cumulant

Figure 83   Issuance of local government bonds

Government · Debt   —— Debt · Ratio

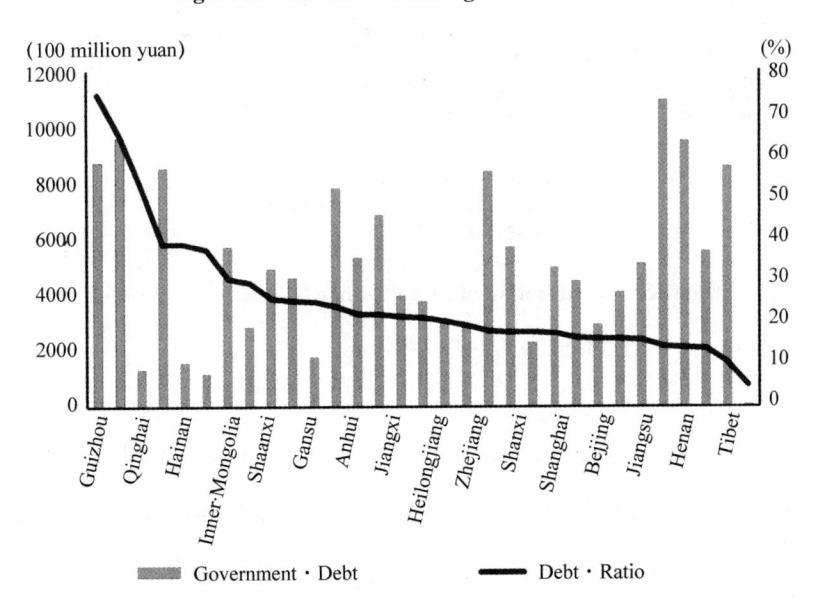

Figure 84   Acute risks of government debt in some regions

Guizhou, Qinghai, Hainan, Inner Mongolia, Shaanxi, Gansu, Anhui, Jiangxi and Heilongjiang are already high, and the sustainability of debt is of concern.

Second, the default risks of corporate debt are concentrated in certain regions. In Shandong, Beijing, Shanghai, Jiangsu, Anhui, Zhejiang, Guangdong, Henan, Liaoning and Heilongjiang, there are serious risks of corporate bond defaults.

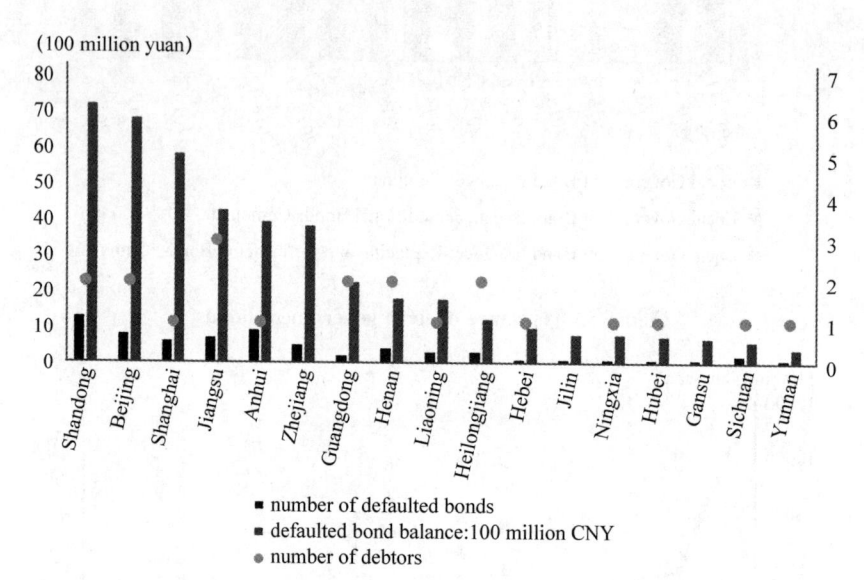

Figure 85 Distribution of defaulted bonds in different regions in the first half of 2019

Third, debt defaults also tend to be concentrated in specific industries and private enterprises. For instance, bond defaults are more prevalent in industries like petroleum, coal, comprehensive industry, construction, multi-field holdings, food processing, basic chemicals,

Chapter Four The Establishment of an Economic Growth Target for 2020 Considering Possible Risks | **335**

iron and steel, seaports, real estate opening, trade and building materials. In terms of ownership, private enterprises and public enterprises both have relatively high debt risks. In the first half of 2019, private enterprises accounted for 88.2% of the defaulted debt balance, followed by public enterprises accounting for 9.5%.

Finally, in the financial sector, small-and medium-sized banks have large debt non-performing loan (NPL) ratios and financial risks and may face greater pressure in 2020. The NPL ratio of rural commercial banks more than doubled from 1.67% at the end of 2013 to

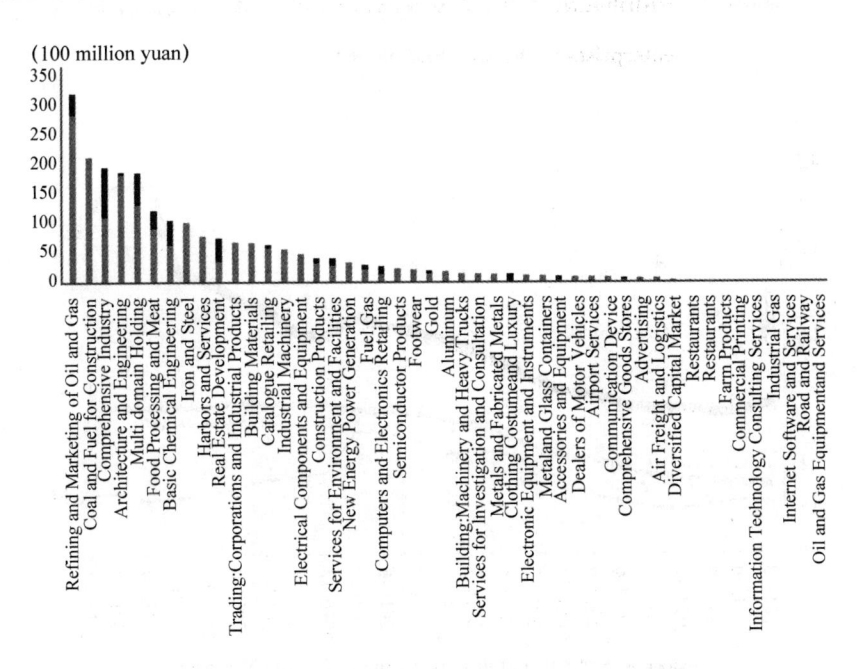

■ Accumulated Defaulted Bond Balance before 2019: Billion RMB
■ Additional Defaulted Bond Balance in 2019: Billion RMB

Figure 86   Distribution of defaulted bonds in different industries in 2018

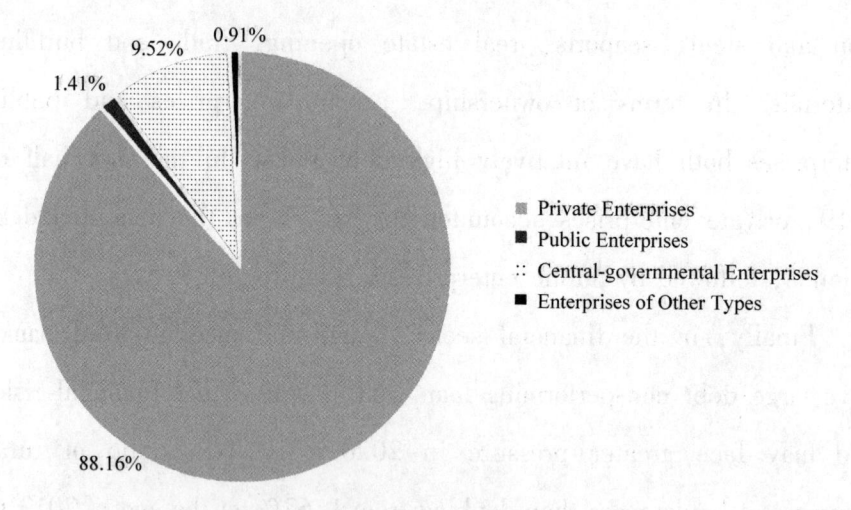

Figure 87 Distribution of default bond balances in different ownership enterprises in the first half of 2019

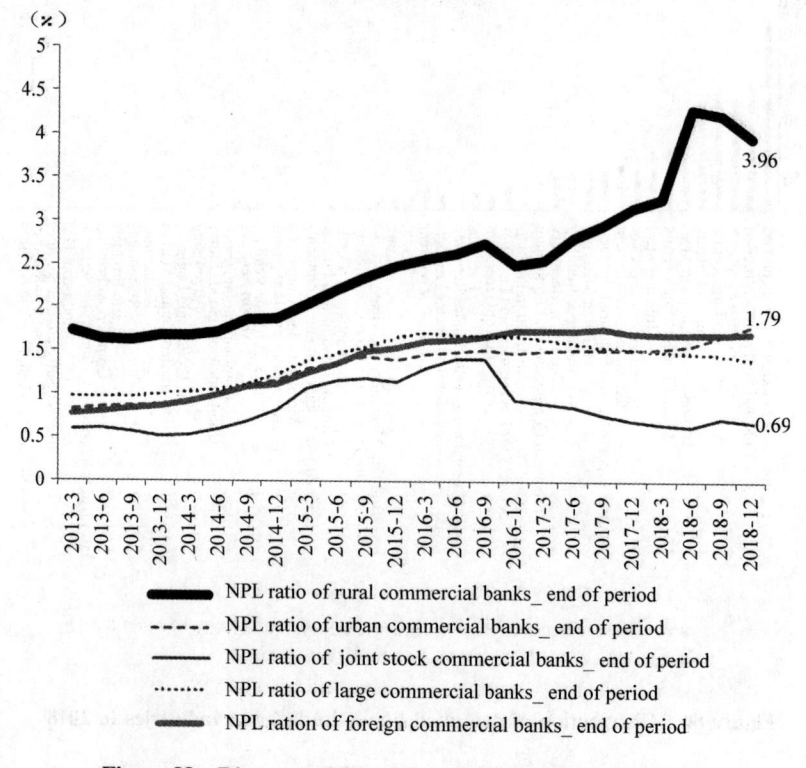

Figure 88 Divergent NPL ratios of different types of banks

3.96% at the end of 2018. The NPL ratio of urban commercial banks also showed a rapid upward trend, which deserves high attention.

Chapter Five Conclusions and Policy Suggestions

As we have seen, China's economic growth has slowed significantly in 2019 while many of the factors behind the slowdown still persist. On the one hand, there have been reforms, but the full benefits of a reform dividend have yet to be realized. The Sino-US trade friction and the global economic slowdown have combined to reduce the positive impacts of the globalization dividend. The decline of manufacturing and the rapid rise of the tertiary industry have reduced the industrialization dividend. And the aging of the population has exhausted the traditional demographic dividend. Consequently, China's economic trends are still in a downward phase, and further shifts in economic growth can be expected over the next two years of structural adjustment. On the other hand, international and domestic cycles and trends will reinforce each other in the current and future periods. Among the most prominent factors will be Sino-US trade friction, a new phase of the global economic downturn, low and unstable investment, financial adjustments, and a new round of market-oriented destocking cycles. Therefore, counter-cyclical macroeconomic policies should focus on countering the effects of these cycles and preventing them from intensifying.

In 2020 China's GDP growth rate will continue to fall and the macroeconomy will undergo significant changes. On the one hand, the downward structural forces in 2019 will continue, leading to a further decline in the potential GDP growth rate in 2020. On the other hand, some downward cyclical forces will begin to turn around. The macroeconomic downturn will ease somewhat, and the downturn will be less serious than in 2019. China's economic policies need to address the following major risks and challenges. First, as the global economy enters a new downturn, a new round of superpower games starts, leading to rising levels of uncertainty in global economic and trade relations. The external shocks from trade will not only directly impact the operation of China's economy, but also have profound indirect impacts on market confidence and expectations. Second, the depression-like effects of structural differentiation may cause downward pressure on local regions and industries. In response, China needs to concentrate on employment issues and local financial risks. Third, the decline in the non-food CPI, the PPI, and the GDP deflator signal a risk of a new round of deflation in China's economy in 2020. Thircl, the decline in domestic demand growth may trigger an accelerated macroeconomic decline. When enterprises no longer expand productive investment, residents no longer increase durable goods consumption, local governments are constrained by heavy debt burdens, and technological innovation is stagnant, China's economic resilience and large-scale market advantages will face profound tests. Fourth, the structural increase in food prices and the accelerating decline in aggregate demand will reinforce each other, which will create serious problems for macro-management and exacerbate market pessimism. Fifth, financial risks may re-emerge. Transmitting financial resources to the real economy remains a problem. And, as the economy further adjusts downward, structural and regional financial risks will rise. Promoting orderly mitigation of financial risks and preventing them from rebounding will be the core of macro-prudential management in 2020.

Based on the characteristics of the current phase of China's macroeconomy, and in response to deep-seated problems and risks, we propose the following eight major policy recommendations.

Firstly, scientifically formulate the economic growth target for 2020, and the recommended target range is 5.5%—6.0%. An important point is that the space between the lower limit of the target and the actual growth potential has narrowed significantly. Therefore, China must prepare for the worst and strive for the best. In order to formulate and achieve the main goals of economic and social development in 2020, three basic principles must be followed: first, high-quality development; second, the completion of the phased tasks under the "two centenary goals"; and third, the basic stability of social employment. After repeated calculations, we have found that the growth target for next year does not have to exceed 6%; 5.5%—6.0% is sufficient to complete the phased tasks under the "two centenary goals", and it can also ensure the basic stability of social employment. This growth target is also conducive to maintaining strategic stability and promoting high-quality economic development in accordance with established guidelines.

(1) Following the principle of high-quality development, the interval management target for GDP growth in 2020 should be set at 5.5%—6.0%. To promote high-quality development of China's economy in accordance with the established guideline, the economic goals for 2020 must be consistent with the medium-and long-term development trends of China's economy. Based on this, macroeconomic policy needs to play the role of countercyclical adjustment to hedge against cyclical factors. It is difficult to achieve an economic growth rate of more than 6.0% in 2020. If China continues to set its GDP growth target in 2020 at 6.0% to 6.5%, it must rely on strong fiscal stimulus policies, loose monetary policies, and relaxation of real estate market control to stimulate short-term growth. However, at present, these three criterion may not be met or be conducive to high-quality economic development in the medium-and long-term. Therefore, from the perspective of maintaining strategic stability and promoting high-quality

economic development in accordance with established policies, it is more appropriate to set interval growth management at 5.5%—6.0% in 2020.

(2) Adhering to the principle of completing phased tasks under the "two centenary goals", the target for GDP growth in 2020 should be maintained at 5%—6% instead of over 6%. According to the current statistical analysis, 6% will be the lower limit of 2020 GDP growth target. However, judging from the data adjustments of previous economic censuses and adjusting the data according to the fourth national economic census initiated at the end of 2018, the economic growth rate from 2014 to 2018 is expected to increase by 0.5 percentage points per year, with a total increase of 2.0—2.5 percentage points in five years. On November 22, the National Bureau of Statistics issued an announcement on revising and increasing the GDP data for 2018 by 2.1%. This means that following a growth rate of 6.2% in 2019, China can achieve the goal of doubling GDP from 2010 as long as the economic growth rate in 2020 is between 4%—5%. Therefore, the growth target for 2020 does not have to be rigidly focused on a growth rate of "breaking 6". A target range of 5.5%—6.0% can achieve the aim of "doubling the GDP in 2020 compared with that in 2010".

(3) Adhere to the principle of ensuring the basic stability of social employment. Maintaining a growth rate of 5.5%—6.0% issufficient to ensure the basic stability of employment. 5.8% is the ideal state, while

5% is the minimum rate necessary to ensure sufficient employment, which may, however, sacrifice the quality of employment. Based on China's GDP growth rate of 6.2% in 2019, if China's economic growth rate is 6% in 2020, the non-agricultural employment increase is expected to be 5.9 million, which is similar to 2018, and employment pressure will be relatively low. If the economic growth rate in 2020 declines to 5.8%, the increase of non-agricultural employment will be 4.8 million, a slight increase from 2019. In 2020, the employment situation should still be intact. If the economic growth rate is 5.5% in 2020, the non-agricultural employment increase will be 3.15 million, which is nearly one million less than in 2019 and a historically low level. Then the employment situation will become critical, but there will be no large-scale unemployment, If China's economic growth rate drops to 5%, then the non-agricultural employment increase will be reduced to zero. Only then will China's employment situation be truly severe. Therefore, a growth rate of 5% is the lowest level to ensure China's employment to be intact, 5.5%—6.0% to ensure the basic stability of employment, and 5.8% to be the ideal state.

Secondly, "expectations management" in the medium-term can be used as an important starting point for various macroeconomic policies. Under the background of a sharp decline in domestic demand growth and new thresholds of structural differentiation, mere pre-adjustments and fine-tuning are no longer sufficient to deal with the increasing risk of accelerated decline in the macroeconomy. Therefore, China must rely on "expectations management" in the medium-term.

(1) It is necessary to stabilize domestic demand, guide market players to form consistent expectations, and ensure that economic growth remains within a reasonable range. As expectations continue to deteriorate, in addition to the overall contraction, structural tightening effects have appeared in the investment and consumer sectors: companies no longer expand productive investment, and residents no longer increase consumption of durable goods. If this continues, not only will the upgraded structural differentiation stagnate, but the depression-type structural differentiation will intensify, resulting in a total contraction effect and localized risks.

(2) A new round of confidence building must start in the fourth quarter of 2019 in full to deal with the further mani-festation of the step-down effect of economic growth in 2020. At present, the institutional dividend of China's economy has begun to rebound. At the same time, the recent mitigation of financial risks and the gradual alleviation of Sino-US trade friction will bring a relatively stable environment of financial markets and foreign trade for next year, providing a critical opportunity to reassure the markets.

(3) Regarding the structural rise of food prices, such as the price of pork, and the risk of deflation in the industrial sector, it is also necessary to strengthen the expectation management and adopt a

combination of macro policies and classified policies. In response to the sharp rise in the prices of individual commodities such as pork, it is necessary to strengthen people's livelihood protection, manage public opinion, and guide market expectations concerning "environmental rectification". Since the beginning of 2019, the "round-robin increase" of food prices has fully exposed the shortcomings of the existing "pre-adjustment and fine-tuning" measures to address the current situation. Leading various macro policies with "expectation management" should not be used to adjust pork prices. Rather, they should be based on overall research and judgment of future price trends and potential transfer paths, so as to guide market entities through forward-looking guidelines. On the supply side, China needs to overcome the constraints of environmental protection and the swine fever epidemic to resume pig production as soon as possible. On the demand side, the poor should be provided with food subsidies or special subsidies for pork consumption. More importantly, China needs to strengthen public opinion management and the guidance of market expectations. For one, to avoid pessimistic expectations, more attention should be paid to employment protection policies and work be done to stabilize residents' future income expectations. For another, opinions of comprehensive inflation amount to noise, which interferes with the formulation and implementation of monetary policy, and therefore should be avoided. As for the deflation risk in the industrial field, it is necessary to make accurate judgments based on the differentiation of various price index trends, to distinguish between short-term livelihood goals and medium-term macroeconomic goals, and to adopt a combination of macro policies and classified policies for comprehensive management.

Thirdly, implement theguidelines of the fourth plenary session of the 19th CPC Central Committee and start a new round of comprehensive reform, including opening-up and supply-side structural reforms to solve the deep-level structural and institutional problems China faces. During the critical period of economic structural transformation and the persistence of deep-seated issues, mere macro-policy adjustments and administrative controls make it difficult to address problems arising from conflicts of fundamental interests and institutional distortions. Basic and overall reforms are still the key solution to all kinds of deep-seated issues in the transition period. A new round of reform including opening-up and supply-side structural reform must be launched with the goal of building a high-standard market economy system.

(1) It is necessary to sort out the boundaries of various issues, distinguish between short-term fluctuations and medium-and long-term growth, external shocks and internal shocks, and accordingly use demand management policies, structural adjustment policies, and basic reform policies. China needs to prevent short-term administrative and macroeconomic controls from circumventing reforms. Macro control of

cyclical fluctuations must be conducted in order to prevent excessive economic fluctuations from deteriorating the reform environment. Industrial and regional policies addressing long-standing issues should continue to cultivate new growth and momentum. Structural reforms are needed to remove resource allocation distortions, reduce market friction, and restore market functions. Finally, basic reforms must be implemented for issues involving conflicts of basic interests and large institutional distortions, which cause serious short-term demand management policies, medium-term industrial policies, and regional policies, to fail.

(2) It must be clear that the core of reform is not to introduce policies or to convene meetings, but to establish a stimulus system of incentive compatibility in which all parties are willingto and capable of reform. The new round of reform must shift from the responsibility and restraint of the past to incentive compatibility and the integration of power and responsibility in the future. It is necessary to establish different second-round reform dividend and cost sharing mechanisms for parties at various levels, so as to fully stimulate the reform enthusiasm of the three types of elites. It is also necessary to carry out periodic summaries in a timely manner, get rid of historical burdens, strengthen the protection of property rights, and solve the original sin problem of entrepreneurs. On the principle of eliminating illegal income, people must face up to the historical inevitability and realistic rationality of

various gray income and shadow activities. China must find a way to reform relevant systems, making them standardized and aboveboard rather than simply banning them. A fault-tolerant mechanism for reform should be established to distinguish between trial and error during reform and violations of discipline and law. Besides, it is a must to redefine the boundaries between top-level design and grass-roots innovation. On the one hand, excessive and over-complex top-level designs must be prevented from completely constraining the potential and vitality of grass-roots innovation. On the other hand, too many grassroots innovations must be prevented from leading to a lack of uniformity and coordination, which may further cause fragmented reforms. China must fully recognize the historical and international position of its economy, and make full use of international issues to open up and initiate a new round of deep-level reforms.

(3) Based on the medium-term planning and design of a new round of reform programs, it is necessary to comprehensivelysummarize the achievements of supply-side structural reform over the past four years, and thus decisively launch a new round of supply-side structural reform. First, it must be realized that the objectives of the first-stage supply-side structural reform have been successfully completed. The content, goals, and means of the five priority tasks of cutting overcapacity, reducing excess inventory, deleveraging, lowering costs and strengthening areas of weakness all require major adjustments in

stages. Second, the second-round supply-side structural reform should focus on "reducing costs and supplementing shortcomings". Third, take marketization and legalization as the mainstay to avoid various problems brought about by administration. Fourth, the solutions to address various supply-side problems must be coordinated with major reforms. Fifth, the relationship among production, circulation, distribution, consumption, and ownership must not be separated, and structural adjustment should not be limited to the production side while ignoring the core role of other links at different times.

(4) Comprehensively position China's macroeconomic policies in 2020 under the framework of reform. First, it is necessary to classify short-term macroeconomic policy regulation, medium-term economic growth policies, structural reforms, and basic reforms, to prevent mismatches in the target allocation and tool selection of various policies. Second, macroeconomic policies should be coordinated with the "great reform and new opening up". The aim should be to create the necessary macroeconomic environment for a new round of reform and opening up, strengthen the capability to deal with the worst, and effectively alleviate short-term shocks. Third, it takes time for reform to channel the macroeconomic policy transmission mechanism and improve the macroeconomic policy system. Therefore, in making short-term policy adjustments, we must consider current macroeconomic reforms, the weakening of macroeconomic policy efficiency, spillover effects,

and the fallacy of synthetic adjustments, so as to avoid macroeconomic control swinging between "over" and "underperforming". This has become one of the core reasons for aggravating macroeconomic fluctuations.

(5) "Expectation stability" is still the core of the "six stability" policy in 2020. While the core of "expectation stability" is "confidence stability", it must be recognized that "confidence stability" does not lie in the short-term stability of certain macroeconomic indicators, nor in the simple loose or targeted assistance of macroeconomic policies. Rather, it requires that market participants have clear, definite and scientific solutions to long-term strategic issues and have confidence that China has carried out real reforms on fundamental issues so as to provide a credible and fair competitive environment for the future. First, the turmoil in market sentiment is not only due to problems in China's market, but also to excessive government intervention, especially excessive expansion of government credit and government-like credit, which has squeezed the market space. Second, the sluggish confidence of private entrepreneurs lies not only in the imperfect protection of property rights in the private economy, but also in the severe squeeze on the room for the survival and development of the private economy. Therefore, the key to boosting the confidence of the private economy is not to provide one-time administrative assistance, but to provide a fair and transparent competitive environment through

systemic reform. Third, the anxiety in financial markets not only stems from market imperfections and large debt NPL ratios, but also from China's method of solving debt problems, which further exacerbates the distortion of resource allocation. Fourth, much of the low confidence is not because China lacks an expectation intervention policy, but rather because many of the signals China has sent are very chaotic and have become the cause of the decline in confidence. Fifth, changes in market sentiment are often forward-looking. While attaching great importance to changes in market sentiment, it must be recognized that market sentiment often exaggerates the difficulty of practical problems because of incomplete and asymmetric information. Scientific analysis of information in market sentiment is vital for macroeconomic "pre-adjustment" and "fine-tuning" management.

Fourthly, there is need to restructure the framework of a sound monetary policy in terms of philosophy, target system, tool selection, prudent management, exchange rate arrangement, expectation management, and policy coordination.

(1) Both the philosophy and target system ofthe monetary policy needs to be restructured. First, monetary policy needs a more active philosophy during the Great Transformation. During a period of shifting forces, the potential GDP growth rate and output gap may be underestimated, so the traditional concept of the potential growth rate needs to be discarded. At the philosophical level, extraordinary times

require extraordinary actions, so China needs to stay open to studying experimental and unconventional monetary policies. Second, during the period of structural adjustment and highly differentiated prices, the goals of monetary policy must shift from the CPI, real GDP growth, and employment to the following areas: nominal GDP growth rate, employment quality and GDP deflator; liquidity stability and big swings in asset prices; exchange rate expectations and arbitrage capital flows. In the current economic structure and statistical system of China, the above traditional indicators can no longer accurately reflect the status of China's macroeconomic operation.

(2) When endogenous decline is accelerating along with weak external demand, it is necessary to clarify new connotations and new measures for a moderate monetary policy. First, amoderate monetary policy should be able to smoothly shift from steady positioning to moderate easing when necessary to stabilize market expectations, break the "debt-deflation" vicious cycle, and reverse the current endogenous decline. Second, because of financial rectification and the deepening of the financial system reforms, prevention and mitigation of major financial risks have been achieved, which will result in a relatively stable financial market environment in 2020. Monetary policy should continue the basic positioning of 2019, but it can be moderately looser. ① When domestic demand continues to fall, external demand has weakened sharply, and financial risks have been mitigated, monetary

policy should avoid an excessively tight orientation. The low interest rate policy is still a very important basis for market recovery, and the decline in the actual loan interest rate is a key to stabilizing investment. ②The M2 growth rate should not be set too low, and room should be reserved for preventing deflation and endogenous contractions of various financial indicators. The current decline in non-food CPI, the continued decline in the PPI and the GDP deflator, as well as the deterioration of corporate efficiency and market expectations, may indicate that a new round of deflation is taking place. It is necessary to pay close attention to the next two or three quarters and adjust monetary policy in a timely manner. It is suggested that the growth rate of M2 in 2020 should be higher than the nominal GDP growth rate, reaching 8.5%—9.0%. Further, the growth rate of the total financing of the whole society should not be adjusted too quickly—specifically, it should be maintained at about 11% to meet the requirements of financial rectification and stronger supervision.

(3) The toolbox and transmission channels ofa sound monetary policy need to be reshaped. First, due to the diversity and superposition of sources of volatility during the Great Reform and Great Transformation, monetary policy tools must be diversified, since conventional policy tools are insufficient to cope with the current pattern. Unconventional monetary policies such as the Chinese version of QE require systematic research. In the future, there may be

unconventional macro policies in China's policy basket. Second, attention should be paid to the impact of currency transfer changes on currency transmission. In 2020, currency placement can be completed by gradually reducing the deposit reserve ratios of financial institutions. Internally, China needs to pay attention to the continued decline in the growth rates of M0 and M1, enrich the channels for central bank currency issuance, and increase the reduction of bank reserve ratios, the supply of China's security assets and the depth of the currency market. Externally, China must pay close attention to the policy adjustment of the Federal Reserve and changes in US financial markets. Third, the transformation of the monetary policy regulatory framework often brings problems such as an unstable base money supply rhythm, uncertain supply tools and opaque supply targets. In order to prevent triggering market tensions and causing unnecessary fluctuations in capital markets and interest rates, in addition to commonly used open market operating tools, monetary policy should be supported by a series of innovative tools such as Standing Lending Facility and Medium-term Lending Facility to inject liquidity into the market as well as strengthen and guide market expectations. Fourth, in the process of controlling excessive debt increases, the choice of instruments for monetary policy is very important. Price-based instruments are more favorable for the adjustment of high-debt companies. Simple quantitative easing still needs to be controlled. Therefore, the current loose monetary policy should be based on quantitative tools focusing on liquidity, with price-based tools as the foundation. Fifth, against the background of increasing downward pressure on the economy and rising uncertainty, LPR reform needs to be promoted alongside with other reform measures to effectively hedge the risk premium of commercial banks. Recently, the central bank passed the LPR reform, lowered the open market operation interest rate, and led the LPR interest rate to decrease slightly. However, commercial banks have increased the risk premium on the basis of LPR, resulting in a higher general loan interest rate for enterprises. Therefore, other reform measures are still needed, and effective hedging should be carried out through a modest reduction of deposit reserve ratios and a substantial reduction in MLF interest rates. Sixth, in the case of highly differentiated prices, especially for CPI and PPI, the actual interest rate differences faced by various market entities must be considered when using interest rate tools. Especially in the context of a negative PPI, the price index corresponding to the productive investment of the enterprise should be used to adjust the nominal interest rate. An asymmetric interest rate reduction tool is recommended.

(4) Make expectation management the starting point for monetary policy. First, with reforms continuing, financial innovations emerging, and interest rate marketization not yet fully completed, monetary policy should be focused on strengthening expectation management and guiding

social expectations to improve the effectiveness of monetary policy. Second, in the face of insufficient aggregate demand, monetary policy must clearly explain the new connotation of stability. The adjustment of monetary policy in terms of exchange rates, deposit reserves, and interest rates should be more explicit about its looser connotation. Third, in order to completely reverse the pessimistic expectations of the market, monetary policy must break the traditional "small-step fine-tuning" control rhythm. The core reason why China's monetary policy has not achieved the "pre-adjustment" goals through "fine-tuning" in the past two years is that market entities do not recognize "small-step fine-tuning". As a result, expectations do not change, and confidence is not stabilized. Avoiding the faster tightening of the financial environment over market expectations is the goal of monetary policy. Fourth, a new round of confidence building must begin in the fourth quarter of 2019. At present, the institutional dividend of China's economy has begun to rebound. At the same time, the recent mitigation of financial risks and the gradual mitigation of Sino-US trade friction will bring a relatively stable financial market and foreign trade environment for 2020, which will provide an opportunity to reassure the market. Even in an environment where long-term interest rates are rigid and financial resources are declining for the real economy, a moderately accommodative monetary policy is necessary to guide expectations, prevent excessive contraction, and cooperate with active fiscal policy.

Fifth, China needs to break the vicious circle of "deflation in production-high debt" and avoid entering a balance sheet recession. The opportunity in the current period to ease monetary policy to a certain level must be seized, instead of adopting an afterthought model in which monetary policy will lose its role of guiding expectations. Once China enters the stage of balance sheet decline, the efficiency of China's monetary policy will also plunge, resulting in huge adjustment costs. The cases of Japan and other countries have shown that the traditional "fine-tuning" model may mislead the opportunity for regulation. China must avoid entering a balance sheet recession and carry out a comprehensive transformation of the direction of monetary policy.

(5) Respond to the challenges of a new global downturn with flexible exchange rate policies. First, correctly identify and respond to the downturn in the world economy and the tide of interest rate cuts of global central banks, especially the resumption of interest rate cuts and QE operations in Europe and the US. The easing of monetary policy in major countries in 2020 will be the norm. In this context, it is necessary to clarify the international orientation of China's monetary policy. The easing of monetary policy should be consistent with the major central banks in order to achieve exchange rate stability, which is central to dealing with the risks of external fluctuations in 2020. Second, internal economic stability is still the basic starting point, to which exchange rate adjustment and reform of the capital account must

both adhere. In view of uncertainties, China's foreign economic policy should adopt a conservative approach in order to stabilize the foundation of China's economy. Third, exchange rate marketization remains the key to cushioning the economy from external shocks and improving its elasticity and resilience. From the perspective of stabilizing financial markets, the government should plan ahead and prepare for the abnormal fluctuation of CNY exchange rates and abnormal capital flows.

(6) Countercyclical macro-prudential policy needs to adapt to the requirements of structural adjustment, strengthening policy coordination and avoiding new distortions. First, the mitigation and prevention of financial risks is the core of macro prudence in 2020. Although financial risks have been mitigated in 2019, the economy will be in the normalization stage of default for a period of time, in which the integration of monetary policy, macro-prudential supervision, financial micro-regulation, and other financial goals is even more important. The institutionalization, integration, independence, and power of monetary and financial authorities are also the prerequisites for formulating a scientific monetary policy. Second, during the structural adjustment period, countercyclical macro-prudential policy needs to strengthen the relationship among currency supply, credit supply and social financing supply, so that monetary policy and financial supervision can be coordinated with each other. It is our recommendation to adopt a combination of moderately easy monetary policy and financial

supervision reform to ensure the relative stability of the monetary condition index facing the real economy. Third, financial stability should be based on the bottom of no systematic financial risk and should not be over-defined. There must be a certain degree of tolerance towards occasional financial problems and risks. Especially at this moment of the Great Reform and Opening-up, the concentrated exposure of local risks is conducive to forming an effective reform path. Fourth, no systematic risk shouldn't be treated as equal to the stability of financial indicators. During the Great Transformation and the Great Reform, various financial indicators must be adjusted; otherwise, it is difficult to optimize the method and structure of resource allocation, and various potential risks cannot be exposed. Fifth, macro-prudential supervision must be tilted from the supervision of systemic financial risk indicators to the supervision of certain structural factors. After the risk mitigation in 2019, the monitoring of debt sustainability risks in key cities and provinces in the next two years, and the monitoring of risks in some industries and products are particularly important. Sixth, easy monetary policy must be supplemented by market order construction. It is an important prerequisite for the implementation of a moderately loose monetary policy to make up for financial market defects and restore the ability of financial markets to allocate resources. Otherwise, bubbles in the financial sector under loose monetary policy are likely to further distract funds from their intended purpose, leading to the departure of the real economy from the virtual economy and the emergence of recession bubbles. Seventh, in a high-debt environment, China should not only maintain a moderately loose monetary policy, but also clear a large number of corporate zombies, restructure debt of high-debt companies, and substantially restructure the balance sheets of banks and related companies. Since stock adjustment is the basis for incremental adjustment, a combination of active fiscal policy, moderately loose monetary policy and strong supervision on the basis of stock adjustment remains China's core weapon to get out of the predicament.

Fifthly, fiscal policy must be precise and targeted. The sharp decline in the growth of domestic demand has exacerbated the vulnerability of China's economy, so fiscal policies in 2020 must be more active and effective. Before the time window closes, China must step up efforts to strengthen domestic demand with precision.

(1) In addition to continuously implementing the existing policy of cutting taxes and fees, China also needs to further increase tax deductions for advanced production equipment and pre-tax deductions for research and development expenses, so as to motivate enterprises to expand their production and R&D investment. Considering the special circumstances of internal and external difficulties and major reforms, it is suggested that the fiscal deficit rate in 2020 be increased to more than 3.0%. At present, the National Bureau of Statistics of China has

revised the GDP data for 2018 upwards by 2.1% according to the Fourth Economic Census, an increase of 1,897.2 billion yuan from 90,030.9 billion to 9,1928.1 billion. The expansion of the total GDP volume means that the room for fiscal deficit will increase in 2020. While maintaining a constant deficit ratio, the public budget deficit can increase by about 60 billion yuan and local government special debt by 60 billion yuan, increasing the potential of leveraging social funding with government funds.

(2) Further clarify fiscal discipline and market rules, and on this basis, give full play to the enthusiasm of local governments for infrastructure investment and public utility investment, promote the recovery of social investment growth and stabilize market expectations. Although the current growth rate of infrastructure investment is stabilizing, the recovery speed is very slow, dragging down the overall investment growth rate and adversely affecting market expectations. Fiscal expenditure in 2020 should shift from investment-oriented to livelihood-oriented and from subsidy-oriented to welfare-oriented. It is necessary to use active fiscal policies to accelerate the construction of a low-level and broad welfare system, and use targeted fiscal policies to boost the pension, health, and mid-to-high-end service industries to stimulate demand. Meanwhile, the expansion of local government special bonds in 2020 cannot be "one size fits all", rather, it must be based on the assessment of regional debt risks and tailored to local

conditions. In areas where the government debt ratio is already high, the replacement and refinancing of government-specific debt can be used to further mitigate debt risks, while the issuance of new bonds can be encouraged in areas with low government debt ratios.

(3) Pay attention to local fiscal revenue collapses, especially the various livelihood issues brought about by sudden changes in grass-roots fiscal revenue. We propose to expand the scale of fiscal stabilization fund and establish a basic-level fiscal assistance system during the transition period. At the same time, moderately weakening fiscal revenue will prevent local governments from increasing the financial burden of enterprises, which is in disguise by the intensified enforcement in tax collection and non-tax revenue. In view of the narrow capacity and imperfections of the local bond market, the core channel for increasing the fiscal deficit level in 2020 should be increasing the central government's fiscal deficit rate and volume of national debt issuance in order to improve government spending capacity for the implementation of reforms.

(4) The focus of tax and fee reduction reforms should be shifted from production to consumption and income distribution to motivate residents to consume. In the new period when savings rates continue to decline, stablizing consumption plays a fundamental and leading role for the stability and sustainable development of the macroeconomy. Great importance must be attached to the internal causes for the current

decline in consumption growth. China must consolidate and expand the consumption base of Chinese residents and give full play to the advantages of super-scale markets. We recommend the following. First, a ctively implement the plan of the individual income tax to reduce the tax burden of the wage-earning class. Second, strengthen the reform of public services to improve their equity and availability. Third, focus on the risks of pork price fluctuations and income fluctuations in 2020 and prepare consumer subsidies for low-income groups. Fourth, develop a strategy for raising the consumption of the middle class. Pay attention to the excessive increase of the leverage ratio of middle-class families, and promote the steady growth of consumption by establishing a corresponding debt risk mitigation mechanism. Introduce special tax and fee reduction policies for the consumption of durable goods such as automobiles. For example, according to the international per capita car ownership and per capita disposable income level, China's car ownership still has room for growth of up to 80%. It is recommended that the car purchase tax rate be reduced from 10% to 5%. The past 10 years of automobile consumption experience shows that reducing the automobile purchase tax has an immediate effect on promoting automobile consumption. In 2009—2010 and 2015—2016, the automobile purchase tax rate was reduced from 10% to 5%, which significantly increased the growth rate of automobile consumption. In contrast, the sharp decline in automobile consumption in the past two years has to a certain extent been related to the increased automobile purchase tax rate rising from 5% to 10%.

Sixthly, the core of growth stability in 2020 lies instabilizing investment, but corresponding policy direction and policy tools must be adjusted. A systematic plan is required to initiate new investment measures. At the same time, the implementation of "playing the key role of investment in optimizing the supply structure" proposed at the 19th National Congress of the CPC is a medium-term task. A package of reforms is needed to optimize China's investment structure.

(1) Increased private investment is the key to investment stability. The key to stimulating private investment is increasing the expected return on investment in the future, which comes from the protection of property rights, newroom for capital investment, reduction of investment costs, and investment expansion of industrial demand. Therefore, the launch of private investment does not depend on any single policy. There must be a systematic policy plan and reform measures, which must be carried out systematically from a medium-term perspective and aim to fully adjust investment expectations. It must be recognized that the low return on physical investment is not only a cyclical phenomenon, more importantly, it is the result of the absence of a series of major reforms. The plan for encouraging private capital must include a large number of fundamental, medium-term reforms. First, the government must gradually shift from its current investment-

orientation to a livelihood-orientation. Second, the investment system and profits of state-owned enterprises should be strategically repositioned, while non-main business investment must be strictly restricted. Third, various controls must be reorganized. Fourth, the market-oriented reform of public institutions and public service systems must be deepened. It must be recognized that the room for private investment mainly in manufacturing has been saturated, and the opening of various market-based and semi-public service areas is very important. It is also important to relax government control in these industries, reduce government investment in non-public areas, and comprehensively shrink the non-main business of state-owned enterprises.

(2) It is important to increase the availability of funds for the investment needs of small and medium-sized enterprises, private enterprises and innovative enterprises. Channeling funds into the real economy is key to increasing the growth rate of real economy investment. However, it is hard to achieve the goal of stabilizing investment, especially the goal of stabilizing private investment, with simple financial consolidation and strengthening of supervision. In the process of managing risks, administrative supervision can easily stifle financial innovation, making a large number of financial resources rely on the traditional system for financing, and shrinking new financing channels. As a result, a large number of small and medium-sized

enterprises, private enterprises and innovative enterprises have difficulty in obtaining financing. Difficult and expensive financing has become a bottleneck to enterprise investment.

(3) In the short term, the country needs to prevent the growth rate of investment in fixed assets from falling too fast. It is still important to maintain the relative stability of government investment growth and real estate growth in 2020. In the medium-term, any expansion of investment policy will bring crowding-out effects through channels such as capital squeezing, industrial space squeezing and political doubts. So not only does market investment not expand, but it shrinks in the medium-term. Government investments and subsidies for various industries cannot be further expanded, instead, it is necessary to tolerate a moderate decline in investment growth.

Seventhly, livelihood policies should be developed to cope with the "dual risks" brought about by the economic downturn and the multiple impacts on people's livelihood. The impact of people's livelihood as well as the decline in aggregate demand will exacerbate market pessimism about the future, which will cause more serious problems for macro management in 2020. Facing the "dual risks", in the short term, China must not only increase livelihood security expenditures, but also pay more attention to employment stability policies, since guaranteed employment is more important than guaranteed wages and cost shocks can be addressed by strengthening wage flexibility. The first task is to develop targeted interventions and guidance for local industries and regions where Sino-US trade friction may induce unemployment risks. The second is to work on special solutions for industries that have recently faced greater difficulties, such as automobiles and mobile phones, in combination with industrial policies, consumer policies, tax policies, and traffic management policies. The third is to attach importance to the operating difficulties faced by enterprises, especially small and micro private enterprises, in order to reduce the financial burdens from multiple dimensions. Supporting policies should be combined with employment goals. The fourth is to appropriately relax restrictions on the stall economy and night economy so as to expand the living space of flexible employment. The fifth is to guide the employment practices of enterprises through tools such as employment subsidies, while paying more attention to the employment of young unemployed groups. The sixth is to restructure the future employment policy system. Employment policies should be more active, with the goal shifting from full employment to high-quality full employment, while passive employment policies should be improved to further enhance the social safety net.

Eighthly, positively respond to Sino-US trade friction, and rethink China's strategic choices during this volatile period of the world economy. The world economy may undergo unexpected changes in 2020, when calls for strengthening international cooperation and policy coordination will briefly suppress protectionism. However, if the effects are limited, protectionism as well as populism will launch a more violent counterattack, causing even more serious damage to the world economic order. During the fission period of the world structure, it's necessary to comprehensively consider China's strategic choices from a medium-term perspective. First, continue to strengthen reforms with high levels of openness to meet the short-term challenges brought about by the fission of the world structure. In the Sino-US trade friction, China must confront neo-protectionism with liberalism, isolationism with multilateralism and bilateralism, and the new cold war with new cooperation. Second, while insisting on meeting challenges with the new opening-up, China must recognize that fundamental changes in various basic parameters of the world economy during the fission period have determined that it cannot stick to the past strategic path. Third, a restructuring of the global industry chain, supply and value chains, is bound to take place. It is necessary to conduct forward-looking researches and adopt a comprehensive strategy, especially for the "Economic Iron Curtain" and "New Cold War" strategies that the United States may adopt. First, China should strategically avoid the rapid emergence of the "New Cold War" and maintain a good international environment for its industrial upgrading. Second, it is necessary to prevent the United States from rapidly forming an international united front of the "Economic Iron Curtain" and the "New

Cold War". So a higher level of integration and liberalization of the regional economy are needed. Third, there must be sufficient plans for the full spread of the trade war in other fields, especially in the fields of technology, talent, exchange rates and security. There must be adequate researches and strategic arrangements. Fifth, prepare short-term policies to hedge against possible deterioration in the balance of payments and the impact of turbulences in international financial markets in 2020. Sixth, in dealing with Sino-US trade friction, there are a few traps to avoid. The first is the trap of "surrender for peace". The second is the "Thucydides trap" of mutual hostility. The third is the trap of high-cost military competition without technical spillover, and the fourth is the trap of political alliance without trade support and economic foundation.